LA GRANDE ITALIA

GEORGE L. MOSSE SERIES
IN MODERN EUROPEAN CULTURAL AND
INTELLECTUAL HISTORY

Advisory Board

La Grande Italia

The Myth of the Nation
in the Twentieth Century

Emilio Gentile

Translated by
SUZANNE DINGEE
and
JENNIFER PUDNEY

THE UNIVERSITY OF WISCONSIN PRESS

This book was translated with the generous support of
the Italian Ministry of Foreign Affairs,
the Istituto Italiano di Cultura of Chicago, Director Tina Cervone,
and published with support from
the George L. Mosse Program at the University of Wisconsin–Madison.

The University of Wisconsin Press
1930 Monroe Street, 3rd Floor
Madison, Wisconsin 53711-2059

www.wisc.edu/wisconsinpress/

3 Henrietta Street
London WC2E 8LU, England

Originally published as *La grande Italia: Ascesa e declino del mito della nazione nel ventesimo secolo*
© 1997 Arnoldo Mondadori Editore S.p.A., Milano

1   3   5   4   2

Printed in the United States of America

Library of Congress Cataloging-in-Publication Data
Gentile, Emilio, 1946–
[Grande Italia. English]
La Grande Italia: the myth of the nation in the twentieth century /
Emilio Gentile; translated by Suzanne Dingee and Jennifer Pudney.
p.   cm.—(George L. Mosse series in modern European cultural and intellectual history)
Originally published as La grande Italia:
ascesa e declino del mito della nazione nel ventesimo secolo.
Milano: Mondadori, 1997.
Includes bibliographical references and index.
ISBN 978-0-299-22810-1 (cloth: alk. paper)
ISBN 978-0-299-22814-9 (pbk.: alk. paper)
1. Nationalism—Italy—History—20th century.
2. Fascism—Italy—History—20th century.
I. Title.   II. Series.
DG568.5.G4513   2009
320.54094509′04—dc22   2008013448

CONTENTS

13   Where Is Italy?   211
14   Pull the Idol Down   231
15   In Search of a Fatherland   250

PART 5: THE COUNTRY OF POLITICAL PARTIES

16   A Great but Small Nation   279
17   A Myth for the Republic   296
18   The Italies of Republican Italy   307

     Conclusion: The Jubilee of the Simulacrum   337

     Notes   357
     Illustrations Credits   387
     Index   389

PREFACE

The Italies of the Italians

There is a reawakening of the cult of the nation in Italy today.

It can be seen and heard everywhere. The Italian flag flies on monuments and government buildings. The national anthem, written by Goffredo Mameli, is played by bands and sung by choruses in the streets and squares. On the Republic's birthday, the armed forces proudly march in the parade to celebrate it and are acclaimed by many. The president carries out the ceremonies celebrating the country's historical moments with stately majesty.

There is a reawakening of national rhetoric in Italy today.

It can be seen and heard everywhere. Even in the political arena, few parties refuse to raise the national flag, or sing the national anthem, or celebrate the national glories, or commemorate the national tragedies.

There is a reawakening of the myth of the nation in Italy today.

It can be seen and heard everywhere. Even in the cultural environment, where few intellectuals refrain from making their contribution to the protection of the national identity, within a generous competition of noble initiatives aimed at building a common history cemented by the memory of joys and sorrows, nostalgia and misgivings, disappointments and hopes.

Everyone can see and hear it: Italy is waking up.

How different Italy is today compared to a decade ago, when all over the peninsula, from the Quirinale and the Vatican, from radio and television, from newspapers and books, from teaching posts and pulpits, from the squares and the parliament, the lamentations that the state was breaking up resounded like the dismal tolling of a funeral bell, the obituary of the nation, predicting the future of a population destined to stray like lost sheep in a chaotic world where large groups continue to migrate under the threat of clashes between civilizations, cultures, religions, economies, nations, and continents.

"Suppose we stop being a nation," was the cry of alarm launched in 1993 by the political scientist Gian Enrico Rusconi, who did much to prevent such an event from occurring. The alarm spread immediately and lasted to the end of the last decade, voiced by those who were ever more pessimistic in a chorus of sorrowful predictions as to the future of the Italian nation.

However, the cry of alarm was neither new nor recent in the Italian Republic, as the last chapter of this book explains. Three decades earlier, when Italy was celebrating its first centenary as a unified country, worried observers had noticed that the national myth and the feeling of belonging to a common fatherland was about to die out or had already done so.

That was the beginning of the nation's oblivion.

In the years following, the oblivion continued and worsened. Almost twenty years ago, in 1987, the historian Renzo De Felice said: "Our country is going to lose its historic past . . . ; national tradition has disappeared and most people ignore the country's origin," while Italy, he continued, "is only a container that is supposed to guarantee some rules for living and working as best it can." No less disconsolate were the considerations regarding the nation expressed that same year by the philosopher Norberto Bobbio: "Italy is no longer a nation, in the sense that, at least for the new generations, there is no national sentiment, or what was recently called love of one's nation. Italy has become little more than a geographical location, and the Italians, and I say this with conviction, 'a dispersed people without a name.' I often wonder why, but I have never found a satisfactory answer."

There was a kind of amnesia of the nation, then, in Italy.

No one celebrated the cult of the fatherland, no one glorified the nation, no one cared about the identity of the Italians. Rarely was the Italian flag seen flying, and when it was, for established ceremonies, it aroused the same emotion as a line of laundry put out to dry. Sometimes the national anthem did have an emotional effect, for example, when it was played to celebrate Italian victories in sport, almost like the background music to a commercial. No one knew the words, but everyone pretended to sing along just moving their lips. The armed forces did not march in a parade on the Republic's anniversary, and the president carried out the country's official ceremonies with the same composed indifference as a master of ceremonies. "The ceremony on June 2nd is a rather dismal one by now," commented the Republican Party organ in 1999.

At that time, culture did not cultivate the myth of the nation. National rhetoric had disappeared from the political arena, replaced by new vernacular rhetoric: in public speeches referring to the Italians collectively, the word *paese* (land) was used instead of *patria* (fatherland) or *nazione* (nation), because these words were considered either old-fashioned or were suspected of being a sign of hidden neo-Fascist nostalgia. And the people who lived on the peninsula, the Italian citizens, were like the noisy, quarrelsome inhabitants of a condominium that was disintegrating due to the wear and tear of time and the negligence of the residents, jealous of their well-appointed private apartments but indifferent to the deterioration of the common areas.

Where was the Italian nation ten years ago?

The answer came when an obituary was unearthed—"the death of the fatherland"—that the jurist Salvatore Satta wrote after September 8, 1943, when he jotted down his painful reflections about Italy, in ruins, during the civil war. The work was published in 1948 under the title *De Profundis* but was soon forgotten until it reappeared in 1980. Midway through the nineties, Renzo De Felice used this formula to explain why the nation had fallen apart after September 8, 1943, and the civil war, which left republican Italy with open wounds, deep divisions and a sense of not belonging to a nation. In 1996 Ernesto Galli della Loggia reworked the "death of the fatherland" in an essay, and it became symbolic of the nation's end-of-the-century crisis. Meanwhile, at the same time, the party-driven Republic was on its death bed, routed by a judicial cyclone that accelerated the course of an irremediable decline due to prolonged internal decay and corruption. Several essays on the future of Italy were published at the time, and, in an attempt to perhaps make the dramatic moment seem even worse, were given lapidary titles in Latin—probably for readers who did not know Latin. *Quo vadis Italia?* was the dubious question of one book title, while *Finis Italiae* was the irrevocable verdict of another.

The *de profundis* for the "death of the fatherland" became a literary genre, of the kind that tends to spread by echoing one another in the never-ending repetition of the same theme.

During this period of dismal predictions and melancholy obituaries, this study of the myth of the nation in contemporary Italy was completed, and the first edition was published in 1997. Over the last ten years the book has been widely commented on and well-received, even abroad, with proposed translations. Its topics and arguments have resonated and led to other studies, and on the whole, the contents seem to have stood up well under the trial of further research and considerations. This book is still the only history of the myth of the nation in contemporary Italy narrated in a single volume. For this reason I think it is useful, especially for younger readers who probably view the events recalled here as belonging to a very remote past. After being absent from book shops for several years, the book is making its comeback in a fully revised edition.

The history of the myth of the nation in Italy begins with the celebrations of the first jubilee of a united country in 1911. It then backtracks to the origin of unification during the Risorgimento, moving forward through the various versions, manifestations, and difficulties experienced in the first ten years as a united country, during the liberal regime, the First World War, Fascism, the Resistance, the first fifteen years of republican Italy, up to the celebrations for the first centenary in 1961. In my notes, the concepts and the method are explained, as well as the spirit with which the book was written, without passing judgment on the past, without polemics on the present, and without predictions for the future.

Although the book was published at a time when there were complaints and obituaries about Italy, it was not my intention to add further painful notes to the chorus of patriotic lamentations, as one superficial commentator wrote (erroneously placing this essay in the "death of the fatherland" literary genre), because I had begun to concern myself with patriotism and nationalism in the history of Italy long before, at the end of the sixties, when *patria* (fatherland) and *nazione* (nation) were not considered worthy of historiographical consideration. It is also true, however, that when the book was published, some did erroneously see it as belonging to the "death of the fatherland" literary genre, a genre that is not always historically accurate and convincing. With this book, I aimed to make a new contribution to considerations regarding the troubled events surrounding the myth of the nation in the history of the Italians, modifying and correcting some hasty judgments on the past, without venturing to make predictions for the future.

Those who read the book will realize how complex the history of the myth of the nation in Italy is and will begin to understand the different, remote, and deep-rooted reasons why forming a national conscience within the institutions of the unified state was so difficult and precarious. It will also be possible to see how far back in time one has to go to discover the origin of the events that led to the birth of republican Italy, territorially united but split up into many consciences, just as liberal Italy and Fascist Italy had been. The book should also give a clearer idea why there was not, in the history of the Italians during the first century of unification, a single Italy, a common concept and image of the nation, in which the people of the peninsula felt united because of their deep love for their country.

The Italians had many Italies in the first century of unification. Each was wed to its own ideology of nation, politics, and state, which set it against the others. As a result they lived together in quarrelsome antagonism that threatened to degenerate into civil war (and sometimes did). However, the same thing happened in the history of other populations organized in state communities, founded on the myth of the nation. Almost everywhere the history of modern national states is one of conflict caused by different concepts of nation that, at times, have driven the citizens of the same state to fight against each other violently, like the worst of enemies, rather than compete peacefully as rivals. There is no congenital anomaly in the history of the Italian state that makes it pathologically different from the history of other national states, but it does have its own peculiarities, both in the history of the Italians and in the myth of the nation, which this book has attempted to reconstruct in the various tormented and often violent vicissitudes.

The book ends with the historic acknowledgment of what the Italian nation was like when it celebrated its first century of unification: "a simulacrum that was carried onto the stage as required by the script for the established celebrations, . . . incapable of arousing ideals, sentiments or collectively shared emotions in the Italians, or evoking in them memories, sorrows and common hopes."

Today it seems the simulacrum has regained vitality.

There is a reawakening of the myth of the nation in Italy today. The Italian flag flies everywhere; choruses sing the national anthem; the armed forces march in a parade on the Republic's anniversary; the president carries out the ceremonies celebrating the cult of the nation, speaking simple but moving words; and almost everyone in politics and the cultural milieu speaks about the fatherland and prides themselves on being Italian. The laments and obituaries have disappeared like a bad dream at sunrise.

In a few years' time we can pick up the threads of history where we left off and try to trace the myth of the nation after 1961, during the decades of amnesia, oblivion, hibernation, or catalepsy, to continue our study of historical events up to the dawn of the current awakening. Only then can we perhaps evaluate if today's cult of the nation and the national rhetoric are the genuine expression of a lasting conscience and

if, along with the waving flags, the national anthem, the marching soldiers, and the celebrations as well as the hospitals, courts, public ser-
vices, and schools, the municipalities and provinces, the regions and
parliament have become the respected symbols of a state that functions,
efficiently and equally for all, as the home of a common fatherland that
exists only if it lives in the consciences of the citizens who are free and
equal before the law.

Many of the protagonists in this book, from the Risorgimento to the
Republic, imagined the Italian state like that and acted accordingly,
hoping to achieve an Italy of Italians. Many sacrificed their lives to do
so. Many survived and were disappointed when they saw what had been
achieved, as often happens in human affairs. Their hopes, sacrifices,
and disappointments are part of the story that this book tells.

E.G.

October 2005

NOTES FROM THE AUTHOR

This book traces the history of the myth of the nation in contemporary Italy along the curve of its rise and fall; it reached its lowest point long before the recent discovery of the nation's and the national state's crisis.

This is a history that is neither for nor against the nation. It only illustrates what the nation's and the national state's problems have been for the Italians of our era. And by "Italians" I mean the supporters and the enemies of the national state, the Liberals and the Catholics, the Monarchists and the Republicans, the Fascists and the anti-Fascists, those who fought in the Resistance and those who fought for the Social Republic. I also include in the Italian Republic, Action Party members, *l'Uomo Qualunque* (the "men-in-the-street" movement), Socialists, neo-Fascists, Christian Democrats, and Communists. The protagonists of this book are the cultural and political movements that racked their brains to solve the problem of the Italians' national identity and who struggled to assert their vision of the nation and its destiny in the twentieth century. In this way, through their ideas and actions, the national myth influenced, for better or worse, the very existence of all Italians.

Between unification and the Republic, the Italians, as citizens of a national state, experienced the most decisive and dramatic periods in their history. They lived through three political regimes, two world wars, profound and irreversible economic, social and cultural changes, with the myth of the nation as their ideal point of reference. Furthermore, during the course of the twentieth century, Italy was the European country that experienced the rise or development of different types of nationalism that were to dominate the scene up to the early years of the Republic. All of the above makes the history of the Italian national myth a particularly important area in the study of modern nationalism.

In this regard, it is necessary to clarify the use of the terms "fatherland," "myth," and "nationalism" in this book. "Fatherland" is used according to its meaning as "the land of our fathers, of our ancestors." By "myth" I mean a constellation of beliefs, ideas, ideals and values combined and compacted into a symbolic image that arouses in the individual and the masses strong conviction, enthusiasm, and the desire to act. By the term "nationalism" I mean to define any cultural and political movement that aims to assert the supremacy of the nation as a historical, cultural, and political entity that is achieved in the organization of a national state, identifying itself with the fatherland. Given this meaning, the term "nationalism" does not involve any ethical or political evaluation. This point of view does not make any distinction between "good" nationalism and "bad" nationalism or between nationalism and patriotism, nor does it consider them opposites, as if they were derived from quite distinct genetic processes, nationalism being the pathological fruit of the cult that worships the nation and patriotism the beneficial result of love of one's fatherland.

Actually, this distinction assumes an ideological choice that could seriously hinder understanding of the problem of the nation and the role that the myth of the nation has played in the history of the last two hundred years. From the historical point of view, the qualification of nationalism and patriotism does not depend on distinguishing between the intrinsic "good" or "bad" nature of nationalism and patriotism but on how they actually manifested themselves when combined with other movements—liberalism, democracy, racism, socialism, totalitarianism—thus giving rise to different forms of nationalism or patriotism. The history of the myth of the nation in Italy is useful to verify the validity of this viewpoint.

I also want to explain the method used to limit the contents of the study. The quantity of material gathered and the complexity and variety of the problems connected with the history of the national myth risked transforming the paragraphs into chapters and chapters into so many books, overloading the notes with bibliographical references that would have doubled the current size of the book. Therefore, the selection had to be drastic and the work had to be contained within strict limits, which may have made the choice of topics and problems debatable. Equally drastic was the decision to restrict the contents of the notes to the bibliographical references of the quotations and the listing of the studies indirectly referred to in the text.

LA GRANDE ITALIA

Prologue

The Fatherland's Jubilee

The New Era of the Italians

In 1911 the Italians celebrated fifty years of political unity, commemorating the birth of the Kingdom of Italy on March 17, 1861, in Turin. The jubilee celebrations of Italy's unification were actually a *festival of the nation*. That is, they provided the most important opportunity to once again solemnly sanctify, at the beginning of the twentieth century, the preeminence of the national myth as the supreme principle of ethical and political inspiration for the citizens of a united Italy. The anniversary was also an opportunity to assess the achievements made by the Italians on the road to modern civilization after unification. Apart from the patriotic ceremonies evoking the heroes and feats of the Risorgimento, expositions, congresses and exhibitions were organized illustrating the economic, social and cultural progress made, to show the world that a Greater Italy, dreamt of by the patriots of that period, was becoming a reality.

Five decades of unification was certainly a modest period of time compared with the fourteen centuries that had passed since the fall of the Roman empire, during which time the inhabitants of the peninsula had been divided and subjected to changing local and foreign domination. And yet, it was this comparison with the centuries of division and servitude that justified the national pride of the young state, which after fourteen hundred years had unified the populations of the peninsula within a single national state, thus beginning their transformation into a population of free citizens.

The birth of the national state was the beginning of a "new era," as Camillo Benso di Cavour stated before the Chamber of Deputies on March 11, 1861, when he presented the bill conferring on Victor Emmanuel II and his descendants the title of King of Italy:

> It is a noble nation that, owing to misfortune and errors, having sunk so low, having been trampled on and flagellated for three centuries by foreign and domestic tyrants, finally rouses itself, invoking its rights, renews itself in a courageous struggle carried on for twelve years and imposes itself before the world. It is this noble nation that, remaining steadfast during lengthy trials, prudent in times of unexpected prosperity and, today, completes its foundation, is united under one regime and authority, united as it already was by race, language, religion, the memories of the suffering borne and hopes for complete deliverance.[1]

Considering Italy's situation in 1861, there was good reason by 1911 to be proud of the results obtained in every field in half a century. The birth of the national state, although carried out by a minority, was a great accomplishment for all Italians: it created the conditions necessary to begin the country's development, it made the emancipation of weaker groups possible and it allowed Italy to reach the status of the more advanced European countries. Despite all the criticisms that could be made against the builders of the unified state, political unity was "in any event the best and most noble thing that had happened to Italy since the Roman empire."[2] This was the judgment of Giustino Fortunato, one of the most pessimistic politicians of the so-called Third Italy. He was well aware of the ancient and recent ills of that society and state, and during his long life spent in politics and as an expert on the problems of the south, he never tired of denouncing them with polite severity. However, he never lost faith in the value of unity and was firmly convinced, despite everything, that political unification had opened the door to progress for the Italians: "Thanks to unity, there has been enormous moral progress."[3]

In fact, having been able to build a single state, overcoming serious obstacles—from the war against banditry to the permanent hostility of the Church, from the unfortunate military campaigns to the violent social uprisings—could be legitimately claimed as a title of merit for the founding fathers of unified Italy. Equally great for their successors was having strengthened the political structure by dealing with the rather serious disorders that had rocked the existence of the new kingdom, and preserving unity by developing the liberal regime and taking it through stormy periods such as the end-of-the-century political crisis, the attempts at restoring authoritarian government and the assassination of King Umberto I. In 1911, the *Times* of London wrote, "Nothing is more notable than the stability of the Kingdom of Italy. By now Cavour's structure is as stable as the most stable in Europe. The concepts of liberty and social order in Italy rest on a strong foundation: actually, in some European countries this has not been achieved yet."[4]

Despite its limits and all its shortcomings, building the national state was the first fundamental step toward a place for Italy in modern civilization. There were still many fractures, both old and new, social and political, that divided the Italians, such that some of them felt, for various reasons, they were not part of the national state. However, even those who did not place the nation at the top of their list of ethical and political values considered political unification a conquest that could not be forgone. "The fifty years of Italian unification have been an illuminating process for Italian workers. Conquest of a bourgeois fatherland was the necessary first step toward a proletarian fatherland,"[5] proclaimed the Socialist Party on the eve of May 1, 1911.

National Pride

In the fifty years since unification, Italy had acquired the fundamental characteristics of a modern national state, even if economic and civil progress had not been made by the whole country. In many regions and sectors of society there were still vast depressed and backward areas. In 1908, Alfredo Oriani, one of Third Italy's most influential nationalist supporters wrote:

> By comparison with Italy today, the country as it was in 1859 has already become part of a legend; the land of singers and the dead, the carnival nation, that foreigners visited either dismally or ironically between brothels and monuments, is one of the most modern and vital countries today. Our population has increased so much that in fifty years it would have almost doubled without emigration, [and] our wealth has increased perhaps tenfold. We have dealt with an unbelievable debt. We have created everything—schools, the army, the navy—we have improvised without having mines, mills or factories but have taken up the challenge of our foreign competitors: considering our poverty, our railroad was an even more wonderful creation than the American one, because we built it without having the money and before other thoroughfares could link places

up. When Turin lost out as the capital, it became doubly important
as an economic center; when Rome became Italian again it was reborn as a magnificent capital.[6]

During the first decade of the twentieth century, the new liberal
course undertaken by politician Giovanni Giolitti and actively supported by the young king, Victor Emmanuel III, had helped accelerate
the state's pathway toward democracy, while the country entered into
a period of intense modernization, economic development and social
change. Ancient and deeply rooted opposition to the national state
seemed to have been overcome or was being solved, and for an ever
larger number of Italians there were more opportunities for freedom
and political participation. Internationally, Italy was playing an increasingly important role in the gatherings of the great powers, which enabled the country to successfully carry out a new colonial undertaking.
The year 1911 was not only the Jubilee year, it was also the year that the
government announced a reform of the electoral system that was to
lead to universal male suffrage. That same year, for the first time, a socialist climbed the steps to the Quirinale for consultations during a government crisis. It was also the year that Italy went to war with Turkey
over the conquest of Libya, with the country's general consensus.

Looking back at their accomplishments, especially in the fields of
production and economics, the Italians of 1911 had good reason to be
proud of industrial Italy. Despite his rhetoric, Francesco Nitti, Minister
of Industry from Lucania (Basilicata), expressed this pride when he inaugurated the World Fair in Turin:

> In fifty years our Italy, overcoming difficulties of all kinds and hin-
> drances by competitors on its small but densely populated territory,
> has witnessed a new industrial era, the budding of a new civiliza-
> tion. . . . A new civilization has been formed only on Italian soil. It
> is as if our land possesses a mysterious power of greatness and
> being. Even if we look reality in the face, even if we are aware of
> what we are lacking, when we view the progress made, we are al-
> most surprised at what we have done.[7]

Apart from the rhetoric, the figures regarding the social and economic activities, which confirmed the country's development, spoke for
themselves. "In fifty years, not only have we managed to confirm our
unity but we have also conquered one of the top places among the great

nations, [and] we have increased our wealth and the nation's assets," observed the editor of a collection of nonrhetorical essays on contemporary Italy, published for the fiftieth anniversary.[8] Economists, little inclined to be enthusiastic patriots and usually critical of the ruling class, shared the same feeling of legitimate satisfaction. The fifty years since unification changed "the face of economic as well as political Italy," declared Luigi Einaudi. However, "whatever the judgment that history will pass about what could have been done better and above all about the many things that could have been avoided, one thing is sure: the comparison between the balance sheet of 1862 and 1911/12 is such that the Italians can be proud," because "we are alone among the great states of Europe (along with England) not to have increased the public debt for a long time and to have accounts that balance." The Turin economist added that, of course, there was still a long way to go to reach the other more modern nations in the organization of the state:

> The Italian people have every right to expect their rulers to provide better and less expensive public services that are less burdened with useless interventions. However, the Italian people have made great sacrifices to give their rulers the means to conduct the war and preserve peace, to honorably meet the public debt inherited from the old states (less than 2 billion and a half but that soon grew to about 15 billion), and to give impulse to culture and the instruments of economic unification, such that even the great men who planned and organized the new Italy could never have thought possible.[9]

Academics and politicians, like Napoleone Colajanni, decidedly hostile toward the monarchic state, also acknowledged the "prodigious economic awakening" recorded in Italy on its fiftieth anniversary.[10]

At the time of the Jubilee, even foreign observers praised the Third Italy, marveling at the strength and vitality of the young state and the progress made by the Italians, although they sometimes delightedly sprinkled salt on the country's still-open wounds. They admired "the huge results that in the short space of time of little more than forty years—nothing in the history of a nation—they were able to obtain," as one English academic wrote, adding: "I don't fear being contradicted by any intelligent and impartial observer of the progress in Italy, when I state that no other European people would have known how to face these difficulties more courageously, and overcome them more satisfactorily, than the Italians have in less than half a century."[11] An unofficial government publication in Vienna, capital of the empire that had been the historic enemy of the Risorgimento and was now an ally, recognized that united Italy "in the last fifty years has developed wonderfully in finance, commerce, industry, education, communications and navigation."[12] The French highlighted the prodigious vitality of the Italian economy, testifying to the admirable effort made by the whole nation: "The economic rebirth of Italy is apparent no matter what aspect of the nation's life you look at, . . . and the ascent that began fifty years ago can be expected to continue." Italy might still encounter some hurdles, but there were no dangers in sight for the stability of the Italian state or the liberal institutions, which appeared to be firmly founded on popular consensus. "The peninsula's population wants to progress, and the pride of the Italian race stimulates its ascent, but taken as a whole, it conforms, despite momentary revolts, to the directions given by its rulers. Italian political life has the same divisions that are to be found in any constitutional state." Furthermore, the continuity of the Risorgimento's liberal tradition was guaranteed by a "very open-minded" king, "a leftward-looking sovereign who follows the ideas of his times and doesn't fear tomorrow." In conclusion, the Third Italy could be considered the "just descendant of its illustrious ancestors."[13]

For believers in the myth of a Greater Italy, comforted by the appraisal of foreigners, the achievements made in fifty years of unity strengthened their faith and increased their self-esteem as a modern population able to look ahead with renewed trust in the future. "We can expect an even greater Italy in the second fifty years of its resurrection," wrote the anthropologist Giuseppe Sergi, hailing the new glory of Italy, which he saw destined to once again carry out "a great mission for peace in the world" as the "intellectual wet-nurse of nations."[14] The nation's pride in fifty years of unity, recalled the historian Arturo Carlo Jemolo, reliable witness of the period, did not rest on "the Greeks and Romans but, finally, on something more realistic; the undertaking in Libya brought together men of different leanings because, rightly or wrongly, they saw it not as simply giving vent to the instinct to overpower but as the beginning of a building process that socialists and even trade unionists could take part in."[15] In 1911 Italy was so proud of itself that it clearly did not tolerate the image many had of it as a museum for past glories, the chosen destination of foreign tourists who admired its works of art but looked down on the people who lived there, seeing the Italians only as waiters, junk dealers, singers, beggars, swindlers and bandits. From the Renaissance on, "we have never lived better nor given more lustrous examples of our worth," observed Angelo De Gubernatis in the pacifist and humanitarian publication "La Vita Internazionale," protesting against those foreigners who visited Italy "just to see the old ruins":

> We certainly do not want to forget any of our past glories. On the contrary, we like to remember all of them; but we no longer want to be that ragged people who wear a threadbare red cape to give a shameful spectacle of our decadence; we have risen to live our own vigorous and powerful life, and we have the right, therefore, to be recognized by the foreigner not as cemetery guardians, or cowardly beggars, or handsome tenors, or novel-type bandits, but as a lively, resolute, proud people conscious of a virtue that wants to rise again and give our national life the mark of new power and new greatness; and it is only thus that we want to, and feel we should, celebrate our fiftieth anniversary.[16]

The Jubilee did not just exhibit the glories of Italy's past. It also focused on the glories of the present, the conquests in production, technology and industry. The Third Italy wanted to show the world that it was ready to compete in the "next industrial and commercial conflict," expected to be "grandiose," with the most powerful nations such as France, England and Germany, "fired by the most powerful fighting spirits: rivalry of race and rivalry in work."[17] Turin, Florence and Rome—the three successive capitals of the Kingdom of Italy between 1861 and 1871—held world exhibitions of the arts, production and industry. The chairman of the organizing committee of the Rome exhibit stated, "The Italians want to show the civilized world today how they, free and united, have wisely used the gifts of liberty and civilization and how they have properly shared out this task between Turin and Rome: in Turin, the most powerful and varied display of the work of all people, and in Rome, a huge celebration of the sciences and the arts, because they have gained inspiration from this city over the centuries and also conferred on it such greatness."[18]

The division of the events between the two cities, "which summarize in their names and in their memories the history of our Risorgimento from beginning to end,"[19] aimed to demonstrate that the sentiment of national consensus triumphed over the spirit of municipal rivalry. In a joint statement, the mayors of Rome and Turin said: "The two cities' commemorative and patriotic celebrations bring together people who are pursuing the road to human civilization, so that the competitors and emulators of the peaceful and fruitful contest of the sciences, the arts and industry are, at once, participants and spectators of the reborn nation's heights of glory."[20]

The Holy Year of Third Italy

However, the fatherland's Jubilee was devoted most of all to exalting the epic of the Risorgimento, which had given birth to the liberal monarchic state. The authors of a popular pamphlet that illustrated the significance of the fiftieth anniversary wrote that it was the duty of a civilized people to preserve the national traditions and keep the flame of enthusiasm burning for everything that had made the nation great. This they were to hand down to the new generations as knowledge for the present and faith in the future, combining worship of those who had unified the nation with "praise of its luxuriant present life."[21]

The patriotic celebrations began in 1909 with a commemoration of the Second War of Independence. They continued in 1910, commemorating Giuseppe Garibaldi's Expedition of the Thousand and the plebiscites that had sanctioned the unification of the Mezzogiorno. And they ended with the inauguration in Rome of the monument to Victor Emmanuel II in June 1911. The aim was to "keep the population's highly patriotic ideals alive," submerging its "mind and heart in a warm sea of sacred memories," to renew the memory of the "sacrifices made for a united Italy" and to "strengthen the faith in its great destiny."[22] They were to hold ever more dearly "the hearts of the Italians in their common love for their country and the sentiment of loyalty to the throne," wrote an English biographer of Victor Emmanuel III.[23] The rites, the symbols and the eloquence of the Jubilee presented the monarchy and liberal institutions to the population as the most authentic incarnation of the Risorgimento's national myth and the only sure means for guiding the Italian nation on the road to progress and greatness, and to the conquest of modern civilization. From this point of view, the celebrations were the greatest undertaking carried out until then by the ruling class to reconsecrate before the whole nation the ideals that legitimized the national state.

Giovanni Pascoli, poet laureate of Greater Italy, was the officiating minister at this consecration, performed in the lay spirit of "religious worship of one's country," and making up the civil creed of liberal Italy. When he commemorated the death of Victor Emmanuel II on January 9, Pascoli declared the year 1911 the country's "Holy Year": "Holy, I repeat. What we and the Italian people are having is not a celebration and a civil commemoration, but a religious ceremony. We are celebrating the nation with a religious rite," the religion "that inspired the philosophy of Mazzini, that fueled the energy of Cavour, that made Carlo

Alberto raise the Italian flag (the tricolor), that made Garibaldi launch his cry for unity, that made Victor Emmanuel unsheathe his sword." In his oration, Pascoli evoked the images of the fundamental elements that made up the national myth of the liberal Third Italy: the cult of father-land and freedom combined with the myth of Rome; the heroic deeds of the Risorgimento that had welded together the conflicting ideals of clashing patriotic forces to achieve unity and independence; the regen-eration and faith in the progress of the Italian nation, risen from the abyss of centuries-long decadence to resume its mission of civilization among modern nations. Inspired by an ancient grandeur to be pro-tected and the hope of a new greatness to be conquered, the poet glo-rified the great Italians of centuries past, the heroes, martyrs, founders, gestures and holy places of the Risorgimento's epic deeds, placing them all in the mythological universe of the reborn country, "so ancient and yet so new, so different and yet the same, like the sun." It was in this uni-verse that the image of Rome was hailed as both muse and goal of the Risorgimento: "Whoever first dreamt, divined, announced and pre-pared the unification was moved by the thought of Rome. Rome and the unification of Italy are one and the same. Rome was not conquered; it was she that united, attracted and unquestionably won over Italy, with all her people of various origins, memories, cleverness and customs: she was the conqueror." The poet linked the cult of tradition to that of prog-ress and hoped that the new generations would be able to "contemplate a knowledgeable and powerful, free and just population in another fifty years."[24]

The myths evoked by the poet were greatly magnified during the Jubilee celebrations. The ceremonial rites and rhetoric emphasized a symbolic representation of the Risorgimento based on the liberal ruling class's assimilation of the different versions of the national myth — ranging from Giuseppe Mazzini's to Giuseppe Garibaldi's — which had been transformed into integral parts of the liberal state's national myth after having been purified of all the elements ideologically incompatible with their own political concepts. Through this assimilation the ruling class aimed to mend the Risorgimento's ideological fractures, exalting the supremacy of the nation, which stood above the parties, to finally build the *fatherland of the Italians*, identifying it with the institutions of a state in which all people could feel they were citizens on equal standing and free before the law despite their different religions, ideologies and social classes. The idea of unity — said a senator commemorating the ex-pedition of the Thousand — "did not belong to a party, here," but "was above tendencies of any kind because it has only one goal: creating a free and unified Italy."[25] It was evident that the ruling class aimed to use the myths predominant in the celebratory rhetoric to shape a national tradition, a common memory of a common history from which no citizen would feel excluded: no citizen, that is, who was above all ready to accept the unified state, the national myth and the principle of freedom identified in the liberal institutions as the supreme value of a civic conscience.

The Harmonious Design of Unity

The most striking aspect of this assimilation was the cult created, and shared by all, for the major protagonists of the Risorgimento, depicted as the architects of a single project that was accomplished by gaining independence, unity and freedom under the protection of the House of Savoy. When on March 10, 1911, the mayor of Rome, Ernesto Nathan, commemorated Mazzini on the anniversary of his death, he exalted the "miraculous combination of separate forces" personified "in the statues standing in the great Council Hall, representing the four most important factors. The Apostle, the Warrior, the King, the Statesman stand watch there over the reborn nation like guardian deities."[26] The bitter struggles that had set the Risorgimento patriots against one another were, thus, hidden in the oleograph in which the faces of Mazzini, Cavour, Garibaldi and Victor Emmanuel II serenely encircled the image of Italy reborn, as if it were a lay image of patriotic devotion. There were no winners or losers among the protagonists of the Risorgimento, only different forces cooperating for the triumph of the national cause. One of the official speakers at the ceremonies in Milan said: "The various movements that crisscrossed life in Italy eventually reached Piedmont and the monarchy, coming from different directions and driven by different forces. Piedmont was home to Italian intellect, nobility, and the kind of strength that bursts forth from the invincible power of an idea, and all accepted or were subjected to that state and that king"; Giuseppe Mazzini, "the most combative, evocative spirit, the most religiously unswerving soul of modern times, who, though distrustful or reluctant, poured the concept of unification into the kingdom's melting-pot"; Garibaldi, "the sweetest of armed poets that ever opened his eyes under the sun," brought "the monarchy a generous people's spontaneousness and severed the dispute over systems and forms with his sword"; lastly, Camillo Benso di Cavour, "the ardent heart, the powerful, calm intellectual, who more than anyone else saw reality clearly, who thanks to a

wonderful balancing act through revolutionary diplomacy organized
Italy's freedom and victory."[27] The prime minister, Luigi Luzzatti,
praised the "Four Founders of the Risorgimento" as heroes of humanity, venerated by free citizens the world over because "no revolution
more than ours is characterized by greatness and pureness; no revolution more than ours has such a brilliant group of forerunners, philosophers, apostles, martyrs, heroes and statesmen; no revolution more than
ours links together four names, each of which would be sufficient for the
glory of a nation: Victor Emmanuel, Mazzini, Garibaldi and Cavour."
The architects of the national revolution were to be held up for venera-
tion by the Italians so that the "cult of the heroes can guide us and help
us during the bleak and difficult hours that are never lacking in the lives
of great peoples; it is sufficient to name these founders of our national
state, and we will be protected from danger. They have given us our
fatherland and will give it to us again in new supreme ventures, as long
as we know how to keep the memory intact and venerate the blood shed
for our country, preserving the cult of our life as one nation in these sublime memories."[28]

Within the framework of the Jubilee celebrations, Garibaldi's undertaking was celebrated as the apex of the Risorgimento. It was seen as the
moment when the aspiration to unification was accomplished thanks to
the combined action of the popular initiative supporting Garibaldi's
type of democracy and the Savoyard monarch's political and diplomatic
action. "For centuries the principle of democracy and that of monarchy
were considered historically irreconcilable. Giuseppe Garibaldi marked
a new era. He embodied Italian democracy in uniform, which held out
its hand to the centuries-old dynasty of the House of Savoy to reach an
agreement based on loyalty, which, fortunately, was never broken."[29]
Thus evoked, the Expedition of the Thousand was considered the
founding event of the national state in Third Italy's mythology. The *Corriere della Sera* wrote that feeling the tie with Garibaldi's undertaking was
"a necessary condition to feeling Italian," because in that undertaking
"the Italian people rediscover themselves after centuries of oppression,
not only in their traditions and their nationality, but also in a sensation
of renewed youth."[30]

The democracy-monarchy combination, which gave birth to the
Third Italy, appeared to be the realization of a "harmonious design
whose starting point was the people's initiative, whose aim was political
unity identified with geographical unity and whose successful civil and
moral completion was Rome."[31] The proclamation of Rome as the

capital of Italy "was the agreement that a legislative assembly signed with the revolutionary demon. Aspromonte, Mentana, the breach of Porta Pia were the necessary consequences," declared a deputy during the commemoration in 1859. Before the grandeur of Rome, "symbol and synthesis of Italy's unity and independence," added another minister on the same occasion, "all differences disappear."[32]

By proclaiming the monarchy-democracy combination intangible in order to formulate the principles and values of a united Italy's civil ethics, the monarchic state could make use of Mazzini's unitarian mysticism, purifying it of its revolutionary and republican spirit, to then include a Mazzini-type "religion of duty" in its educational program as well as the conviction that the national destiny was a civil mission in the name of human progress.

In the "harmonious design" that had led to the birth of the Italian state, the monarchy played an important role that only the antimonarchists saw as an unlawful appropriation perpetrated against the people's wishes. At the time of the patriotic Jubilee, opposition to the monarchy had greatly diminished.

Apart from the Republicans, not even the Socialist Party considered a review of the national state's institutional form a matter for the agenda. Humble and discreet, the young Victor Emmanuel III helped dismiss the fear and suspicion that his predecessor's authoritarian policies had caused at the end of the century. The king's manner conveyed an image of the monarchy that was serene and affable, thus enhancing its function as the best guarantee that the liberal system would develop into a democracy.

Actually, the monarchy had become for most Italians the symbol of unity, in part owing to the national education program carried out by the army and the schools, with their sober state liturgy, and in part, to the spread of the national mythology and the "religion of the fatherland" (*religione della patria*) through Giosue Carducci's poetry and such lay gospels as *Cuore* by Edmondo De Amicis.[33] Despite the fact that the individual sovereigns did not always behave correctly in politics from the liberal point of view, the monarchy contributed to the shaping of a patriotic sentiment, albeit weak, among the population and to a collective national conscience, which during the Jubilee celebrations seemed to increase among Italians of all social classes.

The fatherland's Jubilee gave the official blessing to the image of the national state, which was legitimized as an ideal synthesis between democracy and monarchy, between nation and freedom, nation and humanity, aspiration for greatness and desire for peace and progress. By referring to their common values, to the link between nation and freedom, the liberal ruling class felt that it had solemnly consecrated the ideal union of the Risorgimento's different patriotic forces with the national mythology. On the other hand, only by confirming this indissoluble link would it be possible to build, within the framework of a monarchic national state, a country that an ever greater number of Italian citizens could relate to.[34] Remaining true to the symbiosis between nation and freedom at the beginning of the twentieth century, the liberal state could consider itself the legitimate incarnation of the myth of Greater Italy, daughter of the unity and freedom that had excited Italian patriots since the dawn of the Risorgimento.

PART 1

THE FATHERLAND
OF THE ITALIANS

1

Modernity, Freedom, *Italianità*

The Conquest of Modernity

In the "Jubilee year" of the nation's unification, liberal Italy confirmed its pledge of allegiance to the tradition of Risorgimento patriotism, which, by uniting the ideas of freedom and nation, had found the way to reanimate the Italians' pursuit of modern civilization after centuries of subjection and decadence. "Thus we shall do a great favor . . . to this Italy of ours, which will be called back to new life, finally able to participate in the banquet of nations and contribute its building stone to the great edifice of modern civilization," said Cavour on October 16, 1860.[1]

Uniting the ideas of nation and freedom with the prospect of "civilizing," a word dear to the Risorgimento patriots, had indeed been the matrix of the Italian revolution ever since a political awareness of nation began to develop among small groups of intellectuals, mainly inspired by the French Revolution, at the beginning of the nineteenth century. In that period the awareness of being Italian, which had been a cultural myth since the Middle Ages, turned into a political myth, meaning there was not only the awareness of a cultural nationality but also the intention to act politically in order to free, unify and regenerate Italy through gaining independence and unity.

The Italian patriots' interpretations were conflicting because of the divergent ideologies—moderate, liberal, democratic, neo-Guelph, and federal—that had contributed to forming the Risorgimento movement. Their views on how to reach their goal and the means required to do so were also different and discordant. Even more at odds were their plans for the new national state—monarchy or republic, unitarianism or federalism, centralism or regionalism, lay or confessional—whichever the patriots considered the most suitable for creating a fatherland belonging to all Italians. However, all the patriots would certainly have supported

Mazzini's concept of nation as "a communion of free and equal citizens, united by working harmoniously toward a single aim."[2]

What the chief figures of the Risorgimento movement had in common, beyond the profound divergences separating them (to such an extent that they became enemies), was the conviction that once the nation was reborn it could only be the fruit of a union between "nation" and "freedom," that the national state was to be a nation of free and equal citizens and that the Third Italy was to become a Greater Italy, in the forefront on the road to modern civilization.

Even though the main groups of Risorgimento patriots were inspired by a religious meaning of life, they expressed modern laicism, basing the future national identity on the ideal of individuals able to free themselves of every kind of bondage and become masters of their own destiny.

A lay idea of modern civilization predominated in the Risorgimento's aspiration to nationhood which had merged with the political culture of a liberal state. Modern civilization was mainly conceived as the progress of reason and freedom, as the intellectual and moral emancipation of the individual and humanity, through the progress and emancipation of single nations. "This idea of a moral and free universe, governed by rational law, applied to the life of each single nation, where all peoples are united and have a common destiny, is the essence of our present civilization," stated the Neapolitan philosopher Bertrando Spavento in 1860.[3]

Coming to terms with modernity constantly permeated the growing aspiration to a Greater Italy in all its different phases. We can say that Italian nationalism arose from the need of modernity, placed the conquest of modernity, as we have called it,[4] among its main objectives, and aimed at leaving the mark of a new Italian civilization on modernity. This means that the modernity that Italian nationalism had to face after the Risorgimento was meant both as economic and social development and as cultural and spiritual development—as the creation of a new civilization. The different ways a Greater Italy was envisaged, which we will explore further, arose from the way the aspiration to nationhood faced modernity, that is, how those who believed in a future nation interpreted the process of modernization according to their view of how the Italian nation was progressing. In each of these ways, counterposing the vision of a future state to modernity predominated, while what distinguished them from each other was mainly a different perception of the social and economic transformations typical of modernization, the differences in political culture and the type of state considered most suitable to ensure success for Italy's conquest of modernity.

From Freedom to Modernity through the Nation

The Italian aspiration to nationhood arose from a noble concept of modern man's dignity, which could only be fully recognized in the ethical and juridical condition of a free citizen in an independent and sovereign state. In Cavour's concept of nation is one of the loftiest expressions of this idea of human dignity interwoven with national conscience: "The history of all ages," wrote Cavour in 1844, "proves that no people can reach a high level of intelligence and morality without strongly developed national feelings." He explained that this held good above all for the masses, whose intellectual life "proceeded in a very restricted circle of ideas. The noblest and loftiest ideas that the masses can achieve, after those pertaining to religion, are certainly the ideas of nation and nationality." Only if the most backward classes achieved a national conscience would they rise in society and achieve greater dignity and well-being. Where political circumstances do not allow any expression of the ideas of nation and nationality, Cavour stated,

> the masses will remain in a state of wretched inferiority. However, that is not all: a people that cannot be proud of its nationality will have only some rare privileged individuals with feelings of personal dignity. The classes made up of the masses, who occupy the lowest rung of the social ladder, need to feel important from a national point of view in order to become aware of their own dignity, [an awareness that] is an essential moral element for peoples as for individuals. . . . If we want the emancipation of Italy so passionately, . . . it is not only with the aim of seeing our nation glorious and powerful, but above all so that it may raise its level of intelligence and moral development to that of the most civilized nations.[5]

Cavour's concept of nation, as a means of emancipating both the individual and the masses, was similar to Mazzini's. The Piedmontese statesman and the Ligurian revolutionary disagreed about everything regarding the aims of, and the means and methods required for, the revolution necessary to become a nation-state. However, they could have agreed, at least ideally, on one principle: that the national consciousness, in other words, the sentiments of belonging to a common fatherland, was an indispensable condition to raise the Italians to the dignity of modern men and citizens. Addressing the Italians, Mazzini affirmed,

Without a fatherland you have neither names, nor distinctive
marks, nor votes, nor rights and not even acceptance as brothers
among peoples. You are the bastards of humanity. Soldiers without
a flag, Jews of the nations, you will be neither trusted nor pro-
tected: no guarantors for you. Do not be under the illusion that you
will be emancipated from an unjust social condition if you do not
first attain a country of your own. Therefore do not be led astray
by hopes of material progress that, in your present condition, are
illusions. Only a single and unified fatherland, the vast and rich
fatherland of Italy that stretches from the Alps to the southernmost
tip of Sicily, can fulfill those hopes.[6]

The two architects of the Risorgimento could have agreed, at least
ideally, on another principle, that is, on the belief that political freedom
was an essential and indispensable element for developing the modern
Italian's awareness of nation. Indeed, Risorgimento aspirations held
freedom to be a vital need, not only to civilize the nation but for its very
existence, just as independence from any foreign rule was vital for the nation. Not even the greatness of a country could call for the sacrifice of
freedom and dignity or the subjection of other nations for its own expansion. Mazzini more than any other Risorgimento patriot believed in total
devotion to fatherland, the idea of a nation's moral unity. He believed
that a sense of duty had precedence over citizens' claims to rights in the
framework of civic ethics, and he had the greatest faith in Greater Italy's
supremacy in the mission to guide humanity. Consequently, he firmly
condemned "limiting sentiments only to one's country," sentiments that
gave rise to "rights and duties of citizens, not of men, a spirit of independence and honor, not of freedom and moral improvement." The cult of
one's fatherland had to be secondary to the cult of an individual's freedom and dignity, "because devotion to your country is sacred," stated
Mazzini, "but where it is not governed by a sense of individual dignity
and the awareness of rights inherent in man's nature—where a citizen is
not convinced that he has to bring honor to his country, not take it
away—it is devotion that can make a nation powerful, not happy, splendid in its glory to the eyes of a foreigner, not free."[7]

For a Free Association of Free Countries

What was good for the citizen of a national state was good for a nation
in the international community. The Risorgimento's aspiration to nationhood expressed love of one's country and the idea of nation, which

seem closely linked to the love of freedom and independence for all nations. The right of a nation to be free, united and independent within the borders of its own state derived from the idea of freedom, which had also been maturing in European culture since the Age of Enlightenment. Gian Domenico Romagnosi had stated that the right of a nation to have complete authority over its own territory was a natural right inherent in humanity and in the process of its becoming civilized, whose purpose was "to allow different and naturally unequal people to acquire legal and civil equality."[8] Since nations are also individuals with body and soul, becoming civilized, in their case, consists of gaining independence: "Whole nations independent, masters of all their territories and with only one moderate government, this is the final destiny of the world intended by nature and reason and that leads to internal and external peace and prosperity."[9]

Mazzini was the greatest theorist and the most fervent apostle of the ideal of humanity as an association of free and independent nations cooperating for the progress of modern civilization, each with its own mission. Nation, freedom and humanity formed a trinity that was central to his political theology. Mazzini believed that a nation was not an end in itself but a means to emancipate and set free humanity, which he imagined as

> a vast army moving to conquer unknown lands, against powerful and cunning enemies. The peoples are the different units, the divisions of that army. A place has been entrusted to each one, and each one has a special operation to accomplish. The collective victory depends on how correctly the different operations will be carried out. Do not upset the order of the battle. Do not abandon the flag that God gave you. . . . Your nation represents the mission that God gave you to carry out in humanity.[10]

Mazzini envisaged peoples as "the individuals of humanity" and nationality as "a sign of their individuality and a guarantee of their liberty. Nationality is sacred. Manifested also by tradition, language and by indications of an attitude or special mission, it must seek harmony with the whole and work to better everyone, for the progress of humanity."[11]

Mazzini's concept of the link between nation and humanity inspired the Neapolitan jurist Pasquale Stanislao Mancini, in 1851, to work out a theory of the principle of nationality, setting it "as the rational basis of the rights of peoples."[12] As there are, in fact, a lot of nations, Mancini stated that this principle could only mean the equal inviolability and protection of all of them; and, therefore, as this principle would be violated if our nationality suffered offence from others and was prevented by them from carrying out its activities freely, it would not be less so if, on the contrary, our nationality invaded the domain of others and caused offence against their legitimate freedom. In both cases, equality would be subverted, national independence would be harmed and the rule of rights would be upset.[13]

The loss of freedom causes the death of a nation or reduces it to an inert body. A state "in which many proud nationalities are suppressed by obligatory union is not a political body but a monster incapable of living," just as those nations "whose governments were not born of their own wombs, and which obey laws imposed on them by others, no longer have any legal power. They have already become means for the aims of others, and therefore things. . . . When a nationality's autonomous and independent life is impaired, its whole being inevitably decays and dies."[14]

Formulated to give the Italian national movement legal legitimacy, the principle of nationality required freedom and independence for all nations. The internal life of a nation, like relations among nations, was to be ruled by a single "formula for justice: *Coexistence and agreement on freedom for all men;* which we must translate into the other: *Coexistence and agreement among the free Nationalities of all peoples.*"[15] This ideal of coexistence was considered valid in that it was inherent in humanity's historical evolution, which "shows us that humanity progressively joins forces, and this is a law governing the development of our species." Nationality, "a formation midway between a town and the world," was precisely "destined by nature and civilization as a means to accomplish this transformation peacefully and harmoniously."[16]

Fatherland and Nation

The assumption behind the principle of nationality was the idea of nation expressing a sense of belonging, a desire to belong, which arose above all when one freely and consciously participated in the life, history and destiny of a collective entity recognized and loved as one's own nation. Country and nation thus tended to coincide in the modern concept of a national state. Mazzini stated that nationality was "a common thought, principle and aim." A nation is "an organic whole held together by the same aims and capacity to act, living with its own faith and tradition, strong and distinct from others, with a special tendency to carry out an intermediate mission, secondary to the general mission of humanity. Language, territory and race are nothing but indications of nationality."[17] Achieving unity and independence, that is, creating a national state, is the main goal of the mission for building a single fatherland for all Italians.

Natural and historical conditions, "having territory, origins and language in common at the same time, are still not enough to completely form a nationality as we mean it," explained Mancini when developing Mazzini's idea:

> These elements are like inert matter, capable of living but not yet having received the breath of life. Now, this vital spirit, this divine achievement of a nation coming to life, this principle of its visible existence . . . *is the awareness of nationality,* the sense it acquires of itself that enables it to come into being internally and appear externally. Find as many material and exterior points in common as you like among an aggregation of men. However, they will never form a nation without the moral unity of a common way of thinking, of a predominant idea that makes a society what it is. . . . Until this source of life and strength, with its wonderful qualities, flows into and permeates the shapeless mass of the other elements, their manifold varieties will lack unity, their active capacities will not have the spark of life and will be consumed by disorderly and sterile efforts. Rather, an inanimate body will exist but will still be incapable of functioning as a national personality, of subjecting itself to the moral and psychological relations in each distinct social organization.[18]

This concept became the basis of the aspiration to a liberal state, where the ideas of *patria* (fatherland), *paese* (land), *nazione* (nation) and *nazionalità* (nationality) often tended to blend or overlap. We may be able to deduce the prevalent meaning given to the concepts of *patria* and *nazione* in united Italy from their definitions in the most widely read dictionaries of that period.

For example, in the *Dizionario dei sinonimi della lingua italiana* (*Dictionary of Italian Synonyms*), whose fifth edition came out in 1867, Niccolò Tommaseo pointed out the difference between "fatherland," "country" and "nation," explaining that "nation is, or should include, those born of the same origin, speaking the same language and subject to the same laws. However, none of these three conditions exists in any civilized European nation, and any country closer to fulfilling these conditions is closer to being a nation. A conquered state that loses its public life is no longer a nation, but remains a people," since a people, according to Tommaseo, is distinct from a nation insofar as a people is part of it, even if "the most numerous and noblest part."[19] Tommaseo introduced an important clarification in his definition of *patria* (fatherland) when differentiating it from *paese* (land), revealing not only the philologist but the sentiments of a patriot:

> After all, we can love our own native land without loving our fatherland; love the enclosure we were born in and not those rights and duties that make up one's real country; love out of interest or instinct, not love with reasonable and virtuous affection. More or less everybody loves his own native land, few love their fatherland. We can love our fatherland very much and our native land little. Everyone has a native land that he can call his own, but how many have a fatherland? Many think they have one but they do not. As the love of fatherland fades, so does the affection that every man not indifferent to beauty owes to the beauties of his own country. A native land may be more or less beautiful, but a fatherland is always beautiful to those who feel it is theirs.

In his definition, Tommaseo emphasizes the link between the idea of "a real fatherland" and the idea of the rights and duties that are fundamental to "the reasonable, virtuous affection" that a citizen feels for his country, who loves his "real fatherland" in that he benefits from the rights and duties that are part of it. Thus, someone who does not benefit from the rights and duties of his country can say that "not all the things of our country are ours," as Tommaseo went on to explain regarding the term "*patria*" (fatherland), "all the citizens feel that there are some things (even civil ones and those naturally in common) that do not belong to our country."

What differentiated the idea of fatherland from that of nation was mainly the emphasis on the emotional element, the sentiments of love — with the intimation of filial love — rather than the more strictly historical, cultural, ideological and political elements that were peculiar to the modern idea of nation gradually taking root throughout the 1800s. "Patriotism is the cult of love," according to the definition of the word *patria* (fatherland) in the tenth volume of the *Nuova enciclopedia popolare* (New Popular Encyclopedia) published in Turin in 1848 by the publisher Giuseppe Pomba and that later became UTET. A fatherland is the place "of birth, feelings, traditions, hope and possessions, where different families have common origins, customs, religions and relations; where different communities are united by rights and duties and by the same laws and powers." Patriotism "produces the wonderful harmony of different minds, so that if everyone submits to the common interest, the body of the state will become, if not invulnerable, at least invincible. It absorbs all passions and is nourished and enlarged by everybody's efforts." It is clear from this that slaves have no feeling for their country ("they live in their country like animals in a den"), that patriotism cannot arise in a state where the inhabitants are "voluntary subjects of tyrants," and that only a despot in a despotic state loves his country, but he loves it as "a kaffir takes great care of the prisoner he wants to cook and eat." The "powerful men" in monarchies can love their country for the favors they receive or expect from the prince who rules, but they do not love their country. "A Turk can love his sultan, a boyar can love his tsar, but nobody can love a country he has not got." Not even the great feats of despotic monarchies are acts of patriotism because they are the fruit of thirst for gold and ambition for power. Only in representative states, in the "plebeian" chamber, "is there, if still possible, the love of country," and only from these "political bodies does patriotism spread to all the country."

Therefore only freedom allowed patriotism to arise and spread. This essential element was acknowledged also in the modern concept of nation and nationality, although not explicitly. The same encyclopedia (ninth volume) defines "nation" as "an aggregation of people within a limited territory ruled by the same laws, with customs and language in common. However, sometimes it refers to the inhabitants of the same country who do not have the same government, like the Italian nation that is divided up into many states." Nations "are parts of humanity in the same way as individuals make up nations," so, in these terms, the words "people" and "nation" are often exchanged, even though "it may be more correct to keep the word "people" for the masses united by common origin and ideas and only call "nation" the peoples in regularly established political and sovereign states." Belonging to a nation, whether by birth or by association, is what is called "nationality," which is established "when the ideas and material and moral interests of a large aggregation of people, and above all the aim of their activities, are almost identical. The more united these three basic elements are, the stronger and more vigorous the nationality tends to be. However, when certain ideas are no longer generally accepted, interests divided, and there is no longer agreement on the goal to be reached through common efforts, the nationality weakens and finally dies out." Even though

nations "have tried to incorporate and destroy each other," nationality
has intrinsically "great energy that can be completely suppressed by
force for some time but come back to life at the first moment of hope."
However, at present, the author of the definition pointed out that "the
world of politics has more respect for the nationality of peoples, and it
seems that calling peoples to a holy alliance where all are united by an
aim of love, brotherhood and civility is the prerogative of the divine law
of Christianity."[20]

Substantial changes in the idea of nation can be found in later edi-
tions of this encyclopedia. In the sixth edition (1883),[21] for example, it is
significant that, while the definition of the word *patria* (fatherland) was
almost unchanged, the word *nazione* (nation), still coupled with *nazionalità* (nationality), was extensively modified: the new version clearly reflected the development of Italian and European nationalism, which
had by then become the predominant movement in political and cultural life, even though the word "nationalism" was not yet included in
dictionaries. Furthermore, the new definition gave the highest level of
conceptual and ideological complexity to the idea of nation that the
Italian conscience had acquired after unification.

It was by itself indicative, first of all, that at the beginning most
people were confused by the various meanings given to the idea of nation, and it was only later that an attempt was made to elaborate concep-
tually the idea of nation according to the political, diplomatic, religious,
geographical, anthropological and linguistic points of view. According
to the latter, a nation was an "aggregate of different tribes that used similar linguistic expressions and, when civilized, used the dialect of one
tribe as the common official written and spoken language." The linguistic definition was indicated as the "truly accurate meaning of the word
nation and the only one that should be used" because "it is this meaning
that is used today when the question of nationality has become so
deeply felt as to lead to bloody battles or rebellions among Italians,
Magyars, Greeks, Poles and Scandinavians, and that each day threatens
to create disorders in Turkey and Austria, and perhaps even Russia, and
will have a new political order in Europe as its inevitable consequence."

The linguistic element also prevailed in the definition of what "nationality" was made up of: that is, a group of elements such as "political,
religious, territorial unity, origin and language, as well as the same laws,
customs, historical development, interests and even the same architec-
tural tastes." However, linguistic uniformity was considered the "cornerstone of nationality," and despite the fact that it was "often the only true

national characteristic, it was thought to be sufficient to constitute a nation." Linguistic uniformity, reached through a long process of "civilization," is "one of the factors of nationalities, and the one that fosters territorial expansion more than conquest." Nations, therefore, "are not built by chance, although their creation is independent of the will of individuals"; the making of nationality is always the "result of centuries of aspirations and effort." Creating nationality is a "job that requires hundreds of years, but once it is done, the necessary step forward is to develop the desire for political independence, moving from hope to effort, that is, from concept to action." Once created, all nationalities hope to achieve independence, to set themselves up as sovereign states, to become an "ethnic authority." Essential conditions for the creation of sovereign states are to have "well-defined, easy-to-defend territorial boundaries and a city that is memorable for its expanse, population size or central location so as to facilitate commerce; in other words, a city that can be considered a metropolis, unrivaled by any other." But it was thought to be equally important to instill the concept of duty in the minds of the nation's members, because the independence gained could only be maintained "if the duties incumbent on the members of the great human family were fulfilled. If they refused to perform them, the nation would not be able to keep its independence for long."

Moving from such conceptual premises to the observation of reality at the end of the nineteenth century, it is possible to quickly draw a precise profile of the historic evolution of nationalism from its original linguistic uniformity to the modern idea of political awareness and aspiration that animated national movements at the time, permeating them with a driving force that was to drastically change the order of Europe: "Every nation labors to obtain independence, that is, to become an ethnic authority. This explains the radical changes that are taking place with respect to dynastic rights within national law and concerns the redistribution of Europe into regions already occupied by nations, and not states, made up of groups of people of different nationalities." The strong desire to turn becoming a nation into reality, as happened in Italy, was irresistible, because "once a principle has taken root in the general opinion, governments no longer have the power to oppose it. The wars and rebellions that have caused so much bloodshed in Europe over the past fifty years, with few exceptions, were purely motivated by the desire for nationality." The triumph of this principle would have closed the doors of the temple of Janus, being the "right to nationality, . . . the complete opposite of the right to conquer." A nation that subjugates another or prohibits natural and legitimate demonstrations, commits "a crime against the order established by God . . . and sooner or later will have to pay the penalty," the author concluded.

Looking again at the encyclopedic definitions of the concept of nation, we can now examine the *Dizionario di cognizioni utili* (*Dictionary of Useful Words*), published by UTET in 1914. It was conceived as an elementary encyclopedia based on secondary school programs and was intended for use by families.[22] The first thing we notice is that this dictionary does not contain the word *patria* (fatherland) nor the word *nazionalismo* (nationalism), while it clearly treats the words *nazione* (nation) and *nazionalità* (nationality), defining the latter as the *principio di nazionalità* (principle of nationality), in other words, "the right of every nation to set itself up as a separate political unit (state)." Some important changes and new elements appear in the concept of nation with respect to the previous definition. It confirms the "ideal" nature of the social bond that "links a large group of people who have language, religion, culture and customs in common. Some other elements, based on geography, conquest, common interests, and needs, thought to be essential factors denoting origin, were considered less important as were religion and language. As regards race, this was considered an "important element but not the only one needed to build a nation," because "modern nations, most of all civilized ones, are made up of individuals who belong to many different races." In fact, even the Germans, "who are the most strenuous supporters of a pure race, have many, many Slavs in their nation."

In conclusion, a nation was an "ideal principle made up of elements, one relating to the past, the other extending into the future. The former consisted of inherited memories, sorrows and joys; the latter was related to contemporary consensus, the desire to live together, the expressed or unexpressed will to continue to enjoy the common heritage received." And since "nations are made up of men, who are human beings, the only legitimate criteria to spread nationality is the desire of individuals to do so."

Nation, History, Race

As we have seen, the concept of a national identity as the historical awareness of a common past that gives rise to faith in a common future, became more and more evident in the political culture of liberal Italy. In this sense, a nation was considered the outcome of a history-making process that, in modern times, culminated in the appearance of a "national sentiment," such as Giuseppe Carle, a follower of Pasquale Mancini, defined it: the awareness of wanting to be a nation and achieving it through the organization of an independent sovereign state. By claiming the Italian school of thought to be the father of the definition of the principle of nationality and eliminating anything that remained of "naturalism" in the definition of nation, Carle gave considerable importance to the "historic and traditional element in the making of modern nationalities," because "it is the memory and awareness of a common past that convinces peoples that they will have to cooperate in undertaking a common task for the future and, therefore, convinces them to desire and aspire to become part of the same state in order to perform that very task."[23] According to Carle, a nation derives its origin and legitimacy from history, thus becoming the "initial organizer of the modern state" and "the only worthwhile element that modern states can put forth as the basis of an international right."[24]

History, conceived as the activity that spawned humanity's aspiration and spirit, was the matrix and justification of the desire for nationhood. Aspiration and spirit were predominant factors in the Italian concept of nation: they were decisive factors that enabled all the others—territory, language, religion, traditions and customs—to acquire, so to speak, vitality in the building process of a nation, a building-process that would be completed with the actual realization of the nation-state. The preponderance attributed to the awareness of a common past in forming the modern concept of nation, understood to be its historic formation and not a natural factor, excluded race from the characteristics determining nationality. The idea that prevailed in liberal Italy viewed a nation as a spiritual, cultural and historic reality in which the element of aspiration was essential, decisive and generally more humanistic compared to any naturalistic element. On the basis of this concept, spiritual, cultural and historic factors are more crucial than natural, geographic and ethnic factors in forming a human community that can be called a nation. None of these, even when combined, are conducive by themselves to building a nation unless they are united and enlivened by the awareness of nationality and by the desire to live together to pursue a common aim.

However, there were many interpretations that excluded aspiration from the definition of national conscience in an attempt to dogmatize the idea of fatherland and nation. For example, Francesco Crispi exalted country as if it were a dogma: "There can be no questioning of fatherland—suffice that it exists," he said in September 1900. "No one has the right to disavow it: no code sanctions repudiation of one's own mother. Denationalization is a crime just like slavery—and conquests do not invalidate a right, they only suspend the exercising of it."[25]

Placing the emphasis on the nonvoluntaristic characteristics of a nation never led to defining the same according to predominant racist criteria. In the 1883 edition of the above-mentioned encyclopedic dictionary, for example, identification of a nation with race was clearly rejected, and this element was not even found among those making up nationality, because "race is a word that should be left to zoology only." Also in the 1914 edition we find a clear rejection of the idea of nation as originating just from race: "Anthropology is inept to justify the ideal value of nation."

Of course in liberal Italy there were those who stressed the reference to the Italian race, interpreting the nature of nations and their struggles according to the theories of social Darwinism. However, even they did not define the quintessence of nation as being founded exclusively on racial groups. Even positivist anthropology favored "conscience" over "race" in its definition of nation. Celso Ferrari, a positivist theoretician of nationality, said that it was not race alone that made up a nation but "affinity of sentiment and aspiration that unites individuals who become organized to carry out the functions necessary for the independence of a social body, which must inspire a collective conscience that will relate said functions to its external environment."[26] The nation was the "first and most essential product of all those moral and intellectual factors that aim at the progressive development of social life."[27] In 1906 Napoleone Colajanni wrote: "In the reality of the present time there are no races, only peoples. And more than peoples, today it's nations that live and act on the world scene. . . . Today there isn't a single nation that is the product of just one race. Nations may not be the result of true fusion, but they are, at least, the outcome of the union, overlapping and mixing of different races that were not pure even before the beginning of their historical existence."[28] What characterized a nation, said Colajanni, was the "psychosocial element"; the contributing factors to the building of a nation were "above all social factors and historic elements." Therefore, "there is no nation without a common sense of belonging, where there is not a common intellectual and moral heritage that fosters mutual action and establishes solidarity among its members. Where these elements are lacking there is no nation and there can only be a state or an empire."[29]

Except for some sporadic attempts, the nationalism advocated by the liberal movement in Italy did not embrace any theory of an Italian race, which had preserved its ethnic purity and uniformity over the centuries. Anthropological studies of Italians, which confirmed indisputably that the modern Italian population originated from an ethnic mixture, did not offer grounds for founding a nationalist myth that favored and exalted the racial factor. In 1901, the anthropologist Alfredo Niceforo advanced as scientifically proven the hypothesis that there were "two Italies that do not resemble each other in their customs, civilizations or race; they are strongly bonded by their national conscience and always will be, but they have indelibly impressed in their physiognomy the traces of a vivid physical and moral dissimilarity." This dissimilarity was determined by the fact that "northern Italy was populated—to a large extent—by a different race from the one that forms the majority of southern Italians."[30]

The New *Italianità*

Actually, if there was not a positive myth of an Italian race, there was indeed the "negative" myth regarding the character of the Italians. This idea was supported by the conviction that, in the mentality, customs, habits and the way in which life was conceived by Italians, who descended from centuries of servitude and backwardness and remained segregated from the vital movements of modern civilization, so many faults and defects had built up as to weaken their moral conscience, making it necessary to profoundly regenerate their character in order to allow the emergence of the new Italian, the citizen of a modern national state.[31]

In 1824 Giacomo Leopardi dissected the character of the Italians, highlighting the defects of a nation that was skeptical, cynical, pleasure-loving, superficial and lacking the strong principles and civilized habits of what the poet-philosopher called "society."

> The Italians laugh their way through life: they laugh at life much more often and there is more truth and intimate conviction in their scorn and detachment than in any other nation. This is surely understandable, as life for them is worth much less than for others and because, certainly, such vivacious and warm-hearted characters as the Italians have, become colder and more apathetic when they have to fight against odds that are superior to their strength. It is the same for individuals and nations. The upper

classes in Italy are the most cynical compared with their peers in
other nations. The lower classes are the most cynical of all lower
classes. Those who believe the French nation to be the most cynical
are wrong. No one exceeds or equals Italy in that.[32]

What the Italians were lacking were the common fundamental values
that made up the customs of a national society: They

> have practices and habits rather than customs. Only a few prac-
> tices and habits can be considered national, and those, together
> with the more numerous ones that must be considered provincial
> and municipal, are followed only because people are accustomed
> to them, not because of any national or provincial spirit. . . . Use
> and custom in Italy usually end up with everyone following his own
> practice or custom, whatever that may be.

That is what has led to a "total lack of, or uncertainty about, proper
customs in Italy, including customs that are specifically Italian (a lack
that always accompanies and causes bad habits)."[33] Leopardi concluded
his dissection of the national character, imparting a severe judgment of
moral and intellectual inferiority with respect to other nations:

> As regards morals, Italy is wanting in the fundamental principles
> more than perhaps any other European and civilized nation, be-
> cause it lacks those principles that gave birth to, and everyday con-
> firm as they progress, that very civilization, and it has lost those
> that have been destroyed by the progress of civilization and knowl-
> edge. On the one hand, Italy is inferior to the culturally more ad-
> vanced, better educated nations that are more socially inclined,
> more active and lively, while on the other hand, it is inferior to the
> less culturally advanced, poorly educated and less socially inclined
> countries, that is to say, Russia, Poland, Portugal and Spain, which
> still conserve many of the prejudices that characterized past centu-
> ries and which, due to ignorance, are still able to guarantee moral
> standards to a certain extent, although they lack what society and
> the fragile sentiment of honor can contribute to a moral code.[34]

In conclusion, the poet said, "We should not be at all surprised that
the Italians, the liveliest of all the educated nations, the most sensitive
and warmhearted by nature, have now become the dullest, the coldest,
the most philosophic in practice, the most circumspect, indifferent and
insensible."[35]

The need for the intellectual and moral reform of the Italians was given great impulse by this judgment, which was widely shared among the architects of the Risorgimento, especially after unification. The reform project, variously conceived, aimed to create a new Italian identity. The idea of regenerating the character of the Italians came from the Enlightenment and the French Revolution, which had exalted the "sacred love of fatherland" together with the love of freedom and pride in belonging to a "great nation." According to the patriots of the Risorgimento, it was imperative to regenerate the character of the Italians, corrupted by centuries of servitude, in order to educate them in the virtue of patriotism that binds an individual to his nation. The prophets of the Risorgimento movement had dreamed of the "future Italians" who would be "chosen to perform the major change," as predicted by the Neapolitan exponent of the Enlightenment, Franceso Lomonaco, in 1800.[36] Vittorio Alfieri urged Italy to awaken, in the memory of that "august mistress" that it had once been, and at the same time, scorned it for being "helpless, divided, humiliated, not free and impotent," meanwhile dreaming of the "day when undoubtedly" it would rise up again, "virtuous, magnanimous and united."[37] But to regenerate the nation, the "human plant" that was the typical Italian had to be regenerated. As Melchiorre Gioia said in 1823, the "new Italian" had to be taught that he belonged "to his country, to the nation where he was born, whose name he takes and whose climate, education and habits had imprinted specific national traits on him."[38]

Identification of the patriot with the citizen who was free, hardworking, virtuous, took part in the rights and duties and above all was devoted to his country and ready to die for it became the cornerstone of the civilized ethical concept that was to form the conscience of the new Italians that the architects of the Risorgimento had dreamed of. However, the Italians, thus conceived, had yet to be created. The new Italian, said Vincenzo Gioberti in 1843, "is wishful thinking and not a fact, an assumption and not a reality, a name and not a thing. . . . We have Italy and Italian descendants who are joined through blood ties, religion and the written language, which is well-known, but divided by different governments, laws, institutions, local idioms, customs, ties of affection and practices."[39]

And once again the protagonists of the Risorgimento were divided on how to conceive and put into effect the regeneration of the Italians. Cavour, both as a monarchist and a moderate, thought it should be the responsibility of a liberal monarchy: it was a long, hard operation that was to be realistically conducted through a gradual emancipation process. In contrast, Mazzini was a radical republican who believed the regeneration should be carried out by the Italians themselves. It was to be the outcome of a revolutionary undertaking by the people, who, spurred by their faith in the cult of fatherland, regenerated themselves through struggle, sacrifice and martyrdom.

To the present day, exalting the regeneration of character has been a characteristic of the national culture and has maintained considerable vitality throughout various metamorphoses. After political unification, reforming the character of the Italians was the biggest undertaking that the builders of the new Italian nation had to deal with.

As Massimo d'Azeglio wrote:

> For about half a century Italy has been active, laboring to become a nation with a united people. It has regained most of its territory. The struggle with the foreigner has ended with good result, but that is not the greatest difficulty. The greatest, the real one, the one that makes everything uncertain, is the internal struggle. Italy's most dangerous enemies are not the Germans, they are the Italians.
>   Why?
>   The reason is that the Italians wanted to build a new Italian nation, remaining the same old Italians they were before, with their mediocrities and their poor morals, which have ruined them since ancient times. They think they can reform Italy, and no one realizes that in order to succeed they must first reform themselves. Italy, like all peoples, cannot become a nation, will not be orderly and well managed, as strong against the foreigner as against the internal sectarians, free in its own right, until old and young and middle-aged, each in his own sphere, do their duty and do it well, or at least to the best of their ability. But to do one's duty, which most of the time is annoying, vulgar [and] ignored, requires willpower and the conviction that the duty must be performed, not because it is entertaining or fruitful but because it is a duty. It is this willpower, this conviction, this precious gift that is embodied in the single word, character. Therefore, to say it briefly, the first thing Italy needs to do is to form Italians who know how to do their duty; thus, it needs to form strong-willed, tenacious characters.[40]

The founding fathers of united Italy had placed teaching among the primary duties of the state to cure the Italians of their "old-fashioned ways" and turn them into "modern men," as the Neapolitan philosopher Silvio Spaventa stated.[41] The army and the schools were the principal institutions charged with forming the character of the modern Italians. This was a problem that worried the educators of liberal Italy, to the point of obsession for the most fervent believers in the myth of a Great Italy. In 1875 a competition was even organized, for the second time, on "the importance of forming character in the education of the Italians as the basis of civilian courage, truthfulness and living and working accordingly." The participants were asked to indicate the "principal directives and practical suggestions for achieving that end."[42] The competition was won by Augusto Alfani, the well-known philologist and educator, who was passionately devoted to forming the new Italian. The text describes the ideal type of Italian that liberal Italy wanted to educate in its schools and army, developing, above all, love for one's fatherland, since "those who are not strongly attached to their country are without religion, virtue and character."[43] Love for one's fatherland became the foundation and source of every virtue, every moral quality, both private and public:

> Indeed, any person who, after God, didn't love his fatherland more than anything else on earth would not be worthy to speak about character. In order to form a man who is full of good intentions, sound and vigorous devotion is required, and devotion to one's dear country is among the most important things on earth. It lends goodness and vitality to the devotion to family and friendships, as well as to love of oneself and one's improvement. Who could ever doubt that a people unenamored of its own country should not be worthy of the name, because the very meaning of fatherland is the moral and civilized unity of its people, and their traditions and hopes?[44]

Liberal Italy's state teachers were well aware of the difficult task they had to tackle to achieve moral unification after political unity. "By now we have national 'unity,' but we are still lacking the foundation, that is, 'unification,'" the renowned politician and educator of the Third Italy Francesco De Sanctis told his voters in 1883:

> Unification is that slow process of assimilation that has to try to reduce the distance separating region from region, class from class. Continuing to point out the passions and divergences between the classes and regions is not conducive to this, but rather sows the seeds of hate and envy and encourages feelings of aggressiveness; hate doesn't create anything, but destroys everything; therefore, since this is not unifying Italy but dividing it, it is a crime against national unity.[45]

De Sanctis had devoted much time to the study of the national character in the belief that "it is not ingenuity that saves nations but character and temperament."[46] He was searching for the reasons for the *corruttela italiana*, the Italian tendency to exploit people and situations for one's own benefit. He was searching for its "elements, its widespread existence, its intensity, its causes, its development, its effects, the characteristics it gave to the nation and its aspect, the traces to be seen even today and that keep the nation from moving forward." By studying literature, Italy's greatest educator tried to understand why Italy, "although strong and healthy, was in such a state of dissolution and corruption that in its first clash with barbarians it lost everything, including its honor, taking such a bad fall as to disappear from history for many centuries, casting a doubt today [1869] whether its recovery is real."[47] In the end he was convinced he had discovered the cause of the *corruttela* in the "Guicciardini-type man," as he called him—that is, the typical Renaissance Italian whose life and actions were insincere and hypocritical, whose real aim was to develop his own "personal interests," for which he was prepared to sacrifice country, religion, freedom, honor, glory, or in other words, "anything that encouraged men to be magnanimous and that made nations great." Ever since then, the Italians, who were in a lethargic state, have lacked the "strength to sacrifice, when necessary, not only substance but life itself,"[48] strength that was the foundation of society. It was only during the Risorgimento that the regeneration of the Italians' character began, but even after unification and independence were achieved, the "Italian race has not recovered from its moral weakness, and its forehead still bears the brand of hypocrisy and simulation," the characteristics the "Guicciardini-type man" had so boasted about. "This fatal man, who lives on in the character of the Italians, blocks the way unless we have the strength to kill him in our consciences."[49]

On the other hand, it was not possible to imagine the advent of a Great Italy without having first liberated the Italians from their vices, defects, and the "Guicciardini-like" customs inherited from centuries of conformism, dogmatism, sectarian interference in politics, of outward devotion and inward scorn, indifference and skepticism for everything that concerned politics, to finally form a civilized ethical conscience in the modern Italian, citizen of the Italian state, capable of guiding the nation toward attaining modernity in the twentieth century. It was the duty of the reborn nation "to turn the modern world into our world, by studying it, assimilating it and transforming it. . . . The great effort of the nineteenth century is coming to an end. We are witnessing a new flourishing of ideas, heralding a new creation. Already in this century we can see the outline of the new century. And this time we must not find ourselves at the tail end, we must not take a back seat."[50] This is the mission that De Sanctis left for future generations: "There is still another program. . . . Political unification is useless without intellectual and moral redemption; it is useless to have created Italy without the Italians, as d'Azeglio said. This program was not given to him to carry out, nor was it given to the current generation. It is in the hands of the new generation."[51]

2

Complex of Greatness

God's Chosen Nation

One of the main reasons for the 1911 celebrations was to exalt the contribution that the Italians had made to the progress of humanity through the Risorgimento movement and the creation of a national state. Achieving unity and independence was a remarkable feat that benefited not only the Italians but the whole of humanity, which, with the unification of Italy, was enriched by this great nation's contribution to building modern civilization. The universal value of the Italian revolution sprang from its nature as a movement of liberation and to affirm modern man's dignity, wrote *La Stampa*, a newspaper that did not usually give vent to nationalistic rhetoric. The Italians had taken only "a few decades to accomplish a revolution that all Europe had to accept in the end, almost as its own glory," because "in fact, the spirit of the Italian revolution was universal. We were not content with just changing things silently at home. Once again, even in distress and in the midst of the bitter obstacles of action, we were able to augment the treasure of our common humanity" through the example and deeds of men like Mazzini, Cavour and Garibaldi. These heroes of the Italian Risorgimento who created a new Italy were champions of human civilization because "they were the apostles, warriors, and ministers of the same formidable principles that the whole world fought and suffered for last century."[1]

To understand the meaning of this claim to universality in connection with the mythology of nationhood, we should remember the Italians' acute inferiority complex with regard to more advanced countries like France and England. This complex was one of the main driving forces of Risorgimento patriotism and continued to goad the more restless and ambitious of those who aspired to a Greater Italy.

To offset this inferiority complex, however, a complex of greatness had developed based on the myth of the Italian nation's universal supremacy. Those who supported this idea of supremacy gave history as proof, citing the universal civilizations that had arisen in Italy from ancient Rome to Catholicism, up to Humanism and the Renaissance, the two great spiritual and cultural movements that gave birth to modern man's conscience.

From this point of view, the Italian nation's return to modernity with the birth of a unitary state meant discovering its own roots again and taking possession once more of its original patrimony—modern Italian genius—after it had been assimilated and developed by other European nations.

The Catholic Vincenzo Gioberti made a special contribution to creating the "myth of Italian supremacy" ("*il Primato*") when he maintained that in achieving unity and independence and thus rising again, Italy was only carrying out the duty assigned to it by God, returning to its universal mission as a teacher of nations. Gioberti called geography and history to witness to maintain that, because Italy was the seat of the papacy and a Catholic nation par excellence, "it can be rightly hailed as the mother nation of humankind."[2]

Italian supremacy was proven by the geographical position of the peninsula, at the center of the sea that had been the cradle of civilization, chosen by Divine Will as the seat of the universal Church; it was proven by the creative genius of its poets, philosophers, artists and politicians; and it was proven by Italy's capacity to repeatedly rise again, after temporarily declining, to give humanity the gifts of its creative and liberating virtues.[3] "Since the fall of the Roman empire history has shown the Italian nation to be a creator and liberator of peoples,"[4] because "the principle of liberation is innate in Italy, because of all peoples only Italy has always risen again through its own virtues after falling, and enjoys immortal life, and because other nations took the seeds of their own rebirth from Italy."[5] The universal virtue of this principle had never ceased, not even in the darkest periods of Italian history: even when "the Italian sun seemed close to setting, and when the setting was followed by a night that many thought would be eternal, decrepit Italy was able to bring forth some intellects that would be enough for the glory of a flourishing people."[6] "Italy was always civilly or religiously the most cosmopolitan of nations," declared Gioberti with unshakeable faith.[7]

Prophet of a religion of the fatherland, Mazzini had been equal to the Catholic philosopher in glorifying the universal vocation of the Italian nation, and he also called on Divine Will, geography and history.[8]

Italy had to achieve unity and independence not only for itself but also to carry out the duty assigned to it by Providence, the mission of "unifying Europe": "the Italian nationality is an indispensable part of the educational plan assigned to mankind, and is a duty, a special mission to be fulfilled in the collective life of humanity."[9] While fulfilling this mission, Italy's universal function was renewed for the third time, after the Roman world and Catholicism: "Italy is the only land that has twice cast the great unifying word to separated nations. Italy's life was everybody's life."[10]

The myth of supremacy and mission derived from a universalistic vision of a Greater Italy, where the nation was considered part of the human family, as a brotherhood, not as an animal of prey that ardently desires to conquer and subject other nations. Gioberti pointed out that assigning "civil and moral supremacy over all peoples in the universe" to Italy did not conceal any plan of "political domination." Pride in one's own nation did not in any way imply hate toward other nations.[11]

Deriving from Mazzini's and Gioberti's theories and penetrating various cultural and political movements, the myths of mission and supremacy merged permanently with that of a Greater Italy and became its most tenacious and seductive motives. We can find them throughout all the twentieth century, in different situations and new versions, passing through numerous metamorphoses, mixed with the ideologies of different cultural and political movements, even those with nationalist tendencies, which, during the twentieth century, competed for the privilege of interpreting the destiny of the Italian nation in the modern world.

Italian Rome

After being the greatest driving force of Risorgimento patriotism, the myth of a Greater Italy continued to fascinate united Italy. Of those who governed the national state, not even the most realistic, aware of the country's real condition, accepted the prospect of a future for united Italy similar to Switzerland's. For example, Marco Minghetti, a leading member of the ruling class, disdainfully rejected the advice of those who suggested neutral nations like Switzerland and Belgium as models for newly risen Italy to follow: "A great country," he had replied, "cannot concentrate its activities on itself like that. Youth needs to grow and expand. If it is not offered some great prospects, it will become embittered, then corrupt and dissatisfied."[12]

Feelings of pride for one's own nation, which launches itself from an imaginary or real past greatness toward an equally great longed-for future, is certainly the driving force of every kind of nationalism. Probably nobody wishes to belong to a nation he deems inadequate, wretched and despised. Pride is a sentiment typical of a national conscience that intends to assert itself as political will, and without a spark of national pride, a lasting and vital myth of nation is unlikely to arise. Gioberti maintained that a nation "can only take its rightful place in the world if it believes it is worthy of it; where excessive modesty is sometimes praiseworthy in individuals, it is blameworthy in public life, like the modesty that fatally saps the strength required by virtue and magnanimous deeds."[13]

Centuries of the peninsula's history offered the Third Italy's myth of nation a depository well stocked with supplies of pride to nurse its ambitions: the myth of greatness was embodied above all in the tradition of Rome. Rome handed down to the Italians the "awareness of being ministers of a tradition of greatness deriving from God," Mazzini affirmed,[14] and the Third Italy drew its rightful reputation, which placed it in the vanguard of modern civilization, from the universality of Rome:

> Twice Rome was the metropolis, the temple of the European world: the first time when our conquering eagles crossed unknown lands from one end to the other and prepared them for unity with civil institutions; the second time when, subdued by the power of nature, of memories of greatness and the religious inspiration of the northern conquerors, the genius of Italy was embodied in the papacy and, from Rome, carried out its solemn mission—which had come to an end four centuries before—to spread the word of the unity of all souls to the peoples of the Christian world. Today a third mission is dawning for this Italy of ours: the Italian people, the free united nation that you must found, will be much farther reaching, greater and more powerful than those of the Caesars and popes.[15]

It was united Italy's duty to restore to a Third Rome its universal mission, leading Italy back to Rome and Rome to humanity, so that "Rome would become the earth's mind: the word of God among races."[16]

United Italy was born with a Rome complex. Celebrating Rome was the great passion of the Third Italy's men of letters, especially Giosue Carducci, and they kept the myth of a Greater Italy alive in the prosaic politics of the new state. Perhaps not even Cavour, who was usually allergic to passions for myths, was completely immune to the fascination of the myth of Rome, declaring it "the noble capital of reborn Italy,"[17] although he confessed that, "among the most splendid monuments of ancient and modern Rome" (as he was not very "artistically inclined") he would miss "the austere and unpoetical streets of my native land."[18] In effect, not all those who governed united Italy and the intellectuals shared the enthusiasm for the myth of Rome, especially when this enthusiasm sprang from admiration for the glories of antiquity. For example, Ruggero Bonghi engaged in controversy with those who loved "memories of ancient Rome," reminding them that ancient Rome was "the glory of Italian history, but we are not the continuers of ancient Rome."[19] Others urged to forget "ancient Rome and console ourselves with gaining freedom and national independence and being able to feel what we like and say what we feel."[20] However, because of its noble ideal and moral value in the national culture of the Risorgimento, it was not easy to resist the myth of Rome and it would have been even more arduous to try and get rid of it completely. Even a Piedmontese like Quintino Sella, an engineer and member of the government who was usually unmoved by rhetoric, confessed that "when we speak of Rome, our old bones are galvanized."[21] Although he himself was a man of science, he knew that sentiment in politics was very effective, championing the myth of Rome against its superficial disparagers on at least one occasion. On March 14, 1881, he said to the Chamber:

> Who made us what we are? Who taught us to want a fatherland? Rome, nothing but Rome. Others taught us the cult of beauty, of goodness and greatness, but we owe everything we know, everything we think, everything we feel regarding patriotism, to ancient Rome. Consequently, when we old men come here to Rome who was our teacher, we feel an unimaginable veneration. . . . Don't be surprised if our old bones are galvanized when we speak of Rome. . . . I had not been to Rome, but the cult we had for this town was immense . . . ; we are Italians by virtue of Rome, because if it were not for the sacred name of Rome, the many misfortunes, the many acts of hostility that Italy suffered would have broken its back, annihilated it. It was Rome that kept Italy alive.[22]

Nevertheless, even though those who governed united Italy exalted the myth of Rome, they did not intend to exalt the Rome of the caesars and popes. Rather, they nursed the ambition to create a Third Rome, an Italian Rome, which was not inferior to those preceding it as regards its civilizing functions. The "greatness of this new Rome" was "something identical to the greatness of all Italy." It was a new greatness that was due to Rome "as the emblem of the present national unity."[23] This new Italy called for "the resurrection of Rome's genius, . . . revived by the breath of the strong, free life of the people's modern spirit and not by the genius of papal or imperial Rome, or of a Babylonian Rome with gold and bronze thrones whose magnificence is dazzling but whose corruption is infectious."[24]

A new rhetoric, no longer humanistic but modernistic, no longer literary but scientific, and above all anticlerical, flourished around the myth of Italian Rome. Those who created this new rhetoric were the men who aspired to making the capital of the new state the universal center of free thought and science, the symbol of democracy and freedom against the dogmatic obscurantism of the papal theocracy. The modern world had to consider Italian Rome "as the beacon of civilization," said a Roman deputy to the Chamber on March 10, 1881: this new Rome, the capital of Italy, was not to be famous for its past glory but for its future glory as a "great lay Rome," a symbol of freedom, equality and the emancipation of humanity. Italian Rome's mission in modern civilization was to attain the principle of nationality.[25]

With the end of the papal theocracy, Rome's achievement was the new Italy's contribution to the progress of modern civilization: "here we have resolved the biggest problem of the last twenty centuries, a problem that seemed unsolvable, which the most civilized nations in the world have not had the courage to resolve, not even free England—that is, the problem of making a clear distinction between rights and conscience."[26] When the period of absolutism and theocracy ended, the word of science was to spread throughout the world from the new Italian Rome. As Guido Baccelli, the Minister of Public Education, stated in 1881: "Here is the Third Rome. Indeed, it is impossible not to realize that, once the wars of conquest are over, from now on only the sciences will make up the sole aristocracy possible among nations."[27] It was the duty of the new state to continue the work of modernization in the new capital: "to eliminate every vestige of the Middle Ages in which Rome has been buried for many centuries while the modern world has continued to progress. Churches should be substituted with schools, the syllabus with freedom of thought and conscience, monks' orders and sloth with dignifying work, privileges with equality before the law and the sovereignty of cardinals and princes with that of the people."[28]

In short, it was impossible for the Italians of united Italy to escape from the myth of Rome, whatever meaning it was given. The "young Italian nation," observed the nationalist sociologist Mario Morasso in

1898, was carried away by "the utopia of Rome," which "always towered over the core of the Italian soul," because it is "the greatest symbol
that the history of civilization can boast, the most majestic and far-
reaching result that has emerged from the imagination and the united
efforts of all peoples in twenty centuries of human life," which "has incorporated the two loftiest ideas that the human mind has conceived,
the ideas of universality and immortality."[29] Yet the nationalist sociologist rebelled against the myth of ancient Rome, prefiguring "the outline
of a new Rome, uprooted from the past and the first stage of the future,
between the oblivion of memories and the rise of a renewed conscience,"[30] yet wondering if "introducing Rome into the Italian nation
was an advantage or disadvantage."[31] He reached the point of questioning the myth of Italian monopoly on Roman tradition. "Above all,
Italy as a whole has not any tradition; it has not a single historical root.
All tradition and all the past are summed up in Rome. However, that is
not Italy's past but the world's," so Rome "was not, is not, cannot be the
capital of a nation, of a race or of a people."[32]

King Umberto I voiced pride in Italian Rome when, on the occasion of the celebrations for the fiftieth anniversary of the statute in 1898,
he proclaimed the originality of modern Rome. "We do not consider this
new greatness modest among the majestic remains of Rome's ancient
greatness, which, for the spirit of the times, was universal, while this new
greatness is national. A Roman Italy rose from the former, an Italian
Rome from the latter. Rome's ancient greatness expressed force; this
Italian Rome expresses rights."[33]

The height of glorifying the new Italian and modern Rome was
the so-called fatherland's Jubilee in 1911. This was an occasion that
easily exposed the new state to the danger of a torrent of rhetorical references to past greatness, so it wanted to show, rather arrogantly, that
the Rome of the Italians was not at all inferior to the Rome of the
caesars or popes. On the contrary, it was even superior, because it was
the Rome of rights, freedom and modern science; it rose above imperial
Rome, founded on force, and above theocratic Rome, an enemy of free
thought. In the speech Victor Emmanuel III delivered in the town hall
on March 27, 1911, he quoted his predecessor's words confirming that
the work of "the nation's liberators cannot seem less exalted than the
two preceding civilizations of Rome." The president of the Chamber,
representing the national assembly of deputies, echoed these words in
his message to the king: "Immortal Rome is cloaked in different glories;
if before it kept Italy united with mighty imperial power, now it is the

symbol and guarantee of civil freedom for an Italy united by the con-
cord of minds."[34]

The Appeal of Might

The myth of Italian Rome was not only and completely in harmony
with faith in freedom, rights, reason, science and progress. The myth of
Rome also cast the fascination of might and expansion, and this height-
ened its attraction in the age of imperialism. Bear in mind that even
Mazzini had crossed the threshold between the Roman myth of a civilizing mission and the myth of expansion when he imagined a reborn
Third Italy that, once it had reached its own borders, would assume the
role of a colonial power in the Mediterranean area, following in the
footsteps of the Roman legionaries to conquer and civilize the African
populations.[35] Francesco Crispi, a republican revolutionary converted
to the monarchy, was the most important slave to, and then victim of,
the myth of might and expansion. After unification he became the principal coryphaeus of Italian imperialism.

Crispi was certainly the most enterprising of all the statesmen of
the liberal regime in foreign policy and had the ambitious purpose of
sending Italy along the road to colonial conquests. This purpose, which
ended rapidly with the disastrous defeat at Adua, was not only one man's
megalomania but reflected a concept of nation and foreign policy, intended as a policy of might, that was spreading throughout Europe at
the end of the nineteenth century.[36]

Convinced that he was the most faithful interpreter of the reborn
nation's will, Crispi believed that Greater Italy's destiny was a vocation
for might and expansion and accused those who opposed his foreign
policy of being enemies of the country because they wanted a defence-
less Italy, "weak and impotent, therefore prey to conquerors, as it had always been since the fall of the Roman Empire." They wanted Italy to
continue being "an artist's studio, a museum of antiquity, and not a nation."[37] Crispi believed that relinquishing the policy of might and expansion meant undermining and endangering the very unity of the nation: for this reason he treated all the "micromaniacs, who want to keep
Italy closed in its shell, segregating it from the great Nations, inhibiting
all those laborious initiatives whose development will one day lead to
Italy's achieving its glorious destiny,"[38] as subversives and "negators of
their nation," just like anarchists and clericals. Wanting might and greatness for Italy had been "an original sin for us, which only reactionaries

will be unable to forgive, and the sin of those, led by Mazzini, who worked to transform the whole of Italy into a united state."[39] If Italy gave up its role as a great power, said Crispi in Palermo on May 27, 1892, when unveiling the monument to Garibaldi, it was destined to succumb: "A nation of 31 million inhabitants, which withdraws, hides, and does not count for anything in the world, is just a geographical figure and not a power. Now, this position would be too humiliating, and we will not be the ones to encourage it." And right up to the end of his life the old statesman, defeated and isolated, was convinced that an "Italy huddled within its borders, that abandons the seas that surround it to foreign fleets, that does not speak at the assemblies of civilized governments for fear they will not trust it, that closes its eyes for fear of the light, cannot be the Italy to which Mazzini, Garibaldi and Victor Emmanuel aspired."[40]

Loyalty to Freedom

Despite his imperialist ambitions, not even Crispi, the most authoritarian of the Third Italy governors, went so far as to sacrifice his faith in freedom as the foundation of the national state, remaining firmly convinced that a "modern state cannot live without freedom in all its social classes and in all the manifestations of its political life." He called those who accused him of wanting to "begin an antiliberal movement and give up achieving civilization" puerile.[41] After his imperialist plans collapsed, the elderly democrat confirmed his long-standing Risorgimento faith even more strongly: "Unity is not everything, and for independence to be real and substantial, freedom is necessary," he declared on April 12, 1899. "A state whose people does not feel the dignity of its own rights is weak and exposed to the invasions of anyone who wants to rule over it." Borders are not enough to protect it without "the faith that springs from freedom, like clear water gushing from a fountain."[42]

The fusion between nation and freedom was the essence of liberal Italy's myth of nation. The ruling class of the liberal state believed that creating a national conscience through freedom was the only way to also achieve a new Italy capable of reaching the forefront in the competition of modern nations for the progress of human civilization, which the prophets and creators of the Risorgimento had so strongly desired. From this point of view, monarchic Italy's myth of nation can be considered a direct and legitimate descendent of Risorgimento patriotism. The new Italy's idea of greatness was not unrelated to faith in the values of freedom and reason, as values inherent in modern civilization. "We are not the ones that make nations, they are the fruit of reason and freedom that, by making men free again, claim their own rights, violated by tyranny and ignorance. We can, rather we must, cooperate with this grandiose work of human civilization; and we did a great deal in the 1860 revolution," stated Giovanni Rapisardi in 1868 in a reader that was intended to teach the new state's young people "how to be Italians."[43] The authoritarianism and statism that characterized the political line of conduct of the ruling class after unification never reached the point of explicitly rejecting the link between monarchy and liberalism, nor was the fascination of might ever so strong as to lead the ruling class to destroying the ideal pact between the nation and freedom, which had been the foundation of the Italian state. Not even the kings of the House of Savoy violated the liberal principle, which had legitimated their ascent to the rank of sovereigns of the Italians, despite the authoritarian drive behind the personal politics of Victor Emmanuel II and Umberto I. At the opening ceremony of every new legislature in liberal Italy, the king's message renewed the reigning House's oath of loyalty to the "cult of fatherland" and to the cause of freedom and modern civilization. "Reborn in the name of freedom, we must look for the secret of strength and conciliation in freedom and order," declared Victor Emmanuel II to the Chamber on November 27, 1871.[44] May respect for "the dignity of those free institutions, in which my House has faith, . . . inspire you when preparing the sound and radiant future of the Italian motherland,"[45] Umberto I confirmed on June 10, 1895, to the members of parliament of the nineteenth legislature. Straight after the failed attempts at authoritarianism in which he himself was personally involved, the sovereign acknowledged that the link between nation and freedom was binding and that it guaranteed the future of the Third Italy: "Italy owes its great progress to the fact that its free institutions have worked properly, notwithstanding the events fraught with misfortune in this last half century. Nevertheless, we still have a long way to go to reach and then keep the high position that is rightfully ours among the most civilized nations at an economic and social level."[46] His successor confirmed his "unswerving trust in freedom" as an instrument of progress and human emancipation. "The experience of these years," said Victor Emmanuel III in his royal message on November 30, 1904, "has confirmed it and convinced me that only freedom can resolve the mighty problems that peoples now have to face and that derive from their new social aspirations and expectations."[47] This declaration concurred with the new awareness of social issues and the world of work typical of the so-called Giolitti era (1903–1914), together with the desire to foster the liberal institutions that were both a guarantee and condition for economic and social progress.

At the beginning of the twentieth century, the Italian nation's return to modern civilization through freedom seemed accomplished: now the Third Italy aspired to having a more important role in the progress of humanity. "Italy is and will be an element of order and peace among nations," declared the senators in their message to the king for the fiftieth anniversary of Rome as capital. "But Italy must also leave a shining mark of its accomplishments, visible to future ages. Our national genius and industriousness can be freely expressed in a country [that is] master of itself and its own destiny and [can] contribute efficaciously to universal civilization."[48]

3

The Italies of Monarchic Italy

The Apotheosis of Unity

The celebrations for the Jubilee of the fatherland reached a climax on June 4 when the monument to "the founding father of the nation," Victor Emmanuel, dedicated to the "freedom of the citizens" and "the unity of the nation" (as written in the Latin inscription) was solemnly inaugurated.

The monument was only part of a farther-reaching and more complex plan, which the creators of the Third Italy and their successors had worked hard to develop and implement, to build up a mythology of the nation aimed at forming the Italians' collective identity and conscience and teaching them the "cult of fatherland." Schools, the army, literature, monuments, rites and symbols were to popularize, spread and foster faith in the values of nation, freedom and progress among the masses. With this plan in mind, celebrating the Jubilee and inaugurating the monument were the most ambitious and grandiose undertakings in the task of building up a mythology of nationhood. All Italy's political, social, cultural and artistic efforts in the Jubilee year seemed to be concentrated on building the monument, a "mass of shaped and sculptured marble," to the "father of the fatherland." It expressed "somehow or other, all the ideals of greatness and might that had flashed through the minds of the Italians between 1870 and 1914," the journalist Giovanni Ansaldo remembered in 1945, when meditating on the ruins of the myth of a Greater Italy in a German concentration camp.[1]

Inaugurating the monument to Victor Emmanuel was also the apotheosis of the monarchy, with the bronze equestrian statue of the king standing out at the center. Present at the inaugural ceremony were all the members of the royal family, the government, the highest state authorities, veterans of the Risorgimento wars, representatives of the armed forces, mayors from all over Italy, school children and an immense crowd, the like of which had never before gathered in the capital for a civil celebration. The press of that time spoke of two hundred thousand visitors in Rome for the occasion, a city that then counted six hundred thousand inhabitants.

It was the duty of a politician, Giovanni Giolitti, who was absolutely allergic to any hint of myths and who had succeeded Luigi Luzzatti as prime minister, to deliver the official oration. He spoke rhetorically (something alien to his nature), evoking Roman greatness and the epic deeds of the Risorgimento, praising the magnificence of the monumental work "that will remind future generations of the greatest event in the history of Italy," celebrating the "long way reborn Italy has come in every field of civil progress and in the world's esteem," and renewing the government's faith in the future of the country. He spoke, too, of renewed faith in the future of the Italians, "who feel a sense of national solidarity more strongly every day, while the political order, founded on the principle of the greatest freedom possible, makes every kind of progress attainable." Moreover, Giolitti spoke of the improvement in the economic conditions and standard of living of the poorer classes as a guarantee of social peace. He urged his fellow citizens to overcome minor issues and take care of "the important interests of the country to make it greater and more prosperous and more esteemed and loved by all civilized peoples." He ended his speech by sharing the sentiments of the Italian people who recognized "the symbol of the fatherland's unity, the guardian of its independence and freedom, and the sure guide toward its lofty destiny"[2] in the king and the House of Savoy.

Inaugurating the monument was the most solemn and important ceremony of the Jubilee, as it represented the myth of nation symbolically, both in the way it was carried out and in the significance given to the monument itself—the consecration of the Savoy monarchy as symbol of the nation. The ceremony was a great collective rite, the nation celebrating itself through the mystical communion between governors and governed, united by faith in the nation and freedom. The liberal press gave great and rather exaggerated emphasis to the crowd's participation, indicating it as confirmation that the masses gave widespread and unquestioning support to the myth of nation. In this atmosphere of a collective rite, wrote one observer, even the "smallest things took on a broader and more profound life than their material one; they became symbols; everyone was credulous and moved."[3] The June 4 event, stated *La Stampa,* was above all a patriotic ceremony and not just an act of homage to the monarchy. As such, it was "to be recorded among the best pages of our national life."[4] *L'Illustrazione Italiana* wrote that it was "really a secular triumph, the fighting spirit and civil triumph that all the Italians celebrated to honor the virtues of their origins."[5] The *Corriere della Sera* declared that the national state had inaugurated "the crown of its glory, the temple of its memories" with the monument, while the Italians, represented by the Romans and those Italians who had flocked to Rome from all the regions, had once again enthusiastically confirmed "the strong ties that still linked the nation to its dynasty."[6] In this sense, the fact that some Catholic deputies and a socialist mayor were present was seen as a good sign. On the occasion of the commemoration of Garibaldi's Thousand, the *Corriere della Sera* observed that, all told, fifty years after unification the monarchic state offered the image of "Italy, united and in harmony on these fateful days," when "a whole people, the whole people" gathered "behind a single flag, behind the fascination of a single idea and behind the call of a single duty. This is because we should really lose hope for ourselves and our destiny if different kinds of people with different opinions could not, for once, get together as unanimous supporters of a single duty, within the bounds of their own history and race."[7]

The Other Side of the Jubilee

Nevertheless, among the chorus of praises, there was no lack of criticism deploring unsatisfactory performance, delays and every kind of shortcoming scattered throughout the whole series of Jubilee celebrations. When the monument to Victor Emmanuel II was inaugurated (although not yet completed), it was strongly criticized from an aesthetic point of view. Also, the deplorable events that had taken place during the long and tormented period of its construction were brought up again. The grandiose monument seemed to make visible the reborn nation's unsatisfied aspirations to greatness, with the excessive rhetoric of its dimensions, the allegorical statues and the decorations—marble and bronze used to celebrate the myth of a Greater Italy that was, in reality, still far from being a common fatherland for the Italians.

The adversaries of the liberal state took their cue from this to pronounce that the national unity on show during the Jubilee was false, commenting ironically on the obsession with greatness on the part of a state that had not yet managed to create a fatherland for everyone. "Today socialists and clericals are arm in arm," observed *La Stampa*, "and this emphasizes the fact that the monument is unfinished, meaning that the symbol of the nation is still incomplete, in the sense of agreement among parties and the evolution of civilization. It does not matter. The monument is a work of great beauty; the people have sensed this and today have taken it to their hearts."[8]

The contrast between reality and rhetoric in Italy on the fiftieth anniversary gave rise to sarcasm from those who had commented ironically on the "plethora of commemorations" in the Jubilee year, "the year of miracles," as the man of letters Giovanni Rabizzani called it.[9]

As a matter of fact, behind the facade of "rampant and overelaborate rhetoric,"[10] in the Jubilee year, Italy was anything but united or of one mind when professing faith in the country and the institutions and principles that legitimized the national state. Observers who were not at all inclined to pessimism or ideologically or emotionally hostile to the national state and monarchy were aware of the real situation, and this awareness was in contrast to the patriotic and triumphant rhetoric and the image of a united nation. Benedetto Croce wrote in 1911:

> I believe that any careful and unprejudiced observer of Italy's present spiritual life cannot but be struck by the evident decadence in the feeling for social unity. The high-sounding words that expressed this unity—king, fatherland, city, nation, Church and humanity—have become cold and rhetorical, and as they sound false, we avoid pronouncing them, almost as if an intimate sense of decency warns us not to name sacred things in vain. As these words fall into disuse, there is a similar and general decadence in the attitude toward social discipline: the people no longer feel linked to a great whole, part of a great whole, obedient to it, cooperating with it or attaining their worth from the work they carry out within the whole.

Without overcoming this decadence, warned the philosopher, it was "a vain hope that these or those contingencies can improve society and make Italy great."[11]

In fact, on the occasion of the Jubilee celebrating unification, many protested strongly, from the right and left, denouncing the false image celebrating a united, harmonious and prosperous Italy, intent on continuing its way toward modernity in the name of the myth of nation embodied in the liberal state, parading the idea of nation and freedom as the supreme principles and values guiding the rise of the Third Italy toward greatness.

The Lie about the Nation

Socialists, republicans and Catholics did not take part in the "festivities for the nation," because in no way did they recognize their fatherland in the monarchic state. Some Catholic deputies were present at the inauguration of the monument to the king as a personal initiative, but these were isolated cases. "That Italians from the various regions, orderly, organized and militant in defence of their religion, were absent, is an undeniable, deliberate and openly declared fact," noted the *Rivista di Roma;* or rather, the Jubilee had highlighted "that kind of intimate uneasiness suffered by a whole community of Italians, as, undoubtedly nobly inspired, they would like to reconcile their religious faith with the cult of their country's past."[12]

The Jesuits of *Civiltà Cattolica* were among the most contentious in disputing the "Jubilee of the fatherland," particularly the celebration proclaiming Rome the capital. The periodical called the "din of the fiftieth anniversary" a "Masonic stunt of exhibitions, shows, inauguration ceremonies, commemorations, competitions, congresses and merrymaking," which meant only one thing: "to spite religion, the Church and the pope, the vicar of Christ."[13] Furthermore, calling the unification celebrations a "Jubilee," the term used by the "poet with pagan tendencies," was considered blasphemous, "insulting both religion and the nation," and expressing a typical "frenzy of sectarian joy, as it called to mind the vote on March 27, 1861, when the deputies of the Chamber in Turin, some knowingly, others unwittingly, gave cosmopolitan masonry the hope to see the capital of the Catholic world transformed once again into the pagan capital of Italy." For "true Catholics," the fiftieth anniversary of Italian unity was "a year of religious mourning" and proof that the work of the founders and rulers of the new state was a "shameful failure."[14]

The strongest argument in the Vatican controversy against the celebrations was the call to Catholic patriotism, which could ensure the greatness of Italy more efficaciously than liberal patriotism. This argument was to become the core of the Catholic myth of a Greater Italy, opposing the myths of nation of lay culture. In the "long centuries of Italian history, . . . the glory and greatness of Italy was constantly combined and associated with the destiny of the papacy, which a vain attempt is now being made to portray as an enemy of Italy," wrote *L'Osservatore Romano.*[15]

To confirm these accusations, the Holy See's publication cited the protest demonstrations organized by the socialists during the Jubilee celebrations to show that liberal patriotism "too often did not know how to reflect the real interests of Italy and the Italians." It also observed that "this much-discussed patriotism, which should be like the *diapason* that sounds throughout the whole land, has not yet managed to penetrate the working classes." They must certainly have received a "distressing impression" from having to assist at "the flag-waving, banquets, inauguration ceremonies and illuminations that cast a sinister light into their small, dark and simple rooms where poverty and perhaps hunger still reign." Only by letting the workers share the economic advantages of the modern world, the Vatican publication warned, would they be able to understand the "patriotic sentiments that are now the prerogative of the wealthy," and only then would the progressive proletariat "choose between sound and flimsy patriotism," while for now "the patriotism of the masses consists of resisting as best they can in the daily struggle to survive."[16]

The socialists would not have had any difficulty in supporting the Vatican's observations that the proletariat had no part in the liberal bourgeoisie's festivities. They celebrated the fatherland's Jubilee in their own way, organizing public transport strikes, protest rallies against the high cost of living, agitations for universal suffrage, and processions of demonstrators against militarism. The organizers of these demonstrations intended them to symbolically set the fiftieth anniversary of the proletariat against the Jubilee that the bourgeoisie had organized to "be admired by other national bourgeoisies and by themselves."[17] Even if by then the socialists accepted the unitary state, they believed that there was no reason to celebrate the fiftieth anniversary of unification, which was in fact very far from being achieved: "Independence, economic freedom and political rights—the Italian, the worker, the citizen—are ideally inseparable terms of the liberating trinomial. If each one is separated from the other two, it is a falsehood." And "the celebrated political unity" of the country was a "falsehood" for the socialists: "North and South are two nations; and one of them, the poorest, flees overseas. Cities and the country are two nations: turbid and melancholy Vendées still seethe around the meeting places of industrial areas. Voting privileges foster criminal gangs, fraudulence, corruption and massacres. With so much of the population excluded from political life, the fiftieth anniversary seems a reckless anticipation. One fatherland does not yet exist."[18]

Giuseppe Mazzini had first mentioned "the lie about Italy" regarding the unitary state immediately after unification, because the unity of the state, carried out with Machiavellian artfulness by the Savoy monarchy, lacked "the fecundating breath of God, the soul of the nation."[19] The republicans, Mazzini's heirs, did not in any way recognize a Greater Italy in the principles, values, institutions and political line of conduct of the monarchic state, which lacked effective patriotic unity because it lacked effective popular consensus. When commenting on the commemoration of Mazzini in Rome's city hall, the republican newspaper *La Ragione* wrote that, while territorial unification had been rapid, "only that moral unity that is founded on a civic religion, on feelings of duty, can strengthen the virtues of the Third Italy's mission in the world."[20] In the same way, fifty years after the political unification of the country, "nothing, absolutely nothing, has been done in this half-century to modernize its economy."[21] The republicans protested against the figure of Mazzini being appropriated by the Savoy mythology, with "posthumous honors" that falsified "the clear and profound concepts of the master."[22] The republicans also condemned the educational purpose of the celebrations, which aimed "not only at putting the irremovable seal of the people's will on the achievement of national unity after half a century" but also "at glorifying men and institutions that cannot receive the unanimous judgment and approval of the Italians," mixing up "all the men who took part in the great work of the Italian revolution in a single apotheosis."[23]

Mazzini's descendents thus confirmed their position as exiles in their own country, psychologically foreigners in a state they did not recognize as legitimate, even if they made a distinction between their opposition and that of those who "would like to see the unity of the nation destroyed in order to restore a theocratic government on its ruins, the negation of God and civilization." At the same time as the inauguration of the monument to Victor Emmanuel, the republicans had organized a counterdemonstration, "taking the oriflammes of the Republic up to the Janiculum, sacred to the Third civilization of Rome."[24] This is how the republicans intended to oppose the celebration of a myth of nation they considered a deformation and a betrayal of the authentic myth of a Greater Italy, longed for by the patriots of the Risorgimento revolution. The latter was uncompleted owing to the Savoy monarchy, which had carried out territorial unification to its own exclusive advantage, usurping the people's will and giving life to a soulless state. Furthermore, the republicans considered the official ceremonies of the Jubilee to be acts

of "monarchic usurpation": they were solemn, pompous and cold, "like
all celebrations where the people's soul is absent."[25] The monarchy's festivities were "for pleasure seekers and scroungers, not for the people,
who feel the need to satisfy their hunger rather than enjoy themselves."[26]
And according to the republicans, the "public conscience" had rightly
isolated official Italy, responding "to Savoy rhetoric with an indifference
that means much more than immense demonstrations": "it is the agony
of an institution, not the apotheosis of the fatherland."[27]

The "Two Italies"

Young intellectuals of the cultural avant-garde had also joined the
protest against the "lie about the nation"[28] being a united Italy while, actually, observed *La Voce*, "the moral disorganization of the nation is profound, widespread and general, it strikes all institutions and classes." The
Florentine periodical commented ironically that future historians would
remember 1911 as the "sad year": besides the fiftieth anniversary celebrations, there had also been a cholera epidemic that was not checked in
time and had spread over the whole country, revealing the backward
state of hygienic conditions everywhere, the neglect and deficiencies of
the authorities, and ignorance of the facts and real problems. "The insincere, hypocritical Italians who were indifferent and unknowing observed the country's tribulations from their hideouts, especially from
that costly, futile and useless exhibition of Rome, which has done nothing for Italy's progress or future" apart from drawing the Italians' attention even more to their "glorious past. It is surprising that we have not
gone mad paying so much attention to it."[29] Disputing the "puppet
show of the Jubilee,"[30] and reminding Italians of "the biggest, most serious, important and original problem of Italian life,"[31] *La Voce* solemn-
ized the anniversary in its own way by publishing a special number on
the Southern Italy issue, which opened with an article by Giustino Fortunato with the emblematic title *The Two Italies*. The expert on problems of
Southern Italy wrote that Italy was "fortunately united; but there is anything but agreement between one part, which, having reached a considerable state of affluence, feels hampered and obstructed by the other's
slow progress, and in turn, the other, which suspects that its brother's
prosperity is not entirely due to its own good qualities or to natural
superiority."[32]

The controversy over the unification Jubilee aroused a great deal
of interest in the issue of the "two Italies," adding new elements and

arguments to what was to become another important aspect of the myth of nation, which clashed with the official version especially in the early twentieth century. This other aspect comprised various versions of the contrast between the "two Italies." One was the Mazzinians' ethical-political version linked to the Risorgimento myth as an unfinished revolution. Another was the political and institutional version of the conflict between "legal country" and "real country."[33] Yet others were the sociological and economic version of the clash between North and South, and even the anthropological version, with racial overtones, of Northern and Southern Italians. The fact that there were "two Italies" seriously wounded the Third Italy's pride, stated Eduardo Cimbali, the antinationalist jurist:

> It is distressing to admit, but the irrefutable and bitter truth is that the Third Italy has not yet been able to find the right path to do good service to itself and to others in half a century of independence and national unity. [This is because], on the fiftieth anniversary of its national unity, which it is striving to celebrate even with world exhibitions, the only exhibition it can truly offer the world of visiting peoples is the antiunitarian and antinational show of two Italies that are still completely and pathetically different: of two Italies, one of which is all rich, healthy, well-educated, advanced and civilized, the other all poor, segregated, malarial, illiterate, backward and barbaric; of two Italies, one of which is the European Italy and the other the African Italy![34]

On the opposite side of the political lineup, the question of the "two Italies" was taken up again, but in a completely different way, by the militants of the nationalist imperialist movement organized by Enrico Corradini. Not even these nationalists were enthusiastic about the Jubilee, even though they extolled the economic and social progress achieved by united Italy and praised the nation that, on the occasion of the fatherland's Jubilee, had been able to recover quickly, as the nationalist sociologist Scipio Sighele observed, from "one of the most horrendous catastrophes that history could remember" (the earthquake in December 1908, which had razed Messina and Reggio Calabria to the ground). Furthermore, Italy had gone on to give "the spectacle of three exhibitions in the Jubilee year celebrating its unification, . . . which expressed the extremely high level reached in trade, industry and the arts," in addition to inaugurating "a monument to its great king, which is incomparably the most beautiful in modern Europe."[35] Nevertheless, the nationalist followers of Corradini condemned the ruling class of the liberal

state because it had come to a standstill after achieving unity and independence and had been incapable of setting another common aim
for the nation. Speaking in Rome on June 2, 1911, the nationalist philosopher Bernardino Varisco stated that, if it was right to celebrate the
birth of the unitary state, "our joy degenerating into arrogant lethargy"
should have been avoided, "as if history had ended with the formation
of the state, and there were no more opportunities for engaging in further activity." The purpose attained, said the philosopher, loses its value
"if we do not use it as a means to achieve a higher purpose." And that
did not happen in Italy after unification, because since then "world history has gone on," but still "without our having any influence on it, as
before." In "fifty years Italy has missed many opportunities to play an
active part, and they will never return." Varisco blamed all this on the
government and on the lack of a public opinion aimed at achieving a
higher goal than its immediate interest, that is, a Greater Italy and its
very vitality. A "collection of people who live in a well-defined country,
who speak the same language and who have the same government" is
not yet a nation if "a collective will to work in agreement for a common
aim has not developed." Only the ideal of a new purpose, besides preserving unity and independence, could keep the national conscience
alive, and this ideal could only be making the country great.[36] The tendency to identify the essence of citizenship with total devotion to the
greatness of the nation, typical of imperialist nationalism, became
firmly established in the years before and after the Jubilee of the fatherland. This tendency made it increasingly clear that only a patriotism
that subordinated any other ideal, even freedom, to the greatness of the
nation could be the myth of a nation, worthy of a Greater Italy in the
twentieth century.

The Jubilee celebrations gave Corradini the chance to launch an attack on the ruling classes and on "this wise and limited liberalism of
ours, reflecting domestic common sense, narrowmindedness and immediate usefulness." Corradini was certain he recognized "that there is
feeling for Rome in the hearts of the Italians" because they took part in
the Jubilee celebrations, and he thought this was a good sign for the
coming of a Greater Italy, as "every time Italy shares interests with
Rome, it improves. And this is the best result of the recent Jubilee celebrations," which had left "thrills of the Italian revolutionary spirit" in
the nationalists, "the flash of their aspiration for an hour of enthusiasm
that is not completely for the past, but for Rome and its forefathers."[37]

Faced with the squalor of liberalism, which the Jubilee celebrations had accentuated when the government crisis brought Giolitti back to power on the eve of the commemorations for Rome the capital, the imperialist nationalists burned with enthusiasm for the myth of Rome and prepared to fight against "the official and ruling Italy, the parliamentary Italy of the proletariat and bourgeoisie" in the name of a productive Italy. These nationalists thought they were the only legitimate repositories of the national conscience, the only authentic interpreters of the nation's will and the true coryphaei of a Greater Italy in the twentieth century. The main targets of their crusade for the rebirth of the nation were not only the ruling class and liberalism but the Risorgimento concept of nation itself on which the unitary state was founded.

The nationalist movement had begun at the beginning of the century, inspired by the conflict between the "two Italies," productive Italy and political Italy, presenting itself at first as a kind of movement of opinion and social protest representing the productive bourgeoisie and the mass of workers who emigrated all over the world. They were against the bureaucratic and inefficient state as well as the parliamentary political class. In 1904 *Il Regno*, the first nationalist periodical, declared:

> We believe that the heart of our national life does not reside in the erstwhile papal palace where our five hundred and eight representatives spend a lot of time putting together mediocre laws. . . . That is the sick and weakened part of the country, the bourgeoisie that only knows how to talk and spend, with the acquiescence of the other bourgeoisie that works and earns. Italy's life is in those courageous industrialists . . . who increase our production, beat England on the markets and conquer Asia Minor and South America. Italy's life is in those Apulian peasants, in those Romagnese and Venetian laborers who board ship in Genoa, Naples and Marseilles and spread all over the world, boring tunnels, forming colonies, tilling land, digging mines, setting up companies and every year sending hundreds of millions of lire to their families back in Italy. . . . The false life of words lies above all this real life of activity; the workshop of words at Montecitorio lies above the workshop of machinery in Legnano.[38]

The nationalism of *Il Regno* intended to give a political conscience to the productive bourgeoisie and extol its ruling function, with an open appeal for an antisocialist and antiliberal reaction:

Between these two Italies—one that passes its lethargic life repeating the daily intrigues and the sterile clichés of the old generation,
the other that acts, grows and augments the country but is unaware
of itself, without important objectives, poor in politics, poor in art,
poor in thought—between the two Italies, one habitually rhetorical, cavilers and profiteers, the other, foolhardiness bursting with
energy but aimless, we must be both the force that destroys the former and the light that shines upon the latter; we must be a torch
that burns and illuminates.[39]

In the period of Giolitti's governments, there was much talk about
conflict between productive Italy and officialdom, a new version of the
myth of the "two Italies,"[40] and one of the main points of the anti-
Giolitti controversy. The anti-Giolitti daily *Corriere della Sera* also gave importance to this conflict during the Jubilee celebrations. As proof of the
country's political decadence under Giolitti's "dictatorship," the Milanese newspaper deplored the government crisis on the eve of the celebrations, sparked by Giolitti's majority to bring its leader back to power.[41]

The myth of the "two Italies" was greatly strengthened by the variety of issues brought up, acquiring decisive importance from the interpretation given to it by the new cultural and political movements that
gave rise to a violent reaction against the liberal state in the years of
Giolitti's governments. These movements accepted the supremacy of
the nation and national state but did not acknowledge any correspond-
ing evidence of that supremacy in the liberal state, in its ideology, in its
ruling class and in the way it handled home and foreign policy. Above
all, they did not consider the liberal state suitable for achieving the myth
of a Greater Italy and leading the nation to the forefront of modern civilization. "Our duty is to be strong in order to become great"; this was
the precept that a master of the new generations, Alfredo Oriani, gave
the Italians of the twentieth century. "Expand and spiritually conquer
through emigration, treaties, trade, industry, science, art, religion and
war. Withdrawing from the competition is impossible: therefore we must
be victorious."[42] By conquering Libya, Italy had joined the contest, had
accepted the challenge of the imperialist competition. The consequences of this choice had immediate repercussions on the development of the myth of a Greater Italy

PART 2

WHICH ITALY?

4

The Metamorphosis of a Myth

Toward a Greater Italy

In the year 1912, the victorious outcome of the colonial undertaking crowned the fiftieth anniversary festivities, confirming Italy's rise to a great power on the international scene. As the liberal historian Adolfo Omodeo later recalled, "a satisfied assessment of fifty years of unification and the superb Libyan undertaking, while not creating a triumphant form of nationalism, have created a strong national conscience, particularly in those who were opposed to the policy and yet were destined to bear the greatest strain of the war."[1] The war in Libya, in addition to the fiftieth anniversary rhetoric, sparked the flame of nationalist enthusiasm throughout the country but, by means of political journalism, literature, academic culture and the theatre, was much more effective than the fiftieth anniversary celebration in making the myth of Greater Italy known. Furthermore, in November 1911 Giovanni Pascoli began expounding his national-populist rhetoric with the "great proletariat has marched forth" formula, and with the start of the war Gabriele D'Annunzio's sumptuous epic, the tumultuous *Canzoni delle gesta d'oltremare*, began to appear in the *Corriere della Sera*.

For many of those who believed in the myth of Greater Italy, the conquest of Libya was a dream come true. "The dream of my imagination," wrote Scipio Sighele, "has fortunately come true: the national conscience of a new Italy has been born. Now all Italy is nationalist," because that "sentiment and desire to gain power and greatness for the nation, which few had [expressed], and even fewer dared to express, before September 1911, have today—after the war—come to be the general feelings that lend luster to all the parties."[2] News of a "new Italy" revealed by the colonial war also came from *La Vita Internazionale*, a journal founded and edited by Teodoro Moneta, who had received the

Nobel Peace Prize in 1907. While lamenting the "sad event of the necessary war that the kind people of Rome were fighting on the Libyan
coast," the journal praised "the Italian soldiers and citizens who live,
fight and die with words, gestures and attitudes that, in their ingenuous
and sometimes rough simplicity, are to be found only in the history of
ancient Greece and Rome."[3] In the face of Italy's war experience, even
Giustino Fortunato, who had always been opposed to colonial ambitions and Third Italy's "excessive number of grandiose plans,"[4] was full
of praise because, as he told a friend, when he spent time among the
peasants in Basilicata and Puglia during the colonial undertaking, "for
the first time in my life I saw and realized, with a joy never experienced
before, that they, too, now know they are Italian."[5]

The colonial undertaking brought some innovations to the rhetoric
of Greater Italy, preparing the mythological apparatus that would be
used on a wider scale in propaganda during World War I.[6] The war was
celebrated as a necessary temporary rite, the cleansing of the nation in
sacrificial blood, to consecrate its rise to the rank of a great power. The
colonial war was hailed as the new resurrection of Italy, to redeem itself
from the shameful performance at Adua and the mediocre battle performance of united Italy in other military campaigns, through the sacrifice of its sons. The Italian soldiers fighting in the Libyan desert were
transfigured into the heirs of the Roman legionnaires, champions of the
race's rebirth, the real life model of the "new Italian" and not an invented one. In order to justify the colonial war, the myth of the mission
to civilize was relaunched, and it loomed as an historic duty over Italy,
heir to Rome and the chosen seat of Christianity. This myth was combined with the more recently coined myth of a proletarian nation,
driven to expansion and the conquest of colonies by the unrestrained
demographic vitality of the race, never again having to disperse its own
blood and productive energy far and wide in foreign lands with the hundreds of thousands of Italians who emigrated each year. Furthermore,
the scarce and ineffective opposition to the undertaking within the
country was considered proof of the Italians' great national solidarity.
United in their support of the nation at war and hoping for victory, the
Italians had overcome divisions of class and ideologies. Last, there was
renewed faith in war ethics as a way to regenerate the nation and generate energy and the desire for power.

Apart from the real consequences, the victorious conclusion of the
war was immediately exalted as the birth of a new Italy that was finally
leaving the safe haven of its national boundaries and proudly progressing

toward the conquest of renewed grandeur. The Italians, stated *La Vita Internazionale*, were no longer "the losers, defeated at Adua, ruffians always on strike, and above all, an impotent and resigned population."[7] Giuseppe Prezzolini, editor of *La Voce*, said something similar: once strenuously against the colonial undertaking, at the end of the war he recorded the positive effects on the country. In 1912, he wrote that the war "had given new life to Italy, revealing to the European nations and Italy itself, that the Italians had acquired a new conscience. . . . The war was a revelation to everyone. Both the parties against the war and those favorable to it, both foreigners and Italians, have realized that there is a new Italy."[8]

Looking at it from afar, Italy really did seem to have gained new vitality with the war against Tripoli. Roberto Michels, a German sociologist who loved Italy, was astounded at the change that had come over the Italians. "In order to see the extent of the change, it is sufficient to pronounce a single word: Tripoli. The word Tripoli means the enthusiastic and virtually unanimous approval of an impressively bellicose expansionist policy by a most peaceful population."[9] The conquest of Tripoli changed the national spirit of the Italians, who from a meek and resigned people became proud and aggressive. With the "unexpected awakening of an imperialist sentiment":[10]

> Italian imperialism was born, first of all, out of the full awareness that the Italians were naturally proud, that they were politically, morally, militarily and civilly better than the rest of the world thought they were, and of the legitimate desire to stop playing, once and for all, the hateful role of Cinderella, assigned to it by other populations. Little by little, in more recent years, a certain psychological necessity had been forming in Italy to go and occupy a suitable position for the Italic lineage among the more advanced European nations, given its civilization and ingenuity, cost what it may.[11]

However, moving forward with an imperialist policy created many problems for a national tradition that had developed mainly around a concept of nation founded on "fatherland and freedom" as well as on the principle of nationality. Despite Giolitti's assurance that internal policy was a priority, with the colonial undertaking foreign policy became much more important and weighed heavily on the way a nation was conceived and on its future in the new era of prodigious development of the industrial civilization and the international contest among the great powers. The year 1912, marking the conquest of Libya, can therefore be considered emblematic of a decisive period of change in the history of the national myth and in the very way the ideal of Greater Italy was conceived. It was the beginning of a new era that ended with the crisis of the liberal state and the rise to power of Fascism in 1922.

The Crucial Decade

The decade between 1912 and 1922 is particularly significant in the history of the national myth. On the one hand, the war in Libya and intervention in the First World War marked the height of glory of the national myth, as conceived traditionally by the Risorgimento and as it had been reworked by liberal Italy in an attempt to build a single fatherland for all Italians, creating an original synthesis between nation, liberty and modernity. On the other hand, new concepts of nation evolved and took root. They rejected the humanistic essence of the Risorgimento-type tradition, contributing to the radicalization of the political struggle and thus preparing the terrain for the birth and rise of Fascism. It must also be remembered in stressing the importance of this decade, not only as regards the national myth but for Italian history of the twentieth century in general, that most of the political movements that played a role on the Italian political scene, either directly or indirectly, up to the present time were born and established during this decade. All of them, in one way or another, had to face the matter of the nation in order to determine their ideologies and policies.

During this decade the Italian political arena was dominated not only by conflicts between supporters and adversaries of the national myth but also by contrasts among opposite concepts of the myth. Moreover, between 1912 and 1922 the national myth underwent a change brought about by international and internal events and, generally, by the profound social and cultural changes due to industrialization, modernization, the society of the masses and imperialism. The international events that led to World War I invigorated the national myth, making it, once again, the center of political debates. Despite the hold taken by imperialism, one of the sparks that set off the outbreak of the European conflict was the principle of nationality, fulcrum of Risorgimento nationalism. It was also that same principle that made up the ideology of the war, fought by the democratic states against the central empires, and that, after the war, was considered the foundation on which to reconstruct Europe.

After the war in Libya, important internal events brought the myth of the nation to the forefront again. With the electoral reform that introduced universal male suffrage, the democratization of the liberal state received a further impulse, opening the doors of politics to the new masses. It also imposed on the ruling class the need to find new ways to continue the construction of the "fatherland of the Italians" at a time when the future was seen as troublesome, despite the euphoria of the Jubilee and the nation's pride in having won the colonial war. The slowdown of economic growth, the intensification of social conflicts, the radicalization of political struggles and the emergence of new antidemocratic and antiliberal forces caused a crisis in the precarious equilibrium that had characterized the democratic process started by Giovanni Giolitti and led to a long series of crises of the liberal state. In 1912 the Socialist Party decided to abandon its reformist policy (which might have been conducive, at least empirically, to a compromise between socialism and nation) and espoused resolutely revolutionary ideas, engaging in an all-out battle against the national state. After 1912, a plan developed among the bourgeois lay liberals (and thanks to the work of Sidney Sonnino and Antonio Salandra, who replaced Giolitti as head of government in 1914) to update the liberalism professed by the right wing as an alternative to the Giolitti-style democratic liberalism. The intention was to safeguard the concept of tradition bequeathed by the Risorgimento, adjusting it to the needs of mass politics so as to strengthen the national state and the bourgeoisie's leadership with respect to the Socialists and Catholics. This plan for a new "national policy," according to the definition given by Salandra, was to culminate with Italy's participation in the European war, a decision based on the principle of nationality and the "sacred egoism" of the nation.

As the backdrop to these events, there were some very important transformations of the national myth. At the same time, the conditions for a separation between national state and liberal democracy developed. During this decade the idea of nation conceived in the nineteenth century as developing around the principle of nationality and liberty was increasingly challenged by an idea of nation as developing mainly around the myth of power and expansion. The myth of a single fatherland for the Italians, without ideological, religious or ethnic discrimination, was opposed by the supporters of an authoritarian concept of nation as an organic whole. They defined nationality according to criteria that linked different ideologies to anthropological differences and, therefore, as such, presaged the future attitudes of racial discrimination.

In choosing to assign a unitarian significance to the decade 1912–22, it was not the author's intention to give less importance to World War I in the history of the national myth. It is conceivable that without the First World War, the parable of the national myth in Italy would have followed a different course, and both the destiny of the liberal state and the outcome of the attempt to build the fatherland of the Italians within its framework would probably have been very different. Actually, the importance of World War I in the history of the national myth is better highlighted if we place it within the unitarian perspective of the decade 1912–22. To a certain extent, the presence of new and different forms of nationalism prior to World War I played a crucial role in the interventionist-supported mobilization and, from the very beginning, contributed to consideration of the conflict as a "great event" full of implications for the nation's future. Most of the national myths of democratic, liberal or imperialist interventionism already existed before the war. However, it enriched the constellation of the national myth with new myths that came from the war experience more than from intellectual considerations. Also, the categories used to define World War I as a revolutionary event had been formulated by the culture of a new nationalism during previous years, although the war experience was able to enhance and publicize them. And finally, World War I played a crucial part in the history of the myth of the nation because it became the main battlefield on which the different concepts of nation clashed. These concepts, which had matured during the first decade of the new century, came into conflict in the postwar period, leading to a civil war that saw many politically active Italians take sides in support of opposing revolutionary myths, some in the name of the nation and some in the name of socialism or in support of other national myths representing incompatible visions of Italy and politics.

The Residue of the Myth

During the decade 1912–22, the liberal ruling class's attempt to create a national state that would be the fatherland of all the Italians, founded on harmony between liberty and nation, without ideological, political or religious discrimination, came to an end. Before examining the most important aspects of the change in the national myth that occurred during this decade, the significance of the liberal state in forming a collective national conscience must be considered.

One verdict that seems to have been accepted by all, including histo-riography, and that assessed the first fifty years of unification positively,[12] was that the liberal state did not manage to become the fatherland of all the Italians, despite the widening of the electoral base and the involve-ment of more and more strata of the various social classes in politics and civil life. Adherence to the national state had involved a small part of civil society, even if not the most backward or least modern part, whereas sizable sections of the bourgeoisie, the middle classes and the proletariat did not acknowledge their fatherland as being the existing state for religious, ideological and social reasons. According to socialists, Catholics and republicans, the liberal state was not the "real Italy." They saw the liberal bourgeois government—a mere instrument of an oligar-chy that hid behind the national myth in order to continue its exclusive class domination—as an unlawful one that claimed it represented the nation. Their opposition had created many obstacles to the ruling class's efforts to realize a fatherland for the Italians based on the principles and values of liberalism. During the first twenty years of the twentieth century, these traditional adversaries were joined by new radical move-ments, not all of which were authoritarian oriented but that all chal-lenged the existing state, which was basically considered a dictatorial sys-tem of power, corrupt and guilty of bribery, lacking impetus of ideals, moral coherence and a higher vision of the nation's future, such as em-bodied in the person of Giovanni Giolitti. These movements did not ac-knowledge the legitimacy of the national state, born of a compromise between the monarchy and democracy, because they felt it was the out-come of an abortive revolution, a bungled construction, the result of cunning more than faith, put together more by chance and with foreign help than by national energy and virtue.

These new adversaries, who would eventually find themselves to-gether on the side of Fascism, were more efficient than the traditional opponents because they fought the liberal state, setting themselves up as the genuine interpreters of the nation's wishes against a ruling class of senile parliamentarians, guardians of an old ideal of nation and state, by now inadequate to realize the myth of a Greater Italy in the new era of imperialist powers. Furthermore, they scorned the ruling class that had governed the country during the first fifty years of unification—making an exception for Crispi—reputing it an incompetent, wretched and hypocritical oligarchy concerned more with preserving their own power than increasing the country's, and they ridiculed the parliamentary and bourgeois *Italietta* (a petty Italy), seeing it as terribly inferior to the myth of the Greater Italy, which was gigantically enlarged in their imagination.

The presence of so many adversaries, however, did not mean that the liberal state's attempt to build a fatherland for the Italians would have failed in any event, even without the turmoil caused by World War I. Despite its limits, the liberal state had created the conditions for democratic development, which became more and more effective during the fifty years of unification. Meanwhile, nostalgia for the Papal State and for other preunification states faded away, all criticism of unification died down, and the principal political forces no longer had on their agenda the matter of constitutional changes in the republican and federal sense. Fifty years of life as a unified state, guided by the ideals and morals of liberal patriotism, had familiarized an ever larger number of Italians with the myth of the nation. The army, schools, cultural events and the press carried out a collective educational process centered around "the religion of fatherland" and the civic ethics of duty. This educational program, albeit limited and lacking, helped increase the participation of Italians in politics, making it possible for a yet elementary national sentiment to take root in an ever wider segment of the population. The national sentiment was certainly sounder in the bourgeoisie and middle classes, but was not altogether lacking in the proletariat. Thanks to the national state, the overall "civilization" of the country and the conquest of modernity dreamt of by the Risorgimento's patriots and the founding fathers of the Third Italy had made such progress that Italy was no longer considered the underdeveloped country it had been prior to unification. Moreover, the national state had fostered a sense of human dignity, independence and personal responsibility as well as an individual and collective civil conscience in an increasing number of Italians.

These changes had come about mainly because the liberal state also brought with it the formation of a national political dimension, which allowed united Italy to achieve an acceptable level of modernity and democracy, considering the context at that time. Even the most intransigent challengers of the liberal state were able to take advantage of this situation, exploiting their struggle not to dismantle the unified construction but to occupy it themselves and transform it according to their own idea of state and ideal of nation. Speaking of the unified state as the "lie about Italy" after half a century could have been a way to criticize the state for those who absolutely refused to acknowledge its origin and its very existence. However, an impartial evaluation shows that even the socialists and Catholics recognized that the liberal state had enabled its very adversaries to grow, act and gain followers. The Italians had reached a standard of living within the framework of the national state that was still lower than that of other more advanced European nations but much higher than the standard before unification. In conclusion, while taking into consideration the limits and intrinsic weaknesses of the liberal state, which became dramatically apparent after World War I, it cannot be said that after fifty years of unification the Italians' level of civil conscience was the same as in 1861. It must also be admitted that among the population there was the feeling and knowledge that they belonged to one nation, above and beyond the boundaries of their villages and regions, and this was amply demonstrated by Italy's participation in World War I.

The First World War was the first mass experience for millions of Italians, their first collective national experience. Many did not share the patriotic optimism of the interventionists, nor did they accept the ideals and policies that motivated the intervention. Many protested against the war, while others returned from the trenches wanting to rebel, feeling deeply resentful of those who had led them into such a tragic experience. However, on the whole, the patriotic education received in fifty years of unification was proof of their loyalty during Italy's three years of participation, especially at such difficult times as the defeat at Caporetto. The ideals of the Risorgimento's national myth, the fatherland, freedom and the greatness of the new Italy, even in a simple and emotional way, were perceived and experienced by a large part of the population as never before. Perhaps for the first time, the Italians felt they were citizens of a single fatherland during the First World War. Unfortunately, it wasn't to last long.

Intervention in the European war was the last action taken by the liberal ruling class to complete the building of a unified state. Meanwhile, the radical antagonism that existed among believers in the national myth, which aggravated the divisions and political contrasts, undermined the foundation of the liberal regime. Basically, the last sparks of vitality of the Risorgimento's national myth went out with World War I. When the liberal philosopher Guido De Ruggiero reviewed Antonio Salandra's war speeches in 1922, he identified in the considerations of the man he defined as "the last politician of the Risorgimento" the patriotic characteristics typical of the ruling class that had created and governed the national state for half a century: "The fatherland is like the family! This is the romantic basis of the political ideals of the Risorgimento. . . .

It is still the fatherland for a few people, those whose destiny and industriousness gave them a house, a piece of land, and with this first possession fueled a greater passion. But others—the homeless, those without land, in other words, history's underprivileged—did not feel this was
their fatherland."[13] The few, however, had the "strength to undertake a
higher, almost coercive representation of the many, a representation that
did not interpret the desires and thoughts of knowledgeable men but
was superimposed on a childish, uneducated, underage population with
sublime deceit, the germ of a future reality. There was great pride, but
also abnegation because that representation meant work, responsibility
and sacrifice." Thus, the "fatherland was built and the Italian State created. The protection of the ruling class continued but became less and
less generous" with the turbulent advance of new interests "cloaked
in the robes of the country's interests" and mixed with the highest and
most noble sentiment of liberal patriotism, or so De Ruggiero stated. By
choosing to enter the war, he continued, Salandra ended the era of liberal patriotism: "In agreement with the ultimate triumph and death of
that old-fashioned, patriotic liberalism that he had represented, he led
the country to vote unanimously in favor of entering the war. In doing so
he involuntarily and unknowingly opened up a new era; the era in which,
more than an echo of the past, we are attracted by the tumultuous and
tormented real-life experience of a population without a fatherland,
until now."

When the world conflict ended, many of those who had been thrown
into the "great vortex" of the war, returning home safely and proud of
the sacrifices made, felt stronger ties with the nation they had fought for
but did not identify it with the liberal state. As a matter of fact, they
fought against that state to radically transform it and build one better
suited to represent what they considered to be the real Italian nation.

Varieties of Nationalism

During the decade before the First World War, there were political
clashes among movements with very different concepts of nation. In
many ways this was a direct consequence of the evolution of the myth of
the nation through its various changes, and this, in turn, led to the birth
of different types of nationalism. These were hostile to one another and
quarreled over the Italian government with other movements that, more
and more radically, took up anti-nationalist or decidedly internationalist

positions because they considered the myth of the nation and the national state simply the expression of a bourgeois dictatorship that had to be toppled so as to build the proletariat's universal fatherland.

The founding of a political and intellectual movement that defined itself as nationalist and imperialist; the birth of progressive cultural movements that tried to create a new national culture to modernize the Italians' collective conscience and enable them to face the challenges posed by the new century; the heated debate that arose in the democratic left over the possibility of combining the idea of nation with an internationalist ideal or on the compatibility between patriotism and socialism; the surfacing of a "national question" and a nationalist line of conduct in Catholic circles; the conversion of groups from the revolutionary left to the national myth by means of interventionism; all these developments show how important the myth of the nation was, right from the beginning of the twentieth century, and how it influenced culture and politics. Confirmation also comes from the widespread use of the word "nationalism" at the time. In fact, people spoke of "democratic nationalism," "liberal nationalism," "radical nationalism," "Catholic nationalism," and "humanitarian nationalism," all of which led to much confusion and the need for clarification by turning to adjectives and making distinctions, particularly for the difference between "patriotism" and "nationalism," between "true" and "false" nationalism, or between "healthy" and "perverse" nationalism.[14] In 1913 Edoardo Giretti, a liberalist and anti-imperialist economist, observed that nationalism had become "a banner hiding the most varied types of goods."[15]

During the first decade of the century, various forms of Italian nationalism began to bloom.[16] They did not identify with or consume themselves in the new, bellicose, imperialist version but, rather, related to the different revolutionary movements of the Risorgimento and to more recent concepts of life and man, which interpreted the national phenomenon within the framework of a renewed humanistic and universal version of modernity. As Giretti commented, nationalism "is neither necessarily unjust, nor aggressive, nor provoking," but if it is interpreted as the "high ideal of a great, prosperous, respected nation, . . . it can be a powerful influence on moral and political cohesion and at the same time a splendid goal toward which our best, united efforts should surely be directed."[17] In the same manner, the philosopher Giovanni Vidari supported a "healthy and knowledgeable nationalism" that would combat and win not wars but battles "against the external difficulties created by the civil superiority of other peoples in commerce, industry and the sciences, . . . against the ignorance and poverty of our plebeian emigrants, against the lack of culture, the mischievous, unruly bourgeois classes, against the rancid and nauseating rhetorical and sectarian speeches of our political parties."[18]

It was perfectly acceptable to use the word "nationalism" in democratic environments. In fact, "democratic nationalism" was often mentioned in the publication *L'Unità*, founded in 1911 by Gaetano Salvemini, Social Democrat and federalist. Against imperialist nationalism, said a collaborator, there is "idealistic and democratic nationalism. The latter, being nationalism, does not deny the realities of life in the nation and its true problems."[19] Another collaborator said that the movement "was and is nationalist with Mazzini-type inspiration."[20] On his part, Salvemini cut short these discussions about the meaning of nationalism, saying that he thought there was only one kind of nationalism and that it could be identified with "conquering, militarist, antidemocratic imperialism" that has a "megalomaniac vision of Italy's real capacities, a chauvinist erethism": in this sense, Salvemini wrote, the nationalist is a "clairvoyant who now sees an efficient Greater Italy that may be a reality some day in the future; I am a citizen of 'Little Italy,' the Italy of today that is only now beginning to emerge from many centuries of intellectual, moral and economic poverty. "[21]

The Lega democratica nazionale (National Democratic League) professed "humanitarian nationalism,"[22] which drew inspiration from Risorgimento tradition as conceived by Mazzini and Gioberti and was against imperialist nationalism. The League was a Catholic movement that aimed to combine Catholic democracy and nationalism. Meanwhile, within the new, revolutionary, left-wing syndicalists there were those who were in favor of imperialist nationalism. In fact, during the war in Libya, some union leaders supported the colonial undertaking.[23] Angelo Oliviero Olivetti, one of the main theorists of revolutionary unionism in Italy, declared he was opposed to a nationalist party but wholly in favor of nationalism, "interpreted as establishing the race's aspiration to live and be powerful."[24] Another theorist of the revolutionary syndicalism, Arturo Labriola, declared in 1914 that nationalism "exists when the people who are part of a given cultural unit feel more distinctly and intensely that they belong to this cultural unit. . . . In some ways socialism is a factor of nationalism, in so much as it advocates better education for the working classes and, therefore, arouses in them the feeling that they belong to an historic and cultural unit."[25]

Ideologizing the Nation

The spread of the national myth during the period ranging from the beginning of the century to the rise of Fascism was more conflictual in nature than conciliating. Instead of encouraging a feeling of national unity and consensus of the liberal state, it accentuated and worsened divisions among the Italians. In actual fact, the propagation of the myth of the nation, in its various versions, had its effects on the crisis suffered by liberalism and on the traumatic failure of its attempt to build a fatherland for all Italians, because it increased the number of people who, in opposition to the ruling class, claimed they were the only real interpreters of the nation, the expression of the "real Italy." Starting from the beginning of the twentieth century, the national myth followed new courses instead of spreading in the wake of the Risorgimento-style tradition that was faithful to the values of nation and freedom. The new courses led to the creation of decidedly antiliberal and antidemocratic nationalist movements. During the decade prior to World War I, clashes between old and new believers in the myth of the nation became more and more inflamed, each side proposing its own ideal of nation and state and condemning that of the other as a false expression of the nation, and even "anti-nation." This situation degenerated progressively into violence, lasting through the period of the so-called *Biennio rosso* (Red Biennium, 1919–20), from World War I to the Fascist rise to power. In this way, during the Giolitti period and, above all, after the First World War and because of the effects of the Bolshevik revolution, the ideologization of the nation was accelerated and accentuated. This process, present in the history of modern nationalism since the French Revolution, came about within the sphere of a more general ideologization of politics resulting from the radicalization of the conflict between opposite and irreconcilable visions of life and politics.[26]

The "ideologizing of the nation" is a process wherein the national myth is monopolistically appropriated, explicitly or implicitly, by a political movement, which defines the nation according to its own ideology exclusively. It acknowledges the right to be a member of the nation only to those who share the same ideology, at the same time claiming to be the sole interpreter and legitimate administrator of the nation's aspirations. Consequently, in the case of Italy, the process of ideologizing the nation led to a rigid interpretation of the elements making up the *Italianità* and the criteria for defining the necessary prerequisites of national identity. These were made to coincide basically with the principles of a particular ideology, thus creating the basis for transforming ideological identity into anthropological identity and, therefore, opening the way to a, more or less, explicit introduction of the racial factor in the definition of nation. By doing so, the nation, which according to the national myth of the Risorgimento and liberal Italy had been conceived as the "prerogative or monopoly of no one person" but was "presumed to be common to all," as De Ruggiero wrote, became a "pawn in a game that transcended the limit, the stakes in a gamble" at the hands of "fanatics who, not able to propagate, stuck obstinately to their useless pride and attacked all of those who would not let themselves be organized, either by destroying them or wearing them out." This gave rise to the "necessity to exclude, eliminate and even identify oneself with the nation, to assume the absolute monopoly of truth and reality."[27]

By involving an ever wider area of Italian culture and politics in the contest to decide who represented the "real Italy," the ideologizing of the nation exasperated the mutual incompatibility between the movements and antagonistic ideologies, particularly between nationalists and internationalists, creating the conditions for turning the political conflict into a potential or open civil war. This is what happened in 1919–22 and in 1943–45 after Fascism had collapsed. We do not believe we are stretching our interpretation of historical reality, nor is it the result of reading the events backward, if we see a link between the radical antagonism that existed between 1912 and 1922 and the civil war that was to devastate Italy from 1943 to 1945. It is sufficient to recall that the movements and ideologies clashing during these periods were largely the same and that, in both cases, albeit different situations, the civil war was conceived, experienced and fought, on both sides, to support the "nation" against the "anti-nation."

The Torch of Civil War

The spreading of the various types of nationalisms and the clashes among the different concepts of nation and state during the ten-year period between 1912 and 1922 contributed to the popular belief in the myth of the "two Italies," bestowing on it an increasingly conflicting nature with such hostility between the two entities that they could not coexist; the life of one necessitated the death of the other. The myth of the "two Italies" was the common denominator in the complex group of themes, motives and movements that we have called national radicalism, which was fertile ground for cultivating new versions of a national myth in which there was strong opposition to the liberal state.[28] These new versions departed from the Risorgimento's Mazzini-type myth, seen as an unaccomplished revolution, and accused the liberal ruling class of not having been able to accomplish the moral unification of the nation along with its political and territorial unification. Therefore, it had not provided the Italians with a national conscience or integrated the masses into the state, nor prepared the nation to face the challenges of modernity so as to create a Greater Italy capable of taking a leading role in the progress of modern civilization. National radicalism maintained that the unsuccessful attempt to realize a national revolution, as Mazzini had dreamt of, had originated the ongoing conflict between the "two Italies," the one embodied in the liberal ruling class, and considered narrow-minded and incompetent, the other formed of "real Italians," the genuine interpreters of newborn Italy's vocation as missionary and intransigent champions of its supremacy.

From the ideological point of view, the myth of the "two Italies" was the banner under which all the new movements, left and right, contested the liberal state, sustaining the need to overcome the antagonism by wiping out the forces and ideas that represented Italy of the past and bringing into power the "real Italy," the young nation that in every field of productive activity manifested its vitality, its energy, its desire to rise up and conquer. These movements, both cultural and political, pursued Mazzini's concept of the unaccomplished revolution and adapted it to a new vision of the myth of Greater Italy, which was strongly influenced by the perception and interpretation of the new realities of modern life created by industrialization, modernization and imperialism.

From the social point of view, the myth of the "two Italies" expressed by these movements reflected the aspirations of young intellectuals, a new middle class and sections of the productive bourgeoisie that wanted to play a greater role in national politics and running the state at a time when, owing to the rise of an organized proletariat and the mobilization of the Catholics, the supremacy of the lay and patriotic bourgeoisie came under discussion. The new generations, born at the end of the nineteenth century, did not recognize the existing regime as the nation's legitimate representative. They considered themselves the genuine expression of the new Italy that was emerging from the modernization process and felt they had the right to be considered its knowledgeable chosen elite, the new ruling class, whose job it was to lead Italy to new grandeur. Consequently, they clamored for a radical transformation of the political system to build a new state, capable of mending the divisions that still separated the Italians, and to undertake the moral regeneration of the Italian character more effectively and with greater intensity to form the new *Italianità*. This would enable them to proceed more quickly and decisively with the forming of a collective national conscience and to integrate into the state the social classes that had been excluded after unification. The new state was to be a state of the masses, capable of turning the ideal of a renewed Italian greatness within modern civilization into reality.

In this way the myth of the new state became part of the mythological constellation of Greater Italy, reviving all the other myths, from supremacy to the regeneration of character, from mission to the conquest of modernity, and at the same time, renewing its cultural and political presence more energetically and efficiently. Actually, rather than accelerate the process of the nation's unification, the myth of the new state also contributed to radicalizing the ideological and political conflict among the "various Italies" that existed under the monarchy.

Ironically, the radical protest against the liberal state worsened right after the fatherland's Jubilee celebrations, which were intended to consecrate solemnly the identification of liberal Italy as the fatherland for all the Italians, without any exceptions. As we have seen, Italy's political reality at the time of the fiftieth anniversary was very different from an imagined fatherland where the Italians were united and in accord. Speaking before the Chamber on September 9, 1913, after the first elections with universal male suffrage, Arturo Labriola concisely and efficiently described the ideological gaps that divided the Italians: "We are at the atomic collision of all the political elements. . . . There is a Catholic Italy, a Socialist Italy, an Imperialist Italy: there is no Giolitti Italy. That Italy is a mediocre parliamentary combination, born in the corridors outside the Chamber, good only to prevent, incapable of creating. That Italy has to disappear."[29]

The deep-rooted conflict between the "two Italies" became a violent clash, the battlefield for interventionists and neutralists. In the postwar period, it turned into episodes of civil war, first between Socialists and bourgeois, then between Fascists and anti-Fascists. It ended with the victory of Fascism and the suppression of the liberal regime. However, even before the outbreak of the war, there was a certain propensity for a civil war that would solve, once and for all, the antagonism between the "two Italies" and build a "new fatherland," as Adolfo Omodeo wrote in 1912 in a letter to his fiancée. He was then a young student in the Christian religion, full of Mazzini-type passion for the myth of the Greater Italy and animated by heroic fury against Giolitti's Italy, which he felt was the most dangerous opponent to this myth.

> A new fatherland: this is what we need, not the old fatherland, the fatherland of orators, but a fatherland that is alive, that feels, aspires to a renewed soul. The fatherland, Mazzini used to say, is the conscience of the country. . . . Our nation, now politically an aggregate of the old regions that are badly welded together, national life that has disintegrated into single, egoistic individual activities, a moral life swamped in shoddy interests; everything needs to be recast; everything needs to embrace, bind and converge on a profound desire to unite, to create the nation, even by lighting the torch of civil war.[30]

The invocation petitioning a civil war might appear to be the irrational outburst of an angry young man. But if we consider it one of the possible effects of the extreme contrast between the "two Italies," it has a more important meaning. Radicalizing the myth of the "two Italies" into antagonism between opposite and incompatible concepts of the state and nation left the door open to a possible degeneration of the political conflict into civil war, intended as the armed conflict between groups of people belonging to the same nation or the same state, each proposing its own model of nation or state, which could only be achieved by annihilating the adversary, considered an enemy with which no compromise was possible. At the origin of all this, at least from the point of view of the history of the national myth, there was, on the part of the new left-wing and right-wing nationalisms, the desire to form the national conscience of a new Italy, capable of facing the challenges of modernity in the twentieth century so as to play a prominent role in world politics and take the lead in a new civilization.

5

Italianism and Modernity

Modernist Nationalism

The different ways the new nationalism appeared on the scene, starting at the beginning of the twentieth century, were partly expressions of cultural and ideological efforts at modernization. Like the Risorgimento patriots and the founders of the national state, these efforts had to deal with the same problem of achieving modernity that had tormented the patriots of the past, but the terms were new and the situation completely different. From this point of view, the new nationalism was not a rhetorical display of provincial culture that had remained on the fringes of the modern European movements, nor was it produced by intellectuals incapable of understanding modernity and who continued to dream of resurrecting ancient glories in humanistic idleness. While these aspects did exist, they were marginal compared with the pressing need of modernization fueled by the vision of a new world that was being shaped by the prodigious development of the industrial civilization. The confrontation between the myth of the nation and modernity in the twentieth century was a general trend throughout Europe from the end of the century to World War I. This period marked everywhere the height of nationalism, the meaning of which had progressively moved away from the principle of nationality, identified with a national state, to be linked with imperialism and intended as the enforcement of expansionist policy and a national state's powers.

The spread of the new nationalism was not circumscribed to political circles in Italy. In fact, the national myth was, more or less explicitly, central to the philosophical revival proposed by Benedetto Croce and Giovanni Gentile's new idealism[1] and evident in the new historiography,[2] in the pedagogical school of thought,[3] and above all in avant-garde culture, such as Futurism and the "La Voce" group.[4] To a certain

82

extent, it could be said that the myth of Greater Italy had originated the avant-garde movement in Italy, orienting it clearly toward political activism. This became evident in more or less pronounced forms of radical nationalism that was hostile toward the liberal state and vaguely advocated an Italian revolution, a political, moral and cultural revolution all mixed together—capable of regenerating the Italians, forming a sound national conscience and preparing Italy to, once again, take the lead in world history by creating a modern civilization.

Politically, the new nationalism manifested itself in a variety of stances, ranging from authoritarian to democratic. However, the variety should not let us lose sight of the fact that there were some important common traits that influenced the change that took place in the myth of the nation during the first two decades of the century, bringing up again the question of tradition in the Risorgimento and liberal sense.

In liberal Italy's culture, the ideal of modernity was summarized in three elements, "nation, liberty, progress," and identified politically with a parliamentary regime, considered the most suitable institutional form to govern and guide the nation in its move toward modernity. When King Victor Emmanuel III inaugurated the twenty-third legislature (1909–1913), he said that the huge transformation that took place after the unification was due to the "beneficial effects of liberty and its educational value, because not only the individual but the social classes and the whole population acquired, together with the sentiment of their worthiness and dignity, awareness of their own duties and responsibilities." Only a policy of "widespread liberty has guaranteed a peaceful social climate by improving the conditions of the working classes, without stopping or delaying industrial and commercial progress: but the benefits of liberty must be associated continuously with the regular application of wise reforms, which Italy has been undertaking wholeheartedly and carefully in this past decade." And we must continue to pursue this "policy of liberty, progress and wisdom so that the state can proceed more vigorously and flexibly in promoting and regulating the many types of activities of modern life."[5]

However, many people, particularly the young, felt that this political trend did not respond to the needs of the nation at the dawn of the twentieth century. They also thought that liberal Italy's progress toward modernity was too slow. Italy was lagging behind other modern nations, slowed by the weight of ancient ills never cured and by the internal problems of a largely backward society. It suffered social and political conflicts that were often violent, showing how far from reality a single

fatherland for the Italians was and how distant was the advent of a
Greater Italy that could really take the lead on the international scene
and be capable of helping to solve the problems facing the new era.
"The value of a population is measured only by its cooperation in solving the problems that it is confronted with; therefore, it expresses its
greatest power of superiority and glory through its foreign policy," declared Alfredo Oriani at the beginning of what he prophesied would be
"a great century."[6]

Paradoxically, Italy's pride in having made so much progress during
fifty years of unification aggravated its inferiority complex with respect
to the more powerful European and non-European nations, which were
competing for a greater international role. For those who were not resigned to accepting, realistically, a role suited to Italy's effective human
and natural potential, the cause of this inferiority complex was not the
scarcity of material energy and means but the government's lack of will
and capability. Populations with a weak collective conscience, explained
Francesco Nitti, who turned to the younger generations as the new century dawned, with the authority of a *nouvelle* Italian Fichte, are destined
to stay behind in the modern industrial civilization.[7] As a result, it was
necessary to form a "greater national soul."[8]

Nitti was a democrat and did not cultivate imperialist ambitions. For
this reason his attitude helps us to better understand the deep-rooted
motivations of the state of mind that was at the basis of the new nationalism. This state of mind was common to those who, above all among
the younger population, had great faith in the nation's potential, thanks
to its economic and industrial development, and wanted to accelerate
modernization and intensify the creation of a collective conscience to
enable Italy to keep pace with the advent of modern civilization. The
young, modernist, avant-garde intellectuals wanted the nation to be
ready to throw itself into the "vibrant turbine" of the "grandiose device
of modern life,"[9] and they were convinced that only the ineptitude of
the ruling classes, the inertia of the masses, the absence of a suitable cultural background to understand and face the realities of the new modern life that was forming with such confusing rapidity prevented Italy
from reaching the more advanced nations.

The predominant sentiment in the new nationalism was enthusiasm
for scientific discoveries, technological development, the acceleration of
time, the new dynamic sense of life and the vitality that came with the
desire for individual and collective power, which spurred competition

between people, classes and nations, drawing everyone, willy-nilly, into the vortex of modernity. New lifestyles came into being as a result of the "rapid and widespread growth of big industry," with repercussions on all classes, societies and countries, upsetting "millennia of world balance, . . . not only from the economic but also the political and moral points of view,"[10] observed Mario Morasso in 1905 in his extremely bombastic description of the great transformation that involved the whole world during the imperialist era and the upheavals it caused in all fields of individual and collective lives, customs and consciences. Modern man was living "in a new world among newly deployed unpredictable forces . . . that had transformed not only the foundations of people's political lives and moral conduct but also the whole system of economic relations" and had had "an enormous influence on other types of relations, on man's very sentiments and habits, on human nature, on the government's functions, creating a new conscience and a new political attitude toward the new energy thus generated." The major cause of this transformation of human conditions was the growth of big industry, which was anonymous and collective, and as a result had "deep repercussions on . . . the trend of public and private lives, on the regime of our sensibility and our activity;" "human life has come out of it completely changed, centuries-old customs have been destroyed, profound tendencies of our soul have gone astray, . . . the social order has been upset so that it can be reorganized in view of a new future."[11]

From the new confrontation between national myth and modernity, a multifaceted form of cultural and political modernism emerged. "Modernism" is intended as an ideology, a culture, a movement that, starting from the perception of modern reality as a period of irreversible change, wanted to face and resolve the human, cultural and political problems arising from industrial civilization and modernization, by working out solutions coherent with its own view of modernity. The new Italian nationalism had perceived positively both modernity and the desire to promote a cultural and political movement capable of modernizing the Italian nation and enabling it to face and win the new challenges of modern life. In this sense, we can speak of "modernist nationalism" to define the direction being taken in Italian culture and politics by the new versions of the national myth between the beginning of the century and the coming of Fascism to power. The new myths were being created under the effects of the new modern lifestyles resulting from industrialization, imperialism and the society of the masses and

were influenced by Italy's considerable economic progress in the years
of its industrial growth between the end of the nineteenth century and
the early twentieth.

Modernist nationalism combined the idea of nation with enthusiasm for the new civilization; it was the outcome of the industrial revolution and modernization; and it was characterized by an irreversible
transformation process, an explosion of human and material energy
unprecedented in the history of mankind, and an intensification of individual and collective lifestyles that disrupted and affected every aspect
of society, causing antagonism and conflicts between nations and continents in a world contest for power and supremacy. Modernist nationalism did not reject modernization and industrialization but wanted to
promote these processes in order to consolidate the nation's cohesion
and increase its participation in world politics. Modernizing the nation
meant not only giving it new instruments for economic and social development but also regenerating it to eliminate obsolete customs assimilated during centuries of servitude and to form, by means of a new culture, a conscience and character better suited to the style and rhythm of
modern life, within which the nation could grow and expand its power
and civilization. The main modernist trait of this nationalism was the
attempt to reconcile spirituality, generically considered the prime characteristic of culture, ideas and sentiments, with the realistic acceptance
of industrialization and the society of the masses, but retaining these
processes within the borders of the nation so as to use them for the nation itself. To this end, modernist nationalism sustained the necessity to
accompany the industrial revolution and modernization with a spiritual
revolution in order to shape the sensibility, character and conscience of
a "new Italian," so that he would be able to understand and deal with
the problems and challenges of modern life, keeping a firm grip on the
superiority of spiritual forces when faced with the development of the
material and technological ones. This would be the only way to guarantee the nation unity and a collective identity and to contrast the negative
consequences and disintegrating effects of the crisis affecting traditional
society, which in Italy, compounded the defects inherited from a national revolution considered incomplete because it did not result in the
regeneration of the Italians and did not create a new national conscience
or common faith. The revolution of the spirit was to create new character aristocracies capable of leading and dominating modern life, calling
upon the power of sentiment and emotion rather than reason, by reacti-
vating mythopoeic capacities. A new lay religion was to accompany the

nation's modernization process to increase awareness in the masses of their spiritual unity.

Modernist nationalism did not have the fetishlike cult of tradition, although it used historical tradition to create new mythical universes in support of the "religion of the nation"; it did not look back nostalgically on the past as being perfect, to be preserved or restored to counteract the changes brought by modernization; it launched itself toward the future tragically optimistic that the nation would become so great as to satisfy its desire for power. In this sense, the importance given to the myth of *Romanità* (Romanness) in modernist nationalism enabled it to coexist with the creativity of futurist myths that also exalted the nation with the aim of generating new values and principles in a new universal civilization and proclaimed the supremacy of the spirit, and celebrated the realism of force and even hailed the brutality of revolutions and wars as the makers of civilization. Modernist nationalism saw war and revolution as the major factors accelerating modernity, the testing ground for the new elitist energies, classes and emerging nations endowed with the desire for power. War and revolution, conceived as instruments for regenerating the nation, meant spirit of sacrifice, exercise of discipline, battle readiness and sublimation of the individual in his devotion to the nation: all these were elements of a national ethics oriented toward austere antihedonism, a "cult of the heroic,"[12] a tragic and agonistic vision of existence, life to be lived in continuous tension and perpetual conflict in order to affirm the nation's desire for power.

The first indispensable requirement for participating in the contest to conquer modernity, according to modernist nationalism, was to form a sound national conscience that would strengthen the nation's forces, so that it would be ready to face world competition. Italy had made great progress in economics and social life, but the collective national conscience was still weak, and this risked keeping the nation out of the race for modernity. Therefore, it was necessary, wrote the philosopher Giovanni Amendola in 1910, "to clearly go beyond Italy as it is now"; there was a "profound need for resurrection," which was to be found in the "practical and continuous quest for the highest ethical value that gives significance to life and transcends the boundaries of the individual and allows, or rather encourages, the very sacrifice of life." Without this "ideal passion capable of transforming life and elevating it, . . . one has a gathering of men, not a nation."[13] The problem of regenerating the nation needed to be dealt with by first forming a new religious conscience. In 1911 Amendola wrote:

We want to establish in the granite of moral life, the ethically strong construction of the new Italian history by means of a religion that will link us to the deepest and purist reasons for human existence, which by emerging from our daily humility will establish itself over the centuries. . . . Our future as a nation will depend on this choice: and it is this choice that is maturing obscurely in the depths of the national conscience. If we had a way to influence this profound spiritual choice, we would also be able to create the Italy of tomorrow, an Italy that would allow people to forget forever the poverty of our past.[14]

Italianism

Modernist nationalism was inspired above all by a renewed faith in the myth of Greater Italy. Italianism—that is, the conviction that Italy should have a role in the twentieth century as one of the great protagonists and be in the forefront of a new national and universal civilization—was the lay creed of the new generations who considered themselves the new aristocracy of the spirit and character, destined to lead Italy in the conquest of modernity. "A Third Italy without an important ideal in the world would be the most absurd miracle in modern history, a resurrection without life, a reappearance of ghosts just passing by,"[15] stated Alfredo Oriani, who was, for the new generations, one of the most popular writers praising Italianism. "In our modernity, which attenuates all the limits from class to class, from nation to nation," Italy needed to establish its own new origin as a nation, no longer dependent on its past: "At one time, Italy had distinct, rival physiognomies in its regions and classes, cities and rural areas, which the centuries passed over, making them all the same; the national spirit leveled the surface and condensed the bottom; therefore, the new Italy needs to conquer a new origin in the world, otherwise the ancient one will remain stamped on its forehead like a label on a vase."[16]

Those who believed in Italianism were proud of Italy's industrial progress. They were not afraid of modernity nor opposed to modernization. They did not dream of a return to a nostalgic past of lost grandeur but wanted to adjust the Italians' conscience, sensibility and culture to the living conditions brought by modernity and prepare them to face its challenges by competing, even warring, with the other large European nations. The greatest ambition of Italianism was not only to attain military power or conquer colonies, but also to create and be acclaimed throughout the world for Italian modernity.

At the origin of Italianism was the conflict between an inferiority complex felt by the new generations when comparing Italy with the more advanced European nations and their faith in Italy's inborn quality of grandeur, which was giving signs of recovery, thus refuting ancient and consolidated prejudice regarding the decadence and inferiority of the Italians. In 1905 Amendola wrote, "Italy has made great strides as regards its affluence, but it cannot maintain it unless its potential moves forward at the same pace and at the same time."[17] This sentiment was common among the young nationalists, convinced that now Italy was ready to make the big leap forward, to take the lead in humanity's march toward the future. The avant-garde cultural movements that had appeared in Italy early in the twentieth century were certain that Italy was destined to play a leading role during the new century. "Italy must be acclaimed for its spirit, it must give birth to a modern civilization,"[18] proclaimed the editor of *La Voce*. His ambition was shared by the journal's collaborators, animated by the conviction that Italy "was a great nation, a nation under pressure from the urgent needs of world competition, and a country that had declared that it accepted the challenge and hoped to be victorious."[19] These young people wanted to "change the national character," because, as Amendola wrote, "in Italy there is little national dignity. There are shopkeepers, . . . hotel keepers and servants."[20] It is necessary to regenerate the Italians and form a national conscience of modern Italy, putting "a bit of organism into this atomic chaos that is Italy."[21]

Similar expressions were to be found in the manifesto of the Futurist artists, published at the beginning of 1910: "For other populations, Italy is still the land of the dead, a huge Pompei gleaming white with tombstones. Instead, Italy has been reborn, its political resurrection followed by intellectual rebirth. In the country of the illiterate, the number of schools is increasing exponentially; in the country known for its *dolce far niente*, now you can hear the roar of numerous workshops; in the country of traditional esthetics, what stands out is the striking inspirational flight of innovation."[22] The Futurists wanted to give Italy "a conscience that would turn it into a country based on hard work and ferocious conquests. May the Italians finally experience the intoxicating joy of feeling alone, armed, very modern, in conflict with everyone, and not the sleepy descendant of a greatness that is no longer ours," and experience the "wonderful young atmosphere that is forming, in which Italy is going to turn out to be a great, hard-working, military power," wrote the Futurist painter Umberto Boccioni.[23] The nationalist tendency predominated in

the Futurist movement. After the war in Libya, the anarchist and Futurist artist Carlo Carrà converted to nationalism, explaining that to deny
"nationalism means subjecting oneself to the nationalism of others."[24]
The Futurists did not want to be confused with authoritarian and traditional nationalism, so they professed their nationalism, libertarian and
revolutionary, and that they were antisocialist, because socialism was
pacifist and internationalist, while they wanted to combine emancipation of the proletariat with "national pride, energy and expansion," as
proclaimed in the first Futurist political manifesto published during the
1909 elections. Futurism did not exclude the possibility of an agreement
with the revolutionary left, made up of anarchists and union leaders, to
fight the common enemy — the liberal bourgeois society. However, Italianism was a prejudicial factor that always influenced the ideas and
political choices of Futurism and prevented it, despite its intentions and
attempts, from overcoming the diffidence of the proletariat and subver-
sive members of the left to establish a common action. In the political
manifesto published during the 1913 elections, Filippo Tommaso Marinetti, Umberto Boccioni, Carlo Carrà, and Luigi Russolo proclaimed
the dogma of the Futurist political creed: "The word *Italy* must dominate the word *Liberty*."[25]

The avant-garde culture, permeated with Italianism, wanted to "link
up again the new expectations of Italian civilization with the great economic growth that we have been witnessing for several years,"[26] wrote
Giovanni Papini and Giuseppe Prezzolini in 1906. The intellectuals, according to Amendola, should unite with the Lombard industrialists, the
Genoese shipping magnates and the merchants and bankers of northern Italy and work together for "our country's success in the struggle
among the various countries currently competing for the world."[27] To
this end, the avant-garde movements thought a radical process of moral,
cultural and political regeneration was necessary to give birth to a "new
Italian," with a strong national conscience and a sound faith in his future. Even Croce, with his realistic and antinationalist temperament,
addressing the young people who dreamt of "carrying Italy to a higher
destiny," warned them that only a new faith, capable of contrasting util-
itarianism and materialism, could "improve society and make Italy
great."[28]

National pride, sparked by the progress Italy had made in the first
fifty years of unification, was fueled by every event that testified to or favored Italy's becoming a greater and stronger nation. Even success in
international sports events was hailed as an expression of the "abundant

Italian energy that continues to increase the industrial power and vitality of the race, which has gone a long way to correcting old prejudices regarding our irreparable decadence as Latins and to reminding everyone how Italy is now racing . . . toward the future." That was what the *Corriere della Sera* wrote in 1908.[29] It also mentioned Arturo Toscanini's triumphs at New York's Metropolitan Opera, praising Italy as "intellectual and vigorous, artistic and industrious, young both mentally and physically, in addition to having a luminous tradition of genius and strength, a new Italy that deserves a review of the judgment it has been burdened with for too many years, and passed by more fortunate, richer, more powerful populations. . . . The Italians challenge these comparisons. There is the raw material for building the greatest of futures."

Italianism also revived the myth of supremacy and mission, with greater confidence in the possibility of realizing them and, therefore, with more determination to do everything necessary to enable the nation to carry out its mission. In 1912 Bernardino Varisco declared: "We want Italy to carry out, within the human race, the function its history and capacities have assigned to it by right and imposed on it as a duty. We want it to live its own life, not subordinated for any reason to anyone. As a matter of fact, we want Italy to exercise a leading role in the lives of human beings, on equal footing with any other nation."[30]

Even the classicist intellectuals, such as Gabriele D'Annunzio, became inebriated with modernity at the prospect of imperialism. They were looking for the source of a new mythopoeic art in modern life that would give the function of creating the national mythology back to artists. D'Annunzio was enthusiastic about modernity. As an esthete he admired the spectacle of industrialism and imperialism, merging the images of modern life with a mythical view of a Greater Italy, of which he elected himself poet, prophet, poet laureate and creator. In his oratory upon the death of Giosue Carducci, he said:

> Here is the new world, here is the Divina Commedia of the new transfigurations; . . . an extraordinary amount of spiritual energy is about to erupt from the tumult to assume the pose of unknown beauty. In the numerous factories that rise up from the earth, in the mines that sink deep inside the earth, in the ships that in ever greater numbers ply the rivers and the seas, and in all of the instruments of work, profit, games and war, the new images and rhythms are being prepared. . . . And life was never so rich, the spectacle of the earth so proud, the drama of the races so vehement. . . . And everywhere the commercial battle, the battle for wealth, brings the

danger of martial conflagrations. . . . Never more crudely have the
rights of the less powerful races been violated by such arrogance
and avidity. Above the continuous din of the workers you can hear
the barking of warfare. The whole world is stretched like a bow.

Fascinated by the sight of the large nations leading the new modernity, D'Annunzio encouraged the Italians to emulate them. The models
he chose to follow were imperialist powers like Japan, "an unprecedented example of a transformation that was more like a profound
creation"; Germany, "concerned with showing off new means of conquest every day, more valid and rapid than before, with opening new
commercial channels for trade, preparing for the supreme victory of the
future with a series of minor victories," with its cities that "are fervently
productive, magnificent industrial centers," with its governors who,
"wisely, are always ready to try to find new and larger outlets for its huge
output," with its "old Prussian military tradition" onto which it has mi-
raculously grafted the novelty of industrial competition," with its people
who "in concordance and fortunate in employment . . . has strengthened its instinct to predominate and adapted to the weapons of a different war"; or like England, which under the effects of an "almost frenetic
exaltation of the national conscience, extraordinarily full of the race's
virtues," has established its power, "by immeasurably increasing its colonial territory, indefinitely enlarging the boundaries of its Empire," while
"all of the lively forces of such a people, inebriated by a poet, see it as
the image of a 'Greater Britain.'"

In the midst of the "formidable conflict" that was upsetting the
world, the poet questioned himself on the future of Italy. He was over-
joyed at the "many efforts made by Italy in the past twenty years by virtue of its own inherited instinct alone." He added, however, that that had
occurred "despite the ineptitude and blindness of those who guided the
future of a nation that had given birth to and helped advance a science of
state and an art of government not founded on false scholastic methods
and childish illusions but on reality, fact, experience and the detailed
study of men and institutions, their analogies and their relationships."[31]

Much more significant than D'Annunzio's patronage in understanding the importance and propagation of the modernist myth of a new
greatness was the presence of Italianism also among the new left of the
revolutionary syndicalists, who were particularly sensitive to the myths
of power in their vision of the future society of producers, conceived by
mixing Marx and Nietzsche. In 1907, the revolutionary-syndicalist review

Pagine Libere published an article praising the "minds of our people, so pure and accurate, combining naturalism and good common sense, questioning all physical and experimental truths, initiators of humanism in the first and second Renaissance—minds that anticipated modern science during the troubled seventeenth century. . . . We who invented scientific politics, demolished the Papacy, remained immune to infatuation with the Reformation, . . . we owe it to the internationalism of modern life to find ourselves. This is the aim we have set for ourselves; revival of *Italianità* in the nation's way of thinking, so cosmopolitan and universal in its origin and expression."[32] At the same time, in 1909, and with similar feeling, the future head of Fascism, then antinationalist and internationalist, praised the new Italy that was "losing its sepulchral characteristics. Where at one time lovers dreamt and nightingales sang, today the factory whistles are blowing. Italy is accelerating its pace in the stadium where nations are running the marathon of world supremacy. Heroes have made way for producers. After having fought, people are working. The hoe cultivates the earth and the pick demolishes cities. Italy is getting ready to fill a new era in the history of mankind with its own story."[33]

6

Italian Imperialists

From Nationalism to Imperialism

The "discovery of imperialism"[1] by Italian culture played a decisive part in transforming the myth of nation, giving impulse to the birth of imperialist nationalism, which redefined the myth of a Greater Italy in terms of exclusive criteria, with policies of might, expansion and conquest. A consequence of this new direction was the plan to found the national state again on an authoritarian basis, to harness all the productive forces, with the aim of accelerating the industrial revolution and preparing the nation to face imperialist competition in the world of economics and on the battlefield. Despite the classicized rhetoric enveloping its ideology, Italian imperialist nationalism was imbued with modernism and aimed at modernizing the country by using authoritarian means, considering the liberal state incompatible with the requirements of modernity in the age of imperialism. The latter was considered an inevitable outcome of industrial civilization, which greatly changed the idea of nation and its role in international life.

In 1901 the liberal journalist Olindo Malagodi wrote that the "new imperialism," which had sprung "unexpectedly and disquietingly" from industrial civilization, was "an excellent achievement but charged with dangerous strength and will, the conscious and imaginative ambition to be great that, heady with self but still unsatisfied, is reflected, projected and magnified in the dark mirror of the future."[2] The great world powers competing for industrial, economic, trade and political supremacy expressed this ambition in the desire to expand and rule. "They are world powers because the theater of their actions, the field of their ambitions, is no longer a continent and a civilization but all civilizations and the whole world, because the streams of their expansion spill everywhere into the four corners of the earth."[3] Malagodi observed that, if at

94

first the industrial revolution had fraternized with national revolutions and had supported the "sacred right of nations to educate and govern themselves," laying down that "a nation's territory was its perpetual and inalienable birthright," this new imperialism ruled that "no nation possesses perpetual rights over the territory it occupies."[4] By becoming imperial, even in the form of democratic imperialism as in England, industrial civilization no longer recognized the principle of nationality as valid. Roberto Michels pointed out that, on the contrary, the theory of the principle of nationality "is only a symptom of weakness" because as soon as a people "has overcome the phase of defending itself ethnically and achieved its own national unity, the very vitality that it feels flowing in its veins emboldens it to the point of starting to destroy, by dismissing it, the theory that was the foundation on which this people rose to the dignity of nation. Or rather, sometimes peoples appeal to the principle of nationality and, at the same time, to the right to care nothing about it."[5]

Thus the supremacy of the principle of nationality was undermined in international relations after being the cornerstone of the Risorgimento's aspiration to nationhood, to which liberal Italy had remained basically faithful. This was so even though diplomatic requirements had obliged liberal Italy to play down the claims of the Irredentists, who had been the most aggressive champions of the principle of nationality after unification.[6] However, in the past some had already expressed doubts about the theoretical validity of the principle of nationality, as Crispi did, defending the "objectivity" of a nation with respect to the will of individuals, or Gaetano Mosca, who supported unprejudiced realism and wanted to highlight the merely ideological nature of this principle.[7] Even an anti-imperialist like the Trieste writer, Scipio Slataper, a scholar of Irredentism, expressed well-founded doubts about whether the principle of nationality could be applied, just when it had become the ideological banner of most of the Italian interventionist movement with the First World War.[8] At the beginning of 1915 he realistically wondered if it was possible "to practically resolve, I do not mean all, nor some, but one of the European national issues in a strictly national sense, that is, not causing new rights and new intentions to arise, not a new national issue for every one that is finally resolved." As far as he was concerned, Slataper doubted that "the national principle" could be "a sufficient political rule when it is not a matter of nations conceived theoretically or sentimentally and not a part of history (that is, of reality) but of nation-states, that is, concrete in their traditions and aspirations." It had to be kept in mind that the principle of nationality also had its historical occasion, in that it arose historically against a monarchy of Divine Right, "when some great nations still had to assert themselves outside the extremely vague and inadequate 'allegiance of subjects.'"

The problems brought up by the Trieste writer found an answer in imperialist nationalism, which rejected the principle of nationality as an obsolete Risorgimento ideology, giving importance to what the state required. The state was an expression of the will and power of an organized nation and was, therefore, destined to expand its borders and its economic and cultural influence and also to increase its possessions so as not to succumb to the inevitable expansionism of other states. Some even went to the extent of wondering if the principle of nationality was an obstacle to the development of an Italian national conscience, as it expressed an ideology that was not at all indigenous but derived from English and French liberalism. The principle of nationality had to be reconsidered in the light of the new international reality dominated by the struggle for power and expansion, but it was also necessary to keep in mind the need for autonomy of the national state's collective conscience. Thus, in a profile of Crispi in 1922, Arturo Jemolo identified the reason for Italy's weakness compared to the great powers in a primal defect: the abstractly doctrinaire nature of the principle of nationality.[9]

Indeed, faced with the success of the national state as an expanding power, the principle of nationality seemed destined to decline, just as the new reality of imperialism seemed to require reconsideration of the principle of freedom in the relations between a state and its citizens. Turning into imperialism, the myth of nation had to necessarily abandon liberalism. At least this was what the first champions of Italian imperialism, like Mario Morasso, believed.[10]

The new imperialism placed the relations between citizens and state in a new perspective as well, completely to the advantage of the latter, which took on an increasingly predominant role in organizing and running Italy's collective life, launched as the state was toward imperial conquest and subordinating the rights and interests of the citizens to this aim. What was characteristic of the "imperialist sentiment," stated the sociologist Giovanni Amadori Virgilj, was that all the energy and strength of the state and its citizens were concentrated on the imperialist aim, which "directs the greatest efforts of everyone toward domination,"[11] seen as carrying out a mission. The new aim of the state demanded the maximum abnegation and sacrifice of its citizens through a kind of "nationalization of private lives based on individual freedom," because the imperialist ideal "needs concordant energies" and, therefore, demands the rejection of internal divisions, class hatred and personal and political struggles that undermine the nation's harmony: "The imperialist aim requires internal peace, and the more prepared an individual is to sacrifice his resentment to it, the stronger future domination will be."[12] Thus, imperialism tended to question another cornerstone of the Risorgimento myth of nation, that is, an individual's freedom, even if, in fact, the experience of England, France and the United States showed that imperialism and parliamentary democracy could go hand in hand. There were Italian imperialists, like Scipio Sighele, for example, who believed that Italian imperialist nationalism should be based on democracy, and there were expansionists, like Amendola, who remained loyal to the liberal state in any case. However, the prevailing tendency among the supporters of imperialism was favorable to limiting or even suppressing an individual's freedom in order to strengthen the unity of the nation. This was considered necessary above all for a young nation recently established as a state, which had not yet become unified or cohesive, with its own sound national conscience, and which therefore had to speed up the process to be able to take part in world competition.

Founding the National State Again

In the new century, the domineering brutality of imperialism, the growing predominance of the myth of might and racial superiority with respect to the myth of justice and equality among nations, the realistically oriented advance of ideological and political analysis, the idea of modernity as an explosion of vitality and strength that undermined the progressivist optimism of humanitarianism, all led the Italian imperialists to believe that the principle of nationality, valid for claiming rights for one's own nation, was less so, or was not valid at all, for recognizing the rights of other nations. Furthermore, the principle of nationality had to take second place to the expansionist requirements of demographically fertile races, the fecund "proletarian nations," needing new lands as an outlet for their proliferation.

The idea of a national community bound together by moral solidarity and social unity, capable of being a protagonist on the world stage in an age where imperialism was flourishing, was the dominating inspiration of Italian imperialist nationalism, together with enthusiasm for modernity. Enrico Corradini extolled the vitality of modern life and the spirit behind it:

> In this age, the pace of life is extraordinarily violent and lightning-
> swift. . . . The spirit that in the guise of a storm assailing the world
> moves unwitting multitudes is the spirit of the new life [that] seems
> to sweep everything away, because new men who understand and
> whose minds are equal to the new world order and who are
> stronger than the new forces, have not yet appeared. This is the im-
> mense tragedy of the present, and the epic deeds of the future will
> be the fruit of man's victory over tools and the forces of life, for-
> midable as never before.[13]

This was the core of the nationalist modernism of the new imperialists who had gathered in the Italian Nationalist Association that sprang
up in 1910 and who later joined the Fascist movement in 1923.[14] Corradini was a fairly realistic observer and also a fertile producer of myths for
Italian imperialism, like the myth of a proletarian nation and of "national socialism," where he condensed his concept of nationalism, identifying it with imperialism. He derived his idea of nation, described as "a
matter of spirit surrounded by supreme moral values,"[15] from the concept of imperialism, but in fact it was based on a strong foundation of
positivist naturalism, which Corradini counterposed to the idea of nation in the Risorgimento tradition. The principle of nationality was only
a point in time in the life of nations, before they embarked again on the
struggle to hold sway in a perpetual contest for domination, because a
nation is nothing but "a unity of forces whose natural objective is to
dominate. Because those who do not wish to dominate end up being
dominated." The instrument required to dominate was inevitably a war
of conquest. Imperialist nationalism had a cult of war. It believed in the
"need for war" and extolled preparing for war as the essence of national
education: "War is a supreme act, but upholding the need for war means
recognizing the need to prepare for war and be prepared for war."[16]

Imperialist nationalists, convinced that Italy would be excluded from
imperialist competition and degraded from its rank as a great power for
lack of an ambitious and aggressive foreign and colonial policy, aimed
at fostering the development of a national conscience and the adoption
of a resolute foreign policy supported by strengthening the productive
and armed forces. "True nationalism," "pure and straightforward,"
stated the Turin newspaper of monarchic trade-union nationalism *Il
Tricolore* on June 1, 1909, summing up the whole program of imperialist
nationalism in blunt, concise sentences:

> Italy cannot and must not hold back. It must compete with great
> nations and must not succumb later. However, to avoid this, it
> needs a policy of strength, of great undertakings, of expansionism:

the victorious policy of great peoples. It is the traditional policy of
Rome, conqueror and ruler in the world, against intrusive and vul-
gar demagogy, against the leveling madness of socialism, against
the cowardice of radicalism, and finally against idle and dishonest
parliamentarianism, worthless and immoral, which no longer rep-
resents the national conscience and does not understand the new
functions of the nation in the world.[17]

To carry out this program, admonished Corradini, nationalism had
to take lessons from its main adversary, socialism, for its methods of mobilization and struggle, transferring them from the proletarian to the
middle-class world, from class conflict to war among nations. Nationalism had to take on organizing the conflict of the proletarian nation,
"the socialism of the Italian nation in the world,"[18] organizing the Italians through an iron national discipline, preparing them morally and
materially for the war of conquest, and launching them in the conflict of
nations.

The national imperialist concept held that all this led to glorifying the
role and function of the state as the political organization of the nation.
Overcoming a former generic antistatism, when nationalism was above
all social and political protest, the imperialists favored the productive
bourgeoisie, opposed a weak and inefficient bureaucratic and parasitic
state, and became ever more determined champions of a strong state—a
national state. The latter was to bring about the close-knit, moral and
productive unity of all the classes, subjecting them to an intense nationalizing process of education and discipline and thus equipping the nation, economically, militarily and morally, to face world competition. In
1911 Luigi Valli, one of the first nationalist theorists, stated that the main
function of the state was "to gather and organize the forces of the nation
for predominance in an economic, moral or military conflict against all
the world."[19] As far as this was concerned, the national state could only
be an authoritarian and aristocratic one as regards power and the ruling
class, which was identified with the intellectual and productive bourgeoisie. The wavering of some imperialists when defining the relation between nationalism and democracy was overcome by the jurist Alfredo
Rocco, a former militant of the Radical Party converted to imperialist
nationalism,[20] who worked out the definitive national imperialist theory
of the state.

Rocco's definition of a nation was somewhere between a positivist
concept that considered belonging to a nation as an organic community
that had "necessary origins and is linked to a fact not depending on individual will,"[21] and a voluntaristic concept considering that "nationality

is something spiritual, not physical. Those who are born and live on
national territory do not belong to the nation, only those who feel spiritually bound to it."[22] In fact, Rocco's nationalism was based on straightforward naturalism: he considered nations as racial organisms, dominated by the principle of the struggle for survival and supremacy in
their relations, in a perpetual cycle of birth, development and end, like
the perpetual cycle of nature. Rocco believed that the supreme principle
of nationalism was the idea of society as an organism, that is "an aggregate of elements destined for an aim that is outside the whole, and that
pertains to the whole." Society had higher aims than the interests of the
single individuals making it up in a particular historical period; its existence "goes beyond that of individuals and extends into centuries and
sometimes into millennia." The only spiritualistic element in Rocco's
nationalism was the state, which expressed the principle of organization that, opposing the principle of disintegration, enabled the nation-
organism to rise, establish itself and expand. Human beings lost their
individuality in the nation-organism launched necessarily toward expansion and became nothing but transient cells, instruments and not
the purpose of society. Individuals were "organs of society's aims." The
largest society in the modern age was the nation, "a community of all
the individuals who, through following generations, live permanently on
a particular territory, and thanks to their common ethnic origins, common language, traditions and interests, have become aware that they belong to a single community, with their own aims and duties to carry out
in the development of world civilization."[23]

In internal politics, the imperialist nationalists praised the productive bourgeoisie's ruling function and urged it to react against socialism
and democracy in order to reassert its predominance and role as interpreter and guide of the nation, claiming its monopoly of the myth of
nation. However, at the same time it urged the bourgeoisie to intensify
nationalizing the proletariat, so that all the productive classes would
close ranks, like a single block of faith and will, concentrating all their efforts on foreign policy and imperialist expansion. Everything was to be
subordinated to this aim, which was the greatest reason for a nation to
exist. The civil ethics of a nationalist state demanded the individual's
total devotion to the nation, because a state, said Bernardino Varisco, "is
the nation that has the strength to carry out its destiny, and that, therefore, creates the conditions to have this strength. There are many of
these conditions; but one is fundamental: that everyone has an alert
and vigorous awareness of national unity, of the obligation to sacrifice

lesser interests, if necessary, to the interests of the orderly nation, that is, of the state."[24]

The Nationalist Revolution

The imperialists believed that instilling new spirit into character played an essential part in reorganizing the national state to mould a "new Italian" completely subject to the policy of the nation's might. Imperialist education taught anti-individualism, the ethics of sacrifice, hierarchy, discipline and a religious cult of nation idolized as a lay divinity. The citizen had to be brought up with a single aim: to make his nation great and powerful and to be ready to sacrifice himself for it in the inevitable wars of expansion and dominion. The imperialists were convinced that sacrificing an individual's freedom for the might of the nation was a necessity imposed by modernity. The national state had to make up for the historical delays that still burdened the spirit of the Italians by increasing the work of nationalizing their consciences, saving them from the influence of new ideas that could hinder the formation of a solid and close-knit national unity, or even act against it. The modernistic note is predominant, however. It was wrong for faith in the future to be based only on the memory of past glory, protested *La Grande Italia,* the Milanese organ of Irredentist nationalism with imperialist tendencies.[25]

An important part of imperialist pedagogy was assigned to the mobilizing function of tradition and myths, drawn from the glorious past of the nation's origin, going back as far as Roman times. Classicized rhetoric went hand in hand with extolling modernity, identified with the productive and expansionist power of imperialist nations, especially the new ones like Japan and the United States. The nationalist syndicalist Mario Viana stated that "a nation cannot aspire to greatness, power and glory if it does not venerate its past, glorify its own strength, and arm mighty armies and colossal ships launched on the waves of infinite seas." This reference to the past inevitably conjured up Rome, "the mistress of the world," "the torch that lights up our hopes of greatness and glory: because the greatness of Rome was the greatness of our race, which must rise and dominate again in order not to be overwhelmed."[26]

This was not a chance reference to race. Ideology led to anthropology in imperialist nationalism, and in some cases, to racism, with the aim of establishing the distinctive and discriminating features of the "real Italian," in order to attach the myth of nation to something—descent (*stirpe*) or race—considered permanent in time, with its genetic patrimony of higher qualities. So an idea of nation no longer based on ethics but mainly on ethnicity or race was gaining ground through the Italian imperialists, who often spoke of descent, blood and racial superiority. Viana affirmed that the feature of imperialist nationalism that differentiated it from patriotism was "the superiority of the race and the supremacy of the nation in conquering world markets. The nation is an organ of civilization and a producer of wealth that is successful if the solidarity of individuals is closely knit."[27] Sighele, echoing the French nationalist Maurice Barrès, stated clearly that nationalism was based on the scientific principle of determinism:

> We can be nationalists in that the nation is conceived as an organism living and developing on its territory, like a plant that grows in the soil where it was born, finding the conditions necessary for its growth in this soil and the surrounding environment; and in that we think the successive generations in a nation are nothing but the leaves and branches that the plant renews every year: periodic proof that it is continually rising.[28]

The imperialists advanced from ideology to anthropology to define the nature of the "new Italian," starting from the naturalistic belief that man is essentially an aggressive animal, moved by bestial instincts to conquer, and innately egoistic. However, this can be overcome when a society passes from the "individual state to the national state," using Corradini's terminology: then national solidarity develops through the discipline of the state, and "each one of us becomes a particle of the nation, when suddenly our fatherland appears in us. . . . Then, for our fatherland, we get lost in the chaos of distant generations with the same blood as ours, who breathe and will breathe under the same sky as ours."[29] Mario Morasso recognized the racial model of the "new Italian" in D'Annunzio's imaginary description of Garibaldi in his *Canzone di Garibaldi:* "the eternal hero of the beautiful and dominant Aryan race," "tall, as blond as golden Italic and Hellenic sunsets, eyes as blue as his Tyrrhenian Sea," endowed with "all the excellent and enduring qualities with which the Aryan race dictated its law, imposed its dominion and its supremacy in the world."[30]

This collection of ideas clearly reveals the distinct separation of imperialist nationalism from the Risorgimento tradition, with liberalism and democracy explicitly disavowed and individualism condemned. The Italian imperialists refused to accept the humanist and universalist vocation of the nation, the right to nationality and freedom of the individual:

all ideas that weakened the unity and discipline of the nation had, therefore, to be quashed in the national state, which was organized for a policy of might and expansion. *La Grande Italia* explained that the nationalists believed "the *nation* is not an abstract and sentimental body, which
was the patriots' idea of fatherland, but makes up the powerful and solid
collective unity on which world conflicts in all fields of human activity
are based and with which they are carried out in the present historical
period."[31] According to the imperialist viewpoint, the myth of mission
and supremacy was also redefined as a policy of might and dominion,
wielded in the world by the "chosen people": "A sovereign law takes the
chosen people at the first nucleus of their national formation and, from
age to age, continually urging them on, encouraging and making them
greater, leads them to becoming an empire. When there is an empire,
nations enter the service of world civilization."[32]

When the European war broke out in 1914, it was naturally greeted
enthusiastically by the imperialist nationalists, who demanded intervention not so much with the intention of completing the national borders
by reuniting the Irredentist lands with the mother country as out of desire for grandiose territorial conquests and predominance in the Mediterranean area. They were also strongly determined to free Italy of the
liberal, democratic and socialist ideologies that had prevented the national state from being achieved. Immediately after the war the imperialists had finished working out their concept of nation, finalized by a
collective test—the war examination—which, they thought, definitively
confirmed that their idea was valid. In 1919 Alfredo Rocco summed up
the core of this concept very clearly and concisely, a concept that Fascism was to appropriate: "The purpose of political action is to develop
the nation, considered not as the mere sum total of living individuals but
as a summary unit of the indefinite series of generations. The necessary
and absolute preeminence of national aims over the aims of individuals
or groups of individuals (categories or classes) implies the absolute supremacy of the state, which is precisely an organized and functioning
nation, the unyielding achievement of its authority over individuals and
classes."[33]

With the First World War and the Fascists coming to power, the imperialists saw their aspiration successfully completed, their myth of the
Italian revolution put into effect, with the creation of a national state of
organized and disciplined masses for the greater might of the nation. In
1923 Corradini declared that, from the defeat of Adua (1896) to the
March on Rome, "the process of ethnic rebirth" had been carried out.

It had begun with the Libyan war, when Italy was "in a state of grace that was excessive compared to the importance of the feat, but that was divine," and now continued, after Italy's participation in the world war, with the victory of Fascism.[34] The imperialists thought it was completely natural to join the victorious Fascist movement, entering with the attitude of forerunners, of the firstborn, of the elder brothers and of the first apostles of the "cult of nation." Fascism had finally provided them with a broadly based party with which they could carry out their dream of a Greater Italy as it marched to gain an empire. Imperialist nationalism and Fascism had quite a lot in common, but there were also differences of opinion: what they unquestionably shared was the conviction that a Greater Italy could be achieved only by denying the Risorgimento tradition, because the union between nation and freedom was not compatible with the formula they were proposing to raise Italy to the rank of a great imperial power. Freedom had to be sacrificed on the altar of a Greater Italy.

7

The Man and the Patriot

Humanist Nationalism

Looking back and highlighting the groups that had contributed to the development of Fascism, its success magnified the place of imperialist nationalism in the history of the myth of nation. As far as imperialist nationalism was concerned, it contributed to this exaggeration with its excessive, self-important propaganda, claiming merit as the firstborn as regards Fascism, leading historians to give much more importance to its role than it really deserved. Thus, all the other expressions of the new nationalism that had developed in the Giolitti period were overwhelmed, or wiped out of the image of *nazionalfascismo* (National Fascist union). All of them were suspected, in one way or another, of being infected by the imperialist or authoritarian virus. This viewpoint started the tendency to identify the myth of nation with authoritarian or imperialist nationalism, confusing it with Fascism: a tendency that became established over a long period, even in historiography.

In fact it was a distorted perspective that overshadowed other versions of the myth of nation, in which, although modified many times, the Risorgimento tradition stayed alive beside the myth of a Greater Italy. Various expressions of what could be called humanist nationalism referred directly to the Risorgimento. Up to the period immediately after the First World War, humanist nationalism was an alternative to imperialist nationalism, sometimes keeping close to a modernized and rejuvenated liberalism, sometimes looking for new ways, as happened with national radicalism, to reconcile freedom and nation, the individual and the national state, democracy and the myth of a Greater Italy. Humanist nationalism included a variety of positions that differed in their particular political choices but shared the purpose of strengthening

105

both a sense of nation and a sense of humanity as inseparable and complementary aspects of creating a modern Italian conscience. Benedetto Croce, who lay claim to the task of forming "a modern Italian conscience that would be both European and national,"[1] summed up this tendency very well when he wrote that it was right "to keep the individuality of the national conscience alive, as it is first-rate historical strength" and "is changing and becoming more modern and cosmopolitan. However, this transformation must start from a vital center or nucleus, which eliminates some elements and absorbs others," because if it does not do so, "the change will be superficial and false: the modernity and cosmopolitanism frivolous."[2]

We think it is quite legitimate to speak of "nationalism" in terms of these groups, because their culture embraced the ideal of a Greater Italy, the need for the modern Italian's character to be reborn in order to create his national conscience (underscoring the positive aspects of national civilization in relation to the progress of modern civilization, accepting colonialism as protection of national interests in international competition and as an instrument of civilization), and the moral concept of war as an eventuality (sometimes inevitable) for the life and development of the nation.

Furthermore, there is a "humanist" element in this nationalism, because it deemed safeguarding the dignity and freedom of the individual an integral part of the myth of nation. The idea of nation, in fact, did not cancel the individuality of a human being, reducing him to a cell of the national organism. Rather, it considered creating a universal human conscience a priority, an essential requirement for a modern national conscience. Humanist nationalism did not want to close the doors and windows to prevent ideas from other nations circulating; on the contrary, it looked for lifeblood in Europe to revitalize the nation's spiritual and cultural life.

And last, this idea of nation, even in the tragic view of life as an eternal struggle that could lead to war, kept its faith in the emancipation of humanity toward more spiritual forms of civilization. Although humanist nationalism contested the existing parliamentary regime, it did not repudiate the Risorgimento tradition; on the contrary, it confirmed the unity of nation, freedom and modernity in the same way it defended the principle of nationality in international policy, though tempering it with a dose of realism that kept in mind the difficulties that could prevent it from being fully carried out.

The Nation as a Humane City

This was the prevailing tendency in the work of the young intellectuals gathered around *La Voce*. Giuseppe Prezzolini's periodical was the main cultural meeting place where the various writers expressing humanist nationalism met and exchanged ideas in the years before the First World War and where there was a more intense effort of the new generation to find a formula capable of creating the national conscience of the Italians. This formula was to regenerate their character, preparing them to face the challenges of modernity consciously and realistically, keeping before them a high ideal of individual and collective life, which found its concrete accomplishment in the entity of the nation. The contributors to *La Voce*, the so-called *vociani* (writers for *La Voce*), believed that the Italians had not yet become a nation: "This is what above all Italy suffers from at present," stated Amendola, "that the nation is little more than a dying myth and a rising hope."[3]

Most of the contributors to *La Voce* wanted to reconcile nationalism and cosmopolitanism, patriotism and humanism, on one hand referring back to the Risorgimento tradition and, on the other, to the new idealism of Croce and Gentile.[4] *La Voce* expressed an idea of nation that was related to the ideal of a "humane city," as Amendola[5] called it, within which the existence of countries was recognized and respected, in the name of the universal essence of the human spirit. "There is something greater than nation and it is the human conscience,"[6] declared Prezzolini. Referring to the Risorgimento tradition, he condemned imperialist nationalism as the "theory of a nation for itself and not for others," as "repugnant and narrow-minded," "greatly different from the patriotism of our Risorgimento," which "wanted a fatherland for everyone": "Patriotism was Kantian, in a sense, because an action taken in its name could serve as a universal principle. Nationalism is a positivist and Nietzschean doctrine, egoistic and particularistic, which can only serve a single nation exclusively."[7]

A humanist vocation was the motive that inspired the myth of nation of *La Voce*, conceived in essentially historical, spiritual and cultural terms, without any inclination to deify or objectify the nation in naturalist forms nor to cloak it in the florid rhetoric of past glory, as the historian Antonio Anzilotti stated.[8]

Starting from these ideal presuppositions, even if they were not always coherently expressed or shared by all the contributors, *La Voce* intended to carry out an ambitious program of national regeneration, taking on the task that Francesco De Sanctis had entrusted to the generations of the new century, that is, reforming the Italians' character following criteria, methods and aims that were distinctly different from those of imperialist nationalism. In fact, the writers for *La Voce* refused to base the modern Italian's conscience on an exclusively nationalist inclination, taking a stand "against those who take the empirical fact of our being born in a historical tradition as the basis of a national education":

> There is only one kind of education, that of man. It makes no difference what their age or sex, nation or period is. You cannot make good Italians if you do not first make good men. You cannot create citizens useful to their own country if first a conscience is not created. The human values of truth, beauty, the sacred and the good do not have the form of race, sex, period, and nation, but only the matter and content of race, sex, period and nation.[9]

And that, in the program to instill new spirit in the Italians, meant tending above all to "form the man in the Italian, to develop an open, well-informed and critical conscience."[10]

Setting out to pick up the unfinished Risorgimento revolution, the periodical gave priority to internal political problems and to moral and cultural revival, eschewing a policy of might and territorial expansion, which it judged to be too ambitious considering the country's condition and its real needs. Creating a national conscience required, above all, resolving serious internal problems like the southern issue, reforming education and the centralized state—to overcome all the persisting divisions among the many Italies, without suppressing freedom in any way. The aim was to bring out a common public spirit, a "national discipline," from the free development of a citizen's personality rather than from adopting an authoritarian education. "True nationalism," wrote Anzilotti,

> can only be this: a fertile approach to the real country, an effort aimed at arousing a more profound national interest against class particularism, against the atomism of democratic degeneration [and] automatically rejecting those fanciful and rhetorical exaggerations in bad taste more or less crammed with ridiculous imperialism.[11]

La Voce thought that creating a national identity was the spontaneous result of a confrontation, even lively, among its many brighter and more original writers rather than the product of a nationalization process imposed by the state. Prezzolini maintained that developing a national conscience required fighting ideally for principles, values and concrete programs: "The greatest nations were divided in the finest times of their history."[12]

In this sense, giving importance to the variety of regions as an essential part of the Italian national identity was significant, set against the concept of nation as a homogeneous organism incorporated in the centralized state. "Provincial life," declared Prezzolini, "can be called Italian life. We are still provincials compared to central Europe, with provincial defects and virtues. . . . Italy is a country of provinces, a union, a federation of provinces, and if it achieves something, it will do so as it is provincial. That is because it will have local color, bonds with the land and with places of origin, and that sense of quiet, long and convinced maturing that is characteristic of provinces."[13]

The periodical opposed the rhetorical revival of the myth of Rome according to the imperialists with a crusade against Rome itself, considered a bureaucratic capital, symbol of a parasitic Italy that suffocated productive Italy:

> Rome is the central bloodsucker of Italy, the least productive town, the meeting place of all sluggards and spongers, the center of corruption and meanness of spirit, the neutral point that attracts swindlers, weak consciences, rascally lawyers, pettifoggers, paid cuckolds, pimps, political careerists, journalists "for hire" and complaisant clerks: Rome is the basic cause of all our economic, moral and intellectual deficiencies, and in its very origin is a tribute in imbecility that we pay to our rhetorical and slapdash tradition. There is nothing in or outside Rome that comes from Rome; not even a five-lire piece circulating in the kingdom is produced by any Roman activities. Rome is the city that exploits all of Italy, and the best way to celebrate Italian unity would be to take away from Rome three-quarters of the Mafia power it holds, giving the provinces ample autonomy.[14]

Prezzolini maintained that it was necessary to decentralize, so as "to take power away from Rome and give autonomy back to the provinces. . . . I believe that autonomous regions would be well received in Italy, where deep down there is still a certain regionalism, suffocated by insincere waves of unitary rhetoric; that would be quite useful to the progress of all the regions alike, without exception."[15]

However, the writers for *La Voce* did not think that defending the provinces and decentralization meant sacrificing the national country for the provincial one. As Alessandro Casati wrote, the *La Voce* writers opposed parochial-minded regionalism and sharp local business practice with "true regionalism that did not deny the 'greater country' but gave it content."[16]

The humanist propensity of *La Voce* nationalism was also present in its attitude toward foreign policy. Even though recognizing that the tendency to "base all politics on national interest" was the right reaction "to humanitarianism without backbone," the periodical judged it "impossible" to imagine the life of a nation that was not founded "on more humane and ideal principles, and above all on respect for other nations and on sympathy for oppressed peoples that have a strong culture and civilization, a hope of liberation."[17] Consequently the *La Voce* writers were constantly engaged in controversy, which was often bitter, against imperialist nationalism. "Nothing is further from us than the Roman spirit. . . . We are anti-imperialists," declared Scipio Slataper, ridiculing the expansionist ambitions of the imperialists: "an enormous program, as we know—the Adriatic, the Mediterranean, beyond the Alps, even toward the interior of Europe, as far as Italy is capable of expanding and the imperialists have energy to go—the infinite and the indefinable."[18] In the same way, Slataper confirmed that the bond between nation and humanity was spiritual, against naturalist and racist ideas of national superiority.[19]

For these reasons, the periodical was not only immune to the fascination with modern imperialism but also published articles strongly condemning it. President Theodore Roosevelt, the champion of American imperialism, was branded as a symbol of "man back to brute," with the "glorification of everything that is rotten and reactionary in our civilization."[20] The periodical accused imperialist England, which protested about the atrocities committed by the Italians in Libya, of being a hypocritical race that

> destroyed the natives of Australia and North America in cold blood and with premeditation by importing strong liquor, gunpowder and certain diseases; that is trying to get rid of ten million negroes by any means, including lynching; that has brought to subjection two hundred million Indians, drowning their revolt in blood; that about ten years ago flaunted before the world—in South Africa—the shame of concentration camps; that hangs not only the living but even the dead (as Lord Kitchener did with Mahdi's body) when this is to its advantage; that does not count the dead

and wounded if it bombards cities because it would take too long
and . . . time is money—in short a race that has erected a monument
to might on the solid pedestal of implacable egoism. And today this
race raises its voice to take us to task, scandalized by our excesses.[21]

In the same way the periodical condemned pan-Germanism, with
its theory of racial superiority, prophesying that Germany would end up
victim of its ambitions, like "an imaginary mortar in which, sooner or
later, all European nations would pound like pestles at the same time."[22]
Although it opposed the war in Libya, *La Voce* had not opposed the
colonial conquest but had warned the neocolonizers that, if they
wanted to do something important in Libya, they should "continue the
work of the Arabs and take advantage of their 'civilization,' without
cherishing fond hopes of being able to apply all our cultural systems and
way of life," because "we have not gone to barbarian countries but to
countries of people with another civilization"; because "what we take
for symptoms of a backward civilization are simply the most useful instruments that a millenary civilization has thought up when faced with
certain climatic and environmental conditions."[23]
Other groups of intellectuals and politicians had much in common
with the nationalism of *La Voce.* They tried to strengthen and broaden
the national conscience within the sphere of lay and liberal culture,
keeping the Risorgimento tradition alive and trying to adjust it to the
needs of a society made up of masses. Right on the eve of the First
World War, faced with the decline of conservative liberalism and Giolitti's liberalism, the National Liberal group gained ground. Its main
mouthpiece was the Milanese periodical *L'Azione,* to which a number
of *La Voce* writers contributed, committed to reviving liberalism and
strengthening the myth of nation, without adopting the idea of nation
as an idol to which everything had to be sacrificed, making it something
concluded and definite, something abstractly homogeneous and exclusive.[24] At the end of 1914 the historian Gioacchino Volpe explained that
the National Liberal group did not believe "they could advance a doctrine of nation and nationalism. We do not feel like brushing aside social
issues in favor of foreign policy and expansion; we think it is against our
traditions and interests to foster a spirit of imperialist oppression in ourselves and so encourage it in others. This spirit is a bit like the past Germanic *faustrecht* modernized, which will be a danger for smaller and
weaker nations like us, and we shall certainly remain relative to other
nations."[25]

The ideal justification for Italy's intervention in the First World War, requested by most of the *La Voce* contributors and similar groups, was mainly the aspiration to revive and strengthen the nation without sacrificing freedom to it. Many of them left as volunteers, because they believed that the war was a test of moral maturity for the Italian nation and wanted to demonstrate Italy's capacity to be a protagonist of world history, not by conquering lands and subduing other peoples but by cooperating with other nations to build a new civilization founded on the freedom of the individual and of nations.

The Two Kinds of Patriotism

One of the clearest signs of the prestige achieved by the myth of nation in the first decade of the century was that the left-wingers paid increasing attention to patriotism. Within the democratic left emerged the search for a synthesis between nation and modernity, founded not on the myth of gaining power through war but on the myth of civil and industrial progress, of overcoming conflicts of power on the international scene, where the means and aims of competition were to be the development of industrial and democratic civilization in favor of human emancipation. As Giovanni Vidari stated in 1910, the democratic left also acknowledged the need "to instill a more alert, solid, active and even aggressive attitude in present day Italians toward their nationality, their rights and their duties to modern civilization," while also understanding the real nature of "modern nationalism." This "is not a memory or a simple continuation of the dislikes and antagonism that were once aroused between one state and another over religion, dynastic interests or territorial aspirations, but something new, brought about by the development of contemporary society, which liberates and unifies national energies and launches them in the new tumult of modern living, so that they can throb with new and more intense life." Vidari added that if modern nationalism were aware of the "positive reality it springs from, it could only be internationalism at the same time, that is, a tendency to both assert and surpass itself in the clash between nations," not by competing in war and might, but by "developing and intensifying the very characteristics of contemporary society, that is, science and industry, or generally speaking, work, as achievement, exploitation and transformation of natural energies for the benefit and glory of man."[26]

So this denied that the only expression of modern nationalism was imperialism: on the contrary, it maintained that imperialist nationalism itself, with its warmongering myths, clashed with the essence of modern civilization, which tended to go beyond armed conflict to reach higher forms of international cooperation. In this progressive and democratic version of the myth of nation—which did not propose the great imperialist powers as models for the new Italy but rather Switzerland, Belgium, Holland, Norway and Sweden—solid faith in the nation was considered completely compatible with humanitarianism, pacifism, democracy and freedom.

Instead of considering the myth of nation a residue of past ages, destined to disappear in future internationalism, an effort was made to reform the myth of nation and patriotism in order to relate them to the needs of a new age. As the socialist Angelo Crespi observed in 1908, "being aware of the transition from an old to a new order of things" was more than ever acute in this new age, after the "disintegration of the old ways of seeing life, the world, society and family, of living, working, thinking, feeling and acting." So, too, was the awareness of the beginning of a "period of reconstruction" with the industrial revolution, "distinguished by new and definitive ways of subjecting nature to man."

The idea of the common good, meant as "fatherland," also changed and broadened to an international scale, where, under the banner of the common progress of humanity, the differences between nations ceased, as did the differences between individuals and classes. "What, then, does a nation become? It becomes the ideal of cooperation among all the citizens of a particular country, with the aim of showing the world how to bring up the greatest number of men to be physically, morally and intellectually strong and happy, and to prove this by supplying it with the greatest number of good ideas, discoveries in all fields of knowledge and products of all kinds, destined to increase the well-being of men everywhere." Thus serving one's own country meant serving humanity; aspiring to the greatness of one's own nation meant making one's own country work "as the organ of the highest level of humanity."[27]

Now, this definition of patriotism was not at all "incompatible with the love of humanity."[28] On the contrary, it was just in this humanitarianism that "true patriotism" was expressed, as Teodoro Moneta then declared, "not rhetorical, not hot-air, but practical and efficacious patriotism," capable of "guiding individual and collective life toward harmony between individual rights and social duties. This patriotism, which intends all citizens to be aware of their duties, ready to sacrifice their lives when their country is in danger, sees justice as effectively equal for all, so that everyone can free his own energy without needing the state to protect him at every step."[29]

This "patriotism of peace lovers," as Moneta went on to call it, was not a generic and abstract statement of love of one's country. On the contrary, it claimed to follow the specific tradition of Risorgimento patriotism, "the finest and purest revolution that history recalls," aspiring to make the new Italy a great and modern nation, among the great and modern nations which are protagonists on the world scene, yet believing that "the true greatness of a nation no longer consists in expanding its territory but, rather, in its morality and the virile, strong character of its citizens, in love of fruitful work, in developing science and culture, in the arts, in industry and trade: only from these can wealth and general well-being be achieved." Although the patriotism of the "peace lovers" opposed "bellicose patriotism," it was not pacifist to the point of sacrificing the country on the altar of peace: even considering peace "as the supreme good, they would never sacrifice to it the independence of the country and justice in international relations."[30]

The essential core of democratic interventionism derived from the humanist nationalism trend and maintained that Italy should enter the first world conflict in the name of loyalty to the principle of nationality and the Risorgimento tradition. The aim was to achieve the territorial and political unification of Italy by liberating Irredentist lands and at the same time to build the new international order of humanity on the basis of the principle of nationality, thus carrying out Mazzini's ideal. In 1919 the republican Arcangelo Ghisleri pointed out that Mazzini's concept of nation "was the most modern idea of the necessary solidarity among peoples,"[31] founded as it was on a spiritualistic assumption that resolutely refused any mingling with racist criteria. The democratic interventionists foresaw future humanity on the way to a higher idea of civilization, to a "new kind of free political organization," by freeing individuals and nations, as Salvemini's *L'Unità* stated in 1917, no longer dominated by rigid national states. In fact, the latter would become obsolete on an international scale, just as Greek cities and Italian city-states became outdated on the scale of national states, believing that "persisting with past ideals out of season is often fatal, and the very cause of greatness can become the cause of ruin."[32] Immediately after the war and before the triumph of Fascism, Prezzolini thought it was still possible to have faith in the future of the humanist concept of nation, going beyond the nation itself, as he wrote on March 30, 1920:

I do not believe that an education and ideas that go no further than the concept of nation, are possible. I cannot feel I am Italian, only a man born in a specific historical climate, but aware of its limits, who does everything to raise himself above it. . . . Humanity, dissatisfied with state and national egoism, races toward new solutions. At present, the national problem is not the main one and above all is not the key problem. Only a sincerely supranational view can give a solution to national problems. . . . There is nothing more ridiculous today, and more impossible, than a national policy. The interdependence of nations is one of the most obvious requirements at present. There can only be a world policy.[33]

The heart of democratic interventionism—humanist nationalism—emerged again after the war in the democratic wing of the belligerent movement before being overwhelmed in the civil war between the antidemocratic myth of the Communist revolution and that of the Fascist revolution. The attempt to revive the national liberal myth carried out in the postwar period by Giovanni Amendola, was also overwhelmed by Fascism. The future leader of the anti-Fascist opposition had been an interventionist because he considered war a means to complete the work of the Risorgimento, not only by freeing the Irredentist lands but also by extending and consolidating the basis of the national state through democracy and converting the masses to a sense of nation. In 1922 Amendola stressed that war "is really the approval given by history to the rebirth of our millenary people and to establishing the unitary national state!"[34] Considering Amendola's ideological journey, we can also include his anti-Fascism among the last manifestations of humanist nationalism, inspired, as he stated in 1924, not only by his faith in the liberal tradition but also by an "impassioned and unwavering faith in the national state, conceived as the only really revolutionary creation in the millenary history of the Italian people. It is also the only feasible guarantee for its future, [with] the conscious intention of bringing all the people into the life of the state, broadening, deepening and consolidating its foundations spiritually in the Italian conscience."[35]

The Catholics Lay Siege to the Myth of Nation

In the years under Giolitti, the Catholics also became more aware of the issue of nation. As the Church had, by then, set aside its disapproval of the myth of nation born of the French Revolution, considering it the expression of a new principle of people's sovereignty against monarchic sovereignty of Divine origin,[36] the Church (and increasingly larger groups of Catholics) were committed to building their own myth of nation, thus accepting the existence of a unitary state. The Catholics followed two directions in this task: on one hand, they continued their intransigent opposition to the Risorgimento tradition and the liberal state, criticizing the lay concept of nation and state, which in their opinion had developed into a new heathenism of state worship and the deification of the nation. On the other, they worked out a Catholic idea of nation and fatherland that stressed the religious factor in forming the national identity, at the same time proposing to resolve the relation between nation and humanity in a higher spiritual synthesis than the one proposed by liberalism and lay humanism, maintaining that reconciling men and patriots could be completely and sensibly expressed only by Roman Catholicism.

The Catholics' determination to take over the myth of nation derived from the fact that Christian doctrine and ethics were completely compatible with a citizen's duties toward his fatherland and state and with the nation's aspiration to greatness. In 1915 *La Civiltà Cattolica* stated that, by linking "the love and cult of one's fatherland and relatives to the love and cult itself of God, Roman Catholicism will make us the stronger and more industrious for the real good of the country and nation the more we distance ourselves from the excesses and ambiguity of a second-rate nationalism and patriotism."[37] In 1918 Father Agostino Gemelli, the founder of the Catholic University, wrote that Catholics considered love of fatherland "a virtue, and it belongs precisely to the virtue of piety, as it is considered part of the filial cult that we owe to the principles of our being, to the creators of our lives and formation. . . . Catholics believe that the source of love of fatherland is God himself, as one's country is the instrument of power, goodness and Divine Providence, [and, therefore,] it is clear that, for Catholics, love of fatherland is included, like the least in the most and the detail in the general, in the cult that is God's right."[38]

Consequently, Catholic doctrine did not oppose patriotism, intended as "the expression of a fully developed and mature conscience" and as the active will to defend national sovereignty and territory and everything that "seems to be a product of national development, therefore political formation, social organization, tradition, aims and hopes, in short the whole spiritual heritage of the nation."[39] The essential and unrestrainable component of this heritage was the Catholic religion: "as religion is part of the national tradition, it is one of the most solid fundamental principles of national unity."[40] And as loving one's country "is wanting our political, social and religious beliefs (that is, those convictions that we believe are the true ones, those we think respond to the needs and aims of our country) to inspire our national life," and "only they enable the fatherland to become great," it was totally unjust to accuse Catholics of being unpatriotic. On the contrary, they wanted to reconcile national sentiment with Catholic doctrine precisely to uphold the greatness of the country, to carry out its universal civilizing mission according to the plan of Divine Providence: "We believe that love of fatherland turns into active desire for our country to be Christian, in order to be great and worthily continue the glorious traditions of past centuries."[41]

Having thus rejected the accusation made by secular culture of being unpatriotic, the Catholics aimed to show that the Church and Roman Catholicism had left an indelible mark on the formation of national identity and had been the greatest expression of Italian greatness for centuries. By exalting the Italian role of the papacy in the history of Italy, in the development of its civilization and the defense of its freedom, the Catholics presented themselves as the oldest and most authentic expression, and the most genuine interpreters, of the Italian nation. Only by returning to its own Christian essence, respecting and strengthening the religious supremacy of Roman Catholicism, would the Italian nation take its place in the forefront of nations, carrying out a mission of universal civilization and complying with a Divine providential plan, since nations, Gemelli explained, "are neither the arbitrary product of an individual nor a fact of nature" but are "wished for by God-Providence, who regulates the lives of individuals and peoples, established on physical, historical and moral foundations. . . . Each nation has a mission to carry out in the world, entrusted to it by God."[42]

The main interpreter of the Church's tendency to define the cornerstones of "true nationalism," of a "solid patriotism" in harmony with Christian doctrine, was *La Civiltà Cattolica*. The Jesuit periodical condemned both liberal nationalism and imperialist nationalism, maintaining that the theories of the Nationalist Association militants were "a new phase of the old liberalism carried to the extreme, harsh consequences of pagan 'imperialism.'" The Jesuits believed this "because not only do the Nationalist Association militants keep the old principles of liberalism, they also aggravate them with pagan ideas of imperialism, conflict and 'egoism,' in short, with Greek and Roman state worship." Even though the imperialist nationalists recognized the importance of religion in moulding the national conscience and criticized hedonistic individualism, liberal secularism and socialist materialism in the name of spiritual values above the egoistic interest of individuals, they had a pagan, egoistic and materialistic concept of nation, which led to glorifying war and conquering and subjecting other nations. Therefore, their ideas were absolutely incompatible "with true love of fatherland, with good nationalism, and, we shall say it in one word, with Roman Catholicism": "Without this, nationalism, like ancient paganism, wrongly wants to sacrifice the individual to its chimera of God—the state—and return to an uncivilized state where human life had no value, the individual did not count, the family did not exist, and the state was everything."[43]

To forestall the accusation of being unpatriotic, condemning state-worshipping nationalism was taken up again in the 1920s, above all against triumphant Fascism, although it was accompanied by condemning every form of cosmopolitanism and internationalism. Continuing to work out a Catholic idea of nation, in 1923 the Jesuits' periodical stated that it wanted "to put the sound idea of country and patriotism on the right path again, as proposed by the doctrine of Christian ethics," and that it recognized the universality and "eternal consistency of the love of fatherland," while it judged humanitarian cosmopolitanism inconsistent, because never, not even in the form of "a universal Christian empire . . . would it manage to wipe out the love that binds us to the people we were born of and the land they live in."[44] Catholic doctrine thought that, with its ethics, it could give a moral basis to national patriotism that was much more efficacious than civil powers in "suppressing individual egoism, bending and subordinating it to the common good of the country. . . . The morals and action of the Church in working out and refining the consciences of individuals, purifying and freeing them from egoistic corruption, facilitates abnegation for the common good, which is the heart of true love of one's country." Therefore, accusing the Church of being against the nation and undermining the citizens' national sentiment was wrong. On the contrary, only if "brought up with the precepts of Catholic morality" would the individual conscience "open and grow, becoming aware of national solidarity." There was no conflict between religion and patriotism, because "the Christian idea of the goal of a future fatherland is so far from opposing the ideal of an earthly fatherland that it is rather its most valid defense." The Church firmly and clearly opposed a patriotism that had degenerated into "exaggerated nationalism," that is, "a tendency to return to those old, ferocious and implacable forms that Christian feeling has always condemned."[45]

The Church rebelled against this "pagan concept of a deified nation," instigator of confusion, anarchy and war on the international scene, preaching a kind of patriotism that did not at all annihilate the man in the patriot, as "exaggerated nationalism did," in the same way as Catholic universalism did not annihilate the patriot in the man, acknowledging "that it was morally impossible for the idea of nation to be absorbed by that of humanity." Patriotism and humanitarianism were both reconciled in a Christian concept of nation, the core of "true nationalism," a "properly understood nationalism," which was so only if it recognized and respected other nations and did not preach the cult of nation as "past state worshippers did, imitated by modern politicians and nationalists": the true patriot "must above all want and obtain the good of the true religion for the nation. That is, he must want the true religion to be propagated, defended and maintained in the nation in all its strength and industrious capacity to pacify and unite the minds of men, furthermore educating peoples and promoting every real progress," so that "for a Catholic, what is against the Church cannot be good for the nation."[46]

An increasingly greater interest in the issue of nation and nationalism of politically committed Catholics was taking root, in harmony with the doctrinal orientation of the Church. In the period preceding the First World War and especially with the war in Libya, marked nationalist tendencies had spread among the Catholics, inspired by the myth of the civilizing mission of Catholic Italy.[47] At that time, the will to establish religion as an essential part of national life, of "the life that a people with one name, race and organism lives, produces and develops," as Luigi Sturzo, a Catholic priest and mayor of Caltagirone in Sicily, said in 1905, prevailed among those who supported the political commitment of Catholics.[48] The time had come to abandon the old, sterile position that was purely "antagonistic and conflictual and enter directly a political and ideal dimension of the unitary state "on a level with other parties on the national scene, not as the only depositary of religion or as a permanent army of the religious authorities that goes to fight a war but as representatives of a national popular tendency to develop a civilized way of life,"[49] imbued with the moral and social principles of Christian civilization, but definitively freed of the preliminary antinational issue. "Today we can state that unifying the country was a good thing and that it was right to have fought for it,"[50] declared Sturzo forthrightly, thus setting a plan in motion that aimed at reconciling Catholic principles and values, on one hand, with the principles and values of the nation and state on the other, with full political autonomy from the Church but also proposing a radical reform of the liberal state. With this prospect in mind, Sturzo gave his approval of the war in Libya, which he thought resolved "the problem of Italy's greatness," "by remaking the country historically, economically and politically," and by recognizing "its rights over the Mediterranean and Adriatic seas and over African lands."[51] Together with his strongly anti-Giolitti position, these latter points were the basis of Sturzo's interventionism and political commitment, after the war, to reform the unitary state without questioning the myth of nation again, but reviving it following the Catholic idea of nation and patriotism.

The political theory of the founder of the Partito Popolare (People's Party) revealed ardent patriotic pride, faith "that this country of ours— which we fight and work for—will leave behind the troubles afflicting it, and which will continue to afflict it for some time, with its moral unity, indestructible strength and civilizing mission reborn."[52] For this to take place, declared Sturzo after the First World War, it was necessary to strengthen the Italian nation, "which has superb resilience. It has a population of 40 million with an exceptional density of almost 140 inhabitants per square kilometer, an industrious, versatile and extremely adaptable population; its geographical position in the Mediterranean is such that Italy should be its center and life force"; and it has gained "political unity, normal and safe conditions at its borders, and an effective participation in international agreements together with the states that at present dominate and govern the world."[53] In his plan to reform the state, Sturzo opposed Fascism, stressing that the bond between nation and democracy was immutable. He was convinced that the national effort to preserve traditional institutions and moral and political positions both within and outside the country was identified with "the historical value of a people, with its very tradition, with an idea of its own autonomy and independence, and with the awareness of the mission and principle of civilization." However, to intensify this effort, Sturzo explained, it was essential for the people to take an active part in the life of the state. "Moral, cultural and economic improvement; free functioning institutions; the strength of the race should be nurtured to the utmost: the more a people is aware of its strength, the better it participates in its collective life, as everyone can communicate freely with anyone else from anywhere." In the same sense, Sturzo confirmed the value of the principle of nationality against imperialism, declaring that nations, "as political unities, are a product of democracy, that is, of a people's government. From this point of view, nationalism should deny imperialism." Acknowledging that "every civilized nation, that is, one that has reached a certain level of civilization and autonomy, must govern and make the most of itself," means that "it can only admit the same right to another nation that is at, or has reached, the same level. Imperialism, as dominion over civilized peoples or rather over those peoples aware of themselves, is suppression of others' nationalism."[54]

When Fascism came to power, the creation of a Catholic myth of nation could, by then, be considered essentially accomplished, as celebrating the love of one's country implied that the reality of the national state had been accepted. Loving one's country, Agostino Gemelli explained, "means wanting our political, social and religious beliefs to be realized in it, leaving their mark on the nation's life. For each citizen, patriotic feelings are nothing but the firm will (rarely present, often imminent, always possible) of the country's political, social and religious way of life, which is believed by the citizen to contain the source of his country's greatness."[55]

The Church and Catholics had passed the first stage of a long journey toward conquering the myth of nation as a means of regaining hegemony within the unitary state, envisaging for the future a Catholic refounding of the national state. It was an ambitious plan, thought up with the intention of opposing lay culture on its own ground, competing with it in the search for convergence between fatherland and humanity, nation and freedom. At the same time, regarding the liberal ruling class, the Church claimed older and stronger roots in the national tradition than those of other lay forces recently formed, which descended from ideologies not of Italian origin. As the oldest expression of the Italian identity, the Catholics maintained they were the true interpreters of the nation, besides being the surest guide to lead Italy to new greatness.

Socialism and Nation: An Unfulfilled Union

Even though less fraught with consequences for the history of the Italian myth of nation, other attempts to reconcile the man and the patriot were made during the Giolitti period, within the democratic left and among the socialists, as well. From the outset, the neutralist stance of the Socialist Party as well as its later infatuation with the myth of the Bolshevik revolution nipped in the bud the efforts of some socialists to create a blend of nation and socialism based on the idea of patriotism. A preference for the term "patriotism" when defining national feeling presumed an explicit conceptual and ideal distinction between the idea of fatherland and that of nation.[56] The need to make this distinction had been felt more strongly by those who, in an effort to reconcile the national entity with an internationalist vision of modern civilization, spoke in favor of socialism converting to patriotism or at least recognized, as socialists, the historical and ideal value of nation and fatherland, like for example, Cesare Battisti, who was inspired as well by his particular personal experience as an Irredentist of Trent.

From the beginning of his political activity, Battisti believed it was possible to reconcile the idea of nation with socialism. Or rather, he assigned socialism the task of humanizing and universalizing the idea of fatherland, divesting "national sentiment of that barbaric pride that sullies it" and fighting the fact that a single class should have the exclusive possession of the idea of fatherland. As he wrote in 1895 in an article titled "Patria e socialismo" (Fatherland and Socialism): "Socialism does not want the iniquitous custom of honoring one's own great while disparaging those of other nations to be repeated, and only the heroism and magnanimity of its own country's martyrs to be acknowledged while heaping insults on the national heroes of other peoples. Socialism demands that all feelings of hate be put aside and that the best and good be accepted wherever it comes from, Austria, France, England or America."[57] Socialism and nationality were not totally irreconcilable, but on the contrary, according to Battisti, socialism could nurture a more authentic and realistic sentiment of nationality through the emancipation of workers: "A country that draws its intimate essence from its language, traditions and history needs to be strengthened by the bond of the reciprocal affection of all those who work and suffer in it."[58] In short, Mazzini and Karl Marx, adversaries in life, could be reconciled in a fusion that united socialism and nation in the fundamental idea of man's freedom and emancipation. Fatherland and national sentiment could not be denied or ignored, insisted the socialist of Trent in 1905, because "a feeling for one's nationality . . . has such deep roots in our consciences that it often blurs our view of things and makes us swear by it even in the language of those who glorify and wrongly exalt the nation,"[59] thus acknowledging that "national prejudices abound even among the socialists." However, Battisti repeated in 1907, to counter nationalist arrogance, socialism had to work things in such a way that love of one's country did not remain the monopoly of a few, and it had to claim the defense of a nationality "whose necessary basis is freedom, and that acknowledges every political and social right that depends on it."[60]

The myth of nation in Battisti's Irredentist socialism, and above all in his defence of the principle of nationality against the Hapsburg empire, revived the purest Risorgimento tradition, assigning Italy the mission of resuming the task of freeing peoples. Moreover, there was an ideal upholding European unity behind Battisti's interventionism, founded on the conviction that only by fighting Teutonic militarism and overthrowing the Hapsburg empire in the name of freedom of nations "can what was so longed for by Mazzini and Marx's program become reality: a federation of the states of Europe," as Battisti said at a conference in October 1914.[61]

The socialist Tullio Rossi Doria had also followed in the wake of Mazzini's humanitarian patriotism, explaining to the socialists "that love of one's country does not destroy but strengthens the love of humanity, and that the good of humanity cannot be achieved without starting from love of one's country"[62]: "If we socialists want to reach humanity, we cannot, we must not, exclude our country. And it is within our country that we must carry out our class war to better the national economy, by improving the living conditions of the workers and raising the standard of civilized living of all the classes."[63] Rossi Doria thought that nationalism was nothing but national egoism, which used the idea of nation only as a "political and economic instrument to conquer and dominate."[64] The very word "nation" was reduced to a mere "technical term to indicate a particular country insofar as it has certain limits and geographical, ethnic, historical and commercial characteristics," in short, a word that "can call up factual data but not arouse feelings," because "it is a word given an inflexible and cold meaning, and thus it should remain. It is not a kind, loving, lofty or solemn word. . . . We do not die for our nation. We do not live for our nation, our feelings are not aroused for our nation, we are not unselfish for our nation but selfish, we ask our nation for life but do not give it our lives, emotions or fortunes."[65] Nationalism was not patriotism, but rather the opposite, said Rossi Doria, contradicting Enrico Corradini, who had exalted the superiority of nationalism over patriotism in the name of the selfishness of nationalism compared to the unselfishness of patriotism. Rossi Doria insisted that it was necessary to oppose nationalism, which, "with its doctrine of dominion, war and the particularly violent expansion of the national ego, strives to continue a tradition of barbarity in an age of civilization." Furthermore, the "loftiest and most fertile" patriotism of those who "want the country to be great not through war but through peace, who want it to be powerful, certainly, but for justice and not for violence, who want to ensure the good of its own citizens, not by harming the citizens of other nations,"[66] should not be denied but strengthened.

This and other speeches pleading with Italian socialism to adopt the
idea of nation had no influence on the direction taken by a party that, in
1912, had chosen revolutionary intransigence with Benito Mussolini,
strengthening its own internationalist myth and ignoring or openly
denying and deriding the nation and patriotism. Mussolini, the internationalist socialist, had ridiculed nationalism and stated that it was not
in the proletariat's interest to worry about patriotism. In 1909 he said
that the problem of nation "is one of the most serious and distressing of
those to be faced by the socialist conscience. But here, too, an effort
must be made to reach an extreme, unequivocal denial." And although
he recognized the nation as "the highest collective organism reached by
civilized ethnic groups," he called "socialist patriotism" "ambiguous."
Bourgeois capitalist organization and workers' internationalism had
abolished borders. "The first to abolish the nation were the bourgeois.
Patriotism is an idol. The bourgeoisie offered the first idol to be adored
by the multitude: parliamentarianism. Now that this god is declining,
here is another idol: patriotism. But too late by now, because the proletariat is unpatriotic by definition and through necessity." Not even in the
case of war should socialism have chosen patriotism—it should have declared insurrection.[67]

Both reformist and revolutionary socialists were, on the whole, indifferent when faced with the problem of nation. The socialist movement
did not bother to work out its own myth of nation, as the Catholics did,
and ignored the question of nation in an international context, despite
a few attempts made in this regard by those with authority in the party,
like Leonida Bissolati.[68] The great majority of socialists continued to
consider the myth of nation nothing more than the mask of bourgeois
dictatorship, the national state nothing more than a class dictatorship
destined to be surpassed by socialist internationalism, and the nation as
an ideological invention or an indefinite cultural and historical entity
that would merge with socialist humanity.

The new situation created by the European war in 1914 raised serious political and moral problems for the Socialist Party, obliging it to
clarify more precisely its own position toward the issue of nation regarding the problem of defending the country in war, but it did not change
its traditional attitude. By first ascertaining that the idea of nation and
fatherland "is far from having the same meaning for the two major
classes," the Socialist Party found no difficulty in maintaining, as the
syndicalist Enrico Leone did at the beginning of 1915, that on one hand,
the bourgeoisie thought the nation was an exclusively political idea,

determined by the class interest that ruled the national state; on the other hand, only the working class, "because of its particular living conditions, freed from systematic contact with the state and with its strength, has worked out a concept of nationality, ethically raising it from an idea that was born simply to justify class interest to the value and dignity of a principle."[69] The Socialist Party's neutralist stance itself could have been justified as patriotic, made to claim Italy's "unique record" as an "independent nation, old and young at the same time, not to be classified either among the great powers or among the minor ones," but just for this reason, the reformist Giovanni Zibordi explained at the end of 1916, "should have felt particularly proud and aware of its duty, its historical strength and virtual future energy, and take a position outside and above the conflict, alone and at the same time with everyone, to carry out a function and wield its own authority, drawn from centuries-old experiences and from new ideas, against the vain stupidity of war, for peace in Europe and to civilize the world."[70]

The reformists' neutralist and internationalist consistency did not prevent them from suffering patriotic feelings after the defeat of Caporetto. At that time, Filippo Turati's periodical *Critica Sociale* declared that "family, country and humanity must not be ignored" and, faced with the threat that his country could be oppressed, called on his fellow socialists to be "determined to fight, to resist to the last," but without being influenced by other kinds of patriotism and without recanting their own beliefs. He explained that "proletarians have their own reasons for suffering for their invaded country" but they "violently contest formal beliefs to sift the basic principles of life and love out of them. They do not disavow their ideas and save the country!"[71]

However, all these emotional rather than ideological experiences were to no avail in changing the Socialist Party's attitude toward the myth of nation. Mussolini's conversion to interventionism had no influence on the Socialist Party's orientation, as it not only remained indifferent to the myth of nation but stressed its antipatriotism by starting off an anti-interventionist controversy. After 1917, its infatuation for the new internationalist myth of the Bolshevik revolution turned this indifference into hostility and contempt for everything connected to nation and fatherland, not even sparing the veterans of the First World War. This is how the socialists helped Fascism to gain the monopoly of patriotism. Then, intending to defend the fatherland, the Fascists declared war on its "internal enemies," above all identifying them with those who believed in the myth of internationalism.

The Revolutionaries of the Nation

Mussolini's conversion to interventionism at the end of 1914 was extremely important for the history of the myth of nation. His experience, in fact, emblematically sums up the formation of a new meeting point between the myth of revolution and the myth of nation, which came about through the First World War. The importance of Mussolini's conversion does not concern just the political course of events of the most important protagonist in Italian history between the two world wars. This is because when the leader of the revolutionary group of the Socialist Party passed to interventionism, the result was the formation of a composite and heterogeneous grouping of tendencies and movements. By abandoning the myth of revolution—meaning social revolution— this grouping discovered the world of nations as a consequence of the war and were converted to the myth of nation. Some, like many revolutionary trade unionists, reached this conversion after an autonomous process of ideological revision, mainly influenced by Italianism and the myths of modernist nationalism. Others, like Mussolini, were converted because they were dazzled by the sudden revelation of the reality of nation, after noting that socialist internationalism had failed when faced with the patriotic choice of almost all the European socialist parties.

In November 1914 on the eve of his expulsion, Mussolini urged the Socialist Party to accept the reality of the nation, convinced that the war was revolutionary: "We socialists have never studied the problems of nation"; now it was necessary to see "if it is possible to find common ground to reconcile nation, which is a historical reality, and class, which is a living reality," because "the nation is a stage in human progress that is not yet over. . . . Sentiment for one's nationality exists, it cannot be denied! The old antipatriotism has had its day."[72] For many interventionists the European war was the long-awaited "great event" that was supposed to start off the Italian revolution, the transformation of the state and the rebirth of the nation. Only through war could the Italian nation show it was a great protagonist of modern life. "In short, we must make up our minds: either war or, if not, let's stop the pretence of being a great power. Let's set up gaming houses, hotels and brothels and get rich. A people can have this ideal too."[73] If we stay neutral, Mussolini stressed in February 1915, "Italy will be a despicable and doomed nation, a condemned nation, without autonomy or future. The world will continue to consider street singers, toadies, lodging-house keepers, shoe shines and street musicians as typical Italians."[74]

When Mussolini and other left-wing revolutionaries were converted to the myth of nation, they did not abandon their faith in the myth of revolution. Dissociated from socialist ideology and shifting from the supremacy of a social dimension to a national one, drawing as well on Mazzini's ideas and the myths of national radicalism, the new revolutionary nationalism worked out a new concept of revolution as a process of national palingenesis. This was supposed to radically renew not only Italy's political, economic, and social set-up but also its culture, mentality, and character, building a new state and creating a "new Italian." However, Italy's universalist vocation was not to be abandoned but transferred from socialist internationalism to the myth of a Greater Italy. The firm belief that, through the revolutionary experience of war, a renewed national conscience would finally give modern Italians a sense of their civilizing mission in the contemporary world as well as the ambition for a new supremacy was an important catalyst in the union between the myth of nation and the myth of revolution.

By taking this new direction, the interventionists from the revolutionary left marched with the *La Voce* writers, the Futurists and the militants of idealism, together forming that composite lineup of the small but active groups of the nation's revolutionaries, ideologically and politically different but united by the myth of the Italian revolution. That is, they shared the desire to act, using any means, even violence in the streets, to radically transform the existing situation, so as to create the conditions necessary to establish a new and Greater Italy in the world. They all believed that taking part in the war had consecrated the new reborn Italy in blood. "It is a matter of passing our examination. Up to now we have been a nation aspiring to be great. Now, not even this is the issue; it is much more: we have to find out if we are a nation," declared *La Voce* in 1914.[75] Mussolini the interventionist was convinced that the war would reveal the new Italy to the Italians and mould the "new Italian" of a Greater Italy:

> It is Italy's first war. Of the nation Italy, of the Italian people, united by now in a solid union from the Alps to Sicily, . . . it will be a great test. War is the examination of peoples. . . . The war must reveal Italy to the Italians. Above all, it must disprove the ignoble legend that the Italians do not fight: it must cancel the shame of Lissa and Custoza; it must show the world that Italy is capable of fighting a war, a great war. . . . Only this can give the Italians the idea of, and pride in, their being Italian; only the war can make the "Italians" d'Azeglio spoke of. Oh, revolution![76]

The war, the philosopher Gentile declared in 1918, had marked the coming of a new Italy and had helped the country to enter "the great history of the world."[77]

Most of the revolutionaries of the nation joined the Fascist movement and contributed to working out its totalitarian ideology. However, if we consider their attitude toward the problem of nation in the period between interventionism and the early postwar period, it is clear that the need to reconcile the patriot with the man still prevailed among the revolutionaries in an idea of nation and citizen that again proposed Mazzini's ideal of the new Italian, but in modern terms. This ideal foresaw a patriot who was a free man in an independent and sovereign nation, among independent and sovereign nations. Discovering Mazzini again was another important catalyst of the new fusion between the myths of nation and revolution proposed by the various movements that had arisen from interventionism and the war, like national trade-unionism, the movement that arose from the taking of Fiume, and the first steps of Fascism itself. In particular, national syndicalism worked out a new idea of Mazzini's concept of nation in view of a future "International of free countries," opposed to socialist internationalism, which denied nation or thought it could be surpassed. In 1918 *Il Rinnovamento*, the national syndicalist periodical, stated:

> The nation cannot be denied or made obsolete, but it must be experienced in all its reality and power. . . . There can be no international agreement between weak and humbled nations and powerful oppressive nations, between enslaved peoples and dominating peoples. The war has broken the spell of proletarian universality against capitalist universality and, with this bloody demonstration, has reminded us of the eternal and unchangeable reality of nation and race. There can be no international agreement for alliance if there are no nations, as there can be no alliance between individuals if there is no individual, with his own conscience, intellect and will, a man fully aware of his personality, dignity and capacity. This is what the war taught us with the convincing violence of a shining revelation, and we and the interventionist proletariat wanted the war to defend our freedom as a people, the freedom of peoples — an indispensable condition for a new and more sincere international alliance. Consequently, we did not think that the war conflicted with our socialist principles: consequently, we wanted the war in order to defend our most sacred heritage of ideas.[78]

The revolutionaries of the nation thought they were the vanguard of the new Italy, reborn from the experience of the war, and that they were therefore destined to govern the nation to complete the Italian revolution, to finally carry out, as Gentile declared, the "redemption of that old Italy known proverbially among the European peoples for its faint-hearted nature, its individualism, its poor sense of state and its tendency to withdraw into private egoism or the infinite abstract of art and intellectual speculation."[79] It was necessary to destroy the "internal enemy" hidden within the character of the Italians, all those in the world of politics who represented the old skeptical and individualistic Italy and all those who repudiated their country in the name of foreign ideals of social revolution. The war was only the beginning of the duel to the death between the old and the new Italy. In December 1918 Gentile wrote:

> And here is the dilemma. On one hand, easy-going, idle Italy, steeped in the skepticism of a superficial culture that cannot be either religion or character: the old Italy. On the other hand, the Italy that, digging in at the Piave and on Mount Grappa, did not budge and drove the attackers off the Montello saddle, and then reached them on the other side of the river and destroyed them, the Italy that won only because it wanted to win, and surprised the world and the Italians themselves with the stupendous proof of its obstinate resistance: the new Italy. Which of the two will remain? The old man is not dead and is lying in wait for us, enticing us and getting in our way. We must fight and destroy him. This is a bitter struggle, because this man is so much a part of us.[80]

After experiencing the conflict between interventionists and neutralists, the new revolutionary nationalism proposed a new version of the myth of radical conflict between "two Italies." Before Italy entered the war, it was the violent contrast between neutralists and interventionists, and after the war ended, it was civil war between the revolutionaries of nation and the revolutionaries of socialism.

At the same time as the conflict between nationalists and internationalists was raging, the myth of the Russian revolution, the most formidable and aggressive rival of the myth of nation, spread among the masses, exerting a powerful fascination. The struggle between these "two Italies" was seen by both sides as a decisive conflict for the future of Italy and degenerated into real civil war when each side aimed at wiping out its adversary. He was no longer considered an Italian with a different ideology but an "internal enemy" whose very existence threatened the safety and the future of the nation.

The postwar ideological struggle was so bitter that it prevented any possibility of an orderly return to political life within the structures of the liberal state, with a shared sentiment of belonging to a single fatherland the same for everyone. Even among those who believed in the myth of nation, the ideological divisions, now deepened by the effects of the war experience, led to contrasts and conflicts. The Fascist movement emerged from these conflicts the winner, with the strength of violence and the attraction of a new faith in the myth of nation, arrogating to itself the privilege of being the only and incontrovertible interpreter of the nation's will and the only representative of the new Italy born from the war.

In a certain sense, although it was the heir of various nationalist groups of the Giolitti years, Fascism was something new, born directly from the war experience, which left an indelible mark on its very essence—on its way of conceiving and actually perceiving its myth of nation and its vision of a Greater Italy. Born of the fusion between the myth of nation and the myth of revolution, Fascism was the expression of a totalitarian revolutionary nationalism that, once in power, put a stop to the liberal attempt to create a common fatherland for all Italians.

Giuseppe Garibaldi on his deathbed. From *L'Epoca*, June 1882.

King Victor Emmanuel III and Queen Elena of Montenegro visit the Jubilee exposition of 1911 at Castel Sant'Angelo.

Announcement for one of many events associated with the "Festival of the Nation, 1911."

Jubilee exposition, Campidoglio, March 27, 1911.

Inauguration of the monument to King Victor Emmanuel II, Rome, June 4, 1911.

An array of Italy's neighbors portrayed as coveting the Italian peninsula. From *Prima l'Adriatico* (Florence: Ferrante Connelli, 1915).

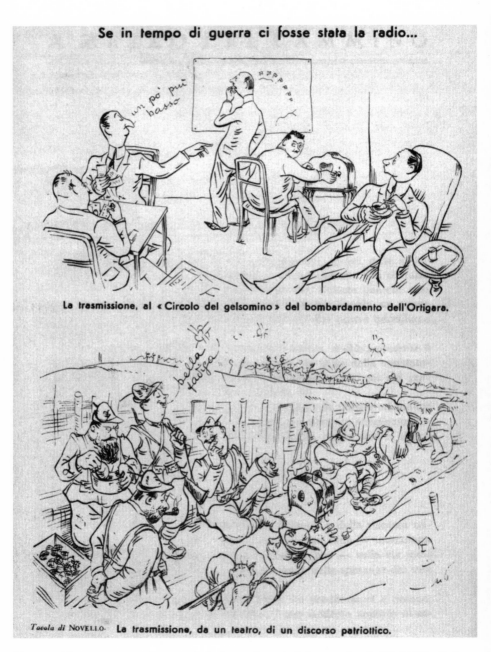

Humor with a message: caricature of the home front and the trenches in World War I. From *Angelo Monaresi, Aprite Le Porte: copertina a colori di novella illustrazioni in bianco e nero di novello, ricci, vellani-archi, angoletta, vitali, minardi e ciotti* (Rome: 10 Reggimento Alpini Editore, 1933).

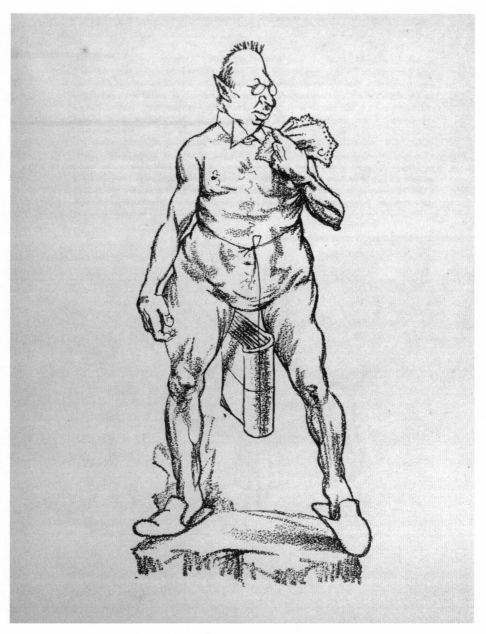

Caricature of Benedetto Croce. From *Emilio Settimelli, Sassate: Antilibro con 100 disegni di musacchio* (Rome: Casa editrice italiana, 1926).

55

Caricature of don Luigi Sturzo. From *Emilio Settimelli, Sassate: Antilibro con 100 disegni di musacchio.*

A Fascist era postcard from Italy.

Mussolini's visit to Berlin in 1937. From *Il Gazzettino Illustrato*, Venice, October 1937.

PART 3

THE FASCIST NATION

8

Italy in Black Shirts

Fascism and the Nation

The myth of the nation embraced all aspects of Fascism right from the beginning: the culture and ideology, the concept of the individual and the masses, the relationship with the state and society, internal and foreign policy, the sense of tradition and the attitude toward the future. However, as we will explain in the following chapters, we are convinced that the national myth in Italy began its decline precisely with Fascism. This was due principally to Fascism's desire to proceed with a systematic and deliberate ideologization of the nation, which led to the identification of the nation itself with Fascism. Before we study the Fascist national myth, however, it is necessary to make some preliminary considerations regarding the overall matter of the relationship between Fascism and nation and, in particular, the novelty and specificity of the Fascist national myth within the history of the Italian myth of the nation.

First of all, it must be pointed out that, despite the importance that the national myth had within Fascism and for Fascism, and despite the influence that the Fascist experience had, in turn, on the parable of the Italian national myth, the question of the relationship between Fascism and nation has remained almost entirely neglected so far. When evaluating the nature and significance of this relationship, most have deemed it sufficient, up to now, to follow the current interpretations that, like all generalizations, are thought to be sufficiently convincing and, as such, appear indisputable. We can take as an example the interpretation, agreed upon by many, of Fascist nationalism as the ultimate manifestation of the degeneration of European nationalism, which culminated in imperialist and racist totalitarianism, thus proving the similarity between Nazi nationalism and Fascist nationalism, both being the expression of a common concept of nation. Also within the sphere of such

143

generalizations are statements affirming, from an even more restricted viewpoint, that the historical significance of Fascist nationalism consisted in the attempt to strengthen the national state after the upheaval of the First World War. From a different but more limited point of view, there is the interpretation that sees Fascism as a commonplace phenomenon bereft of its own historic individuality, therefore denying that Fascist nationalism had its own specificity. This interpretation maintains that it was nothing more than a rougher and more aggressive continuation of the liberal state's nationalism, or little more than an imitation or derivation of the ideology of Enrico Corradini's nationalist movement. In this way, what is being ignored is everything new that Fascism introduced in the evolution of the problem of the nation and national myth: the advent of the society of the masses, the development of industry and modernization, the unparalleled upheaval of World War I, the Bolshevik revolution, and Fascism itself.

If we leave these superficial interpretations and proceed with an in-depth historical investigation, we realize that in actual fact the physiognomy of Fascist nationalism is much more complex than thought up to now, precisely because of the novelty and peculiarity of the way in which the Fascists conceived the nation. A better understanding of the relationship between Fascism and nation is, however, indispensable if we are going to judge with greater knowledge the significance of the Fascist experience in the history of the Italian national myth and the effects it had on the attitude of the Italians toward the nation and the national state during the twentieth century.

Many elements of the previous nationalist traditions flowed into the Fascist national myth. They were mixed up and united in a new and original synthesis, even attributing characteristics to the myth of Greater Italy that only in part coincided with the previous versions, although we do find in the Fascist myth the same group of ideas taken from the myth of supremacy and mission, from the myth of regeneration of the Italians, and from the myth of the conquest of modernity. What disappeared was the link between nation and liberty, rejected contemptuously by Fascism, which explained away the substance of the Risorgimento tradition, while preserving the rhetorical rituals that recalled the great creators and heroic deeds in the struggle for independence and unification of Italy. The link between nation and humanity also disappeared, where the supremacy of the politics of power was asserted definitively over any humanitarian ideal of peaceful coexistence founded on the liberty and equality of national states and on the respect of all nationalities.

Consequently, the principle of nationality disappeared as the foundation of international law and as a guarantee of freedom and independence of nations, as did the ideal of a single fatherland common to all Italians regardless of different political convictions and religious beliefs, based on the concept of a national identity that acknowledged its essence and vitality in the liberty of its citizens.

From its birth, Fascism expected to be identified with the nation exclusively and without question. This claim was an integral part of the essence of Fascism as a revolutionary and totalitarian movement, on which its national myth was founded. This claim, however, was not confined to the abstract world of ideological disquisitions because it influenced internal and foreign policy choices, as well as the attitude and behavior of the Fascist party toward the national state, inherited from liberal Italy, and toward the real-life nation: that is, the men and women in Italy who for twenty years experienced and in the end paid for the consequences of Fascism's totalitarian ambitions.

By arrogating the monopoly of patriotism and expecting to identify the nation with itself, Fascism gave a strong impulse to the process of ideologizing the national myth, which had long-lived consequences on the collective consciences of the Italians and on their way of perceiving the nation and the national state. As we have seen, ideologizing the nation was not just a Fascist or an Italian phenomenon, because it had begun before the First World War and continued during the postwar period, with greater impetus, because of the effect of the Bolshevik revolution. In the case of Fascism, however, this process seems to have taken place faster and more obviously owing to the revolutionary and totalitarian nature of Fascism, which inevitably led it to absorb the national myth within its own ideological universe and to exclude irrevocably the conceptual possibility of a different way of feeling and conceiving the national myth. Thus it was induced to identify itself with the nation and to grant the rights of full citizenship only to those who professed and practiced their faith in the Fascist religion.

The ideal of a "fatherland for all the Italians" conceived by the Risorgimento and liberal Italy was replaced by the ideal of a Fascist nation—a country where only the Fascists were recognized as having *Italianità*, while Italians who opposed Fascism were expelled from the national community, excommunicated and rejected. In the years of the regime, any Italian who did not declare his faithfulness to the Fascist nation was treated by the regime as a foreigner: in the end, this Italian, a foreigner in his own country, no longer felt it was his duty to feel loyal and faithful to a national state that treated him as an internal enemy, even if this enemy professed faith in the fatherland and the nation as ideals of collective life and as the principles of civilized ethics.

The logical consequence of the nation's subordination to Fascism, defined in theory according to the formula "the state creates the nation," was the anthropological revolution that was carried out to regenerate the Italians, to "remake" their character and create a new spiritual and racial identity for the nation.

The advent of Fascism's national myth was entirely conditioned by its totalitarian nature, even if the Fascist national myth did not feature uniformity but rather had many different configurations during the parabola of Fascism. The changes were due to the logic of its development as a totalitarian movement, affected also by the influence of situations and events that Fascist Italy had to deal with both in internal and foreign policy. That does not mean, however, that it isn't possible to identify some specific traits that emerged from the synthesis of ideas, myths and images that the ideologists of the Fascist culture, from the great intellectuals to the masses of organizers and propagandists, were producing in their way of conceiving and experiencing Fascism.

To better highlight this complex evolution (anything but uniform despite the apparent monolithic image that Fascism had of the nation) and to better identify the elements that, from time to time in the different periods of its history were prevalent and characterized it, it may be useful to distinguish different phases in the stand that Fascism took regarding the idea of nation, although we realize how schematic such distinctions are. Depending on the predominant motivation in each phase, we can distinguish (1) the *rebirth of the race*, which corresponds to the very first period when the Fascist movement was forming; (2) the *national restoration* phase during the years between the fight to gain power and the founding of the regime; (3) *totalitarian regeneration*, which took hold, above all, after the mid-twenties, with the regime's internal policy oriented toward increasingly extensive and pervasive "educational" intervention by the Fascist Party in the lives of the collectivity; (4) the *imperial civilization* phase, which developed particularly after the conquest of Ethiopia and during the war years; and (5) *the revolutionary war*, which coincided with the Second World War and the final collapse of the regime.

These phases were not distinguished by sudden, radical changes, but they flowed into each other in a kind of spiral development, like points of time in the Fascist culture and policy, each one presenting a particular

way of conceiving the nation in relation to other fundamental ideas of
Fascism.

The Rebirth of the Race

Fascist nationalism had existential rather than theoretical origins. It was
born of experiences, emotions and sentiments rather than theoretical
reflections on the nation. Fascist nationalism was born of a "state of collective excitement," that is, an experience of exaltation that involved
both the interventionists and those who fought in the First World War.
They were convinced they were the protagonists of a "great event," the
initiators of a new era. "We—and I'm speaking of those who are between twenty and thirty—are enraptured with *Italianità*," said Mussolini
the day after victory. "We feel Italy's dynamic qualities in our veins, in
our innermost parts. And the war has revealed us to ourselves."[1]

Mythically transfigured into a "great palingenetic event" in the typically modernist view of the war as a regenerating catastrophe,[2] right
from the beginning Italy's participation in the world conflict became
symbolic of the rebirth of the race in the Fascist mythology. And it was
from this that a new Italy arose, ready to carry out a mission of civilization of the modern world. The Fascists considered themselves the precursors of the war-generated Italy, claiming the privilege of guiding the
nation toward new and greater triumphs. For the first Fascists, the nation was felt emotionally, above all, as their own country and it was a
symbol of faith, a myth, in which all the sentiments, emotions and ideals
generated by the war experience were concentrated. Fascism's idea of
nation expressed first of all the feeling of pride, sparked by the victorious participation in the war that had crowned Italy's rise to the rank of
great nation.

Mussolini said in 1920:

> In the last fifty years Italy has made wonderful progress. First of all
> there is a given fact: and that is the vitality of our race. . . . The
> main pillar of Fascism is *Italianità*, that is, we are proud to be Ital-
> ians, even if we go to Siberia, [and] we intend to yell out loud: We
> are Italians. . . . Now we are claiming the honor of being Italian,
> because in our marvelous and adorable peninsula—adorable al-
> though there are some inhabitants who are not always adorable—
> the most prodigious and wonderful history of the human race took
> place.[3]

Mussolini wanted to emphasize the existential origin of Fascism's idea of nation, explicitly declaring, in 1922, its mythical characteristic as the symbol of faith: "We have created our myth. The myth is a faith, a passion. It is not necessary for it to be a reality. It is a reality in the fact that it is a prod, that it is a hope, that it is faith and courage. Our myth is the nation, our myth is the greatness of the nation! And it is to this myth, to this greatness, that we subordinate all the rest that we want to convert into a complete reality."[4]

From the beginning, Fascism bestowed a dogmatic nature on the myth of the nation, assuming the privilege of being the custodian and defender of this dogma against anyone who dared to deny or belittle it. "What stands as a tangible and intangible truth—and what some want to deny simply because it exists—is the nation, which is already feeling the first quivers of a new life that is going to explode into such greatness as only the Italian genius knows how to conceive and realize in conquering humanity."[5]

The original nucleus of Fascist nationalism developed by sinking its roots into the fertile terrain of national radicalism. It had also absorbed a large part of the myth of modernist nationalism, which, although at times ambiguous and contradictory, was to permeate the entire evolution of Fascist nationalism, fixing some essential characteristics and influencing the logic of its subsequent development.[6] In fact, from the very beginning, Fascist nationalism can be considered a new manifestation of modernist nationalism, linked to the same typically modernist idea of the rebirth of the race generated by the war. Instead of rejecting modernity in the hope of a return to the past, Fascism accepted the challenge because its ambition was to conquer it so as to be the active and creative protagonist of history in movement, projecting itself toward the future enthusiastically, with a desire for power that wanted to assert itself by participating in the building of a new reality. The Fascists had the myth of the future rather than the myth of the past: they did not intend to be the custodians of an inherited tradition, albeit glorious, but wanted to be the creators of a new tradition, a new civilization, that would be perpetuated in time, challenging time with its ability to continuously renew itself. The Fascists enhanced tradition, acknowledging that it was "one of the greatest spiritual forces of populations" only if it was "the subsequent and constant creation of their souls" and not something "sacred and unchangeable and intangible."[7] Even the myth of Romanness, a fundamental component of Fascist nationalism, was interpreted modernistically as a myth of action for the future. As Mussolini said on April 21, 1922:

> Celebrating the birth of Rome means celebrating our type of civilization, it means exalting our history and our race, it means resting firmly on the past to better launch ourselves toward the future. Rome and Italy are in fact two inseparable words. . . . Of course, the Rome that we honor is not only the Rome of monuments and ruins. . . . The Rome that we honor, but above all the Rome that we are dreaming of and preparing, is different: it does not consist of famous stones, but live souls; it is not contemplation of the past, but hard work for the future.[8]

The "new Italians" that Fascism wanted to forge were supposed to be the Romans of modernity.

Finally, the Fascist concept of nation as a political myth was modernist and, as such, not bound to any particular theoretical, historic or sociological definition, but was flexible in adapting to the needs of Fascism. As we shall see, Fascism eventually considered the nation not as an existing reality but as its creation and instrumental in satisfying its desire for power. Fascism was permeated with Italianism, and it believed that the mission of Greater Italy was to play a leading role in modernity. However, modernity was conceived by Fascism as the expression of a new Italian modernity that identified the nation's future with its own as a movement and regime. In the Fascist concept, the myth of Greater Italy did not coincide with and was not satisfied with establishing the supremacy of the nation, conceived as an historic and moral entity, supreme to Fascism itself and destined to survive it. Fascism's greatest ambition was to be the principle creator of a new imperial civilization founded on its totalitarian principles, values and institutions. By overcoming the dimension of nation and national state, judged near to decline, Fascism wanted to acquire a universal dimension, like Romanness and Catholicism, so as to impress the brand of Italian genius on a new era of modern civilization.

There is another element that characterizes Fascist nationalism in its first phase, but that, unlike others indicated so far, rapidly disappeared in the transformation of Fascism from a situational movement,[9] that is, a movement made up of veterans with recent war experience, to a movement of the masses, organized militarily to form a militia party. In this transformation the libertarian element, characteristic of Fascist ideology in 1919, disappeared. For early Fascists, the supremacy of the nation did not involve establishing an authoritarian concept of the state but seemed to combine well with an antistate, free-market and libertarian ideology that came mainly from Futurism and Italian syndicalism. It was from the latter that in 1919 Fascism derived the principle of complementary factors between social and national questions, the rejection of antagonism between classes detrimental to national interests, and the representation of the nation as a huge union of productive forces cooperating to increase the nation's wealth and power. However, little was left of the federalist and libertarian ideology found in national unionism after Fascist nationalism was transformed into a party. And the few existing traces disappeared entirely with the totalitarian state. The revolutionary syndicalists who followed Fascism in this transformation, making a very important contribution by bringing their political culture, had in effect made a complete U-turn as regards their principles. Allegiance to the totalitarian state meant rejecting the essence of antistate and antiparty principles that were fundamental in the synthesis between socialism and nationalism brought about by interventionist syndicalism.

National Restoration

The restoration phase of the Fascist national myth began in 1921 with the activity of *squadrismo* (action squads). It coincided with the rise to power and transformation of the regime. In this phase, Fascism appeared as the party of believers and fighters, who proposed elimination of the nation's "internal enemies" to restore the authority of the national state and the supremacy of the nation in the lives of the Italians.

The national Fascist Party statute, drawn up in November 1921, established the supremacy of the nation as the supreme value and the principle according to which state existence was organized: according to Fascism, the nation is not the "simple sum of living individuals, nor the instrument of parties for their own ends, but an organism that includes an indefinite series of generations of which the single individuals are transitory elements; it is the supreme synthesis of the material and immaterial values of the race"; as the "juridical incarnation of the nation," continued the party's statute, the state's principle duty is to defend, protect and establish the supremacy of the nation, instilling the cult of fatherland in its citizens through the schools and the army.

Proclaiming itself to be the "nation's militia," Fascism arrogated the privilege of interpreting the general desire of the new Italy, born of the war, and undertook, furthermore, to accomplish the building of the national state with integration of the masses and collaboration of the classes, all in the common faith of "religion of fatherland." "The contrast," said Mussolini on the eve of his march on Rome, "is between nation and state. Italy is a nation. Italy is not a state." Italy was a nation because of the "fundamental unity of our customs," language and religion, unity consecrated by the war, "and if these wonderful unities are sufficient to characterize the nation, the Italian nation exists: full of resources, very powerful, projected toward a glorious future. But the nation must give itself a state. And there is no state."[10]

In its guise as the restorer of the nation, Fascism was welcomed by the patriotic bourgeoisie of Risorgimento tradition, which, having misunderstood the nature of the new party, was under the illusion that the Fascist government was transitory. The bourgeoisie was convinced that it would be possible to give new life to the liberal state by injecting it with Fascist youthfulness and, then, return to the building of a fatherland for all Italians after defeating the internationalist subversives. Fascism, however, had no intention of melting into the framework of existing institutions, ending its revolution in the restoration of a state that still identified with the liberal tradition of the Risorgimento and with the ideals of a ruling class that had governed Italy after unification. On the contrary, the Fascists claimed that liberalism and its ruling class were the cause of the state's weakness and that the unaccomplished Italian revolution was due to the failure to instill a collective faith in the "religion of fatherland," to the failure to integrate the masses into the nation, to the spreading of foreign ideologies and to the prevalence of antinational parties. It was only by repudiating liberalism that the nation could aspire to founding a real national state on a solid basis, capable of facing and overcoming the challenges of modernity. The next step after repudiating liberalism was to belittle and even deride the ruling class that had founded and governed the unified state which Fascism did not consider a "national state" because it was built on foreign models and was represented by an oligarchy unable to rouse the masses. Italy was weak and incompetent because, being at the mercy of the vicissitudes of a parliamentary regime, it was exposed to the continuous protests of individuals and associations working openly against the state as an authority and against the supremacy of the nation. The scorn Fascism held (particularly its hardliners) for the liberal state and Giolitti's "*Italietta*" allowed a considerable deterioration of the Risorgimento as an unaccomplished national revolution,[11] on the wave of Mazziniism and national radicalism. However, faced with the accusation of being anti-Risorgimento, Fascism proclaimed instead that it was the heir, the continuer and promulgator of the Risorgimento's revolutionary ideals, but interpreted in a nationalist, state control and antiparliamentary key. Therefore, the state was severed from its liberal component, judged to be grafted from foreign, individualist and materialist ideologies that had prevented the formation of a national conscience and sense of state among the community.

To establish its own national revolution as being the "true" one and to claim the monopoly of patriotism due to its pretension of being a sort of messianic movement born out of the "great event" of the war, Fascism chose to refer to the First World War and not the Risorgimento as the beginning of Italy's rebirth. At the beginning of 1923[12] Mussolini stated: "The eclipse of our race was torn open in 1915, and all the virtues that were dormant, but not dead, sprang to the forefront, giving us an immortal victory." At the same time the idealist review *La Nuova Politica Liberale* wrote that the war was "a first awareness of our country's national status."[13] Apart from the rituals of respect and the perorations of the House of Savoy historiography glorifying the monarchic Risorgimento, in the Fascist historic mythology, the creation of the unified state was, in effect, relegated to events that took place on the "eve" of the nation's rebirth, prelude to but not the effective founding event of the national state: interventionism, the war and the "revolution of the black shirts" were the founding events of the national state.

"Who does Italy belong to? To us!"

When it came into power, Fascism, which had legitimized its anti-Socialist, antiliberal and antidemocratic revolution by declaring that it was entrusted with the mission to restore the nation's supremacy and the state's sovereignty, demanded exclusive control over patriotism with respect to all other national or antinational parties. Then it took more decisive steps toward putting the totalitarian experiment into effect. It no longer considered itself just the nation's restorer. Having effectively ensured control over political power through the building of a totalitarian state, it aimed to combine in an indissoluble union the "true Italians" and the Fascist Party activists.

In the beginning, the tendency to identify Fascism with the nation did not occur without disputes within Fascism itself. The clash between the dissidents, the revisionists and the fundamentalists was one of the many crises that affected Fascism after the march on Rome and was sparked by the ideological dispute over Fascism's attitude toward the nation and the consequences that that attitude had on the party's and the Fascist government's political choices. Active resistance, which developed into political opposition, at first came from those who had adhered to Fascism believing that its function, entirely transitory, was to restore the nation. For example, according to Massimo Rocca, after having renovated the nation, Fascism was "to melt, submerge and dissolve in the new, widespread, firmly rooted national conscience," because the Fascist revolution had been "carried out by the Fascists for Italy and not for the Fascists themselves."[14] In contrast, according to the fundamentalists, the purpose of the Fascist revolution was to conquer the state, thus realizing total identification between Fascism and the nation. However, this process was not supposed to lead to the dissolution of Fascism in the nation and the dismembering of the Party. It was to lead to the "Fascistization" of the nation, institutionalizing the role of the party as the pillar of the new state and creator of the new Italy.

The battle was won by Fascist hardliners (*integralisti*), but the matter was never completely overcome, for it surfaced from time to time among the ambiguities and contradictions of numerous debates on the relationship between state and nation, on the national or universal features of Fascism, on Fascism's role in the history of Italy or on the function of the Party, debates that considered not only the leanings of the various cultural factions of Fascism but also the tensions and conflicts within the regime. In November 1925, for instance, Mussolini's review *Gerarchia* published an article that foresaw the day when Fascism "would disappear completely among the population because the masses had been converted and, therefore, it had achieved its aim."[15] However, such statements became increasingly rare, while the tendency of Fascism to overlap the myth of the nation with its revolutionary myths increased, raising doubts and concern in those who, although they had adhered to the regime, had been educated in the traditional patriotism of the Risorgimento. Similar sentiments were shared by those who cultivated a "sense of state" over and above parties. These doubts were shared as well by the Fascists who, either for political reasons or religious conviction, did not agree with the strengthening of the party totalitarian dictatorship, with its personalization of power or with worshiping the nation as a deity of the Fascist religion. And they were shared above all by the former nationalists who did not fully accept the totalitarian logic of Fascism because it placed the Fascist party ideology above the nation.

In the early thirties, Gioacchino Volpe complained that the Fascist propaganda placed too much emphasis on the "miraculous nature of Fascism, the Fascist revolution and its men: that it was doing Fascism a wrong to describe its structural substance as mediocre, or to make Fascist Italy's destiny appear to depend too much on events brought about by human beings." Volpe suggested that the propagandists would do better to publicize Fascism "not as a superimposition on Italy but as something generated from Italy, its strong points, traditions, and aspirations," that would present "Italy today, Fascist Italy as a continuation, development, elevation of yesterday's Italy and not, in substance, the opposite."[16] Volpe, like many intellectuals and politicians coming from pre-Fascist nationalism, conceived Fascism not as a party and regime that pursued its own revolutionary ends beyond the interests of the nation but "as a way to renew the Italian nation." And it was only in this sense that they were willing to identify Fascism with the nation:

> It must be admitted . . . that there is deep harmony between the Fascist movement and the Italian nation, solicited by an energetic minority, expression coming from its own bosom, and with an immediateness and readiness far greater than there could have been between the small group that brought about the Risorgimento and the great mass of the Italian people who, more or less unknowingly, followed. In this difference lies the significance of the great progress of Italy in sixty years of unification.[17]

Like many other Italians born under the myth of Greater Italy during the years of liberal *Italietta,* which seemed to them to be limited and modest, Volpe embraced Fascism because he felt it expressed the highest, proudest, national sentiment and the country's desire for greatness. However, as he later wrote, he "felt first of all Italian, and did not accept, as I do not accept, that sort of identification Italy-Fascism, which soon took hold, so that in actual fact, *Italy* was virtually overtaken and conditioned by the qualification 'Fascist.'"[18]

Most of the Fascists coming from the nationalist movement felt the same way. Even if Fascism was indebted to the nationalists because they contributed their philosophy to the development of the Fascist ideology and the construction of the regime, these debts were paid off quickly by laying claim to the novelty of their revolution as well as their attitude toward the idea of nation.[19] The nationalist movement had influenced the Fascist concept of nation considerably during the restoration period, particularly through the legal doctrine and the Fascist laws drafted by

Alfredo Rocco, the foremost theoretician of the authoritarian state as conceived of by imperialist nationalism. But this was only one of the factors that contributed to the making of Fascist nationalism. After having assimilated the nationalist doctrine, Fascism developed along other lines, emphasizing the revolutionary and spiritual concept of nation within the framework of an increasingly conscious totalitarian policy. It clearly and explicitly distanced itself from what it considered to be the conservative, naturalist concept typical of the nationalist movement but without the creative impulse that animated Fascist nationalism. Soon after the unification of the two parties, Camillo Pellizzi stated that, for the Italian Nationalist Association theorists, the nation was a "presupposition, a given myth" and, therefore, used in the conservative sense, whereas for Fascism, the nation was a revolutionary myth, "an instrument of really new actions, much more Italian in substance and more widespread."[20]

On the other hand, the diffidence of the former nationalists toward Fascism's totalitarian pretensions of absorbing the nation rather than the nation absorbing Fascism was never completely snuffed out. Enrico Corradini, making the observation that "there is too much talk about Fascism and too little of Italy," entrusted to unpublished notes his concern regarding Fascism's totalitarian trend and the negative effects this might have on the attitude of the Italians toward the nation. In 1927 he wrote, "less Fascism and more Italy, less Party and more Nation, less Revolution and more Constitution." This observation led to a series of particularly sharp comments on the Fascist regime and the negative effects of identifying Fascism with the nation. The progressive accumulation of dictatorial powers in a "one-person absolute government," observed Corradini, is such that "large areas of national life remain outside surveillance and are at the mercy of corruption," while there has been an "extraordinary increase in flattering and obsequious behavior."[21]

Most of these doubts and expressions of dissent remained personal thoughts and only rarely, and very cautiously, were they heard in public. Therefore, they did not in any way slow down or prevent the totalitarian "Fascistization" of the nation. It was only when the war took a turn for the worse, when Fascism was discredited and defeated, that this dissent changed to open opposition, so as to establish the supremacy of the nation, uncontaminated, and not to be confused with movements or their relative regimes.

9

Remaking the Italians

The Fascist State Creates the Nation

The identification of Fascism with the nation was fully accomplished when the party-state was founded. Its ultimate goal was to overcome the dualism between state and society with the consecration of the totalitarian state's absolute supremacy over the nation. As former nationalist Maurizio Maraviglia explained in 1929, the Fascist revolution had overcome this dualism, a fundamental requisite of the liberal regime, by conceiving the state and nation as an indivisible whole. The nation, conceived as the "historic continuity, as the will to live on and perform the civilizing mission of the Italians, in other words, as *Italianità* that continues and spreads," is realized in the state.

The Fascist state's totalitarian policy was derived from this identification, inspired by the principle that "no political power may exist outside the state." This was because, "having the state absorb all of the national spirit and being unable to pursue any of the nation's objectives outside the state, it follows that the state must consider illegitimate all parties and all political movements that tend to destroy the state doctrine, gaining political strength with respect to the state." Consequently, Maraviglia continued, the state "can recognize only one party: that which espouses the same doctrine, and it has the specific task of safeguarding and preserving it from any attempt to adulterate or pollute it ideologically, as well as diffuse it and teach it to the new Italian generations." With respect to the parties, the state should act "as the Church did with heresy; it cannot allow groups that are substantially divided about the fundamental principles of the state to cohabit in the same political community; just as dissidents cannot be allowed within a religious confession. Anyone who is against the Fascist system, which is the state's system, is automatically outside the national community." The unitary theory of state and nation led, therefore, in real politics, to establishing "the people in the state organically." And speaking of "people," Maraviglia specified that Fascism did not refer to an abstract entity, to the population "in its ideal continuity," but to the "real masses of living Italians." This inevitably sparked Fascism's actions to achieve its own identification with the nation in everyday life, virtually extending "the state's interference and authority over all manifestations of people's lives, without, however, stifling the spirit of initiative."[1]

The identification between nation and Fascism was formally sanctioned in one of the new regime's fundamental documents, the *Carta del Lavoro* (Labor Charter) promulgated in 1927. It began with an official definition of the Fascist idea of nation: "The nation is an entity that has goals, life, means of action superior to those of the single individuals or groups of individuals that it is made up of. It is a moral, political and economic unit that is fully achieved in the Fascist state." Therefore, the making of the Italian nation could only be achieved completely within the Fascist state. This was the outcome of theories of the national state that had found the greatest consensus within Fascism. Despite much talk about the supremacy of the nation, the nationalists themselves had reached the point of favoring the state as an entity, within which the creation of the nation is completed, thus guaranteeing the existence of the nation for the individuals within, perpetuating the collective life of the nation in time beyond the existence of living generations. According to Rocco, who drew up the basic principles of the *Carta del Lavoro*, nations were natural entities with a life cycle: they were born, developed, decayed and died; whereas the state was eternal, the supreme incarnation of the principle of organization, which ensures the nation's lifespan in the perpetual struggle among human societies and the creation of civilization.[2] The implicit corollary to this affirmation of Rocco's statism, which was not very congenial with Fascism because of its naturalistic coarseness, was the definition of state as the constituent component integrating the Fascist concept of nation: in the Fascist concept there could be no completed nation without the state, and, one might add, there could never be a completed Italian nation without the Fascist state. This was a firm conviction of Mussolini's, who had stated in 1924: "Without the state there is no nation. There are only groups of human beings, susceptible to all the disintegrations that history can inflict upon them."[3] And this concept was widely echoed as, little by little, he progressed with building the totalitarian state, transferring to the state the attributes of the nation, turning the state into the nation's conscience. The state, the Duce announced in 1929, is

> the guardian and transmitter of the population's spirit just as it developed in the language, custom and faith for centuries.
> The state is not only the present, but also the past, and above all, the future. It is the state that represents the nation's immanent conscience, transcending the brief limit of individuals' lives. . . . The state educates the citizens in civil virtues; it makes them aware of their mission; it urges unity; . . . it takes men from the primary life of tribes to the highest expression of human power that is an empire. . . . When the sense of state declines and dissociates and centrifugal tendencies prevail among individuals or groups, the sun starts to set on national societies.[4]

Until the end of the twenties, however, the myth of the nation held a predominant position in Fascist ideology, as is evident in the catechism-like text of the Fascist doctrine written by the PNF (National Fascist Party) secretary, Augusto Turati, for Fascist draft recruits. Reference to the nation and fatherland is frequent, and a whole chapter is devoted to the definition of nation. The question "What is the nation?" required the recruit to answer, "More than fifty million Italians who have the same language, the same customs, the same blood, the same destiny, the same interests: a moral, political and economic unit that is realized completely in the Fascist state: that is the nation."[5] The rapid advance of the totalitarian process in the thirties led to a new concept of nation and its relationship with the state, to the extent that the supremacy of the state over the nation developed considerably within Fascist culture's hierarchy of fundamental values. Whereas in the restoration phase "Fascism-party" appeared to interpret the nation's aspiration to become a state, in the totalitarian phase "Fascism-state" proclaimed itself the creator of the nation. The idea of nation, with respect to the state, also suffered a sort of de facto devaluation from a conceptual point of view. In 1941, Giuseppe Maggiore, philosopher of law, maintained that, in the face of the juridical and historical reality as well as the conceptual rationality of the state, the nation "was a sentiment, and nothing more than a sentiment," and that it was "not at all conceptual, but all told, only a spontaneous, immediate state of mind, . . . in other words, purely irrational."[6]

As regards reference to the nation, it is significant to note the change that occurred in the Fascist Party's "sacred" texts. In the statutes of 1921 and 1926, the PNF was defined as a "militia at the service of the nation";

this definition disappeared in the 1929 statute, and no mention of the
nation was made. In the 1932 statute, the party was a militia serving the
Fascist state. We know from evidence provided by PNF deputy secretary
Vincenzo Zangara that Mussolini himself substituted "Fascist state" for
"Fascist nation," as was originally written in the first draft.[7] Something
similar happened in the "catechisms" of the Fascist doctrine. In the
Primo libro del fascista (*The Fascist's Primer*), published by the PNF in 1938,
the "Fascist fatherland" is mentioned and the nation is referred to several times. However, there is no section devoted to the definition of "nation," although it is mentioned in the *Carta del Lavoro* under corporative
state. In the 1939 edition, there is a whole section on the "defense of the
race," a theme treated at length in the *Secondo libro del fascista* (*The Fascist's
Second Book*), published in 1939[8] with a paragraph on *La nazione e la razza*
(*The Nation and the Race*).

The idea of nation worked out during World War I by Giovanni
Gentile was a decisive factor in determining the relationship between
the Fascist state and the nation. Gentile's concept of nation rejected any
naturalistic and deterministic interpretation. The philosopher affirmed
in 1919 that to create a nation it was not sufficient to have the elements
usually considered necessary to make the building blocks, that is, a common land, language, political experience and "a collection of memories, traditions and customs in which a population sees itself reflected in
a common past and where it can always find itself . . . or the link that
brings together the individuals of a community in a strongly compact
union, considering the population's faith an apostolic mission." According to Gentile, the decisive factor was a population's conscious desire
and will to become a nation. Gentile postulated the nation not as a
datum but as the perpetual realization of the population's collective will,
conceived in the Mazzini fashion, not as an existing reality, but as a human reality to create. Like the nation, the state was also a continuous
process of forces, evolving historically, according to Gentile.[9] Thus Gentile theorized that the state, nation and individual came together in a
trinitarian-like unity with strong mystical connotations, in which the
state was assigned the function of the nation's prime creator. Unless the
individual fused mystically with the nation and state, he would be like a
living creature without air: "My aspiration is the state's," because if that
were not so "I would feel the ground fall out from under me." The state
is the condition of "life in common," in which the individual is born,
lives and works. Not to recognize the "spiritual substance" of the state
and nation is to sever the "intimate tie that joins and fuses me with this

great aspiration, that is Italy's aspiration."[10] Nationality was not to be considered abstractly, as a "presumed, de facto, natural or historic community and as such "existing before political rights," but, rather, as an existing "dynamic reality that is achieved by virtue of a population's common conscience when the population does not presume but acts to create the common substance of its conscience." A population feels it is a nation "not only in the fantasy of its poets or the memories or hopes of its writers but also, above all, in its desire to be industrious and efficient, so as to show the world what it is worth."[11] Therefore, Gentile clearly perceived the Fascist concept of the nation as "spiritual energy," which was in total opposition to the nationalist movement's concept, because in his opinion, the latter postulated the nation's existence naturalistically, as a reality in itself, and independently of man's conscience and will.[12]

In substance, according to Gentile, awareness of the nation as a spiritual reality and efficacious will, without any sign of objectivistic, sociological or anthropological influence, derived from a synthesis between cultural nationalism and political nationalism where the latter, as the expression of conscience and will turned into effective action, leaves the final mark. For the idealist philosopher, the supremacy of the spirit was also achieved by means of the realism of force. In other words, the nation also acquired conscience and the will to demand respect through the violence of action squads. In the philosopher's opinion, Fascism was the incarnation of the new Italy's conscience that rose out of the war, particularly thanks to the charismatic personality of the Duce; not only did he possess the mystical sense of nation as a community of faithful and willing followers, but he was also capable of turning the nation's mysticism into reality so as to dominate the collective lives of the Italians.

From this idea of nation came the Fascist idea of state, which contrasted with the nationalist movement's concept because, according to Gentile, it founded the state on the nation, taken to be the "entity that transcends the will and personality of the individual, as it is conceived to exist objectively, and has nothing to do with people's consciences; it exists even if people do not work to make it exist or to create it. The nationalists' nation was something that existed not by virtue of the spirit but as a given fact of nature." This naturalist premise was what made the nationalist movement's concept defective and gave its doctrine, according to Gentile, "everything that was harsh, unliberal, backward and crudely conservative," which it had contained "before it was assimilated and amalgamated into Fascism." The Fascist state, "unlike the nationalist one, is a wholly spiritual creation. And it is the national state, because the nation itself is achieved in the spirit; it is not a premise, according to Fascism. The nation is never made, nor is the state, which is the nation itself in its concrete political form. The state is always in the making. Everything is in our hands." It is "put into effect in the individual's conscience and will; it is not a force imposed from above; it cannot have the same relationship with the masses that was postulated by nationalism."

Gentile intensified his criticism of naturalistic nationalism by referring explicitly to the relationship between the state and the nation so as to denounce its conservative nature, which prevented it from establishing a link with the masses. By "combining state and nation, and making the combination an already existing entity that did not need to be created but only recognized, nationalism required an intellectually inclined ruling class, capable of feeling sentiment for this entity, which first needed to be recognized, understood, appreciated and exalted."[13]

Gentile defined the Fascist state as a spiritual, religious, ethical and democratic entity, applying his own personal interpretation of Mazzini's philosophy. In Fascism he saw the descendent of Mazzini's political theology, the idealistic nationalism that could accomplish the work of the "Risorgimento's prophet" and, by means of the totalitarian state, create the new Italian nation and regenerate the character of the Italians from flaws resulting from centuries of servitude, hedonistic materialism and egoistical and skeptical individualism. According to Gentile, these flaws had also dominated the liberal state's moral and political life up to World War I.

Despite lengthy discussions regarding the faithfulness of Gentile's proposed interpretation of Mazzini's philosophy, it is undeniable that some of Mazzini's ideas greatly influenced the development of Fascist nationalism, and not only through Gentile. The religious concept of politics, the pedagogical and regenerating functions of actions taken to structure the population as religious communities, the Messianic and universalist conception of the Italian revolution, and the myth of the Risorgimento as an unaccomplished spiritual revolution were all clearly Mazzini's ideas that went into creating the Fascist national myth, although they had been filtered through a Mazzini-type set of myths and a *mentality* that did not identify with Mazzini's republican tradition and yet formed one of the most influential movements of Italian political culture after unification. For this very reason, perhaps, it spread far and wide, permeating different cultures, ideologies and movements up to World War I when it spilled into the cult of belligerence and interventionist syndicalism's revolutionary nationalism, the cult of boldness, political futurism, the cult of the masses, and eventually Fascism.

Gentile's concept of nation as the foundation of Fascist nationalism was formally consecrated when the Fascist doctrine was published in the *Enciclopedia italiana*. It was written, in part, by Gentile and signed by Mussolini. In the dogmatic manner of those revealing an undisputed religious truth, it stated that, in the Fascist concept, it was not the nation that created the state but the state that created the nation. The nation was not determined by "race or geographical region, but by the historical continuation of its lineage, multitudes united by an idea, that is, the will to exist and be powerful: awareness of self as a being" that "occurs in the conscience and will of a chosen few, or actually a chosen One, whose ideal tends to realize itself in the conscience and aspiration of everyone." This higher being "is actually the nation," but only "in that it is the state," explained the philosopher, because it is not the "nation that generates the state, according to the obsolete naturalist concept that formed the basis for the national state's political legitimacy in the nineteenth century," but the "nation is created by the state," in the sense that the state "gives the people, aware of their own moral unity, the will to exist and, therefore, effective existence." In this way, the philosopher substantially modified the connection between nationality as cultural awareness and the national state typical of romantic and Risorgimento nationalism. In the definition of nation as a "spiritual entity," conscious and active in establishing itself before the other nations, Gentile highlighted the political will factor that is realized in the state, with respect to the cultural nationality factor, and stated that a nation's right to independence "was derived not so much from a literary and ideal awareness of self, and even less from a situation of ignorance and passiveness, but from an active conscience, from political will *in fieri*, and ready to prove its own right: that is, from a sort of state *in fieri*. In fact, the state, seen as the universal ethical will, is the creator of that right" and the nation "as the state, is an ethical reality that exists and survives because it evolves. If it stops it will die."[14]

The idealistic view of the nation as the perennial creation of the state in its perpetual *making* of the national conscience, through the mystical identification of the individual with the state, was basically taken on as its own by the Fascist culture, albeit with distinctions, specifications and differences, despite statements to the contrary by anti-idealist Fascist groups and, particularly, by Catholics who rejected the immanentist idea of nation or the idea of consecrating the myth of the nation as a new secular religion of state.[15] Under the entry "Fascism" written by Mussolini, the Duce reiterated Gentile's concept of the Fascist state, using more political jargon and simpler formulas:

The cornerstone of the Fascist doctrine is the concept of state. For Fascism, the state is absolute, before which individuals and groups are relative. Individuals and groups are "to be considered" in that they are within the state. . . . The state educates the citizens in civil virtues; makes them aware of their mission; calls on them to unite; harmonizes their interest in justice; hands down conceptual discoveries in the sciences, the arts, law, human solidarity; takes men from the primitive life of the tribe to the highest human expression of power, that is, the empire.

The supremacy of the state with respect to the nation was a dogma of the Fascist religion. It was asserted and preached in the most authoritative and frequently quoted doctrinal texts and spread in simple catechistical form by the official propaganda of the Fascist party. Julius Evola, who was anti-Gentile, compared the Nazi concept of state, viewed as a "secondary element" with respect to the *volk*, to the superior value of the Fascist concept because it established that the "state made the people, the national racial community, and the nation."[16] Carlo Costamagna, a jurist who did not belong to the Gentile school, officially confirmed the idealistic concept of nation under the entries *Stato* and *Nazione* written for the *Dizionario di politica* (Dictionary of Politics), published by the Fascist Party in 1940: "For totalitarian doctrine, therefore, the nation is a human group aware of its historic mission; it has its own supra-individual aim to unite, which has taken shape in a given political system, and defends and develops its own identity in space and time through a process that is expressed as the desire for power in a state."[17] In this concept, patriotism itself is defined not in the sentimental terms of filial love but as the expression of a historic identity that has built up over time due to the efforts of political will, that is, of the state.[18] The founding principle and legitimacy of the state are not determined by nationality but "a nationality is determined and achieved in a state and for a state," explained Costamagna. The only sure element by which a nationality can be recognized is its subjective nature, which is the same as saying that it is the very sentiment of nationality that is important, only as the aspiration to realize itself in a state."

The *Dizionario di politica* upheld entirely the concept of state as the creator of the nation, even if this concept did not go so far as to deny the possibility that the nation could exist without the state. A nation can exist as a cultural unit even without the state, but "it cannot be accomplished entirely unless the conscious desire to do so permeates the whole population and is integrated into the whole community, and only a political will, which exercises the power to command, can accelerate and complete this integration process," according to the renowned philologist, Antonino Pagliaro, who was the leading ideologist and editor of the Fascist Party's political dictionary. He defined this "internal integration" as being the "creation of a national totalitarian conscience. This is an equally active and vital aspect of the nation" when it comes under the pressure of "strong political will during the integration process. Once this political will emerges throughout the nation, which has become a single spiritual bloc, you have a totalitarian state, the idealistically perfect state." The state, thus conceived, is the individual's perpetual integration factor, carrying out "ever so deeply and totally throughout the community" the creation of a social relationship that ties the individual to the nation and exercising an "integral function in the community's life because that awakens, sustains and enhances the resources and the individual's will in all sectors of his life. In this way he can become a vital and long-lasting part of the nation, within that spiritual solidarity that combines and increases the spiritual physiognomy of a community and, in time, makes up its history." Therefore, Pagliaro also thought that "a given state creates a given nation by taking action on the nation."[19]

An Anthropological Revolution

Fascism based the legitimacy of its power on this conception of the totalitarian state and no longer on the myth of the nation, as it had done during the restoration phase. It now based it on the revolutionary and pedagogical function of the party-state, claiming that its mission was to create a nation of "new Italians," the Fascist nation. According to totalitarian Fascism, the concept of the state, creator of the nation, was realized in the plan to completely Fascistize consciences by regenerating living Italians. Fascism did not believe in the inborn goodness of human beings; on the contrary, it was convinced of their beastlike instincts. But such anthropological pessimism was not so radical as to exclude the possibility of moral improvement through action taken by the state.

In the reality of everyday life, Fascism was convinced that it had before it a population needing to undergo an anthropological revolution. It was necessary to take action in the lives of Italian men and women to turn them into out-and-out Fascists, on the model of the "soldier-citizen," who would be trained to blindly believe in the sacredness of the Fascist state and would be devoted body and soul to it to the point of sacrificing life for it. The Fascist state presented itself to the nation as the regenerator of consciences and character and the forger of bodies and souls according to criteria of spiritual and physical well-being, which in the totalitarian concept of life, were organized as the total devotion of men and citizens, the individual and the masses, classes and categories, to the state. The totalitarian state's pedagogical action, therefore, aimed to achieve individual and collective regeneration in the minds and character of Italian men and women, so as to liberate the Italian people from what remained of mental habits, customs and traditions that had caused an "eclipse of the race" after the glorious Roman, Catholic and Renaissance periods. The totalitarian state entrusted the party to act as the "great educator," to create the Fascist nation and regenerate the Italians by educating them to have faith in and worship the nation and the Fascist state. In 1927 *Il Legionario,* the official publication of the Fascist organization abroad, announced: "Under the regime the nation is born. Fascism creates the custom from which the nation is born, the Fascist nation . . . ; Fascism is creating the custom through which, and by means of which, it is creating the nation."[20] When planning the anthropological revolution in order to create the Fascist nation, the Duce and the party could have rightly declared themselves fervent followers of Gentile, who even before the advent of Fascism had recalled that the "Italian people" dreamed of by the "Risorgimento prophets" like Mazzini "were not the real people they saw around them but the people of the future that the Italians, themselves, were to create. And they would create them by taking up an idea, the idea of a fatherland to conquer."[21]

The party's aim was to identify the nation with Fascism by undertaking to shape and forge the character of men and women according to its own model of a citizen, and it even reached the point of suggesting the creation of a new Italian race that would be born, physically and spiritually, Fascist. This remaking of the Italians actually introduced a new discriminatory element in the principle of citizenship between Fascist Italians and non-Fascist Italians. Not only was the "denationalization" of anti-Fascists introduced but, indeed, only Fascist Party members were allowed to enjoy exercising what we might call full citizenship in the new totalitarian state. The state, in fact, recognized civil and political prerogatives only for those who belonged to the Fascist Party and denied them for those who did not. In this regard, it must be remembered that being expelled from the Fascist Party, which meant being banned from political and public life, was equivalent to losing full citizenship. An example of the practical consequences originating from the identification of Fascism with the nation was a memorandum circulated in

1937 by the Ministry of Internal Affairs, which established that the Fascist Party membership card was to be considered, to all effects, a valid document just like the identification card.

The various stages of the Fascist anthropological revolution consisted in the campaign to reform customs (the antibourgeois crusade) and above all, the adoption of racism and anti-Semitism as the state's ideology. This led to the systematic discrimination and selection that was to indelibly fix the national identity on the basis of racial criteria, defined in 1938 with the promulgation of provisions for the defense of the Italian race and with the anti-Semitic laws. The nation was then formally identified with the race. Young Fascists were now taught, according to the catechism of the *Secondo libro del fascista*, that the nation "is made up of all the individuals of the same race. . . . The population is the nation when it is compact in spirit and blood"; with racism, love for one's country becomes, first of all, "an act of loyalty to the race, because anyone who really loves his own country will want the lineage to remain pure in spirit and blood."[22]

The introduction of racism into the Fascist state's ideology was not improvised suddenly, owing to the exigencies of the alliance with Nazi Germany, but was the result of a process to develop a national identity in exclusively Fascist terms. Because of Fascism's propensity to identify ideology with anthropology, that identity could not but end up in racism, particularly after the conquests of the empire. Certainly, Mussolini's obsession with the "remaking" of the Italians' character influenced this outcome. The Duce was fanatically convinced it was his mission to "remake the Italians,"[23] as he said soon after he came to power, and his greatest ambition was to transform the Italians into modern-day Romans, capable of challenging the times by creating a New Civilization. He once said, "If I can, and if Fascism is able to mould the character of the Italians as I would like, you can be certain that when the wheel of destiny goes by our outstretched hands, we will be ready to grab hold of it and bend it to our will."[24]

Mussolini had taken the myth of regenerating the Italian race literally, saying in 1923, "we want to take, mould, forge the Italians for all the battles necessary in discipline, work and religious faith." And he devoted himself to the task with maniacal tenacity.[25] In 1926 he claimed, "Fascism has remade the character of the Italians, scraping all the impurities from our souls."[26] In fact, the regeneration was far from being achieved, and Mussolini was tormented by the fact that the Italians had a long way to go before they were close to his ideal of the "new Italian," and

this troubled him more than any other totalitarian project he cultivated in his imagination as a revolutionary leader in power. Again in
1930, he mentioned the same problem when he acknowledged that the
character-remaking process had not yet achieved the expected results:

> We must scrape clean and pulverize the sediments deposited in the
> character and mentality of the Italians by those terrible centuries
> of political, military and moral decadence that range from 1600 to
> the rise of Napoleon. It is a grandiose undertaking. The Risorgi-
> mento was just the beginning, because it was the work of too small
> a minority; the World War, instead, was profoundly educational. It
> is a matter of continuing, day by day, this work of remaking the
> character of the Italians.[27]

The Duce's assessment of the Italians directed his attention toward
the problem of the nation and the totalitarian state's tasks. Like all modern revolutionary figures, he scorned real-life human beings and wanted
to model them according to an ideal "new man." He was convinced
that only the discipline of "heroic pedagogy" could radically transform
character, habit, mentality and sentiment. The Fascist revolutionary
mentality, while proclaiming itself realistic and anti-utopian, always aspired to launching itself in new "assaults on history," as it did in 1915,
depicting future scenarios of unprecedented challenges to power and
civilization, which could only be faced and won by a nation of new Italians, forged according to the Fascist model of the citizen-soldier, devoted body and soul to the cult of state as were the ancient Romans.
Mussolini scorned the real-life Italian, considering him inferior to his
ideal model. Giuseppe Bottai observed, "His antagonist is this population whose history he would like to revise, to remake it his way." As a follower of Nietzsche, the Duce maintained that the Church had "soft-
ened the population, emasculated it, taken away the taste for effective
domination and disarmed it."[28] He accused the Italians of using resistance against "thinking 'big.'"[29] When he gave vent to his personal feelings, his antagonism toward the Italians bordered on a delirious sense of
frustrated personal ambition, taken for, or confused with, passionate
love for the nation:

> No one, I hope, will deny or try to belittle the passion for this Italy
> that I have forged, much of it in my imagination, but much more
> in reality. I am beginning to feel something new that upsets me;
> what is true, painfully true, and what explains my inner sadness, is
> that I am led to establish a clear distinction between Italy and the

Italians. The Italians are proving unworthy of Italy, or naturally, of my Italy.[30]

During World War II, Mussolini increased the remarks he made about the Italians being unworthy of "his" Italy. As far as the Duce was concerned, participation in the war was part of the plan to "remake" the Italian race because such trials were necessary to forge a population of warriors and dominators. He said many times over: "It is a good thing for the Italian people to have to undergo trials that wake them up from centuries of mental laziness by keeping them in uniform from morning to night. And they need the stick, the stick, the stick."[31] Galeazzo Ciano confided to Bottai soon after Italy entered the war that Mussolini "experienced this war in a state of metaphysical exaltation, as if his aim was to harden the Italians with fatigue and sacrifice."[32] As the war progressed, his collaborators noticed the Duce's increasing aversion to the Italians. Bottai wrote in his notes on January 1, 1941: "He keeps on repeating that the reason for his inner torment, which keeps surfacing, is his disappointment in the 'character' of the Italians. . . . 'You cannot overcome, all of a sudden, centuries of political servitude, not even with a revolution.' And he confirmed his intention to set store by this experience 'later on.'"[33] The more military setbacks the regime experienced, the more Mussolini sharpened his accusations against the Italians, with the same anger as an artist who thought himself a great genius but blamed his failures on the materials he worked with. He would say, "It is the matter I'm lacking. Even Michaelangelo needed marble for his statues. If he had had only clay, he would have been just a potter."[34] It never crossed his mind that the sculptor would have been crazy to hit clay with a hammer, as if it were marble. Therefore, he continued to blame the Italians for the setbacks that the regime suffered on the battlefield. "A people that has been the anvil for sixteen centuries cannot become the hammer."[35] At the beginning of 1943, as the total defeat of Fascist Italy became evident, Bottai recorded yet again Mussolini's "polemical refrain against the Italians, their deficiencies, their defects." It was an obsession. "This is where the hereditary defects of the race that were not remediable in twenty years are revealed."[36] He was angry, above all, with the "cowardly" bourgeois and exasperated to the point of imagining an extermination program. As Mussolini said to Galeazzo Ciano in August 1940, "Save more or less 20 percent of them. . . . No, I think I'll get them all and then I'll say what Domenico di Guzmàn said: God will choose his own."[37]

Worshipping the Divine Fascist Nation

In keeping with the cultural premises of their ideology, which established the supremacy of the myth in modern mass politics, the Fascists
assigned a fundamental role to religion, as a system of beliefs, myths
and collective rites, in order to achieve the moral unity of the totalitarian state and instill in the Italians a religious sentiment of total devotion
to the nation and the state.[38] Fascism wanted to have the vigor and function of a religion. It wanted to be a modern form of political mysticism
in the spiritual fusion of the citizen with the nation and state. The Fascist idea of nation, as the mystical union of society and state, was itself
of a religious nature, as Costamagna maintained. The national idea was
an "irrational element, intellectual and moral communion, which ends
in an environment created by political force but develops into a supreme
declaration of love" and "becomes fully aware of itself when facing the
differences with other nations and puts itself forth as the common soul
of the nation, in other words the nation itself, with a common will and
transcendent interest that is a common asset."[39] In this way the nation,
together with the Fascist state, was sacralized and even glorified. The
"nation is divine," proclaimed the idealist Balbino Giuliano.[40]

The ideal model of the Fascist state's national community was the
Roman civilization, held up, in Fascism's symbolic transfiguration, as
the mythical archetype of the new "Fascist civilization."

> Rome—Mussolini had stated starting in 1922—is our point of de-
> parture and reference; it is our symbol, or if you want, our myth.
> We dream of a Roman Italy that is wise and strong, disciplined and
> imperialist. Much of what was the immortal spirit of Rome is re-
> born in Fascism. . . . Now, the history of tomorrow, the history that
> we want to create so diligently, must not be in conflict with, or a
> parody of, the history of yesterday. Not only were the Romans sol-
> diers but also excellent builders who could challenge, as they did
> challenge, time.[41]

Gentile pointed to modern Japan as another model of political mysticism of the nation and state, which he considered similar to the one Fascism dreamt of. It was not mythical like the Roman one, but it actually
existed—it was real and efficient. It was a national state that had been
modernized by an authoritarian system so as to be considered a great
power. It had assimilated the science, technology and productive organization of the Western world, while fully preserving its own religious
tradition, Shintoism, which was the source of spiritual energy and the

strength of national mystical cohesion. Thus it combined the divine with the human in the cult of fatherland, the Emperor, the great fore-fathers and great heroes.

The philosopher was passionately intent on combining and integrating the Catholic religious traditions into the Fascist religion to educate the Italians in the mystical sense of nation and state. He believed he saw affinity between Shintoism and Catholicism, which could encourage the creation of a modern Fascist political mysticism.

> The Japanese spirit also lives on in that unification of the divine and the human, which is the fundamental dogma of the Church; a dogma that encourages in man the hope of doing God's will and acting, therefore, with divine power, creator of the higher life of the spirit. Creator, first of all, for the Japanese, of the sacred reality of the country in its immortal unification of the living and dead. And, perhaps, the resistance originates from the similitude of principle, which is what makes up the strength of the Japanese spirit and bestows upon it an unshakable faith in its mission.[42]

In this way, Fascism came to "glorify the nation" by means of the sacralization of the national myth, wrote *La Civiltà Cattolica*,[43] which was seriously worried about Fascist totalitarianism and its claim to be a political religion.[44] Fascism's sacralization of the nation was consistent with its totalitarian concept of politics founded on the principle "that the individual cannot exist except as a citizen of a state and part of a whole, the necessities of which must be obeyed. Humanity has no importance or significance outside the nation, and each is a separate interpretation of the existential problems. The national community, being a state-population, has a greater value than any other association and constitutes the compendium of all terrestrial and temporal values."[45]

The Fascist nation was to be, first of all, a community of believers, and to create this community, Fascism consciously glorified the nation and consecrated the totalitarian state, conceived as the highest expression of human spirituality, in its myths, rites and symbols. "The Fascist state cannot but be conceived, believed in, served and glorified religiously," because Fascism "makes the nation-state the most glorious Kingdom of God on earth," preached the Fascist ideologist Paolo Orano.[46]

10

A New Imperial Civilization

From Nation to Empire

The Fascists believed that the mysticism of nation, attained through a totalitarian state, was the highest and most modern form of nationalism. However, they also believed that the problem of nation would not be resolved by building a totalitarian state and creating a "new Italian," with the single aim of exalting and increasing the might of a nation in order to make territorial conquests. Right from the beginning, as we have seen, Fascism wanted to be clearly separate from the nationalist movement and the different kinds of nationalism of other countries, because it believed that their ideology of nation was entirely limited to domination and territorial expansion. *Critica fascista* maintained that, on the contrary, the Fascists did not want to limit their own ambitions "to the narrow confines of the nation. We believe that the nation is the necessary first step, the starting point for expansion, and expansion means not so much territorial conquest as, above all, spiritual and political conquest."[1]

In 1931 a young historian, Delio Cantimori, wrote that Fascism was a revolution that had nothing in common with the reactionary and conservative nationalism of the pseudo-Fascist movements: "National sentiment, an awareness of nation and state, are one thing, a nationalist myth is another." "Creating a national conscience is one of the main aims of Fascist action," but a Fascist's awareness of nation "has nothing to do with the fanaticism of the 'Camelot du roi.'" Fascism was not identified or concluded with nationalism because it had the universal, revolutionary vocation "of a new Revolution, which will put an end to modern, materialistic plutocratism," because "a modern revolution, a people's revolution, a real revolution means a universal, European revolution."[2]

The Fascists considered a national dimension too limited to contain the farthest horizon of their revolutionary ambitions, which transcended

the reality of nation, rising to contemplate vast panoramas, both European and worldwide, toward which they could launch the future conquests of the "Fascist revolution," thus reaching the point of questioning the "principle of nation." In 1927 Camillo Pellizzi, a leading Fascist
intellectual, wrote, "It's a matter of establishing if and how the principle
of nation must be one of the inspiring and motivating principles of Fascism. I say it is not. . . . My theory is that the principle of nationality is
based on a myth or empirical pseudo-concept of fortuitous value. . . .
From Fascism on, we must not act for the nation, rather from the nation
toward the Fascist ideal of state and empire."[3]

In Fascism the myth of empire as a center that spread universal civilization was not concocted by the propaganda related to the conquest
of Ethiopia but had been present since the beginnings of the movement. This emerged more clearly, not only through colonialism, but
above all, through extolling the revolutionary function of Fascism as
a universal, not exclusively Italian, movement that aspired not only to
territorial expansion but to shedding the light of a New Civilization
throughout the world. "We believe in the political absolute, which is
the empire," declared Berto Ricci, an ideologist of "universal fascism":
"Therefore we shall be universal and oppose any vestiges of nationalism, we shall be modern and without idols. . . . It is up to our century to
make Italians think in terms of vastness again, to make them love, dare
and dominate ages and nations."[4] According to *Il Legionario*, the periodical of Fasci Italiani all'Estero (Italian Fascists Abroad), the regime's organization that up to the beginning of the 1930s had carried out a plan
to spread Fascism through imperialism, there was a well-known rule
that a nation could exist and be great only if it carried out a civilizing
mission.[5] Both "great" and "small nations" were subject to this rule, but
the historical responsibility of an "infinitely superior task to that of small
nations" was above all up to the "great nations," which "cannot live for
themselves but must follow a natural law and spread their civilization all
over the world. They must spread in time and space with a special responsibility they must not abandon, otherwise they will decline. Some
peoples rise and others die; some peoples fall into decline and others are
reborn: this is the most profound explanation of wars and, ultimately, of
history itself."[6]

Fascist culture avoided giving this "rule" on the destiny of nations an
interpretation following the positivist principles of social Darwinism,
which considered nations on a level with big animals in a perpetual and
unchangeable struggle for the survival of the fittest, but justifying it for

the sake of the civilizing mission that the "great nations" had to carry out. In 1931 Gentile explained that the aspiration to empire was the logical development of a nation, as it was "new spiritual strength," fulfilling a desire for might that sprang from the very essence of a nation's spirituality when it became aware of itself and made its worth known before other nations. A nation "can only keep itself alive if it actively builds new empires, or ever more suitable forms for the whole, necessary development of the original principle of national autonomy, which means asserting itself through willpower and developing a new personality."[7] Postulating an imperial destiny for the nation, Gentile also openly kept his distance from Mazzini's nationalism, which he reproached for stopping at unity and independence, and beyond it saw only "a federation of peoples and abstract humanity that united peoples, similar to the ideas of the French humanitarians." Mazzini's nationalism longed for "peoples to live together peacefully," although it conflicted with his concept of the "spiritual life as a struggle sanctified by martyrdom." Gentile explained that Fascism "arose from an experience that clashed with Mazzini's eschatological vision," because it wants an Italy determined to assert itself "in the field of international competition, where the strength and vitality of nations are put to the test," also through wars of conquest, because "living means to develop, make progress, spread and move forward." In short, "Italy today, our Italy, is clearly no longer the same as the Risorgimento one,"[8] the idealist philosopher who had become a champion of imperialism declared in 1936:

> We also must move on the level of empire. We must not refine sterile boasts and tediously exaggerate magnificent traditions. Comrades, there is the imperialism of rhetoricians and that of peoples. We are for the second kind of imperialism, and we also want to work for the future of this formerly humble Italy, which has now risen to the level of a really great power thanks to Mussolini's Italians. However, Italy must continue to rise, as otherwise it would begin to decline as before.[9]

Precisely by claiming that the vocation of its nationalism was universalistic, Fascism had ambitions to take its place on a level of epochmaking superiority compared to other kinds of European nationalism, presenting itself both as a national and universal revolution, which had nothing in common with the reactionary and conservative nationalism of the various pseudo-Fascist movements that abounded in Europe. Referring to Mazzini's basic inspiration, Delio Cantimori explained that

Fascism assigned a universal function to its national revolution. "The best men of the Risorgimento were aware of its important European dimension, linking up with the revolutionary movement of the city-states that culminated in the culture of the Renaissance, which began modern European civilization: Fascism carries on and renews this action, and that is why it is revolutionary."[10]

In contrast to other kinds of European nationalism, which were still linked to the nineteenth-century principles of imperialism as a pure manifestation of material might, domination and enslavement, Fascism regarded its nationalism as universalist because it looked beyond national egoism. Therefore, *Gerarchia* declared in 1934, it was different from French nationalism, which disguised the *manie de grandeur* and the ambitions of a nation aimed only at asserting the materialistic power of liberal capitalism as egalitarian universalism.[11] And Fascist nationalism was also different from Germanic nationalism, which it considered "adventurous," and dominated by an "expansive, belligerent and conquering" obsession, imbued with pagan, anti-Roman memories. It was certainly animated by a dynamic impulse in the National Socialist version but dynamic only "in a material sense, that is, with a tendency to transfer masses from one territory to another; in a biological sense, that is, by eliminating and excluding so-called 'non-Aryans' from civil life itself in the German world; in a Messianic sense, that is, tending to religious inspiration and justification of the conquests; and in a physical sense, that is, having the incentive of strength and giving it priority over all other considerations of a higher nature."[12]

The Fascist myth of nation was universalist, declared Carlo Curcio, one of the most devoted Fascist scholars of the problem of nation, because it was not conceived exclusively as an "absolute and single coincidence of nature and nation, of state and economic interests, of borders and political interests" but "as the intrinsic expansive vitality of a civilization, as the dynamic (and therefore containing universal motives), diffusive capacity of a race that is intensely aware of its own universality, . . . as the superior, sublime, moral and political expansion of a civilization." As such, Fascism was the forerunner of a new and modern nationalism, of "true nationalism," which consists "in seeing the nation not as an independent part, detached from and opposed to other nations but as the central part of a system, as an element of an organization that is above all spiritual and therefore civilized," which transcends the limits of nationalism and traditional imperialism. "The active nationalism of some peoples, despite the different beginnings of each one

(Italy, Germany and Japan), bears witness to the vitality and universality of this nationalist concept," because these peoples, "although on the whole they do not reject the nationalist principle .·. . nevertheless raise their nationalism to a higher level. That is, they become centers, the driving force and soul of an ideal and political system that, though not limiting or weakening other nationalities, aims at giving a unitary, spiritual organization, in the context of a new civilization, to aggregations of peoples that otherwise would be destined to catastrophe and decline."[13]

Fascism claimed the supremacy of its universalist nationalism even toward these imperialist peoples, showing the historical credentials of a race that had already produced eternal monuments of universal civilization—Roman history, traditions and customs, Roman Catholicism, Humanism and the Renaissance—impressing its indelible mark on what was still vital and eternal in European civilization. "The Italian's country and nation is the foundation, the solid platform that should be increasingly strengthened, of its civilizing action, which aims at the world as well. The Italian is a patriot and nationalist with a universal function."[14]

Toward the End of the Age of Nation

The mysticism of a nation-state, a desire for imperialist might and universal revolution: these made up Fascist nationalism in its imperial phase. Well into the thirties, Fascism aimed more and more at reaching beyond the concept of a national state as a historical, political and moral unit closed in its shell to the idea of an imperial community, bearer of a "New Civilization." The tendency to transcend the myth of nation to reach the myth of imperial civilization with a universal function dominated the debate, which grew heated after the conquest of the empire. The problem of nation was seen not only in relation to the problem of state but even more in relation to the problems of foreign policy, which influenced the greater attention given to the meaning and role of the nation in European and world history. The prospect was that of a "crisis of civilization," as the Fascists believed that the cycle of democratic revolutions started off by the French Revolution was coming to an end and the way was open to creating a New Civilization of totalitarian states modeled on the Fascist state, organized according to the values, principles, institutions and lifestyle of Fascist civilization.[15]

The idea of going beyond the principle of nationality and a national state when building a "New Europe" had been developed further after

1936 by the representatives of Fascist political culture, especially by the younger ones, taking into consideration not only the problem of the new balance of power that was to regulate the reconstruction of Europe but also the need to favor the supremacy of ideology over nation, the myth of social revolution over the myths of Irredentism and colonial expansionism.

During the imperialist phase of Fascist nationalism, and especially at the beginning of the Second World War, the problem of nation and national state became less important, so to speak, in the painstaking elaboration of the future imperial community, the "vital space," the "great space," of the New Order, New Europe and the New Civilization. The subject of nation merged with that of the "New Order" in an increasingly intricate tangle of issues that involved the two allies of the Axis in all aspects of interior and foreign policy, economy and culture, historical traditions, religions and political ideologies. "The problem of nationalities should clearly be incorporated in a higher concept that can only be that of a 'European civilization' to be rebuilt and reorganized," stated Costamagna at the end of the thirties. "By now the problem of nationalities is giving way everywhere to the problem of empire, in the ideal and European meaning of the word," against "morbid" universalizations of past and present radical demagogy, in favor of foreign peoples and civilizations."[16]

In the early years of the Second World War, when victory still seemed attainable by the Axis, the Fascists treated the problem of nation above all with the prospect of building a New Europe,[17] following criteria that most of the Fascists thought would involve definitively abandoning the principle of nationality by denying equal rights for all the nations that had set up or aspired to set up a national state. At the beginning of the thirties, the historian Walter Maturi had already perceived the symptoms of a declining principle of nationality: "Faced with the emergence of non-European nationalities, most present-day Europeans feel more European than integral nationalists. However, whether the concept of Europe is logically reduced or that of nationality extended, the European concept of nationality as it was perceived in the nineteenth century is going to suffer a profound crisis."[18]

The conflict between the principles of nationality and imperialism that had led to the First World War had been resolved only precariously, with the apparent triumph of the principle of nationality. The attempt of the League of Nations to build a universal construction of Europe and the world—an attempt that the historian Ernesto Sestan described as "generous as a generically humanitarian and pacifist aspiration, but poorly conceived and weakly and insincerely carried out"—had failed, because the League of Nations had soon become an instrument "to pre- serve the political order that was the outcome of the Versailles peace treaty" to the exclusive advantage of its main beneficiaries, France and England. The League of Nations, "a church without religious inspira- tion, cannot stop history, or fossilize a political situation, which expresses a transient relation between powers." The principle of nationality, pres- aging new and more serious conflicts, gave way before a conflict that was not only a contrast among national states but also a challenge be- tween the new totalitarian states, the expression of peoples on the rise with Fascism as the forerunner, and democratic states, which expressed the conservative old order of the age of nationalities. In the challenge of the totalitarian states, Sestan saw not so much a conflict of different types of nationalism as a struggle between "revolution and conserva- tism; between old and new Europe," and he wondered if the stakes were not the contrasting interests of national states but, rather, the destiny of Europe itself.

> Totalitarianism is perhaps the contingent institutional structure thanks to which peoples full of vigor and the fervor of determina- tion, urged on by a supreme strength of will, aim at setting up an order that conforms more to their vital potentiality, their sense of justice; it is a matter of building a different balance of power among European nations, or it is a new but not different thread to weave into the old plot that the history of Europe has toiled over since the rise of national states. This history of Europe has really reached a crucial point, [because] it is ever more evident that Europe, until recently the mistress of the world, has reduced the capacity of its vital breath, resigned to living increasingly within itself and count- ing only on its own strength, on its limited territory. Has the time come for peaceful decline, which some great European nations seem resigned to, covering their retreat with the specious pretext of having carried out their civilizing mission? Or rather, are the young and strong nations, which are about to claim their place in the sun, consciously or not taking up the vocation of this Europe that has had a thousand lives and that does not believe the time has arrived to lower its rightfully glorious flag?[19]

The Hierarchy of the New Europe's Nations

As long as World War II lasted, the search for answers to these questions dominated the debate among the various groups of Fascist political cul- ture on the nation's role in the new imperial age, on the universal mission of the Fascist revolution in rebuilding a New Europe and in carrying out the New Order. During the war, there were frequent attempts to work out a concept of the New Europe, which hinged on the idea of Italian supremacy in building the New Civilization, pointing out the way to go beyond traditional nationalism and the concept of a national state itself to reach a supranational dimension. The New Europe would no longer be founded on the principle of nationality but on a hierarchy of peoples, subdivided into the new imperial aggregations of the "great nations," around which the minor nations would gravitate, integrated according to a criterion of racial affinity. In the often conflicting varieties of opinions and prospects, the common belief prevailed that the age of nationalities had by then come to an end and that the nationalism of the "great nations" itself now had to develop on a continental scale: "By now Europe has accomplished the nationalist phase of its spiritual and historical development. The Roman idea of empire has regained its prestige and political function, because it now seems clear that the stable points of united societies and of the convergences of minds and material interests of peoples can only be established in the sphere of some imperial groupings." This was not intended to deny the idea of nation or consider it outdated, "because the Italian nation will always be the soul and physical foundation of the Italian empire, as Rome was of the Roman Empire"; nevertheless, the destiny of the smaller nations, those unable to rise to the level of imperial powers, would be to sink to the rank of satellites in the orbit of the "great nations." There "all the medium and minor nations that cannot aspire to their own political expansion will have to live and develop within the confines of the new empires."[20]

Above all between 1941 and 1942, Fascist culture undertook a discussion of the subject of New Europe and the role that nation and nationalism should have in it. At a meeting on the idea of Europe, organized by the National Institute of Fascist Culture in November 1942, some saw the approaching or actual end of the age of nation, which began when the medieval Christian community broke up. The president of the Institute, Camillo Pellizzi, developed his own personal concept of how empire went beyond nation. Without denying the valuable contribution that the different kinds of nationalism had made to the development of European civilization, he underscored the antithesis between the myth of nation and the universalism of the Roman tradition. The nation had risen from "a rebellion against Rome, against the universality of the Roman and Mediterranean traditions, . . . which contrasted with the universalist spirit that was, and has always been, the dominating, determining and decisive feature of the Mediterranean contribution to civilization."[21] Others maintained that it was no longer possible "to accept the concept of nation today, in 1942, as it was in 1915, and, therefore, as it was taking shape in the early postwar years," because, speaking of a New Europe, it was necessary to keep in mind that "besides the decadence of a certain relative European supremacy" there was "also the historical crisis of the nation."[22] Some defended the nation for its historical value and significance as well as for the role it had had in the progress of European civilization, and which it should continue to have in a new order that fostered understanding among nations. "After all, nationality is one of the live, guiding forces of the history of Europe," observed one of those taking part in the meeting, and when building the New Europe, this was to be taken into consideration as well.[23]

Echoing the topics discussed at that meeting in an article for *Critica Fascista*, unpublished because the regime had fallen and the periodical closed down, Giuseppe Bottai tried to put some order to a subject that appeared quite confused due to the conflicting and contradictory variety of positions. He picked out the key solution to the problem as going beyond nationalism, seen as a narrow and particularistic concept of nation rather than the nation as an expression of a people's identity, and as defining the new order in social rather than national terms:

> When nation and nationality were discussed, terms were used, to be quite clear, that are dear to those who do not want to give up their own Italian identity, even for a moment. However, these terms, taken traditionally, have no place in a plan for continental reconstruction, which, to be the transposition of the principles under discussion to an international context should move the approach to the problem from its clearly nationalistic content to an essentially social one. European countries were to cooperate and have the common goal of integrating European social forces, with the aim of strengthening rather than belittling the contributions that each people can offer the continental community

To this end, it was necessary for "the basic interests of the peoples, to begin to look for social rather than nationalistic forms as a means of expression," overcoming the prejudice that "national needs contain all the higher values of civilization, while considerations from a social point of view, that is, a direct reference to people singly and en masse, should be based on inferior materialism and nothing else." On the contrary "nationalism, as a political category that persists beyond its time—certainly not as an insuppressible spiritual certainty—at a certain point becomes

an obstacle to overall civil development" and a "phenomenon of political disintegration, after expending its possibility to serve the opposite
purpose," and as such, it had to be eliminated. At the same time, "there
is no harm done in preserving the lofty place, which is its due, in the
sphere of spiritual values, and better still, in giving it the function of
stimulating people to compete with each other." Bottai clearly outlined
what was to be the inspiring principle of the future European order. In
the new order, European countries were to cooperate and have the common goal of integrating European social forces, with the aim of increasing rather than belittling the contributions that each people can offer to
the continental community.[24]

The Duce's periodical also took part in the debate on the future of
the nation, with very explicit declarations. "Will nation still be discussed
or will this concept be considered completely outdated?" *Gerarchia* wondered in 1942.[25] The answer was clear: "If nation means any ethnic
group that is approximately homogeneous and has the legal authority
of a state, the concept of nation is of no relevance." The periodical explained that this did not mean denying the concept of nation, which
was "the very soul of history," but recognizing the right to an autonomous life in the new European order established by the Axis only for the
"Chosen Peoples," for the nations "capable of carrying out a civilizing
mission in history." The *Dizionario di politica* of the PNF (Dictionary of
Politics of the National Fascist Party) pointed out that the problem of
nationalities as regards this future order "should evidently be considered
in relation to a superior concept that can only be seen in that of a 'European civilization,' to be reconstructed and reorganized. . . . By now the
problem of nationalities is giving way everywhere to the problem of empires, in the ideal and European meaning of the word."[26]

The events of the new European war confirmed that this declaration on the destiny of the small nations was valid. Carlo Morandi, the
historian, wrote that this had immediately shown "the intrinsic weakness of the minor national organisms" and "the error of the attempted
policy of neutrality." However, even more, it had revealed "that excessive political divisions were the cause of disorder, an obstacle to creating
a compact and organic continental order." Therefore, in rebuilding a
new Europe, it would be necessary to substitute "the abstract egalitarian
concept of all the states and the imaginary vision of a general, perfect
balance with recognizing that a group made up of the main national
organisms should have a leading, active and responsible function guiding and supporting this 'European union' and intervening decisively to

resolve the most important political problems." However, "to be efficacious and lasting," this balance "cannot be based on a utopian equality
of nations but must spring from acknowledging an insuppressible hierarchy of powers."[27]

The outline of a Fascist plan for a new Europe that could not
be ordered according to the egalitarian principle of national states, all
equally intangible in their sovereignty and integrity, can be deduced
from the various prefigurements of the new continental order. "In the
future Europe, the main issue that will have to be faced is that of state
and nation," says a 1941 book on the future of Europe, where the destiny of the small nations was prefigured within the framework of a new
kind of imperialism, like that of the Axis. "National narrowmindedness
and intolerance will have to be overcome, and the state, becoming more
consolidated and extending its powers, will acquire composite forms, inspired by the criterion of a new kind of imperialism that does not destroy, denationalize and assimilate . . . but that is fairly and firmly hier-
archized." This profound transformation of the European order would,
in any case, ensure that, in the new world balance, Europe preserved
"supremacy in civilization and political initiative; better still, it will be
the first time that Europe is represented in the world not by marginal
nations interested in repressing the great Europe, as has happened up to
recently, but by the Roman influence and Germanism, by Italy and
Germany. They left the mark of their errors on the past with their conflicts, but by cooperating, they will ensure that the continent has the destiny it deserves."[28]

Fascist ideologists believed that the new Europe would be organized
according to a hierarchy of nations, or new "imperial communities,"
founded on the supremacy of the "great nations," around which (although preserving their individuality) the minor nations were to gravitate. They would be integrated in the imperial community following
a political criterion of historical, cultural and racial affinities and an
economic criterion of national self-sufficiency and the dominant nations' need of abundant vital space. Thus democratic principles would
be abolished in international politics as well as in internal politics: the
"falsehood of the sovereignty of many small states will disappear," wrote
Carlo Curcio. "Without offending their national sentiment, language,
religion and customs," the "small states" would be allowed to become
part of "broader systems, dominated by powerful spiritual and material
forces capable of keeping order and impressing real civilization on the
mass of coordinated peoples." These systems would be "great imperial

aggregations . . . hinged on the axis (the word has its logical meaning!) of a power that is such through its strength and civilizing capability."[29]

Fascism believed it could go beyond the traditional imperialism of domination and enslavement with the idea of an imperial community, which small states and nations were to join willingly, rotating in the orbit of a great power that spread the principles of a new civilization. Naturally, the sun of this new system would be Fascist Italy, in virtue of the universalistic vocation of its civilization, which placed it on a higher ideological level than its ally Nazi Germany. In the prospect of Fascist Europeanism, the Nazi ideology based on the principle *Ein Volk, ein Reich, ein Führer* seemed "to have had its day," even to Julius Evola,[30] considered one of the Fascist ideologists closest to Nazism. The Nazi ideology could not be the basis of an imperial community of different peoples, which were to join forces hierarchically, bound by a renewed feudal *fides* according to affinities of aristocratic, spiritual values rather than "the brute percentage" of racial affinities.

At a conference in Vienna in November 1941, Pellizzi explained that Nazi Germany would contribute to building the New Order, above all, with "a material and moral impulse that was more evident and decisive than ours. However, when the present war is crowned with victory, which must be transformed into a peacetime order that means understanding and justice for everyone, the contribution of Mussolini's Italy, both revolutionary and traditionalist, may be even more valuable in the great and new work of building a better world."[31]

In fact, one of the factors that made the whole framework of plans for the New Civilization, New Europe, and New Order very fragile was the confusion between the myths of nation and revolution in defining the aims and nature of Italy's participation in World War II. This ambitious project for the future was created by a totalitarian regime that welcomed the supreme test of a war that was to raise Greater Italy to the status of a great empire. However, this regime was not even capable of preserving, let alone kindling anew, that minimum sense of national identity in the Italians that had been achieved by the liberal regime during the First World War, and this after twenty years of unceasing and all-embracing education to regenerate the Italian character.

11

The Fascist War

Revolution Above All

Italy entered World War II under the banner of a revolutionary war that, after the victory of the Axis, was intended to achieve an imperial Fascist community, a New Europe and a New Order. This is why, as the regime's propaganda explained to Italians, the reasons for intervening were substantially different from those of World War I, which had been waged to endorse the principle of nationality, complete the territorial unification of the nation and definitively confirm Italy's role as a great power. Fascist propaganda explained that after rising to the rank of a great power with the victory in World War I, Italy had become not only an imperial power, with world responsibilities and ambitions, but also for the third time in the centuries-old history of the peninsula, the founder of a New Civilization that went beyond the dimensions of a nation and held itself up as a universal civilization.

Even though there were still traces of the Risorgimento tradition "in claiming Italian territories in French and English hands" among the reasons for Italy's intervention, in fact "the predominating impulse was farther reaching: it saw our future as a great Mediterranean, African and oceanic nation."[1] Consequently, Italy entered the war not only to enlarge the national state and enrich its empire with new territories but also to overturn the old order and contribute to creating a New Order, in which the mark of Fascist civilization would be predominant. After having taken over in Italy, the Fascists now wanted to play a major role in reshaping Europe and the world, thus fulfilling the myth of a Greater Italy that would lead humanity to the year 2000.

Indeed, Italy's reasons for participating in the two world wars were very different, the main difference being that the Fascists wanted Italy's intervention and the war itself to bear a revolutionary and ideological

183

mark. This would play down any nostalgia for the Risorgimento, as they believed that history had gone beyond the age of nationality, which had reached its peak during the Risorgimento. Not only were the ideologists of totalitarian Fascism convinced champions of this ideological justification but so too were authoritative scholars like Carlo Morandi. He was convinced that only "in a very narrow sense" could the new war still be considered a "continuation of the Risorgimento," because "the spirit has drastically changed," to the point that the new spirit "limits and reduces the too frequent appeals to the Risorgimento to sentimental motives and to at least partly rhetorical pretexts, even though they have their patriotic and moral reasons, which are anything but blameworthy." Morandi went on to say that the 1915-18 war had already abandoned "the models of the Risorgimento," due to Mussolini's interventionist initiative as he had chosen war for "its strength as a creative revolution," now reaffirmed when faced with a new conflict. In 1940, the war outlook was profoundly changed by the imperial dimensions of Fascist Italy, by the international scale of the conflict and by the epoch-making scope of the challenge between two different civilizations, which were competing for the future of humanity. Where the Risorgimento had been "the noblest European model for the struggle to free nations," Morandi added, on the contrary, "the new war marked the crises of some smaller countries, among other things, and the need for higher-ranking hierarchies and organized units." Morandi pointed out that Risorgimento values were "unchanged and eternal, and it would be better not to succumb to the over-simplified and automatic idea of 'going beyond' them, so dear to certain superficial historians. However, that age has ended, that political climate offers more contrast than affinities with the present one, more differences than analogies. Let us not prolong indefinitely the historical occasion for Italy to transform itself into a free and unitary organism."[2]

The regime's press eulogized the revolutionary significance of the war in its propaganda, as the war was "first of all and above all a struggle to achieve revolutions that create a new concept of state, the individual and work. Ours is above all a revolution that brings a new, even higher concept of life and history."[3] The Fascist war was not only a struggle to free the last Irredentist lands and to achieve Mediterranean hegemony but was also a real religious crusade, an "alternative civilization," a "real divine judgment," as Gentile called it, "to resolve the dispute between two opposite principles encamped in front of each other with the exasperated certainty of *vita tua mors mea*."[4] And it was propagandized to the

Italians as a war of religion, drawing even more attention to its difference from the preceding conflict. As *Civiltà fascista*, the official periodical of the National Institute of Fascist Culture, explained:

> This time, we are not waging the great war with the past in mind and as slaves of past presumptions, as in 1914–18, but with an idea whose broad outline is clear, and which is a revolutionary idea both at a national and international level. . . . Within the framework of the fighting nation, better still, in the greater scope of a Europe led by the Axis, the framework of a new Europe and civilization must be worked.[5]

As had already happened with internal policy, the Fascist myth towered over the myth of nation in foreign policy, to the extent that the myth of nation lost once and for all that preeminence it had had during the Great War. In fact, this was not wholly due to Fascism and was not limited to the Italian situation. Indeed, World War II took on the characteristics of a war of religion in the propaganda of the two armed coalitions, which stressed the fact that the idea of nation was more ideologized than in the preceding conflict. Fascism saw the conflict of power among the national states as transfigured into a war of civilizations, in a challenge to the death between the "plutocratic and reactionary democracies" flanked by materialist communism and Fascist revolutionary totalitarianism. The Fascists stressed "the ideological impetus" of the Fascist state, believing that it would foster the development of a revolutionary and imperialist conscience in the Italians.[6] Thus, during the war, the totalitarian tendency of Fascism to consider the problem of nation only as a phase in the development of its revolution became more marked, as the war itself was seen as a stage in the revolutionary march forward. "This is the war of Revolution: of the Fascist Revolution. . . . It is the 'third part' of the Revolution. . . . It is the Revolution that has become war."[7] Against the materialistic civilization of liberalism and Bolshevism, and against imperialist nationalism based only on the principle of domination and enslavement, Fascism waved the flag of its national and universal revolution, which, by means of the war, was intended to achieve a new civilization based on the supremacy of spirit and on "social justice" among classes and nations. A summary of the reasons with which Fascism justified the revolutionary nature of the war can be found in the book *Nuova civiltà per la nuova Europa* (*A New Civilization for a New Europe*), edited in 1942 by Edgardo Sulis, one of the most faithful and authorized explanations of Mussolini's ideas on the future:

There will not be a new Europe without a universal revolution,
that is, without a new civilization. Only the final, definitive and
total struggle between two ideas can justify a universal war, the
sacrifice of men much greater and more apocalyptic than the
wretched catastrophe of things. . . . Either the revolution is universal or it is not a revolution. Revolution is never national, nor can it
be the sum of national revolutions: it needs a vital revolutionary
space that opens the way to the universal reality of the new idea.[8]

Social War

The revolutionary war was presented above all as a "social war" against
"plutodemocracies." The periodical *Domani* wrote that "geographical
solutions will not be enough" to face the problems of building the New
Order, "nor will the myth of blood be enough to strongly convince nations of the new hierarchical order." Only around the "social myth"
would it be possible to gather "the strength of our universality."[9] The
Fascist syndicalists were naturally among the most convinced champions and supporters of the social war, and they demanded that the
antibourgeois and anticapitalist campaign be continued more radically
to build the Fascist nation. This was meant to speed up the effective
"shortening of distances" between the social classes making up the Italian population and to achieve the trade union and corporative ideals left
in the limbo of theoretical propositions, thus giving the myth of the
New Civilization the concreteness of a modern "civilization of work."
The war, with "its terrible and elementary morality," was to definitively
wipe out "all the kinds of immorality that the money-based society
wanted to continue against the proletarians the whole world over."[10]

During the conflict, the myth of social war was discussed, above all,
by the young Fascists, who strove to establish the nature and content of
the New Civilization, and who were even more enthusiastic than the
syndicalists themselves in attributing the value of a social revolution to
the war. For many of them, the new war confirmed a profound crisis of
the ideas and values that had guided Europe up to the First World War.
"The romantic motifs that have inspired the policies of European governments up to now are coming to an end, the first to go being that of 'a
national state,' followed by the concepts of 'neutrality,' 'moderation' and
'the balance of power.' New ideas are springing up, like 'empire,' 'vital
space,' 'great space' and 'policies in continental terms.'" These young
people shared the belief that the principle of nation, which was chosen

as the foundation of European order after the Great War, had turned out to be fragile, capable of stirring up new conflicts and nationalistic egoism, intensifying and aggravating the breakup of Europe and the social inequalities among the peoples. "Exacerbating the concept of nationality has inevitably produced a breakaway rather than a convergent movement of the nationalities themselves, nor could it have been otherwise." Unhindered, the new war brought down the "merely nominal sovereignties" created after the Great War, "together with the anachronistic dream of some small national communities."[11] There could only be two solutions to the crisis of nationality, "which inevitably and clearly emerged" in the period between the two wars: either end the "cycle of the nationalistic myths, marking the triumph of the principle of internationalism, which calms history forever with peaceful coexistence," or "strengthen those same myths with the introduction of various kinds of supranationalism, which, while pursuing these myths, even through war, impose them as new values on the soul of history." The young Fascists, lined up in favor of the second solution, maintained that Fascism, "in its desire for revolution, must unleash its inner vitality, going beyond borders in a national sense," carrying out the solution of the social problem in a new imperial community through "the supranational organization based on the corporative principle."[12]

The mysticism of nation was given a populist interpretation by the culture of these young people, with marked antibourgeois and anticapitalist connotations. This view gave the war in progress the nature of an examination of Fascism, a supreme test of its political efficacy, revolutionary coherence and morality, to reconfirm, after twenty years of totalitarian regime, Fascism's claim to be considered the creator of a new Italian nation. In this perspective, the war became a radical and decisive phase of the Fascist anthropological revolution. It was to transform the character of the Italians, destroying bourgeois mentality and customs and, in fact, creating the nation as a "community of faith," hierarchically organized by functions and not by class privileges, a nation imbued with a sense of state and a severe civil morality, inspired by the people's collective sense of solidarity. The more radical of these young Fascists railed at "the servant-masters of capital, the fat bourgeoisie that sees nothing but money, those who live ignobly at the expense of the people, exploiting and handling capital for their own exclusive interests, while other fellow countrymen of ours, blood of our same blood, lack the basic means for a decent life." They expected, and fought for, "the principle of work to be carried out completely, as a subject not only of the economy but of all society, and that gold be only a means to obtain the might of the state. . . . We are for a new morality and religion, whose solid base must be the worship, I repeat, the worship of the social factor. Social awareness that is a sense of responsibility, the mastery of competence, the management of technology, the supremacy of spirit and the unrhetorical glorification of honesty."[13]

Thus the nation was in the service of the ideology of the social revolution, becoming a vehicle and instrument of Fascist ideology, as Camillo Pellizzi stated explicitly in Berlin in 1942 at a conference approved by Mussolini:

> Racial and national reasons are recognized as a law that must not be forgotten, because these nations are also entrusted with protecting the revolutionary principle in the future. However, all things considered, the nation, also in its own interest, works for the idea that it personifies and not the contrary. Therefore, the "nationalism" implied in our two movements is a kind that surpasses the very concept of nation that was emerging in democratic and liberal societies. In the latter, the nation contained the supreme values of entire societies, as single individuals represented the supreme value of the internal life of each nation.[14]

When the Italians and Germans discussed the problem of the New Order during the war, the Fascists clearly stressed the differences of opinion as well as the claim to cultural superiority of their Fascist concept. However, this claim was made with ambiguous and sophisticated conceptual distinctions, with the prudence required by the circumstances of the war, so as not to undermine the ideological alignment that the war alliance imposed. However, when talking about the "supremacy" of Latinism and Germanism in January 1941, Bottai remarked that the points in agreement and the affinities between the two revolutions were not to prevail over the fact that "there are two, to be precise, not one":

> Now, at present there are precisely these two doctrines, National Socialism and Fascism, between Germany and Italy. These must be our aims if we want to carry out an organic and lasting work. We must not be content with their undoubted and surprising affinity and resemblance, but go thoroughly into the basic reasons and facts behind both of them, so that both National Socialism and Fascism have their own function in striving to achieve their shared aims. For example, both say "nation," "state" and "people," but each one in its own way, following the dictates of inalienable and

unchangeable traditions. Getting round the problem by exchanging one term with another, state for *staat* or *volk* for *popolo*, would not create relations between us. On the contrary, they would be destroyed by this violation, which would be intolerable and sterile in the long run. The problem is to act in such a way that the different values add up to a whole, in which, rather than disappear, they are strengthened.[15]

The cultural and ideological debate between Fascists and Nazis on the New Order revealed that the ideological comparison was extremely tense, involving what each of the two allies of the Axis would contribute to the new European order and the new political and social order. Foreseeing the future order of Europe and the criteria that were to regulate the founding of the new hierarchy of nations, the Fascists tended to emphasize the cultural, ideological and institutional differences between Fascism and National Socialism as well as the affinities and similarities, with the aim, sometimes made explicit, of establishing the spiritual and ideological supremacy of Fascism.

However utterly academic the discussions on these subjects may seem, in fact, they went thoroughly into the theories of the two regimes, revealing a profound divergence concerning the fundamental problems of the individual, the nation and the state, which the acclaimed affinities between the two totalitarian revolutions barely managed to hide. These fundamental problems were made even more evident in the frequent debates on the future role of Fascism and Nazism, Roman and German influences, in building the New Europe. The debate, which concerned, above all, the relation between race and nation in the theories of the two totalitarian revolutions, was only one aspect of the continuous work of explaining the originality of Fascism compared to National Socialism. This was meant to assert Fascism's European and universalistic supremacy, which the Fascists thought could not be aspired to by German racism, with its biological exclusivism. It was a constant vindication of the differences, as well as the affinities that acquired growing importance in the Fascist debate on the problem of nation and the national state in the New Order. At the center of this debate there was, above all, the problem of racism and the relation between nation and race.

The Two Kinds of Racism in the New Order

"A nation is above all a spiritual entity that goes beyond every question of dolichocephalic or brachycephaloris skulls, of blond or dark hair.

National unity is also a way of being, feeling and living collectively. . . .
History is the essential matrix of peoples and nations in the travail of
the centuries. Faced with this almost religious truth, the presumption of
forced and selective breeding of race with the relative eugenic steriliza-
tion and coupling, is amusing. It may not reach the point of making a
whole people Nordic or Prussian, but at least it holds good for making a
race hegemonic and more powerful, so as to make it a caste of rulers
and leaders of the Chosen People."[16] In 1934 this was *Gerarchia*'s position
on the issue of racism, with a clearly polemical reference to Nazism.
Even after allying with Hitler's Germany and officially adopting racism
as the state's ideology, Fascist culture continued to point out the differences in the concept of nation between the two movements. This did
not block the way to introducing the concept of race in Fascist ideology
and policy when the Fascists worked out the myth of nation, above all in
relation to the plan for anthropological revolution aimed at changing the
character of the Italians. The tendency to consider racism obligatory in
forming an imperial conscience in the "new Italian" gained ground at
the beginning of the thirties, especially among the young Fascists and
even before racism was officially adopted as the regime's ideology. Racism was seen as an "extremely dynamic" element, a "vital ferment of action," as *Campano,* the periodical of the Fascist university students in Pisa,
wrote in 1934. However, they explained that they were not referring to
"absolutely biological racism" but to "historical and above all spiritual
racism," because "the former would be the return of primordial hordes,
while the latter gave out strong intimations of ideal imperialism." Fascist
racism was to be "not only biological realism but also historical and
heroic mysticism. It meant substituting the rational, democratic and
egalitarian myth with an ideal, racist one, substituting the concept of an
idyllic-utopian life with that of a voluntaristic-heroic one."[17]

Officially grafting racism and anti-Semitism onto the Fascist ideology, apparent alignment with the ideology of the National Socialist ally,
had, in fact, introduced new reasons for comparison that regarded, as
we have seen, the basic concepts of the two movement-regimes: nation,
race, state and New Order. Not only was agreement on these concepts
not taken for granted, as the propaganda wanted it to seem, but the
more thoroughly this agreement was gone into, the more difficult it was
to uphold in the long run. For example, regarding the issue of racism,
while excluding the cases of the most servile ideological alignment with
Nazism, the Fascists' ideas, although varied and contrasting, shared a
tendency to stress the difference and originality of Fascist "spiritualist"

racism, with the fairly transparent intention of affirming its ideological superiority compared to the exclusively "biological" racism of their ally, reaching the point of reappraising the universalistic essence of the Fascist myth of nation, with the prospect of a future order of the New Europe no longer based on the mere logic of domination and enslavement. Among the most important aspects of this claim to supremacy, defending the value of nation as a historical spiritual collectivity while rejecting race as a biological naturalistic entity also came up again. For example, Costamagna was not willing to accept the concept of a New Europe based only on racial discrimination:

> The problem that looms over the spiritual conflict and that becomes manifest in the imperial competition among peoples is not that of the mechanical domination of one people over others, imposed through "zoological wars"; rather it is that of "great civilizations," corresponding to the phenomena of the principal races, the great linguistic families and world religions. . . . To be precise, the movement of a national and popular revolution imposes itself against the problem of the great civilizations, supported by a totalitarian concept and as a protest against the hegemonic egoism of the Western powers.[18]

The distinction between "biological racism" and "spiritual racism" became one of the problems most under discussion among the Fascists when the regime decided to adopt racism as an integral part of its ideology and policy, at the same time introducing anti-Semitism as well. Intellectuals and scientists worked hard to define the original characteristics of Fascist racism, not wanting to make it seem a servile imitation of National Socialist racism. Besides, they had to reconcile it with the past public declarations of Mussolini himself, of disapproval and scornful sarcasm toward the racism from beyond the Alps. However, it was anything but an easy task to find an original interpretation of Fascist racism, due to the basic difficulty of having to reconcile the naturalist assumptions of racism, that is, the prejudice of the "purity" of race, with the spiritualist basis of Fascist ideology and its concept of nation, on one hand, and, on the other, the evident "impurity" of the Italian race. Within the limits of our research, the issue of Fascist racism is of interest only in relation to the myth of nation. And in this context, what is evident in Fascist culture is the particular attention given to the distinction between exclusively "biological" racism and racism that claimed to be "spiritualist," even though, in fact, this distinction did not always emerge effectively from the confusion of tendencies that crowded the

ideological laboratory where the attempt was being made to fix the original characteristics of Fascist racism.

Perhaps the need for caution required by the circumstances prevented the Fascists from accusing their allies of wanting to wage a "zoological war" in order to establish their own "hegemonic egoism," of
intending to rebuild Europe based on the exclusive principle of domination and enslavement in the name of racial superiority. Besides, not even
this caution curbed the Fascists' explicit criticism of the concept of Nazi
racism and its interpretation of the New Order. The latter seemed in
clear contrast with the Fascist idea of a New Civilization and certainly
could not be the principle for organizing a "hierarchy of nations,"
called to cooperate in order to defend and strengthen European supremacy in the world. On the contrary, Nazi racism, conceived in terms of
pure domination and enslavement, would be an obstacle to achieving a
"hierarchy of nations" in the New Civilization.

In 1942 *Civiltà fascista* declared that "killing freedom in the determinism of racial inheritability or personality in racial collectivism, or absorbing the doctrine of Fascism in the myth of racism," would not contribute to building the New Order. The periodical denounced "the
danger that the wrong approach to racism, leading to incommunicabil-
ity between one race and another, would create new divisions among
the European peoples and new causes of incomprehension. And this
danger, of ending up in a tower of Babel where every people speaks a
language that is incomprehensible to the others, is much greater for a
race than for a nation, in view of the spiritualistic and voluntaristic basis
of the latter."[19] The concept of nation, appropriated by Fascism, theoretically excluded any reference to naturalistic assumptions, giving the
highest value to history and spirit in forming a national conscience and
assigning a fundamental and decisive role above all to the "political will"
of the state as the creator of the nation. This concept reduced the importance of the ethnic and racial factor, in a biological sense, as an original factor of the national conscience and national state, and above all
did not make it a main criterion for an individual to belong to a nation.

Delio Cantimori insisted on the difference between the two types
of racism and between Fascism and National Socialism regarding the
concept of nation under the entry *Nazionalsocialismo* (National Socialism) written for the *Dizionario di politica* (Dictionary of Politics), pointing
out that the German movement saw the nation as a "political and natural unit, biologically united by blood and race in common." This contrasted with the "concept of nation as a political, historical and cultural

unit proposed by liberalism, the reference point for Italian and French nationalism."[20]

Costamagna, who was above suspicion of hidden antipathy for National Socialism, also rejected the racist premise of nation in the same dictionary, because "the so-called sociological requisites of nationality, including those relating to the same racial type, are, in short, nothing but the product of combining heterogeneous elements in the melting pot of the state; . . . nations rise from the amalgamation of different races and from the sacrifice of preexistent minor nations."[21] Costamagna stressed the priority and supremacy of the "history" factor and of the function of the state to form the nation: "The main problem regards 'peoples,' which are fulfilled in the state as a 'nation.' This is a problem of the spirit, which can be approached only through a synthetic-ecological interpretation of reality."[22] Besides, Costamagna attributed very little logical-experimental value to the biosociological concept of race, which became important only because it changed into a "subjective concept," that is, linking up with an idea of moral value and thus rising to become a myth. And Costamagna pointed out that it was precisely as a myth that "the idea of race has asserted itself and continues to do so more and more energetically, despite the evident impossibility of reconciling it with any anthroposociological or anthropological justification." This is because Italians, Germans or Russians, considered valid examples of the theory of race, "do not at all represent 'homogeneous racial groups' in the biological sense of the word, but groups of races mixed together. Nevertheless, the racial idea has acquired the character of a real 'Myth.'"[23]

All these considerations on the substantial difference between the concepts of the two kinds of racism in terms of the nation, the state and race are set out concisely in an essay by Lorenzo La Via in the pamphlet *Popolo, nazione, nazionalità, razza, civiltà* (People, Nation, Nationality, Race, Civilization), with pretensions to theoretical explanations even though expressed rather cautiously. This pamphlet could boast orthodoxy, as it was published under the sponsorship of the Department of the Interior, Demography and Race Administration, and endorsed with a preface by the Under-Secretary of State for the Interior. The author stressed that the Fascist state was not based exclusively on the principle of race, however it was meant, and that this principle was accepted by Fascist culture only as "a belief and myth, whose fervor leaves no room for the complicated and uncertain problems of biosociology and does not diminish their importance."[24] Furthermore he stressed that the state was supreme in the hierarchy of Fascist values, followed by the nation, and last of all race. However, they all converged in a higher fusion, which was the idea of "civilization," with a Roman and Fascist meaning.[25]

The Nation Makes a Comeback

Insisting on the spiritual, cultural and universal supremacy of the Fascist concept of nation, race and imperial civilization seems even more dramatic, because it emerged more and more clearly from the confrontation on the battlefields which of the two allies of the Axis, in the event of victory, was the stronger, thus having the right to lay down the principles for building the New Order. By supporting the spiritualistic nature of their own racism, the Fascists did not only want to claim their own originality compared with National Socialism, thus rejecting the accusation of following the way of racism only out of ideological imitation or contingent improvisation. Above all, they wanted to safeguard the cultural and ideological originality of their concept of nation and race against an interpretation that seemed to them exclusively naturalist and determinist.[26] This is why the Fascists not only denied that a "pure race" could be given historical and scientific validity but believed that a "merely biological and zoological racism, besides being objectively inexact, could only have a destructive and disintegrating influence."[27]

By making this distinction between the two kinds of racism, the Fascists wanted to bring out, above all, the superiority of the voluntaristic idea of nation with respect to the biological idea of race. "A concrete, universal principle must be on the tips of our bayonets," declared Pellizzi in 1941, "otherwise even victory is useless and harmful for us. We may be able to help our allies, not only with weapons and work but also with this innate and irrepressible genius of the race, which is the instinct and need for the universal," but without denying either the existence of races or the validity of a racist view of nation. Pellizzi repeated that race was a reality and that the principle of race was not incompatible with the principle of nation; rather, it was a necessary element. What made up a nation—rights, language, faith and territory in common—could not establish "the vital bonds of a *civitas* if the ardent sentiment for, and therefore pride in, a genetic bond, or at least a somatic and psychological affinity among its members, is not added to it." However, Pellizzi also explained that the principle of race was worthwhile as a "sentiment" that became "will and principle": it was therefore a driving force for a people to rise to greatness, but not the only factor involved.[28]

Antonino Pagliaro went in the same direction in order to include race in the Fascist ideology, trying to reconcile it with its spiritualist assumptions. Every people, as a historical community, had to keep the features that made up its physiognomy, and among these there was also the feeling of belonging to a "genetic community," which can "become pride, a more or less decisive exclusivism toward other communities, toward all other communities." Movements "based on the assumption of the natural supremacy of one people over others" were born from this particular sentiment, but Pagliaro believed their position "is, in short, inevitably negative," even if it could lead "to temporary successes, because it entails a wrong estimate of the forces opposing it." Pagliaro thought that this attitude was, in fact, fruit of a "naive and provincial pride," aroused by "faith in the values of one's own ethnic unit and the clear intention to keep them immune from contacts that could anyhow confuse and harm them." Furthermore, he believed that "awareness of race" could give a higher and broader value to the concept of people, as long as "the notion of purity" was excluded from the idea of race. This was "because every advanced ethnic unit has undergone more or less profound influences during its development, the same as every linguistic unit." Nevertheless, he maintained that, once race was adopted as a political value, it "required purity" to define and conserve the hereditary characteristics of a people.[29]

In an effort to highlight the originality and superiority of "spiritualist" racism, the Fascists were once again obliged to give importance to the concept of nation in relation to race: "we do not at all intend to destroy or undermine the concept of nation in the name of race: on the contrary, we want the concept of race to fortify and strengthen the concept of nation with new intensity." Only if understood "with a profound spiritual sense" can racism "strengthen the sense of nation, creating a 'cult of forefathers' and the mysticism of the 'tradition of origins.'" If a "differently oriented" racism steadfastly follows its logic right through, it "corrodes and undermines the nation," considering it "a very different entity from race, and infinitely less noble."[30]

On the other hand, the Fascists did not give up distinguishing between the principles of "great nation" and "small nations." In disputing Nazism, Pellizzi even paradoxically prefigured the future hierarchy of nations as a "hierarchy of equals."[31] Faced with Nazi racism, which aimed at destroying nationalities in a kind of "racial international," a kind of New Order based on the primacy of the "Aryan" and not simply "German" race,[32] the Fascists went back to speaking of the supremacy of nation and the principle of nationality as an irrepressible historical and spiritual reality, also in the future New Order.[33] At the beginning of 1942, *Dottrina fascista,* the periodical of the School of Fascist Mysticism, declared that nationality as a historical-political force and nation as a body and political-social organism could not and were not to disappear in the new order but had to "make up the connective tissue of each empire and each great space," because "considering nationality outdated as a "political force" would lead "sooner or later to a situation equally fraught with errors and, therefore, with dangers."[34]

That these were not isolated opinions is borne out by the fact that Mussolini's periodical, through the philosopher Francesco Orestano, also went back to proclaiming the validity of the nation as the foundation of the new European order, holding that "everything that weakens or nullifies the ethnic consistency and the spiritual value of all the European peoples indistinctly" should be "deprecated as detrimental to the whole continent and avoided scrupulously." The reason was that it would weaken the "cream of the white race," which had "to be prepared to defend itself in the intercontinental struggles of the future": "Therefore the new European order must first take this supreme requirement into consideration. It must ensure that all the nations, parts and scraps of nations that live on our continent, both in separate or separable territories and in those promiscuously occupied and indivisible, continue to exist and be capable of developing."[35]

In one of his rare writings published during the conflict, Giovanni Gentile asserted his firm refusal of the idea of a new order based on the racist principle of domination and enslavement. As far as we know, it was the first time the philosopher openly expressed his position on racism, firmly condemning it in the name of the universality of the spirit. At the beginning of 1942, he gave an oracle-like admonition, saying that war was the divine mystery of the gestation of a new order, which involved all the men "moved by fatality, or rather by the necessary logic of history, which is engaged in a supreme effort to overcome the troubles of an enormous crisis come to a head through the development and strengthening of all the energies of the modern world":

> *Novus nascitur ordo.* Which? We will know what it will be when we get there. . . . Sound mysticism, which is but the austere idea we must have of war as of all life, can give us the strength to wait serenely and trustingly. However, a new Asia, a new Europe and a new world will certainly come out of the war . . . for a humanity that, without dispelling the treasures of its greatest traditions, breaks the

chains that prevent or threaten development and progress. And this humanity will recognize the advantage of mutual intelligence and *fraternal cooperation among different races, none of which was born to serve*, but all of which have the right to bring the free contribution of their own industriousness to everyday human work. This will come about as, little by little, they become aware of themselves and thus rise to the level of the world's dominating civilization, which is not the capitalistic civilization of money and machines but that of the spirit.[36]

The philosopher gave prestige and value back to the idea of nation with the Fascist meaning of an historical and spiritual reality, as it was considered the most suitable groundwork on which to build a new hierarchy of peoples. This would not be based on the dictates of a nationalism of might inspired by principles of domination and enslavement, on the basis of racist materialism, but on the principles of collaboration among all the European nations, between the defeated and the victors, called to cooperate in building the New Civilization according to the place history had established for each nation. As *Dottrina fascista* observed, the war and alliance with Nazism put Fascism "in a dilemma between a policy of might for its own sake and achieving the revolution in a new social and moral order in the empire. . . . This is why, also and above all in war, it is necessary to be on guard in order to build the new Europe without repeating past errors."[37]

12

The Failed Identity

Ideological Congestion

During the war, Fascism superimposed the revolutionary myths of the New Civilization and the New Europe on the myths of the Risorgimento-type patriotism, which had sustained the country in the First World War right up to the victory. Caught up in the euphoria of plans drawn up by ideologists and politicians for the organization of Ordine Nuovo (New Order), many Fascists truly believed that the era of the national state was coming to an end. Consequently, the national myth was scarcely present in the propaganda of the Fascist war, entirely concerned as it was with the myth of revolutionary Fascism. However, these myths did not touch the souls of most Italians, thus making the mobilization and moral cohesion of the country, very difficult. On the contrary, together with the illusion of a "short war" and the suffering of a "long war," it helped to create a state of mind that wavered between euphoria, indifference and pessimism, depending on the military situation. As a result, the regime suffered a severe crisis, prelude to its defeat.[1]

The person who best perceived this state of confusion as well as its negative effect on the Italians' moral attitude regarding the war was the philosopher Ugo Spirito, who wrote an unpublished essay in the spring and summer of 1941 titled *La Guerra Rivoluzionaria* which was read by Mussolini. A staunch supporter of the war's revolutionary goal, Spirito went to the heart of the problem, denouncing the tragic effects of the dualism between imperialist nationalism and universalist social revolution, both assumed as reasons for, and aims of, the war.[2]

Actually, the dualism denounced by Spirito did not arise with the war, but was inherent to the cultural and ideological scheme according to which Fascism had developed its attitude toward the nation and, consequently, its political activity conducted for twenty years to Fascistize the country. In the end there was great confusion and the loss of those values, principles and myths that, from the birth of the national state, had nourished the sentiment of a collective identity among the Italians, to varying degrees. The Fascist national myth was a confused mixture of political realism that praised unscrupulous experimentalism in everyday situations but was seduced by anything mythical and understood politics as "the art of the impossible, the marvelous, the miraculous," as Bottai put it after the fall of the regime. Fascism was pragmatic because it scorned utopias, yet it was obsessed with the passion to create a new reality by designing a New Civilization as its own "city of the sun"; it was culturally pessimistic in its contempt of human nature but acted to redeem men and women through a plan of collective moral palingenesis, the totalitarian experiment in anthropological revolution.

Fascism had always professed its faith in the principles of Machiavellianism, scoffing the universalist ideologies and utopias. However, during the thirties it became ever more locked into the mythical, visionary element of its political culture, over and above the requirements of propaganda. As a result, it sailed enthusiastically toward utopias of greatness, imagining future scenarios of great events dominated by Mussolini's gift in constructing new international systems, which Fascism would design and build. In actual fact, if we look at how it developed, we can see that Fascism was dominated by an obnubilating sense of disproportion. Therefore, it confused the boundaries between myth and reality, between the greatness of imagined projects and awareness of the material and moral resources available to realize them, between the fanaticism of a visionary will that conceived politics as the "art of the impossible" and consciousness of the enormous distance separating the nation of real-life Italians from the utopian model of the Fascist nation.

All of this had not remained confined to the imagination and political fantasies but had brought practical consequences and affected the lives of millions of men and women, who, thanks to the teachings and propaganda of the Fascist state, were used to identifying the nation with Fascism and the future of the country with that of the regime. The population had been attracted by the myth of might, the euphoria of internal and foreign successes, which, undoubtedly, Fascism managed to achieve, and also by the myth of a Greater Italy, which during the regime, as never before, appeared to be nearly a reality, owing to the work of the Duce, Italy's "new god."[3]

It would seem that even before Fascism was defeated militarily it was the victim of "ideological congestion," in which both the myth of the

nation and the national state had been entwined and confused, taking
the Italians into an unpopular Fascist war that was to lead the regime to
defeat and the country to ruin. A few belated appeals were not sufficient
to restore prestige and preeminence to the values and principles that
had been mixed with Fascism for so long and were, therefore, subject to
the wear and tear of public opinion's increasing discredit and hostility
toward the regime and the Duce. One of the most important testimo-
nies of the decline of the national myth in the Fascist war was published early in 1942, when there was still hope that the Axis would win,
by the periodical of the Scuola di Mistica Fascista (The School of Fascist Mystics) when realizing that "in the current war almost nobody uses
the word 'nation.'"[4]

The Absent Nation

An almost accidental observation revealed that very few people at the
time had realized how serious the cultural, ideological and psychological situation was, including the Duce. On December 2, 1942, when commenting on one of Mussolini's last speeches before his downfall, Ardengo Soffici noted that the Duce had ended a speech "speaking of the
'Fascist war' and 'Fascist victims' almost as if the war had been waged
for the party rather than to save the people and the Italian nation, while
perhaps it was the case to declare the party collapsed, or at least dissolved, in the melting pot of genuine national forces."[5]

A significant document describing this situation was written a few
days after the Duce's speech by Giuseppe Mastromattei, an "early Fascist supporter," to remind everyone of the nation's absolute supremacy,
thus reconfirming the national nature of the ongoing war:

> This war is the nation's and for the nation, a war in which the ir-
> replaceable political function of the party must necessarily be
> harmonized with a vaster national reality. To this end, the party is
> working in all fields and sustaining the country's war efforts at all
> times. Under the enemy's brutal attacks, which only serve to re-
> inforce our intention to fight and win, there can only be one politi-
> cal reality: that of the nation, committed totally to fight. For these
> reasons we cannot historically distinguish between the party and
> the nation and we must extend the limits, the functions and goals
> so that they are confused with the entire collectivity of fighting
> people. . . . The party must make its greatest effort to preserve
> the ideology in the patriotic and national sense. The inevitable

evolution of the Revolution evidently sees its unsurpassable limits
in the idea of nation, religion and civilization.[6]

This passage is taken from an article, titled "Guerra, Partito e Nazione,"
sent to Mussolini by its author on December 10, 1942, requesting permission to publish it. The Duce immediately answered "No" and can-
celed the passage with a heavy pencil mark.

Twenty years after the greatly publicized identification of the nation
with Fascism, talking about the need to overcome the confusion between
party and nation by restoring the supremacy of the nation, subordinating the goals of the Fascist revolution to the needs of the country and invoking the unity and solidarity of the population in the "national war"
were all equivalent to acknowledging the defeat of Fascist totalitarianism and the divorce between the regime and the country, in other words,
Fascism's failure to be the nation's interpreter, educator and creator. Actually, the totalitarian regime had turned out to be far less capable than
the liberal regime in mobilizing human resources and material to sustain
the nation's war efforts. The liberal regime had also managed to overcome the disaster at Caporetto and led the nation to victory in World
War I. Mussolini himself had to admit in 1940 that there were "substantial differences between the Italians' state of mind in 1915 and 1940. . . .
From the national point of view, perhaps in 1915 the problem was better
targeted than today."[7] However, the headstrong Duce could not find any
other way of justifying this attitude, so he blamed it all on the Italians
themselves. "This war is not made for the Italian people. They are not
mature enough and lack the strength to undergo such a formidable and
decisive trial. This is a war for Germans and Japanese, not for us."[8]

Only when defeat was a certainty, after a vain attempt to bridge the
divide that the military setbacks had wrought between the regime and
the country, and under the illusion that it could mobilize the Italians in
a last patriotic stand to resist invasion by the enemy, was Fascism induced to lower the banner of ideology to rediscover and exalt the nation, supreme above the party and regime.[9] A month before the regime's
collapse, Giovanni Gentile launched a heartrending, dramatic public
appeal for saving the nation "to all the Italians who carry Italy in their
hearts."[10] The philosopher still professed his belief in Fascism but at the
same time invoked a sort of patriotic catharsis for Fascism itself, which
would regenerate it from so many wrong-doings during the triumphant
years and would restore it to its essence and function "to enhance our
Italy."[11]

Nation and Anti-Nation

During the last phase of its decline, when Fascism was clearly on the brink of collapse, it invoked, once again, the myth of a "fatherland for the Italians," placing the nation supreme above Fascism. However, the invocation was useless. It was just an illusion that the situation could be remedied by a belated but sincere and passionate appeal, to right a moral wrong, possibly an irreparable one, produced in the consciences of the Italians by the twenty years of systematic ideologization of the nation, which ended by canceling the very sense of nation. Among the causes of the Fascist war catastrophe, and not the least of them, was certainly the way in which Fascism had faced the conflict, that is, in a state of ideological and political confusion as well as military and moral unpreparedness. All of this made the principle motives and objectives of the war seem extremely vague to the Italians. Not only was the myth of the nation lost in that confused jumble of ideological motivations, overcome by the revolutionary myth, but millions of Italian men and women had lost the feeling that they belonged to a nation and did not feel involved in the Fascist war. They felt it was something foreign, particularly after the short-lived euphoria of an easy and rapid victory. Most Italians viewed the war with resignation initially, then with growing disillusion and fear. They became increasingly indifferent and impatient, not only toward the regime's appeals but also toward anything that had to do with Fascism, including the nation. The Fascist ideologization of the nation ended in the rejection of the national myth identified with Fascism. Ardengo Soffici had already noted in April 1940 that "the *anti-Italianità* of many is due to the fact that Fascism wanted to identify itself with Italy."[12]

This was the accusation made by the majority of the Gran Consiglio (Great Council) against the Duce and the party when on July 25 it voted in favor of the agenda presented by Dino Grandi:

> For us the regime and the party are and were only a means and an instrument useful for the destiny and greatness of the country.
>
> Parties and regimes are ephemeral and, to say the least, transitory: only the fatherland is eternal! Our concern and anxiety are turned exclusively to Italy at this time. If to save the fatherland we should have to sacrifice both the regime and the party and even ourselves, we would not hesitate to do so for a single moment.[13]

The war and military defeat had revealed an irreparable break between Fascism and the Italians. With their vote, the Duce's opponents declared they wanted to save the country and restore the monarchy. The king was the only legitimate representative and a symbol of unity, and by restoring his full powers, of which the totalitarian regime had deprived him, all Italians, without discriminating between Fascists and anti-Fascists, would be called to unite in a last stand to defend the independence and liberty of the national state born of the Risorgimento. Luigi Federzoni told the Gran Consiglio that the Duce and the party were to be blamed mainly for having divided the Italians with their biased ideological discrimination that postulated the identification of Fascism with the nation, and for leading the population into war, "talking about a revolution instead of the fatherland, about the party instead of the state and about Fascism instead of Italy."[14]

By declaring the identity between Fascism and the nation dissolved and breaking the oath of faithfulness to the Duce and the Fascist revolutionary cause, most of the regime's leading exponents also renounced the original Fascist dogma, according to which, from the early days of the movement, they had justified their actions, from squad-led violence to destruction of the liberal state, from the building of the totalitarian regime to the military undertakings. They also destroyed the fundamental principle on which the legitimacy of Fascist power was founded, thus decreeing, inevitably, the end of the regime.

This extreme act of repentance did not, however, cancel their responsibility in having been, up to then, active, conscious and willing protagonists of the Fascist policy and having shared the presumption and privilege with the Duce of considering themselves the unique and exclusive interpreters of the nation's conscience and will. None of them could consider themselves innocent for having approved, from the start of Fascism's rise to power, a policy that, by postulating a monopoly of the national myth, inevitably split national unity right to its foundation, excluding beforehand anyone who did not accept the Fascist monopoly. And criticizing them just at that time was certainly not sufficient to lessen their share of responsibility in the degeneration of the totalitarian party dictatorship during the thirties, which, according to them, was the reason why Fascism engulfed the nation with its ideology and subordinated the country's interests to its totalitarian ambitions.

By breaking the tie between nation and liberty, the Fascist regime had jeopardized the foundation on which the unified state was built without substituting it with a more solid one, despite the totalitarian state's claim of being a more advanced, solid, efficient and modern way to organize the nation. Furthermore, by scorning the values and principles of the Risorgimento's liberal and democratic tradition, which for more than

205204 *The Fascist Nation*

half a century had been the basis for the unified state's civil ethics and which formed the patriotic tenets in the education of Third Italy's Italians, Fascism had not contributed in any way to consolidating the feeling of belonging to a common nation. On the contrary, it brought about divides that would never mend and dispersed the heritage of a modest collective patriotism—even with all its defects—that liberal Italy had somehow managed to instill, as was demonstrated during the First World War. And it was that that gave Fascism much of the consensus it had received from the majority of Italians, sincerely convinced that Fascism was the highest, proudest and most willing expression of the national myth and patriotism.

After twenty years of totalitarian pedagogy and glorification of the nation, most Italians were not at all united nor ready to support the regime in facing what lay in store for the country at war. Disillusioned with Fascism because of the disastrous outcome of the war, Italians desired defeat as long as that would end the war and Fascism. For most people, the latter had become the main enemy, while they prayed for, waited for and hailed the enemy advancing in Italy as the liberator. The anti-Fascist Piero Calamandrei wrote on July 18, 1943:

> This advancing enemy in our land has all the makings of a liberation. Yes, really, we have been living under foreign domination since 1922: When we are reprimanded for not reacting, for not throwing off the yoke, people forget that since 1922 the problem for the Italians has not been overturning a government, which can be done with a coup d'etat and riots in the square. . . . Throwing off the yoke of a foreigner takes a war. . . . But now, we are at the end.[15]

The dissociation of the anti-Fascists from the fate of Italy at war, which they considered a Fascist war, marked the final break with the ideals and morals that the Fascist dictatorship had instilled in the national conscience from the very moment it claimed it had the monopoly over patriotism, thus ostracizing all those who did not acknowledge, submit to and accept Fascism's identification with the nation. As the socialist leader Pietro Nenni wrote in 1944:

> Then a break occurred in the consciences of the nation that was never again mended, and it so deepened under the veneer of sensational events and official engagements that as soon as the war jeopardized the nation, as soon as danger lapped the shores of the peninsula, the whole Fascist scaffolding collapsed. "Italietta, with its democratic and socialist leanings," regained cohesion and

overcame internal contrasts after the defeat at Caporetto in 1917. Mussolini's "iron-clad" Italy went to pieces when Sicily was invaded.[16]

In the opinion of the anti-Fascists who believed in the national myth, Fascism had embodied a "false Italy" for twenty years. It had been the "anti-nation," the true enemy of the fatherland because it had taken away freedom, put the nation into an ideological straight jacket and forced it to speak, think and act "Fascist," dragging it from one bellicose adventure to another until the final disaster, only to satisfy the Duce's greed for power and the party's ambitions. The anti-Fascists reacted against the Fascist claim to the monopoly of the national myth, countering with their own idea of nation and presenting themselves as the representatives of the "real Italy." "Fascism speaks in the name of the nation. We, too, speak of the nation, a reality, but a free nation, not the instrument of the state, the nation open to Europe and the world," protested Carlo Rosselli in 1935: "Fascism exalts Italy and *Italianità*. We also exalt it. But which Italy? Which *Italianità*? The one for which our country counts and has counted in history: its poets, moralists, heroes, Communes, the Renaissance, the Risorgimento, the bitter fatigue of those who reclaimed the swamps and turned them into the Po Valley, those who migrated throughout the world, those who still enable the dictator to squeeze blood and money out of poverty."[17] Soon after Ethiopia had been conquered, Rosselli wrote against the Fascist megalomania, "To you Fascists the empire, to us the nation."[18]

Actually the struggle between Fascism and anti-Fascism was a continuation of the deep-rooted rivalry that had existed for twenty years between the "two Italies" and that also took as reasons for dispute the national myth, the ideal of a Greater Italy and the model of the new *Italianità*. All were interpreted in an opposite fashion, seen as antagonism between incompatible views of the Italian nation, thus making them necessarily enemies. Rosselli proclaimed in 1933:

> In its premise, our anti-Fascism was always this: a struggle to make the Italians a modern people, a free people, and to oblige them to redeem their human essence in an intransigent battle over principles.
>
> This absurdly miserable Fascist fatherland is asphyxiating us!
>
> We will create the new fatherland of free men fighting hand to hand in the villages, districts and in the factories of Italy to transform the servants into citizens.[19]

Among other things, the Fascist ideologization had the effect of inducing the left-wing internationalist movements to emphasize the values
of the national myth, which up to then they had either ignored or fought.
"Italian socialism will have to concern itself much more in the future
with the specific national problems, breaking up the absurd patriotic
monopoly of the so-called national parties," Carlo Rosselli had stated in
1930. At that time he was working out his concept of liberal socialism, in
which he acknowledged the nation as a reality, as a historic entity and
a myth capable of influencing the masses. Consequently, Rosselli maintained that Socialism should incorporate the national values into its own
ideology as the basis for the nonutopian development of an international community.[20]

Even communism was driven by Fascism to discover the value of
the national myth, and in the mid-thirties, incorporated into their propaganda arsenal a large part of all the myths that had accompanied the
development of the Italian national myth, albeit with fluctuations due
to the prevalent instrumentality of the operation.[21] Apart from it being
instrumental, the acquisition of the national myth by the Communists
was also due to a knowledgeable assessment of its value, together with a
realistic self-criticism of the error made right after World War I. Palmiro
Togliatti acknowledged at the end of 1945 that: "In the other postwar
period there were workers' movements that ended their development
and gave in to reaction because we neglected the national element.
The national element cannot be denied. . . . The working class should
not think they will be able to solve the matter of the victory of democracy or the victory of socialism by breaking away from the national
community."[22]

The discovery and enhancement of the national myth by the anti-
Fascists played an important role in forming the unified Resistance
front. It found in the national myth its greatest cohesive factor and
ethical-political legitimacy, which gave the anti-Fascist fight against
Nazism and republican Fascism the characteristics of a patriotic war to
liberate the nation.

A Torn Nation

It was not easy for the anti-Fascists, educated in the cult of fatherland
during the liberal period in Italy, to choose to deny their solidarity with
the country at war and even to desire its defeat. During the Fascist war,
wrote the jurist Carlo Bozzi in 1945, a profound division came about
among the Italians:

There were those who hoped for defeat; those who looked upon the foreigner as the liberator, some even collaborated with the foreigner; there were those who, arms crossed, waited for events; those who heard the voice of the dominating faction in the war and exalted the fight so that the faction could triumph and be consolidated. The most envied national interests were transported or, worse, subordinated to foreign interests, with the incredible repetition of historic events. England, Russia, America and Germany were the center of gravity of our people's passion.[23]

The Italian anti-Fascists—whom Fascism treated as enemies of the nation, forcing them into exile outside Italy or into a kind of interior exile, isolating them and making them feel they were foreigners in their own country—were obliged to invoke the defeat of their nation as long as it would liberate them from the Fascist dictatorship: "We are letting what is called the Fascist fatherland fall because it is no longer the country of our souls, and we will rebuild it together with the cities destroyed, according to the civil ideals proper to Italy that twenty years of tyranny have not destroyed," wrote Adolfo Omodeo in a manifesto addressed to Roosevelt and Churchill, on July 16, 1943.[24] The division was deep and painful in the consciences of those who had to make this choice, above all for anti-Fascists like Benedetto Croce, born in liberal Italy and educated according to the Risorgimento's patriotic ethics. He was taught to place the good and health of the country above everything. He never thought that one day he would wish for the country to be ruined to save their dignity as men.[25]

Many young people also reached this decision. Although they had been brought up in Fascism, "they had become well aware of the situation." Perhaps making the choice was less painful for them because by now they were well on their way to abandoning knowingly the national myth. In it they saw only a "myth," the worship of idols and the principle source of wars and catastrophes that had devastated humanity in the last decades. On the other hand, many young people had been induced by Fascism to go beyond the national myth. The conviction that the era of the national state was drawing to a close, after the collapse of its myths, and belief in the social revolution in a universalist perspective, had led many young people educated by Fascism to satisfy their desire for myths and action in the movements that they thought were the victorious incarnation of an ideal of social or spiritual universalism, above and beyond the myth of the nation and the state.

The totalitarian experiment carried out by Fascism with the ambitious idea of creating a Greater Italy, a new nation and the New

Civilization, ended with the destruction, to its very foundation, of the fatherland of the Italians, the fatherland that had been the ideal behind the Risorgimento and given birth to the modern Italian nation, and was understood as the awareness of and desire for political and moral unity. As Mario Albertini recalled:

> From the first day of the war we hoped with all our hearts for Italy's defeat. We had no alternative, because Italy's victory would have brought with it the victory of Fascism. But we knew, or should have known, that all the Italians would be defeated with Italy and Fascism, including the not-guilty, the humble and the oppressed. Somehow, by choosing defeat for Italy, we were betraying or losing the fatherland, questioning her historic and social identity, and we were accepting a confrontation with ourselves that would see reason keep silent until we really knew what nationality was.[26]

On the part of the Fascists, no confession of responsibility for having caused the destruction could have been more eloquent and tragic than the image of what Greater Italy had become after 1943, as Giovanni Gentile described it in an article written on January 1, 1944. Giovanni Gentile was faithful to Fascism in its last venture, the Social Republic, convinced he was following the fatherland to its fate.

> Suddenly the Italy you believed in, the Italy of the Italians you lived side by side with and wanted to be united with in heart and mind, seemed to have disappeared. For which Italy shall we now live, think, write poetry, teach and write? It will be very difficult, if not impossible, to always open our minds to the expansion of abstract thoughts without the support of the country, that spiritual heritage that we all live on, without participating in the eternal dialogue between the living and the dead, in which the Italians can feel they are Italian. And when the fatherland disappears, you are left without air and cannot breathe. You lack the desire to look at your surroundings, to look anyone in the eye, because they have nothing to say and don't expect anything from you anymore. . . . The infinite disaster of today is not a foreign invasion, the devastation of our cities and the massacre of our families, or the uncertainty of tomorrow assigned to us by the events that are not in our hands. It is in our souls, in the disagreement that tears us apart, in the anguish that attacks us before the ruins of what was our common faith, which enabled us to look at our past with the same eyes and at our future with the same passion: this not recognizing ourselves, not understanding ourselves, therefore, not finding ourselves anymore.[27]

PART 4

NO-MAN'S-LAND

13

Where Is Italy?

The Debris of a Nation

In the days after September 8, 1943, the Italian state, founded in 1861, fell apart.[1] As Pietro Nenni recorded in his diary on September 9:

> Yesterday and today mark the collapse of what remained of state organization after July 25. Not making an appeal to the population has left everything hanging in a void. What is falling to pieces now is the nation's military structure. The soldiers are throwing their guns down. The officers are without guidance. The generals are trying to reach the king, who has taken flight. Nothing is left of the professed values of discipline and order, typical of the Fascist dictatorship for the last twenty years and of the monarchic structure of the state, wholly based on the dynasty-army-monarchy relationship for a century.[2]

Italy's history records few events where, as in this case, the people who lived through, witnessed and remembered those events agreed so pitilessly in describing the tragic and squalid sight of a ruling class abandoning its responsibilities of command to take flight, of a state falling to pieces, of an army disintegrating and throwing away arms and uniforms, of a people losing even the slightest bond with civic conscience and scattering in disorder like a nest of ants in total panic. "The state has collapsed, the real defeat is beginning now, with the Germans in the north and the Anglo-Americans in the south. The Italians, like ants when their nest is destroyed, are running in all directions, on foot, by train, on horseback and by boat. Now we have to save our homes and lives: we have to defend the poor Italy that each one of us carries within him," wrote Leo Longanesi in full flight.[3]

Vittorio Bachelet who was then seventeen years old, was traveling by train in those convulsive days with his father, an army officer, to the

capital: "The breakup of the army, the disintegration of the general
staff, the king's flight, the conflicting news arriving in those long days on
the train, and above all the soldiers who changed their clothes even at
the stations, throwing everything they had on that was military out of
the train windows—caps, sashes, boots and even hand grenades—and
others in this state, in their shirt sleeves and in disarray, stormed the
train with only one desire, to get home as soon as possible." Young
Bachelet had sensed that it was not only the defeat of an army "that has
fought honorably," it was

> the collapse of a gigantic framework that was coming apart, just as
> the framework of the regime had collapsed inwardly a few months
> before. Thinking it over later, it seemed clear to me that, at the
> time, I had a vague sensation it was not only a war lost but also a
> great number of noble and ignoble traditions. Although these were
> on their way out, the Fascist regime revived them and set them
> marching briskly in legionary square formation, but now they were
> falling, like leaves that were one day green then the next became
> yellow and dreary.[4]

If the army and the head of state are the highest symbols of a nation, nothing more than the spectacle of a routed army and a head of
state in flight could give the Italians the immediate impression that the
nation had broken up and was abandoned, at the mercy of foreign occupying armies. And nothing was more natural for the Italians than to
follow the example of the army and head of state: as the servicemen
had thrown away their uniforms, so they threw away their ideals of
fatherland and nation and took to their heels in search of safety, as the
king had done with his government. "From the top of the pyramid, the
cry of 'every man for himself' thrown to the shipwrecked and abandoned nation, was the most significant expression of this repudiation
of patriotism and civil responsibility," wrote Corrado Alvaro, one of
the most sensitive witnesses of the collapse of the Italian nation after
September 8.[5] The peninsula became a battlefield between occupying
armies that fought each other violently in a setting of material and moral
devastation, where, under heaps of rubble, lay all the national ideals
and myths that had inspired and accompanied the difficult rise of Italy
as a modern nation for over a century.

Those who, sick at heart, had wanted their country to be defeated in
war in order to free it of the dictatorship were dismayed and anguished
before the collapse of the national state, as they had not foreseen what
the fate of a defeated and invaded Italy would be after surrendering to

the allies. Benedetto Croce spent sleepless nights, tormented by the thought that "everything the Italian generations had built politically, economically and morally over the last century has been irreparably destroyed," as he wrote in his diary on December 15, 1943.[6] The same thoughts tormented an anti-Fascist of a younger generation, Ugo La Malfa:

> Italy as a great national state inherited from the Risorgimento has been destroyed. Not only a work of spiritual and material enrichment lasting since unification has been destroyed, not only a life full of promise, and with a future, has been destroyed, not only material, spiritual, artistic and scientific wealth built up with great difficulty has been destroyed, not only towns and villages and factories have been destroyed, but also the fundamental organization and functions of a state have been dismantled. Without these a state— all the civil institutions, the legal system, the military and police, technical services and bureaucracy—does not and cannot exist.[7]

The collapse of the unitary state destroyed the national identity. Without a state and nation, the Italians became bewildered, people who had lost their fatherland.

Salvatore Satta handed down to us the "disconsolate vision of a dying fatherland"[8] in tones of biblical desperation:

> Our destiny has come about in a way that not even the most apocalyptic prophet could have imagined. The immense ruins of Italian virtue are not lying in Thracian ashes, as in so many other historical ashes, there lies an Italy without virtue, hated by its own children, despised by the foreigners who flatter it, and what is sadder, indifferent to the wretchedness it has fallen into. Formidable armies that, when advancing and retreating repeat their Vandalic acts of destruction, are camped on its soil, too often called sacred. . . . On either side of the mobile battle lines, there are two Italies, impenetrable to each other, or more exactly, ten, twenty Italies, as many as there are citizens, all waiting for the weapons of others to restore the lost privileges of some, or under the semblance of freedom, to introduce new privileges for others, and each makes his own state from the disintegration of the state, hate laying down the law in the best, greed in the worst, and all of them lacking compassion.
>
> The death of an individual's fatherland is certainly the most important event in his life. Like a castaway tossed onto a desert island by a storm, he feels the ties that bind him to life breaking one by one in the dark night that slowly descends on his solitude. Then a frightful problem that, when his country was alive and working

(even though badly) he was too busy to notice, arises and looms over the ruins: the problem of existence.[9]

Invaded, devastated and shattered, Italy was no longer a fatherland, the land of our forefathers. It had become a no-man's-land, where the war between foreign armies and the civil war between opposing groups of Italians who fought in the name of two states and "two Italies" raged like a cyclone of fire:

> The war sweeps through Italy like a fire through pine woods. Seen from afar, it barely seems to brush over the treetops with wisps of advancing fire, but up close we realize that it has left only ashes behind it. The flames advance inexorably, from sea to sea, leaving behind them villages in ruins, empty cowsheds, barns burnt down, railways at a standstill, devastated ports full of sunken ships and innumerable dead. Politically Italy is between two armies and two governments, undergoing torture like that of a body torn to pieces by two pairs of horses pulling in opposite directions. The republican government pulls all the political and administrative organs of the state northward, while Badoglio's government pulls them southward. Thus tortured, all the institutions break up like torn live fibers. Afterward, nothing will be left: *solo disiecta membra* that will rot.[10]

At the end of 1943, this was how Piero Calamandrei described united Italy, dismembered into two states, each one proclaiming it was the legitimate representative of the nation, the guardian of the country's honor and dignity, and accusing the other of being Italy's traitor and enemy at the service of a foreign invader.

Two Fatherlands at War

However, the downfall of the Fascist regime did not drag the idea of fatherland down with it. On the contrary, it gave impulse to the anti-Fascists' claim to patriotism, which Fascism had denied them. Immediately after July 25 Calamandrei noted in his diary:

> Frankly, the widespread sensation in this period can be summed up quite simply in these words: we have found our fatherland again, our fatherland, meaning friendliness and human kindness among those living in the same country, who understand each other with a glance, a smile or an allusion. This is our fatherland, where we feel close to, and familiar with, each other, thus enabling us sometimes

to trust and be friendly with people we do not know and whose up-
bringing and profession are different from ours, and yet we recognize each other through something in common, something that
unites us. We have found each other again.[11]

After September 8, with the birth of the Fascist Repubblica Sociale
Italiana (RSI, Italian Social Republic) there was a new outbreak of the
civil war between Fascism and anti-Fascism, which Fascism had won in
1922, unduly claiming the monopoly of patriotism and the myth of nation for twenty years. Italian minority groups fought on opposite sides in
the civil war, convinced they represented the best part of the nation and
were fighting for the honor, liberation and salvation of their country.[12]
In this new civil war, unlike what had happened in the first postwar period, communists and socialists took sides, too, fighting for their country
and proclaiming they were the most genuine representatives and de-
fenders of the nation in the name of the working class. This in itself was
something new for the anti-Fascist struggle and for the nature of the
civil war, seen as patriotic. Furthermore it was a novelty destined to have
quite important consequences for what happened later to the myth of
nation after the war ended.

For the first time since the Risorgimento, all the Italians fighting
each other as enemies in the Italian civil war (the tragic irony of history!) declared it was for the unity and independence of the nation, professing faith in their country. Both those who supported the Social Republic and those who supported the Resistance and the Kingdom of the
South fought under the flag of patriotism. From 1943 to 1945, a war of
symbols and myths of nation was also fought on both sides of the civil
war. Fascists and partisans competed for the monopoly of the national
mythology from the Risorgimento to the Great War, each side evoking
the feats and men of the struggle for unification as their own heritage,
declaring they were fighting and sacrificing their lives for the salvation
and greatness of their country. The propaganda of both sides bran-
dished the names of Mazzini, Garibaldi, Pisacane, Mameli and the
Bandiera brothers, extolling the heroic episodes of the Risorgimento
like the defence of the Roman Republic in 1849 and the lives sacrificed
to free and unite the country.

"Two fatherlands" rose from the "death of the fatherland" — once
again "two Italies," both armed, one against the other, each side convinced they were the "true Italy" against the "false Italy," the nation
against the "anti-nation." We can indeed speak of a revival of patriotism

for the Italians who took part in the civil war, as Giovanni Gentile observed at the end of 1943: "The feeling for their fatherland is alive today, even stronger, in the hearts of all the Italians, although widely varying and even contrasting in kind. The war has imposed its harsh reality and ruinous consequences on everyone, the rich and poor, men and women, the old, young and children, with an imminent, urgent threat: the destruction of their defeated fatherland."[13]

The idea of fatherland predominated in the propaganda of the "two Italies" at war. It was in many ways a patriotism peculiar to that situation, a mixture, on one hand, of historical patriotism, a legacy of the Risorgimento tradition filtered through Fascism for the young people who grew up under the regime, and on the other, the new feeling of a spontaneous patriotism, existential rather than ideological, springing from actual experience as an immediate, almost instinctive reaction to feeling ashamed and humiliated by the catastrophe of September 8. This spontaneous patriotism, which both sides evinced sincerely and undoubtingly, was considered simply an individual's human and civil duty, the task of defending one's country's honor when faced with the collapse of the state and the flight of the ruling class, not to keep faith with an ideology but to preserve the dignity of men and citizens. "Never as on that day," wrote Dante Livio Bianco, who organized the partisan struggle in Piedmont, "have we understood what military honor and national dignity are and what they mean: those words that often seemed unbearably conventional and spoilt by rhetoric now revealed their painfully human essence through suffering heartbreak and burning shame. It was an added reason for the anti-Fascists to pass resolutely to action."[14]

Republican Fascism also justified its raison d'être with the need to redeem Italy's military honor and national dignity, stating that it placed fatherland above party and patriotism above ideology. The prevailing patriotism in the RSI's experience did not require following Fascist ideology, even though it did not deny the Fascist experience. Explicitly giving up its claim to identifying the nation with Fascism, the Social Republic tried to propose the image of Fascism reborn and purified by the defeat, risen again only as a militia in the service of the country, ready to receive all Italians, including non-Fascists, determined to fight for their fatherland. "Let us shout it loud and strong that it is not to save Fascism that we must still fight, but to save the fatherland. . . . We must take up arms again beside our betrayed ally for the honor and deliverance of Italy."[15] The main interpreter of the renewed supremacy of fatherland above party was Gentile, even if his appeal for agreement among the

Italians to rebuild their country in ruins and fight for its dignity and honor did not at all imply denying Fascism or doubting it was the Fascist party's duty to "take the initiative for counteraction," not out of revenge but "in an open-handed peace-making and constructive spirit," as it "has the responsibility of power as an organ of the state."[16]

Actually, for many of those who supported Mussolini's Republic, the main reason for their choice was not Fascist ideology but the honor of the fatherland, the need to free the nation from the shame of defeat and "betrayal," the duty to prove their genuine faith in the "cult of fatherland" in the certainty of defeat, even by sacrificing their lives for it. "We want just one thing: the good of the fatherland!" *Il Campano* asserted, launching an appeal to young people: "We are not interested in their color or political leanings, the important thing is that they come."[17]

Women's activism in the RSI was, from some viewpoints, extraordinary, a significant expression of spontaneous, nonideological patriotism, even though grafted onto the Fascist education received during the years of the regime. In some ways Fascist women had revived their passion for "politics," but for most of these activists patriotism clearly prevailed over ideology, which was sometimes clearly rejected.[18]

Dying for one's country rather than sacrificing oneself for Fascism is the vocation that emerges from the letters of the RSI war victims, especially the very young: "I was not born to see my fatherland die without trying to save it, only because I don't know how to try. . . . I can see the storm approaching, I grit my teeth and face it. Anyway, some time ago I decided what the good of my fatherland was," wrote a seventeen-year-old boy.[19] Nevertheless, it was still impossible for many of them to make a distinction, brought up as they were to identify their fatherland with Fascism and Fascism with their country. RSI patriotism still retained *fideistic* acceptance of the Fascist myths of might, of a religious cult of fatherland that absorbs every other ideal and of the myth of a Greater Italy to dedicate oneself to body and soul. The very young patriots of Salò, like a seventeen-year-old militant of the X MAS (10th Marine Division, Italian naval commandos), still spoke of a "reborn Italy."[20]

Fascist republican ideology did not retreat completely before the rediscovered supremacy of fatherland. After all, the idea of the supremacy of fatherland broke apart in the RSI, shattering into a great variety of positions. The alliance with National Socialist Germany and the fanaticism of intransigent Fascism, which predominated in the reborn Fascist Republican Party, wiped out any value and efficacy in the patriotic appeals for the Italians to make peace and for the independence of the country. Clearly these appeals did not seem at all credible for a state that was destined to live as a satellite of Nazi Germany. The legacy of totalitarianism, however much revised or a source of controversy, still left its influence weighing heavily on any plan for a new state, and no appeal to the epic Risorgimento deeds called back the value of freedom as a basis of the national state. The straightforward Mazzinian vision of a free humanity in free nations was excluded from the great number of Mazzini quotations in the political press of republican Fascism. The patriotic catharsis of Salò Fascism did not imply any rediscovery of freedom as a fundamental value for a modern nation, beyond ambiguous formulas. And then there were the Fascists, quite a number of them and no less important, who insisted that "Fascism is the fatherland today more than yesterday," attributing to Fascism "the duty and right to give the fatherland back its habitual nature: that honor and dignity that the anonymous society of five or six parties had ignominiously thrown in the mud."[21] Even though Fascism had given up identifying the nation with its own ideology, the RSI followers were in any case convinced that only they were "true Italians," faithful to the country. Anti-Fascists and partisans were not recognized as belonging to the Italian nation.

Anti-Fascist Italy, on the opposite side presented a mirror image, with partisan patriotism that, in turn, denied that the Fascists and RSI militants belonged to the Italian nation.

The national-patriotic motive, strictly linked to the motive of freedom, was certainly the main factor that united the various and contrasting political forces of the Resistance.[22] With the fervor of neophytes, the Communists extolled the national character of the armed struggle against the Germans and Fascists and were up front when waving the "sacred flag of the war for the independence of the nation," spurring the Italians on for the "sacred war of national liberation! War to save the independence and honor of Italy!" as Palmiro Togliatti declared from Moscow on September 15, 1943.[23]

The flag of patriotism was raised by the anti-Fascists against the invading Germans, but they themselves considered Fascism the main enemy, guilty of enslaving the country, subjecting it to National Socialism, dragging it into a disastrous war and triggering the civil war, thus destroying national unity. "One of the most serious misdeeds of Fascism," Piero Calamandrei wrote right after the regime had fallen, "was this: killing any sense of fatherland. For twenty years this word 'fatherland' has been disgusting. . . . We felt that foreigners occupied the land: these Fascist Italians camping on our land were foreigners. If they were

Italians we were not. A country occupied by a tribe of savages: for twenty years we were under their heels."[24]

Responsibility for the war and the defeat and invasion of the country denied Fascism any right to speak in Italy's name. Only the anti-Fascists could declare themselves the interpreters of the national conscience still faithful to the values of Risorgimento tradition and to the values of freedom and humanity.[25] The image of the Resistance as a "second Risorgimento" became a fundamental part of partisan patriotism, which stressed the analogies of the war against the German invaders and despotism, a war of liberation for unity and independence, waged once again, as in the Risorgimento, under the banner of the trinomial "nation, freedom and humanity," aspiring to create a country of free and equal citizens.[26] Again it was the patriotic motive that echoed frequently in the letters of the partisans condemned to death,[27] expressions of spontaneous patriotism that were rarely tinged with ideology and more often evoked Risorgimento tones and similarities with the patriotic spirit of the First World War. Many partisans declared they offered their lives "for the ideal of a freer, finer fatherland,"[28] or "to rebuild Italian unity and to make our land honored and respected again all over the world."[29] "I die without fear. I am sacrificing myself for a noble cause: it is for my fatherland," wrote a librarian.[30] "Love your fatherland profoundly, too, this country of ours that is so ill-starred. Do not hate but accept the sacrifice of your brother," was the last message of a teacher.[31] A worker who had fought in the First World War wrote: "In the last few days I have often thought about my life, all my life. I may be wrong but I am convinced that my fatherland, my true fatherland, cannot reproach me for anything. My true fatherland, the one I fought for in the other war, the one that has now spurred me to fight against my own country falsified by the Fascists, will always smile on me as on a favorite son."[32]

However, behind the unitary flag of the war of liberation, Resistance patriotism hid divisions and contrasts regarding, above all, the different ways of interpreting the idea of nation itself. Every partisan formation had its own idea of nation, each one condensing different images of the myth of nation, different interpretations of Italian history, the Risorgimento and Fascism, different views of the future Italy and state to be built and rebuilt. The monarchic partisans' nation was different from that of the republican partisans, the Communists' nation was nothing like that of the Christian Democrats, the Liberals' nation had little in common with that of the Action Party supporters. In any case, the partisans' patriotism did not necessarily identify the fatherland with the national state. Communist and socialist internationalism, Catholic universalism and federalist Europeanism ideologically placed ideal fatherland beyond nation, above or outside the national state. Sometimes, even a local, provincial or regional patriotism emerged in the partisans who were the first to take up arms or who thought they had done more for the armed conflict than the others.

Flight from History

The revival of spontaneous patriotism after the Fascist monopoly ended did not succeed in giving a bewildered population a sense of its own national identity. If the anti-Fascist parties were wanting when they laid the foundations for a new national conscience based on freedom, we should add that the ground on which these foundations were supposed to lie—the Italian population—was extremely brittle after being compressed by the totalitarian regime, shattered by the military defeat, broken up and devastated by the collapse of the national state and by an Italy that had become a battlefield and a heap of ruins.

The image of the Italians rebelling en masse, taking up arms and fighting against the German army and the Fascists, belongs to Resistance mythology, which is not confirmed by historical reality. As Leo Valiani, one of the leaders of the Resistance, explained immediately after the war ended, those who took part in the war of liberation were a "really very small vanguard, . . . incapable of linking up with the mass of people they ideally claimed to represent and enthral."[33] Even if the numbers of those in the vanguard may be assessed differently, undoubtedly most of the population was inert, passive and indifferent and tried to avoid danger in all ways and by all means, just trying to survive the fury of the war. In June 1944 Pietro Nenni wondered:

> Where is Italy in the supreme clash between two civilizations and worlds that is taking place on our land?
> Spiritually it is beside the allied nations, and flanks them with its partisans and volunteers for freedom in the underground struggle. However, the part we play is so small in the steady stream of arms and armed men that daily pass before our astonished eyes that nobody can avoid a feeling of national humiliation. . . . [The] surrender on 9 and 10 September, when faced with the treacherous German attack, took all initiative from the nation.
> Since then, the war fought on our mountains has been almost solely a war between foreign armies. Our nation has been all but absent from the battlefields, or confined to secondary activities.[34]

The anti-Fascists who tried to rally the population against the Germans felt "extraordinarily exhausted" by trying to wake the people up from an "age-old inertia that they had difficulty in shaking off, like an enormous rusty wheel."[35] The result of these efforts were not comforting for those encouraging armed resistance. Alfredo Pizzoni, the leader of the Committee of National Liberation Northern Italy, wrote that when the Italian population was faced with the initiative of the few who wanted to organize the struggle against the Germans, up to the eve of the uprising it "showed the mark left by twenty years of Fascism": it was without outlines, formless, a mixture of fear and indecision typical of the weak and fainthearted. All the respected men were absent or ready to get out of danger, all intent on looking for a way out, whatever it was, even the most dishonorable, rather than risk their lives."[36] This is why the appeal to rid the country of the Germans found little response from those social classes that, throughout both the liberal and Fascist periods, were pleased to be identified with the nation, considering themselves its most conscious, responsible and noble part. Pizzoni refers bitingly to the host of "petty, so-called 'right-minded' people, I mean right-minded at all times and in all circumstances of life, who at that time had only one logical and quite respectable problem, but that should never have been the only thing dominating every activity of responsible men and citizens: that is, to go home in the evening with a bag full of meat, rice, butter and flour, necessary to maintain their families."[37]

There was a "third Italy" between the "two Italies" fighting to the death—the majority of the Italians, who were waiting to be liberated by the allied armies, trying to save their lives at any cost, responding to the sole impulse of an innate and basic instinct of survival. "They behave like spectators, as if what is happening does not concern them. They admire the strongest and the richest, and if these are lacking, the most cunning," Corrado Alvaro noted, sympathetically indulgent toward his "unfortunate country that jealously guards its unhappiness," "used to seeing examples of squalor, egoism, cowardice and arrogance in all its representatives," expecting "benefits and favors always from others and never its rights, ready to turn to whoever promises something or shows he is powerful."[38]

This was personally humiliating, intimately shameful for the more sensitive consciences. "Waiting for the British to free us is humiliating. Every day as we scan the outlines of the hills we wonder, almost impatiently: but when will they come? We are reduced to waiting joyfully for foreign soldiers to arrive!" wrote Alba De Cespedes in her refuge on the mountains on October 18, 1943.[39] Piero Calamandrei echoed her from the Umbrian countryside where he had taken refuge, giving vent to his bitter feelings against the Italians, who, though they themselves did not lift a finger, railed against the allies because they did not advance rapidly enough to bring them liberation and peace. "We are annoyed with the British and Americans who are moving slowly, but what are we doing? The eternal Italian mentality that expects foreigners to save them."[40] Calamandrei was honest enough not to exclude himself from the target of his diatribe: "Those Italians who expect freedom from others, who applaud the victor as soon as he arrives and the following day turn their backs on him as soon as his star wanes. Ah, we never change. . . . Always the same, and I who am writing, with them."[41]

Not even the leaders of the anti-Fascist struggle like Pietro Nenni were immune to this sense of humiliation. Immediately after Rome was liberated, recalling ill-fated September 9, 1943, he wrote: "Today there is not an Italian worthy of the name who does not feel a profound sense of bitterness in the euphoria of liberation, in the joy of not hearing a Nazi military policeman or a Fascist persecutor at his heels. And who does not say to himself that freedom given as a gift tastes salty, like the bread of others."[42]

With the shameful collapse of the ambitious myth of a Greater Italy, the great majority of Italians now had no other aspiration than to flee from history, trying in any way, cautiously or faintheartedly, to get away from the war and find any kind of refuge in mere survival, even in biologically primitive conditions. It was as if a whole population had decided to miss its appointment with history by declaring its unconditional surrender in order to look for safety in the most elementary form of existence, reduced to a simple affair of living and surviving. Piero Calamandrei recorded that "it seems that we live in peace here and that the drama will not touch us, once our most animal physical needs—eating and sleeping—have been satisfied. We try to forget. I realize that the most unbearable suffering is physical: once these needs are satisfied it seems impossible that we are almost indifferent to dangers and humiliation like those that have struck us or now threaten us."[43] "As in the difficult times of a nation, everything seems less important, everything loses greatness and humanity and everyone seems very young, inexperienced and pathetic when faced with reality,"[44] Alvaro commented: "Ours is not history, it is biology. . . . The Italians are not in action: they see themselves in action."[45] Thus they hope against hope they have got away with it, avoided a more merciless punishment from Avenging History— which they had rashly attracted on themselves with their vainglorious

ambition, because they had promptly sided with the winners by instan-
taneously changing sides, that is with Conquering History. "There is no
denying it: that stupid war really turned out well for us. It could not have
gone better. Our self-respect as defeated soldiers was saved, by then we
were fighting beside the Allies to win their war together with them after
losing ours," wrote Curzio Malaparte in 1949.[46]

The Plague

In "a hungry and desperate Italy, reduced to the animal reactions of
basic instincts and hunger,"[47] as Nenni described it in September 1944,
there was little left that could evoke a country worthy of respect and dignity in the eyes of the Italians. The fury of the war broke like an apocalyptic scourge:

> A slow and implacable gangrene is devouring most of Italy, reduc-
> ing it to skeletons and ruins and leaving it formless and exhausted.
> Every now and then the gangrene stops, has a rest, then starts ex-
> panding again, in sudden and violent bursts. There is no way we
> can save ourselves. The same destiny befalls all the regions, more
> or less violently and destructively. First there is bombing, then the
> shooting war and with both of these the deliberate plundering and
> devastation of the Germans. It's a kind of plague of modern times:
> we, too, must believe, like those before us, that God sent this war to
> punish us for our sins.

This was written by *Risorgimento liberal*[48] in the autumn of 1944. The
monuments, which the myth of nation had indicated as witnessing Italian greatness over the centuries, had also been destroyed and desecrated
by the occupying armies, thus losing their value as sacred symbols of
the nation. "An enemy army entering a defeated city," observed Alvaro,
"makes not only the most profound values of a civilization waver but
also its symbols, considered eternal, however big they are."[49] Not only
were the countryside and the monuments devastated and destroyed by
the scourge of war, a more insidious and serious plague had also attacked the Italians, wrote Curzio Malaparte, which was destroying their
very souls:

> It was a profoundly different but no less horrible plague from
> the epidemics that every now and then devastated Europe in the
> Middle Ages. The extraordinary nature of this very new disease
> was this: it did not corrupt bodies but souls. Limbs apparently re-
> mained unaltered, but within the casing of healthy flesh the soul

was rotting, coming apart. It was a kind of moral plague that did not seem to offer any kind of defence. . . . I preferred the war to the plague that, after liberation, sullied, corrupted and humiliated all of us, men, women and children. Before liberation, we had struggled and suffered not to die. Afterward, we struggled and suffered to live. There is a profound difference between fighting not to die and fighting to live. The people who fight to avoid dying keep their dignity, all of them ferociously obstinate and jealously defending it. . . . Fighting to live is humiliating, horrible and a shameful necessity. Only to live. Only to save one's own skin.[50]

This moral disease destroyed every fiber of dignity, degraded and corrupted the very souls of the Italians, while they regressed to the squalor of a precarious daily life, dominated only by the inexorable imperative of hunger. Alvaro noted: "I think the allies are staggered by a population that only asks for chocolate, candies and cigarettes. At first, the occupying soldiers threw them from the trucks. . . . I have never heard or seen anything so absurd. It is something like the cult of a fetish, which was the victor."[51] And "prostitution, corruption, fraud and inflation were rampant with the arrival of the victors. . . . The upper bourgeoisie and the aristocracy give big parties and dinners to welcome the occupiers, who form their ideas of the country on these occasions and pass them on to their governments and public opinion. . . . Some newspapers have placed all our national dignity in the campaign against the little shoeshines. And our national honor in the many prostitutes."[52]

Just before the war ended, Italy offered the squalid spectacle of "rampant immorality," even if speaking of a moral crisis "means using a euphemism" Guido De Ruggiero explained:

It is undeniable and would be useless wanting to hide it under a veil of hypocrisy. People of all ages and social classes, all kinds of public and private activities contribute to it. From prostitution to juvenile pimping to ugly family compromises, theft and murder, now habitual means of subsistence, to commerce debased on a form of banditry, to selling favors in lieu of fairly recognizing rights, to a thousand other like undertakings, it is all so rotten that it is rife everywhere, infecting and suffocating us.[53]

Those who were preparing to found democracy, to rebuild the national state on the ruins of the war, were faced with a "seriously ill" Italian society, "with an alarmingly unbalanced structure and some organs that were wasting away and atrophied, while others were overdeveloped and parasitic."[54] Some compared living conditions in Italy after the war ended to those of its "darkest times": we have to go back "probably to before the year 1000 to find such a frightful situation" of criminality, corruption and violence.[55]

The Downfall of Character

The resumption of political activity in liberated Italy came about amid the general indifference of the population. The people were passive and inert onlookers, consequently chilling the enthusiasm of the anti-Fascists preparing to rebuild the national state and working with the fervor of those who were restoring the nation after the corrupting slavery of the Fascist dictatorship. Behind the rhetoric of the people's enthusiasm for unity, which strengthened the new democratic Italy, there was the reality of a divided and confused population, ready to cancel the experience of the catastrophe from its memory and conscience as quickly as possible. The communist archeologist Ranuccio Bianchi Bandinelli wrote that "it would seem that this tremendous lesson was of no avail: everyone seems to find it extraordinarily easy to forget, which, carried to extremes, makes animals happy, but also inferior."[56]

Reflecting on the Italians' behavior after the collapse of the nation led some anti-Fascists to profoundly pessimistic considerations on their attitude and capacity to be free and responsible citizens of a national state, to be and feel they were a nation in a modern political sense. Many doubted that the Italians were capable of picking themselves up after the defeat: "To pick yourself up you need strength. Has this Italy got the strength?" Piero Calamandrei wondered after September 8. And his answer was full of doubts: "I do not know. It seems to me that all of us, old and young, are generally resigned and wishing not to die, and when at a crossroads, to always choose the road that leads to cowardice, as long as we stay alive, rather than to dignity, with the danger of death."[57] Corrado Alvaro listed a series of defects in "the Italians' souls," in his opinion not unlike the "Italic peoples' souls" described by Livius in the history of the Punic Wars: "ready to betray, inconstant in misfortune, unrestrained ambitions, venal, etc."[58] Other basic traits in the Italian character were recorded by Alvaro on the occasion of the 1948 election, including "the worst kind of old Machiavellism, which is the cause of our disrepute and the moral contempt for us in the eyes of the world and which so greatly disgusted Cardinal De Retz, that is, the shady politics that every Italian indulges in, so that he never responds to an impulse from the heart but to childish and complicated calculations."[59]

The negative evaluation of the Italians' political attitudes was reached through a moralistic analysis of their character. Prevailing criticism insinuated troubling doubts about the possibility of raising the Italian people from Fascist corruption and leading them to live as a community of free citizens of a democratic national state. The comparison with the public spirit in democratic nations highlighted Italian defects and aggravated the sense of humiliation and discouragement in those who were preparing to rebuild a new national awareness on democratic foundations after the disastrous totalitarian experiment. Observing the Italians from London, where he was ambassador, Nicolò Carandini, a Liberal, felt the humiliation of the comparison keenly, giving up all hope that it was possible to educate the Italians, both governors and governed, to the sense of good citizenship of a democratic nation.

On March 17, 1945, he wrote:

> I despair of this spiritual poverty of ours, of this congenital in-
> capacity, of this immaturity that has nothing in common with the
> impetuous freshness of a young people, which smacks of staleness,
> of profound corruption and unwholesomeness. All of us are medi-
> ocre, with no exceptions. Even the best intentioned, the innocent
> souls, lack genius and energy. We go straight from the timid to the
> violent. We lack calm, serene and sure strength. We have no leader,
> no leaders. And the defect descends into the masses, whom no-
> body knows how to rehabilitate. The idea of neo-Fascism is super-
> fluous deceit. The Fascist tendency, which is factious, excessive and
> intolerant, remains in our minds and political practices. The mal-
> ady is more serious than we think and is deep down just because it
> is innate in our nature, in this variety of human beings, of charac-
> ters, of tendencies, of cultural differences, and in this poor sense of
> civil solidarity. This failing causes political competition to degener-
> ate into dispute, it leads every controversy onto the terrain of bad
> faith, it diverts the triumph of political ideals toward the triumph
> of political hegemony, it excludes the possibility of parties coop-
> erating honestly and it deprives political rivalry of any kind of
> generosity. It is necessary to study the malady thoroughly to be-
> lieve in a way to revive the country. Those who will dare to tell the
> Italians the truth, those who will dare to mortify them before rais-
> ing them up, will do the country the only honest and effective
> favor.[60]

In the immediate postwar years, there was no lack of attempts, made above all by writers and intellectuals, to "study the malady thoroughly" and tell "the Italians the truth," taking on the task to discover, reveal and criticize the defects and vices of the Italian character.[61] The collapse of the nation had given new vigor to the so-called anti-Italian moralists who outlined a kind of soul-searching of the Italians in their reflections. These generally reached very pessimistic conclusions on the possibility of an Italian nation as a political and moral entity, established in a sovereign, free and independent state. Furthermore, these reflections were often not very objective, easily open to banal generalizations based on subjective prejudices (and often involuntary projections of the vices and virtues of the fault-finder himself, and of a preconceived idea of the "average Italian"). They were also open to the whims of literary invention and moralistic diatribes, yet were very important to understanding the idea the Italians had of themselves immediately after the Second World War. And these reflections reached a common conclusion: that the prevailing elements in the Italians' character went in the opposite direction to forming a national civic conscience.

Indeed, if there was one thing the "anti-Italians" agreed upon it was that the basic elements of the Italian character (which had emerged over the centuries following the political breakup of Italy after the fall of the Roman Empire) had remained unchanged, even after unification. The efforts made by the unitary state to fuse the many ancient city-states into a new national civilization had been mostly in vain: "Since the city-states came to an end, a national civilization has not yet risen in Italy," the historian Fabio Cusin wrote in 1945.[62] The Communes and seigniories, according to Giuseppe Prezzolini, were "the only original political creations of the Italians,"[63] and the basic traits of their individualistic and factious, ambitious and obsequious, dispotic and anarchic, conformist and quarrelsome character were reflected in them. In Giorgio Fenoaltea's opinion, this was mainly due to the character of the *Italieschi*, as he called the inhabitants, who had "moulded the events of the peninsula" in such a way that "for long centuries it had not formed the history of a nation, but a hundred or thousand histories of provinces and towns, of villages and wards, of districts and people."[64] This gave rise to an individualism that was unyielding to the discipline of common rules, fostering ambition for power for personal use and a tendency to violent party passions in society and politics. Consequently, "it was impossible for political awareness to be instilled as a connecting principle and a profound awareness of the nation in itself."[65]

The horizon of the "*italiesco* politician," as also of the "ordinary citizen," was restricted to defending his "personal interests"[66] and was entirely concentrated on the issue of power for the politician. "What matters above all to the *italiesco* politician? Power. What must he avoid more than anything else? Everything that can make him lose power."[67] Achieving unity and building the Italian state had had little effect on the formation of national civic-mindedness. Risorgimento patriotism, adopted as the highest principle of national education by the ruling class of the unitary state, had not sunk into the Italians' minds, becoming consciousness and conviction: as Cusin noted, it was still ritual and sentimental patriotism, "trifling and occasional patriotism, like one's best clothes worn on fixed days and on important occasions, not a part of everyday life where the cult of fatherland is integrated into daily customs."[68]

Faced with the collapse of the national state, the Italians had reacted by throwing away their best clothes of patriotism, taking refuge once again in "personal interests." Past defects in the Italian character had overwhelmingly come out again with the war and defeat and had regained sway over individual and collective behavior in worse forms. "Today the Italians . . . no longer share a common ideal and have relapsed into an amorphous mass that lives hand to mouth, counting on small Machiavellian ruses typical of provincial politics," the Communist Bianchi Bandinelli wrote in 1945.[69]

Therefore, in reflecting on the Italians' character, the search for the causes of the catastrophe shifted from politics to anthropology, from the responsibility of the governors to that of the governed. The Fascist ruling class was guilty without extenuating circumstances, but the entire Italian population was also to blame, as it had produced, tolerated or applauded that very ruling class. The tendency among the anti-Fascists to put the blame entirely on Fascism for the "malady" that had paralyzed the Italians' political conscience for twenty years and caused moral and civil devastation in their lives was certainly well-founded. Nevertheless, it also had the negative effect of encouraging the Italians themselves to remove Fascism from Italian history and from their consciences by resorting to an act of oblivion, as if Fascism had really been an occupation of the country by foreigners or a malignant foreign body that had attacked the Italian nation, dragging it down to ruin. The fact is, by removing Fascism the Italians thought they could unburden themselves of any responsibility for everything that Fascism had been and produced, posing as innocent victims of the regime and its Duce. The reassuring effect of this act of oblivion arose from the confidence that, once the malady was eradicated, the nation's organism would be restored to good health in the wholesome air of the new democratic Italy.

However, the Italians' declaration that they were innocent clashed with some indisputable facts that, despite all the extenuating circumstances, made it seem pitifully naive, or even simply opportunistic. And these facts highlighted the Italians' involvement, anything but simply forced, in the adventure of Fascism. Certainly, when summing up responsibilities, the greater share went to the ruling classes, the institutions and the men of culture who, with their consent and collaboration, had allowed Fascism to dominate the nation unopposed and construct a system of power that in the end led to the will of one person alone. However, this very "final will of one person alone," as Francesco Flora wrote, was also due to "the mental and moral surrender of the fatherland:"

> All the Italians, except those who died or were buried alive in prisons, were guilty to a greater or lesser degree: not only those who were halfhearted but also those who, though fighting against the regime, did not make every possible effort and failed in their social duty. . . . Italy was ruined by not resisting, which allowed, above all, the continuous reactionary deception of apparent prosperity and order. . . . Italy's holiday from morality had its tragic punishment.[70]

Italy Is Dead

Pondering the catastrophe of the nation after September 8, many reached the conclusion that the Italy born of the Risorgimento had come to an end. The Italians had shown they were incapable of developing national awareness, of knowing how to govern by themselves or unite to face the tragic tests of living together and defending unity and independence. "By now Italy has revealed its limits; it is a nation that cannot govern itself alone. The Risorgimento has come to an end with the most dreadful crash in Italian history. Therefore, some foreigner or other is needed to take Italy in hand, organize it, give it new blood, revive it and, in short, govern it,"[71] wrote Giovanni Ansaldo, who once sang the praises of Fascist imperial ambitions then regretted it. Italy's independence also ended with the defeat: "Italy is really finished, and even if it were formally united and apparently independent in the future, it would be so thanks to foreign imperialism, not to its own autonomous strength."[72] However, it was not only former Fascists who, having changed their minds, considered the Italy created by the Risorgimento at an end. Benedetto Croce also lost all hope in Italy's destiny, even though he had fought against pessimism all his life and still fought it: "Seeing the destruction of the Italy created by the Risorgimento men in which we were brought up, growing with it, is something I cannot accept," he wrote in September 1946.[73] Historian Giacomo Perticone described an imaginary funeral of the Italian nation:

> The fatherland is dead, a large body on a large hearse. It moves with difficulty, evoking grief and physical suffering, even though, as it is a corpse, we should not think of this. But the black hearse moves as if it were motionless, as if it were stuck to the ground, as if it could not break away from the ground without injury.[74]

Actually, the military defeat, the fall of the regime and the collapse of the state not only put an end to ambitions for power and greatness but also seemed to destroy the fragile national identity that, despite its many limits, ambitions and illusions, the Italians had acquired over eighty years as a united nation. From this point of view, the struggle for freedom and the birth of the republic marked a decisive turning-point in the Italians' culture and consciousness. In effect, these two events ended an age of Italian history that began with the birth of the Risorgimento movement and the creation of the unitary state that was given not only political and territorial importance but was considered a supreme set of ideals and values suitable for guiding the Italian nation in its march forward. At the same time, the events of 1943–46 laid the groundwork for a new period of difficult democracy, where "state" and "nation," hopelessly compromised by being too closely identified with the myths of Fascism, were no longer the highest ideals of community life. In 1947 a young supporter of European unity wrote, "The ideal of Italy and its national dignity, is dead."[75]

14

Pull the Idol Down

The Decline of Nationalism

The French Revolution started off the age of European nationalism that reached its climax during the Second World War, a period that also marked the beginning of its decline. Meanwhile the myth of nation found new, very fertile ground in developing countries, becoming the driving force of anticolonialist movements.

The European political order was totally disrupted after the war ended. The two nations that were the main victims of this upheaval were those that, in the nineteenth century, had expressed the extreme triumph of the myth of nation, though in profoundly different ways. Italy and Germany, both defeated, occupied and devastated, had seen their dreams of greatness and their imperialist ambitions collapse definitively. However, it was very soon clear that France and Britain, both of which had once again come out of a world conflict victors, had also lost their rank as great powers, faced with the undisputed supremacy of the United States and the Soviet Union. From then on, the two superpowers, patriotic and proud of being the leader-states that would guide humanity to a better world, wielded real hegemony over the old European national states, who took sides with one or the other superpower according to their ideas of a future world, their principles, values and economic and political systems to make up two hostile blocs. The two superpowers professed opposing ideologies but had universalistic tendencies in common, and each one held itself up as a model for all humanity. In 1949 an Italian observer pointed out that both the Soviet Union and the United States, "deliberately made every effort, through education and in other ways, to substitute narrow-minded national and racial feelings with the idea that an individual belongs to a wider-ranging humanity, held together by common ideals."[1] This was their

231

aim, even though it was easy to see the impulse of a new desire for power behind these ideologies, justified in the name of supremacy and a universal mission, now sustained by the immense strength of new and more lethal weapons. These ideologies did not completely deny the myth of nation but subordinated it to the supremacy of openly antinationalist principles and values. They optimistically foresaw, in the more or less near future, that the divisions and rivalries among peoples, stirred up by armed national states against one another, would be definitively overcome. Furthermore, these states would make peace again under the protection of new international organizations, more effective than the inept League of Nations.

After the war, nationalism was in disrepute, bearing the principal responsibility for the two world conflicts that had inflicted appalling losses on humanity, and becoming wholly synonymous, at least for Western culture, with authoritarianism in internal affairs and warlike imperialist policies in foreign affairs as well as brutal barbarity and inhuman aggressiveness that destroyed the dignity and freedom of men and citizens. Condemning and repudiating nationalism was even more profound in Europe, where it was held responsible for the definitive decline of the centuries-old political and civil supremacy of the old continent, even though nationalism itself had contributed to bringing Europe to the height of prestige and power through imperialism. Torn apart and destroyed by internal nationalist rivalries, Europe had lost its position as mistress of the world, becoming a mere object "of the political game played by the two big imperialist blocs that won the war."[2] Up to then, the myth of nation had made each European state more united internally, but this unity was undermined or broken up into rival groups whose political beliefs were transnational and much stronger than any feeling for their own country. At the end of 1946, Corrado Alvaro wrote:

> The division not only of Italy but of Europe, and within every European nation, so that countries are reduced to political entities from erstwhile national entities, is a state typical of disquiet. Consequently, troubled men are led to choose the political ideals bearing the promise of a stand against new wars and massacres. Today Europe, divided into cliques, expresses nothing but ideals of biological preservation: all its ideals consist in the determination to survive.[3]

Nationalism was unanimously condemned, at least in the European governments' official declarations, just as its members were unanimous in professing their faith in peace and cooperation among peoples to ensure the progress of humanity. In fact since then, no state, at least in Europe, has ever again made a show of brazen ambitions of greatness and might with a display of virile vanity, having banished ambitions of hegemony and imperial dominion to the memories of a tragic past. In this sense, the decline of imperialist and authoritarian nationalism was definitive, at least among the European states, even if some of them have not stopped posing as great powers on the world scene.

Nevertheless, not only was the brutal aspect of nationalism rejected but so too was the myth of nation itself, the idea and feeling that one's nation, expressed through the national state, was something of value. And yet this myth had been an ideal, really decisive factor in the anti-Fascist war itself, rallying peoples against the imperialism of Germany, Italy and Japan. Even Soviet Russia, the home of Communist internationalism, had raised the flag of national patriotism during the war, drawing moral resources from the glorification of the illustrious past of tsarist Russia, a bulwark against the Teutonic hordes.

Indeed, that a national feeling had dwindled, at least compared to the patriotic enthusiasm that in many countries had welcomed the outbreak of the First World War, was evident right from the beginning of the new conflict. In 1946, in an essay criticizing nationalism that was immediately translated into Italian, the historian Edward Hallett Carr wrote that however paradoxical it may seem, the lack of any sign of national exaltation or enthusiasm when the Second World War broke out was undeniable.[4] In all countries this revealed a striking contrast, which drew widespread attention at the time, with the patriotic fervor of 1914—in Germany no less than elsewhere. Hatred between nations has lost its old, open spontaneity and hides discreetly behind every kind of ideological device.[5]

The Axis powers themselves—as we saw with Fascism—fought the war brandishing the myths of a New Europe and new supranational order, holding that by then the age of nationality and national states had had its day.

Is the National State Coming to an End?

To the world that had come out of the Second World War, the future of national states seemed fatally bound to overcoming a unilateral and particularistic concept of nation and state as absolutely sovereign within its borders. Carr stated that the world "will have to adapt to the formation of some great multinational units where most of the power will be centralized."[6] Reducing and limiting the sovereignty of national states within new supranational political and economic structures by means of more or less marked forms of federalism were considered at that point necessary, at least for European peoples. After 1945, a more vigorous aspiration to European unification arose all over Europe, leaving behind past hatred and rivalries and rediscovering cultural matrices and spiritual traditions in common, while recognizing common interests and the search for a common destiny. This was not only to forestall further hatred and nationalistic ambitions from arising but also to find solutions for the evident inadequacy of the national state to cope with the new world situation that had emerged from the war with the success of the superpowers. Federalism seemed the only way for Europe to keep its own cultural identity and enable the Europeans to control and decide their own destiny.

However, was it really possible to speak of an irreversible decline of the myth of the nation in Europe after the Second World War and trust, though without false hopes, that it would soon disappear? Were the defeat, condemnation and repudiation of nationalism in themselves a guarantee of its inevitable decline? The doubts raised by these questions tormented the more realistic European consciences that, though they did not cherish fond hopes for a united and pacified humanity, still felt an urgent need to "cut the claws of nationalism once and for all," as declared by the French editors of a collection of papers published in 1946 titled *Nations ou Fédéralisme*, with British, French and German scholars collaborating on it.[7] These scholars maintained that "to cut the claws of nationalism" there was no other means than by eliminating the causes of rivalry among European peoples. The first step was to go beyond the limited and rigid confines of the national state, which should give up a part of its sovereignty to build a common European house. Nevertheless, they were aware that it was not an easy undertaking and that caution was needed to avoid lapsing into a vague and inconclusive plan for a future world with all humanity united and pacified.

In the early postwar period, European political culture was strongly critical when reflecting on nationalism, nation and the national state. The meaning and role of these entities, once raised to the rank of absolute divinities eager for human sacrifices to satisify their greed for dominion and power, were once again brought up for discussion. The novelty of these reflections was that the attempt to understand why nationalism had arisen did not stop at attributing the original cause to the madness of some megalomaniac or other, whether an individual or a people. On the contrary, for the first time there was a thorough analysis of the events that had led to forming the modern idea of nation and national state as they had developed since the age of the French Revolution. The intention was to ascertain whether aggressive nationalism was a necessary consequence of nation and national state or if it was a degeneration limited to some countries. It was not only a theoretical question: the attitude to take toward the myth of nation depended on the answer. In the former case, the myth of nation would have been involved in the condemnation of nationalism, while in the latter case, not only would it have had no bearing on the issue but it could even have been, once again, considered a valid antidote to nationalism itself, to prevent a return to imperialist madness and rebuild democracy on more solid foundations after the totalitarian experience.

There was another important aspect of the nature of nationalism, which did not concern international politics but, rather, internal politics, and that was the attitude of the national state toward its citizens, in other words, the relationship between individual and nation. Nationalism had increased the power of the state over society out of all proportion, seriously limiting or completely canceling the citizens' freedom in the name of security and power. However, the myth of nation did promote the freedom and equality of citizens. Could it have this function once again?

Italian Antinationalism

In the early postwar years, Italian intellectuals and politicians were deeply committed to dealing with these problems. They brought the issue of nation back to the center of a collective soul-searching that, for the intensity and variety of subjects, could be compared to the ideological turmoil of the first decades of the century. As then, the definition of the national Italian identity and the relation between nation and freedom, the individual and nation and the individual and national state were debated once again, giving rise to a great number of stances and explanations.

After 1945, the Italians were up front in disowning nationalism and repudiating the myth of might, almost as if by publicly abjuring them they might distance themselves, once and for all, from their heavy responsibility. In fact, right after the First World War, they were the first to start off a new form of aggressive, totalitarian and imperialist nationalism, which then became a model and source of inspiration for other

similar kinds of nationalism. Consequently, the old and new parties that
founded republican Italy after the Second World War were unanimous
in condemning nationalism: the only voices not in unison, as we shall
see, were those of the neo- and former Fascists. Nevertheless, the new
republican Italy was also up front in picking up the debate on nation
and the national state again, but this time with a radically different outlook, openly condemning all the ambitions for might that had accompanied the myth of nation from the Risorgimento through the years of
Fascism. In 1946, Alberto Moravia, the novelist, wrote that "the defeat
has definitively sent D'Annunzio and Gentile, Nietzschean heroism and
the nationalism of Barrès, the ideas of the Roman Empire and the ethical state back to the past."[8] The painter and writer Alberto Savinio
added that any claim to greatness had to be outlawed to make the Italians understand that the "enormity of the disaster that has befallen us
is exactly proportionate to the height of the 'rhetorical mountain' to
which our country had been raised."[9]

The myth of a Greater Italy, conceived above all as a great world
power, was certainly wiped out by the catastrophe of the war. Many of
those who had let themselves be seduced by this myth, like Giovanni
Ansaldo, also noted that "the old nationalist myth has been disposed of"
by "realistically accepting Italy's position in the world, which makes our
country small and fatally dependent on the European and transatlantic
giants."[10]

In other words, there were sound reasons to believe that the Italians
had got rid of the nationalist temptation forever. And if anyone was still
slow to believe that Italy's time as a great power was absolutely over,
there was always the indisputable proof of Italy's actual situation in a
world where war had just ended to give a warning, as the diplomat Roberto Ducci explained:

> If we want to be brutally frank, the situation is the following: be-
> tween 1860 and 1940 Italy managed to be included formally among
> the Great Powers, without really possessing the necessary material
> qualities. Since 1940, it has not even been able to aspire to this
> courtesy title, and it would do well to be convinced of this as soon
> as possible. The power scale has grown; and as long as power de-
> cides human destiny, it will be impossible for Italy (and the same
> applies to every other continental European nation, taken individ-
> ually) to be among the protagonists of history's dramatic play.[11]

The Italians were confident that they had gotten rid of nationalism,
and this confidence was strengthened by the belief that all the European

populations, without exception, both victors and vanquished, having suffered in the first person and paid, with their blood, the consequences of nationalistic ambitions and rivalries had finally become wiser or at least had been vaccinated against the risk of nationalist seduction. The attitude of the Italians toward the nation and the national state showed unmistakable signs that all vestiges of nationalism had been expunged. The national pride that still flared up, even among the anti-Fascists, during the controversy over the peace treaty, or when faced with the destiny of Trieste, was aroused by the feelings, rather than by the ideology, of people who had grown up in the cult of fatherland but who had never been among the supporters of imperialist nationalism.

Republican Italy was born with a definite and clear profession of antinationalist faith. After all, antinationalism was congenital with anti-Fascism. If there was one thing all the anti-Fascists agreed upon, it was their aversion to nationalism, just as they were unanimously determined to destroy forever the seed that had brought it to life. "They are anti-Fascists because they are antinationalists," Action Party member Augusto Monti had declared.[12] However, there was not the same agreement among the anti-Fascists when identifying the cause and original nature of nationalism, especially regarding the nexus between nationalism, nation and national state. The debate and controversy over this problem were not limited to the political struggle. It was only by analyzing this nexus, in fact, that strictly theoretical reflections began again in Italy on the subject of nation, on its importance in the history of humanity and on Italian history in particular, with everything that ensued for the destiny of the myth of nation in the new anti-Fascist Italy, as revealed by this study.

The differences of ideas and attitudes regarding the myth of nation were evident starting with the conflicting predictions on the future of nationalism and the destiny of the national state. The optimists prognosticated that "nationalist thought would progressively and rapidly lose all meaning," because in all countries people were beginning to understand that "it is no longer possible to think nationalistically," since "the play of forces in the course of history no longer seems set in terms of nations but in terms of blocs, coalitions, unions and federations, in other words in supranational concepts." This led to the conclusion that nationalism was "fading in people's awareness. It 'sounds false.' It is becoming a provincial ideal. . . . In Europe, nationalism, which was professed up to 1914 by the cream of intellectuals, has sunk to a hoarse 'slogan' of second-rate intriguers, of men who are also morally inferior.

In a certain way, everyone feels that the expression 'every European war is fratricide' is not just an expression."[13]

The destructive monstrosity of nationalism, with the masses of dead and devastation scattered over the European continent, seemed such a convincing argument in itself against a return of nationalism, that it would be madness to take it as a serious possibility. Hope for the end of nationalism, Guido De Ruggiero wrote, had been supported by the belief that

> all nationalisms must have been something against nature if, to put them into practice, it was necessary to suppress the most elementary rights of citizens, to create insurmountable physical and moral barriers, and almost as if this were not enough, to incite men to destroy one another. And it seemed the height of absurdity that the poisonous plant of nationalism had sprouted and grown right at a time when all the expressions of human activity and all the greatest aspirations tended to clear the ground of this plant, typical of stagnant swamps.[14]

However, the optimistic belief that nationalism had been wiped out was denied in some cases by postwar reality, which witnessed nationalistic impulses coming out again both in the ambitions of the nations that won and in the resentment of the defeated. As De Ruggiero himself pointed out, already in early peacetime it was recognized that the war had not at all been "the hoped-for decisive crisis of nationalism, which, on the contrary, had been rekindled and aggravated. . . . We need to be cured of the nationalistic infection, and in the meantime we are forced to stay shut up in our national prisons, hemmed in all around by the nationalism of others. Instead of canceling borders, even tighter ones are imposed on us."[15] The outcome of the war had decreed the defeat of nationalism by liberalism, socialism and democracy, but "now that reducing nationalism to a tragic absurdity is on the way out, too many people still speak in terms of nationalism and imperialism and predict new wars before long, showing they have not learnt anything from the harsh lesson of history."[16] It was right to protest that "the survival of nationalism is so wrong, so nonsensical, that it is difficult to have to admit it as reality." Nevertheless, the philosopher warned, it had to be acknowledged that it "is a reality lying in our nature's irrational depths, which arouses instinctive and passionate impulses, and these keep it alive."[17] Therefore, De Ruggiero concluded, considering the irrationality of human nature, there was still the fear that the passions for nationalism might return, stirring up the passionate depths where "the emotions of the most out-of-date patriotic sentimentalism thrive. . . . It is inevitable that the sharp tips of a surly and irritating nationalism come out of patriotism like claws from the velvety paws of a cat."[18]

The jurist and historian Arturo Carlo Jemolo reached similar conclusions when pondering the "end of nationalism." At the end of 1947 he wrote that, apparently, "nationalism is alive as never before, even in its most harmful forms," because both victors and vanquished had regained national feeling, the former through pride in their victory and the latter "because of the sting of defeat and the humiliation of enemy occupation and economic problems. Their national feeling was not the sound and natural kind, similar to attachment for one's own family, but the anti-Christian one, which leads to saying that one's own country can never be wrong, that it is a duty to be on its side without passing judgment on the aims it follows, without submitting them to moral evaluation."[19]

Uprooting the poisonous plant of nationalism was, therefore, anything but an easy task, and it was dangerous to cherish false hopes of its irreversible decline. To prevent a dangerous revival, it was necessary to wipe out its last hotbeds, too, and tear up the deepest roots and destroy them. It was not enough to ascertain that the ambitions of nationalism had failed disastrously after causing death and ruin: the soil in which the seed of this poisonous plant had sprouted and grown and where it could still find the vital nourishment to grow again had also to be destroyed.

Demolishing the National State

Thus, reflections shifted from nationalism to the national state. And here, as we have already mentioned, many more doubts arose. Was the brutal, totalitarian and imperialist nationalism of the twentieth century genetically different from the nineteenth-century nationalism of the movements for the independence and freedom of nations, or was it a natural consequence? Was Fascist nationalism a consequence of Risorgimento nationalism? And more generally speaking, did nationalism necessarily derive from the myth of nation, always possible everywhere, or did it degenerate from the myth by chance, due, that is, not to the nature of the myth of nation but to a substantial alteration of it in certain situations and countries? And as such, could it be avoided or eliminated if suitable precautions were taken? In short, did the national state contain brutal, totalitarian and imperialist nationalism in its genetic code? And if so, would it mean that this nationalism could still rise again in the

form of ideologies different from those of Fascism and National Socialism as long as national states existed?

The answer to these questions that came from some Catholic and
lay intellectuals heavily criticized the very nature of the modern national state. According to the Jesuit Antonio Messineo, the major expert
of *Civiltà Cattolica* on the national problem, "the idea of the modern
state" emerged above all among the causes of the rivalries that divided
national states and that "inevitably spark off a war at critical points in
time." It was a state that, "under the influence of positivist or idealistic,
individualistic, agnostic or monistic concepts was cast up by political
philosophy, as also by legal theories, to the level of the absolute, deified
in the total autonomy of its will and made into a monstrous idol to
which rights were subordinated." The myth of nation, whose worshippers gathered into various nationalist groups and crowded around its
pedestal, had contributed to strengthening the "myth of state" and to
making it even more closed within its egoism. Consequently, nationalism was seen by the Jesuit as an inevitable product of the modern state's
tendency to justify itself in the name of nation, and in its name "to
absorb parts of the population coming from different cultural backgrounds within its rigidly unitary structure, levelling the differences by
imposing the same language, schools, customs and standard of living."
This tendency was strengthened by the "vast movement of nationalities" struggling for independence in the name of autonomy for individuals and social communities. This was expressed in the "new political
axiom, with the intention of giving it legal content, concerning the right
of peoples to be their own masters," that is, the principle of nationality
worked out systematically by the Italian school of international law. The
myth of nation and of the national state gained substance from these
converging tendencies and merged in such a way that "the nation was
identified with the state and the state with the nation. Consequently, the
shared feeling of belonging to an ethnic group, marked by particular
cultural features, flowed back to the state, which became more intoler-
ant toward the traditional values of the minorities submitted to its regime." Finally, nationalism, which according to the Jesuit was conceptu-
ally "poor but sentimentally rich in vitality," sprang from this source and
set out to transform a natural fact into the value of the national state.
The nation became "the obligatory converging point of all political action, and sacred national egoism the supreme duty of public authority."
When this process reached its climax, which, in the Jesuit's impassioned
description of it seemed to obey the impulse of a devilish desire for

power inherent in modern secular states, the national state had finally emerged, closed within itself like "a castle without windows, within which the population got ready for the conflict against other fortified strongholds, ready to fight for its own success and expansion, to be gained even to the detriment of others' rights. Nationalism, aggravating a sentiment that in itself is legitimate, thus became a disruptive element of the sound unity of peoples in international society."

Summarily, simplifying the numerous ways that the concepts of a sovereign state were formed, the Jesuits' periodical ended up by attributing ambitions of absolutism and imperialism to the modern state, independently of the political regime, the historical situation and the ruling class's choices. Thus the Jesuits quashed any distinction between different expressions of the idea of nation, and between national state and "nationalistic state." They attributed a fatal propensity for war to the modern state founded on the myth of nation, and this propensity was given vent "by making a present of two frightful war cataclysms to humanity." In short, the Catholics believed that only by going beyond the national state would "a true, fruitful and harmonious international society be achieved"; the nationalist error had to be "completely suppressed and eliminated from politicians' minds: Europe must be freed of the nationalist poison."[20]

Even more bitter was the criticism against the national state raised by its secular opponents, among whom the champions of European federalism stood out for their consistency and intransigence. Like the above-mentioned Catholic author, the federalists maintained that the absolute sovereignty of the modern state and the myth of nation were at the root of nationalism. Some federalists thought that the ideas of nation and national state were to be jointly condemned as responsible for nationalism, firmly believing that the age of national states and the principal of nationality itself had come to an end. As the historian Paolo Alatri affirmed in 1946, this was because "the national state, the idol of last century, has by now completed its function."[21] The national state and the myth of nation, which made the state legitimate by giving it an aura of sacredness and eternity, presenting it as the best form of human organization and with unlimited sovereignty, were the still-living matrix of nationalism, and it was unthinkable to destroy nationalism while leaving its matrix alive. Therefore, it was necessary to go ahead and beyond the national state to supranational forms of organization. Some federalists even doubted the existence of the nation as a clearly recognizable historical entity. They started by observing that the idea of nation eluded a clear and coherent definition, as its constitutive elements were uncertain, contradictory and unstable. Others considered the nation nothing more than a political stratagem of which the creators of the centralizing state made use to legitimize its sovereignty.

Silvio Trentin, a militant of Giustizia e Libertà (Justice and Freedom), spoke of "the invention of Nation"[22] by the absolutist monarchic state in order to support its centralizing power, just as the principle of nationality was used to justify "the most cynical initiatives undertaken, which aimed at domination for reasons of state." The new democratic state born of the French Revolution had taken over the principle of nation, which "substituted the monarchy as the depository of sovereignty and at the same time set itself up as its only and immediate source. The nation was expressed through this new state. The nation thus provided many more compelling reasons for entitling the state to subordinate its erstwhile subjects, now citizens, to the authorities, directly and exclusively. The latter are the jealous guardians of the capacities required to govern."[23] With the idealistic theories of Romanticism, "the idea of nation and the principle of nationality as a differentiating and catalyzing principle of the specific individuality of each single people will soon be useful as an idea and pretext to work out the theory of nationalism," in which the nation "ceases to be the subject of a right to freedom and becomes the only authority with the prerogative to dominate." Trentin believed that this was how the democratic idea of nation was transformed into the nationalist doctrine.[24] Both capitalist democracy and messianic nationalism made use of the principle of nationality, reaching the same result, although from opposite directions, that is, strengthening the "monocentralized state and its increasingly aggressive expansion onto imperialist ground." The coinciding results derived from the common origin of democratic nationalism and authoritarian nationalism. In contrast with the current opinion of liberal culture, which believed there was a different origin both for democratic, voluntaristic nationalism and naturalistic authoritarian nationalism, Trentin was convinced that German nationalism, considered a prototype of authoritarian nationalism that identified nation with state, also "comes directly from patriotic mysticism, unleashed and spread by the French Revolution, and it was through the French Revolution that German nationalism adopted the belief that the limits of a state must coincide with those of a nation, and that the emancipation of peoples can only be achieved by means of, and under a regime capable of, putting unity into effect and making it binding."[25] Although the various kinds of nationalism followed different paths, they all aimed at identifying nation with state, affirming the supremacy of the national state over individuals, making the nation absolute above its citizens. In the same way, both democratic and authoritarian nationalism in other countries led to the supposed supremacy of one nation over the others, in the name of a presumed superiority of the "chosen people" to carry out a mission. Trentin thought that this line of development was also typical of Risorgimento nationalism, and he traced Mazzini's idea of nation back to this line of development, though Mazzini had been a champion and model of voluntaristic and humanitarian nationalism, an upholder of the freedom of individuals and equality among nations. Starting from the "rigidity of the *a priori* premises on which he had built his doctrine of nationality so fervently," Trentin held that not only did Mazzini not recognize nationality for all peoples but he "had no doubt about attributing unique virtues to the Italians whenever possible. These virtues seem to destine his country by divine decree to carrying out privileged functions no different from those that Hegel had assigned to Germany."[26] Once Carlo Cattaneo's "fine federalist dream" had ended, it was the mystical concept of the centralizing national state that had prevailed with unification. It was as if "sheltered by and within the rigid walls of a monolithic building . . . , the Italian nation suddenly found it had triumphantly taken the place of the old regional personalities . . . that the Italies had been accustomed to and through which they had persisted in expressing themselves for centuries."[27] The totalitarian state itself was nothing but the extreme expression and the climax of the monocentralizing national state. The only way to ensure a future of freedom for citizens was to break the "vicious circle" that justified the monocentralizing state's unlimited sovereignty by linking it to the nation. "Consequently the true price of freedom is demolishing the monocentralizing state"[28] through a federalist revolution both in politics and in the economic and social field:

> Contrasting interests and political ambiguities contributed to establishing the unitary state on the peninsula in the post-Risorgimento period. Thus established, the unitary state imposed its law, with sovereign power, on that complex and concrete mass of elements, factors, situations and conditions that is conventionally called Italy. Therefore, the problem that arises for Italy today, as for every other civilized country, with increasingly dramatic urgency, is to know whether, despite those aforementioned contrasting interests and ambiguities, it really is a genuine national reality and, if it exists, to

be aware of Italy's needs and find out how it can gain recognition and make its worth known.[29]

   This is how the whole formative process of Italian unity and the history of the unitary state became the center of heated controversy, by attacking the national state and by including the Italian question in the more general issue of the evolution of the modern state. This came about after its symbiotic union with the myth of nation, which had contributed to the increasing expansion of state power to the detriment of the citizens' political freedom.

Against the Myth of Nation

Secular federalism fostered antinationalist criticism organically and coherently, and sometimes with strongly utopian undertones, with the aim of striking at the heart of the national state. The more radical positions reached the point of demanding that the nation in itself as an ideal and political entity, and the principle of nationality as a basis to legitimize the state, be transcended. In other words, the federalists refused to consider the nation an entity existing in and of itself that would be almost eternal. Many were sure that, regardless, the vitality of the myth of nation was exhausted and that it had "lost its potential as a 'creator of states.'"[30] Men of culture who were not politically committed were convinced of this as well. In 1943 Alberto Savinio wrote:

> The idea of "nation," which was originally expansive and therefore active and fertile, and as such inspired and shaped the European nations among which we were born and have lived up to now, has at this point lost its expansive qualities and, on the contrary, has acquired restrictive ones. Hemmed in and wretched, this idea is no longer active but has become passive; it no longer responds to ideas of development, growth or expansion but obeys ideas of impoverishment, restriction and reduction: a sign that the idea of "nation," as conceived by those who built nations, has lost its virtues in the meantime, and from a fertile idea has become a sterile one, from active it has become passive and from a beneficial principle has become a harmful one.[31]

   Radical federalists were very suspicious of the survival of the myth of nation, even though it had been purified and regenerated by federal democracy. They raised the problem more drastically of going *beyond* the nation and not only beyond the national state. The members of the

Action Party believed that not only should "the system of absolute national sovereignties" be suppressed, but not even "new traditions and national and particularistic interests should be allowed to strengthen . . . narrow-minded traditions that lead people to think only of their own country's problems and to consider Europe's problems simply a matter of power and not in terms of lasting cooperation."[32] The Action Party movement was cautiously beginning to evaluate the possibility of a federalist experiment. This would not propose *preserving* the nation, including it within a federal structure, but *abandoning* the nation, that is, to go effectively beyond the age of nation and nationalism by progressively breaking up its constitutive elements, beginning from the territorial basis of the national state. The historian Giampiero Carocci maintained that by breaking up the territorial element "the nation would collapse as a state entity," national barriers would be progressively cancelled, national governments would lose their functions, giving way to more complex international organizations, and at the end of this process, nations would be "surpassed and would merge into a whole, although keeping their individual features. The fusion would not be a sum of nations, as in the nineteenth-century attempts, but the result of their being weakened, that is, surpassed." At the end of the process "there would be a world organization with a functional base, and nations would completely disappear."[33]

For radical federalism, going beyond the myth of nation was a necessary stage in the progress of democracy toward the complete liberation of individuals and citizens. The ideal of democratic revolution as emancipation achieved under the banner of integral secularism saw the myth of nation as one of the last bastions of modern governmentalism besides its historical function in the nineteenth century as a liberating factor of oppressed peoples. In 1944 Altiero Spinelli wrote that modern politics developed precisely along the lines of "continually extending and concentrating the functions of the state."[34] From 1941, when Spinelli founded the European Federalist Movement, he predicted hopefully that rebuilding Europe after totalitarian nationalism had been overthrown would take place on a federal basis, that is, limiting state power to the utmost, both internally and externally. This was because only federalism would guarantee the future of democracy, while the national state, with its centralizing bureaucracy and sovereignty made sacred in the name of the nation, was basically incompatible with democracy. The "problem of democracy's future," Spinelli wrote in 1947, "is, in short, the possibility of building states with limited powers."[35]

In this prospect, the controversy about the myth of nation was not only aimed at the nationalism that caused armed conflict among countries, but at the nationalism responsible for limiting and suppressing citizens' freedom, in the name of the state and nation's sovereignty and security. By being identified symbiotically with the nation, the state had progressively strengthened its power over society and citizens as well as subdued and modeled the nation according to its need to dominate. Thus, the myth of nation had given the state a potentially antidemocratic legitimacy. De Ruggiero observed that the union between state and nation "has given rise to a pathological growth of the state and deformed the nation's historical features" and "has corrupted and deformed nations, driving them downhill in a way that was not natural to their historical mission." However, it would have been disingenuous and antihistorical to think of modifying this process simply by overcoming the side-effects of history. Alternatively, "reducing state functions, thus freeing a considerable part of national energies from an oppressive bond, letting them function spontaneously and autonomously, could have been started." However, freeing these energies completely would have been neither possible nor desirable, because the national state is still alive in the present state of human consciousness." Nevertheless, decreasing the sovereignty of the national state as much as possible could have been taken into consideration, and to do so, "it would be necessary to create a political federation, or a superstate with limited functions."[36] Therefore, the national state was an obstacle to the development of democracy. However, not all antinationalists were convinced that to decrease the sovereignty of the national state it was enough to reduce the power of the state in favor of the citizens' freedom; it was the very sovereignty of the national state—what the symbiosis between the state and nation had produced—that had to be destroyed to ensure the development of freedom.

In *La Nuova Europa* (The New Europe), one of the main publications of secular antinationalism, Mariano Maresca stated that to achieve a democratic state, "a tenacious idol must be pulled down: the national state," because the national state had clearly failed to carry out the function assigned to it by history: "to mediate between the absolute state and the democratic one." However, to do so, the mythological basis on which the national state had built its authority, that is the myth of nation, had to be destroyed. Maresca analyzed the mythical origin of the national state more deeply, giving a psychological interpretation of the formative process of nationalist mythology and the complex of greatness deriving from it. In order to transfer the prerogatives of the absolute sovereign to individual consciousness, so as to make it the "center of autonomous social relations," the realism innate in human imagination" had to pass "through a mythical entity, objectified in space and time, the nation." This is how the process of deifying nation and national state began. "The same characteristics of sovereignty, intangibility and hieratic majesty typical of an absolute sovereign were transferred to them, transforming the nation from a geographical and ethnic concept into "a mythological entity, a transcendental and venerable reality that was not only superior to individual consciousness but a source of obligation toward it, as the nation was a constitutive principle of state authority." The cause of this "overdeveloped idea of nation" was that consciousness was incapable of "stabilizing the achievements of its rational autonomy," feeling unequal to bearing the weight of social reality with its imperative laws." In fact, after the sovereign had been deprived of his absolute prerogatives, human consciousness "rejected what can only exist in a state of consciousness, ideas, feeling and spiritual tension and moved them into a transcendental mythical reality." This attitude in the national state turned into a "crisis of national infantilism caused by retarded development," meaning that the national state produced a prolonged infantile mentality in people, giving rise to "national self-centeredness comparable to the self-centeredness typical of the infantile mentality," and this was expressed as "national-centeredness," that is "seeing everything related to national interests." This gave rise to all the displays of nationalist megalomania, even the most abnormal ones, because "national egoism leads to losing contact with reality and, as in children, creates an imaginary universe fostered by delirious visions of greatness and persecution and by confused feelings of superiority and presumed messianic tasks of universal imperialism." To cure this kind of national infantilism, Maresca saw no other therapy than to abandon national-centeredness, favoring the socialization of peoples through federation in an "international democracy," because this would be the only way to develop democracy in every single state.[37]

The theory according to which "to destroy nationalism from its foundations, the national state had to be done away with and a federal state established" was supported by Agostino Trabalza, another collaborator of *La Nuova Europa*, this time causing the publisher to declare his dissent, although he agreed with the author's basic theory: "The absolute sovereignty of the national state, which can be found everywhere, even today, ends up necessarily in nationalism." Also Trabalza took the mythical aspects of the national state into consideration, implicating the principle of nationality itself from a historical rather than psychological point of view. His reasoning was carried out with remarkable intuition of the part played by the myth in legitimizing the national state and in the nationalist education of the masses. He aimed mainly at showing that the need to destroy the national state in order to uproot nationalism could not avoid harming the principle of nationality in some way. Even if this principle did not coincide with nationalism, by legitimizing the national state, it contributed to making the nation absolute in the eyes of the citizens and to claiming its superiority over other nations, in the name of national egoism or of the supremacy of a civilizing mission. In contrast to those who made a genetic distinction between "good" and "bad" nationalism, hoping that the "sad malady of nationalism will no longer develop from the strong body of nationality," Trabalza declared that, studying "the degree of kinship between nationality and nationalism" more thoroughly in the light of very recent experiences, "we should say that nationality gives birth to nationalism," seeing that the "nations that won show they have been infected by the same malady we suffered from and made others suffer so much." Even though its champions thought that "nationality was to tend toward humanity, through the nation," it actually turned out that "since nations have become free, independent and sovereign, we men tend above all to the nation, forgetting humanity." Wherever there was a national state, its main problem regarding its citizens was to educate them nationalistically, through the school and the army. History was thus transformed into a mythology of national glorification "to influence minds and win them over to the mystical idea of the nation-country," which "after a few years, will have to ask those still-unknowing souls to make the greatest sacrifices in their power, to the point of offering their lives. We can even give our lives for a faith or a myth: that is why a myth must be created and spread among the masses through national education given by the school and army, which has to improve our military awareness," thus detrimentally glorifying the myth of nation even more. "The most fanatical religion does not extol its idols so much as military education extols the nation-country," while the ignorant "poor soldier, influenced by this idol, whether it be beneficial or dreadful, submissively bows his head." Everywhere there were far more citizens of the national state both educated and uneducated "than one could believe . . . influenced by the myth of nation": or rather, "we are influenced or fascinated by the nation-country from the cradle to the grave." As "every myth creates fanaticism" and "all fanaticism falls easily into aberration," Trabalza concluded that "in the climate we live in, nationalism is the natural, necessary degeneration of nationality. It would be a dangerous illusion to believe that nationalism is wiped out with the defeat of the nations that put it into practice in a given historical point in time. Free, independent and sovereign nations are in the best condition to fall into nationalism. Not falling is pure chance; falling is natural."[38]

15

In Search of a Fatherland

From Italy to Europe

It was not sufficient to bring down the idol of the national state to prevent nationalism: it was also necessary to bring down the idol of the national myth that supported and legitimized it. This requirement was shared by the many different sectors in republican Italy's political culture, both lay and Catholic, who agreed that the main condition for preventing a dangerous nationalist trend and ensuring the development of democracy was, in any case, a drastic limitation of state sovereignty within wider international or, at least, European-wide supranational organizations. This could be obtained by reducing state power to a minimum level vis-à-vis citizens and by abandoning the national myth as the principle legitimizing the state's sovereignty and justifying the territorial division of peoples. A middle-of-the-road solution, that is, a proposal to refound the democratic Italian state, thus removing all that had made the national myth incompatible with democracy up to then, was suggested by most of the anti-Fascist parties. These parties included both those of Risorgimento origin, even those that had opposite view points, as, for example, the Liberals and Republicans, and parties not born of Risorgimento tradition, such as the Christian Democrats.

In order to find a solution to the crisis of the national state without renouncing national unity, the lay parties suggested moving forward from decentralization of the national state toward participation in a European federation, with limited sovereignty and functions. In turn, the national myth was to be regenerated from Fascist manipulation so that it could be restored to its original Risorgimento matrix and to the tradition of Mazzini and Cavour. Once again the nation was to be reconciled with liberty, and the country with humanity, by means of an experiment in a European nationality in which citizens would feel that the country was more aware of their experiences and problems, as in local and regional tradition, and at the same time they would belong to a country with a wider scope determined by the many different national traditions that had formed European civilization over the centuries and established its cultural supremacy.

This was what Benedetto Croce had hoped for when nationalism began to rise so aggressively and triumphantly in the mid-thirties. Forcing his anguished soul to be hopeful for the future of liberty, the philosopher scrutinized the signs that he saw "already all over Europe," where there is the "budding of a new conscience and a new nationality." Stressing the concept that "nations are not natural data, but states of mind and historic formations," he imagined that "in that same way seventy-odd years ago, a Neapolitan belonging to the old kingdom or a Piedmontese from the House of Savoy became Italians without renouncing their backgrounds but extolling and resolving their origins in the new collective and spiritual entity. So the French, the Germans and the Italians and all the others will begin to think as Europeans; they will turn to Europe and their hearts will beat for Europe just as they did before for the smaller countries, not forgotten, but better loved." Croce expected the unification process of Europe, "which is directly opposed to the competition derived from nationalism and against it and one day will be able to liberate all of Europe, at the same time freeing it of the psychology linked with and supporting nationalism, generating similar manners, dress and actions" to also confirm the dominion of liberty. [1]

Taking up the wish expressed by Croce, the Liberals had sustained a plan to "reestablish the smaller countries" within a European federation in the postwar period:

> Wherever peoples have been free to manifest their will without pressure from the state, we have witnessed the longing to set up the small countries again, to reestablish their independence and revive the region, the small country, the religion of language and native customs. . . . In the big unified states as well, from the oldest, such as France and Spain, to the most recent, such as Germany and Italy, there are vigorous signs that they aspire to a freer regional life, unencumbered by the many oppressive bonds of centralization, not anti-unitary separatism but the aspiration to feel different in a unified country. [2]

For this reason Luigi Einaudi, who in 1948 was elected as the first president of the Italian Republic, did not hesitate to bring up again the principle of the sovereign state's intangibility, making no allowances, however, for the possibility that political unity might come apart. National unity, for Einaudi, was a "dogma exempt from dispute," but acceptance of this dogma did not exclude at all "the need to allow the Valdostans, Piedmontese, Ligurians, Sardinians and Sicilians to decide their regional matters without asking approval of someone in the capital, who had command over his own affairs and, that is, the nation's." Only by dismantling the centralized state, "a disastrous aberration," could vitality be restored to the national unity that had "actually died in the hearts of the Italians because of the enforced, abnormal Napoleon-like uniformity" and that could now be revived "in the openly acknowledged diversity of neighborhoods, towns, districts and regions." It is in "this diversity that we will be able to reconstruct the unity that is so dear to us."[3]

Dismantling the centralized state and fostering European federalism were the only points that the Liberals and the other lay parties, originating from or inspired by the Risorgimento, had in common. Having put aside Mazzini's unitary mysticism, the Republican Party championed a federal state founded on national unity, conceived as a synthesis of the regional varieties. What the Republicans proposed was a different kind of federalism from that of the Risorgimento, given that they did not consider "making Italy a confederation of states today, because to do that would mean dividing up the country politically and then reuniting the various states under a confederative bond, and that would be absurd. Instead, the idea is to make Italy a regional state that would be the institutional synthesis of the two requirements needed for unity and a federation."[4]

From the very first, the Action Party advocated a "return to the Mazzinian tradition of the Risorgimento and suggested redirecting intentions toward a European Union that would dissipate insane nationalist tendencies and the narrow-mindedness of ignorant fanatics," said Adolfo Omodeo.[5] Manlio Rossi Doria added that it was necessary to reduce "the sovereign prerogatives of the states, linking them to one another with sound federative bonds," if the idea was to overcome "the ruinous antagonism between nations" and to foster "the free exchange of power and civilization" that would eliminate "the periodic reappearance of war, which destroyed all aspects of life in society."[6] In 1944 *Italia libera* (Free Italy) maintained that a federation of democratic European states would make it possible to put an end to the "anarchy of the thirty or so sovereign states that share the continent," at the same time saving the "center of Western civilization" from the danger of "drowning in the miserable chaos of scattered members." Then it could be "reborn as the United States of Europe, thus enabling it to once again be the home of law and freedom, which had their origin in Europe."[7]

Restoring Christian Europe

Several exponents of the Democrazia Cristiana (Christian Democrat Party) reached very similar conclusions. In this party the battle against the survival of the national state and the political myth that legitimized it was waged by the leftist group headed by Giuseppe Dossetti. The Dossettians launched an all-out attack on the myth of the nation using arguments that were similar to those of the secular federalist periodical *La Nuova Europa*, but from a totally different ideological angle. Their aim was to reestablish the basic Christian principles of a new international order by transcending the nation in order to proceed with the unification of Europe.

The Dossettian criticism of the national state combined the Italian issue with European and world matters, considering them different aspects of a single problem—transcending the national states by creating international institutions. This would make it possible, as the Christian Democrat leader wrote in 1946, to put an end to "clashes between great imperialist powers, aggravated not only or so much by old-fashioned nationalism as by the desire to govern the whole world, seeing that as fundamental in order to keep the single systems of the two main blocs alive," each one claiming to have the ideal formula for the future organization of the world; very often behind these formulas there was a "certain amount of ambiguous imperialist egoism."[8] In this context Dossetti examined the problem of postwar Italy and the problem of the profound crisis of the national identity caused by the collapse of the unified state. He considered the Italian problem the expression of a phenomenon that was actually affecting all the national states, undermining them in the citizens' consciences. In 1951 Dossetti wrote of this new postwar situation that "the people see such unifying factors as traditions, ideals and sentiments dissolve. Until a few years ago these factors linked individuals, families, cities, regions, categories and classes to a common idea to form a single population." In his opinion, the crisis of the national state was the apex of a progressive shattering of the people's unitary conscience, partly brought about by the many divisions and oppositions that had jeopardized the unification process conducted by the state under the banner of the national myth.[9]

In this situation, the destiny of the national state appeared to be characterized by irreversible decadence, because it had failed in its historical function and its ability to provide unity in politics and ideals in the consciences of the people. "The state and its historic limits are experiencing a crisis of body and soul. For example, sharing the nation has been surpassed, in both blocs, by an international class-conscious community. It is necessary to invent a new soul (no more nationalism, but even the Strasbourg Europeanism is not sufficient) and a new body (even the continent's dimensions are not sufficient)."[10] While waiting to invent a "new soul" and a "new body" for a dreamlike future international system so as to cure the "incurable ills" of nationalism, the Dossetti group's publication *Cronache sociali* intensified the dispute with the national state that was still alive. According to the publication the problem of the national state was, first of all, a matter linked to the destiny of Europe and its future role in the world. By choosing that perspective, the Dossettians manifested their disparagement of the national state and even went so far as to attribute the "failure of the Resistance" to the fact that it had not been given pro-European importance but "contemporaneous national, social and world level importance," thus ignoring the problem of European unification. This was indicative of the continent's serious decline because it was a victim of nationalism. In 1949, the publication affirmed that Europe

> is currently experiencing a crisis in its political structure; the national state, founded on the concept of absolute sovereignty, is an outdated form of government at a time when history is witnessing an increase in political unification. Therefore, the risk in maintaining it is that Europe would be left in a state of uneasy weakness; a change would open up the old continent to a new course of history that, although in a different form, would grant it the importance worldwide that equals its traditions and real strength."[11]

The Dossettians had no doubts about the by-now final, irremediable crisis of the national state. The cause, wrote the *Cronache sociali* in 1949, was to be found in the historical transformation process brought on by "man's growing desire to possess the world," the latest manifestation of which was the creation "of two great intercontinental empires, the American and the Soviet empires. This by itself "emphasized the anachronism of a political organization originating from the break up of the Holy Roman Empire" on the old continent, overrun and occupied by the armies of two empires, where the strongest national state was deprived of its political unity indefinitely. In the face of such a reality the political myths that had supported the "old system of national states" were meaningless; first among these was the myth of nation "intended as a spiritual and biological reality and linked with a sense of universal mission in the world."

Starting from these premises, the publication quickly traced a detailed profile of the historic function that the national myth had had in the creation and evolution of the national state, particularly in Italy: "It is with this myth that the historic cementing takes place between traditional hierarchical authority and the new bourgeois classes within the various countries." "Nation" and "universal mission" are the two terms of the political myth upon which the unified Italian state was founded. Nations, seen as "dynamic myths and the lifeblood of political systems," had "exhausted their function a long time ago: their political structures survive like bodies without souls," and they embrace democracy as their "official ideology." According to the publication, however, democracy was not "currently a dynamic and vital ideal but a skeptical and static one, chosen as the least of ills by the many European countries' systems, but without profound advocates." The weakness of the democratic ideology was due to the fact that it worked inside structures, those of the national state, which were foreign to it because it consisted of a "framework of structures that the state had not created, and which time and things had by now emptied of any significance. . . . Today democracy is an *intermezzo;* it is the formula for a crisis."

Given Europe's weakness, the publication did not exclude the risk of a return to nationalism, even perhaps a nationalist tendency not concerned with foreign policy but "mainly focused on internal policy," "not nationalism with a mission and inclined toward dynamism but isolationist and tired, of the kind that is manifested in such irrational myths as anti-Communism, etc.," nationalism such as that of the Franco regime and France's General de Gaulle, with "a touch of *politique de grandeur* of times past." As a matter of fact, the very presence of these movements allowed the publication to realistically comment that "nationalism in the European countries is not dying out, because it is *"the natural political expression of the institutional structures in Europe,"* that is, the national states, which are still able to influence public opinion. "Liberalism and democracy are ideological formulas, while the national state is a reality."

In the light of a vague democratic ideology the Dossettian publication proposed the elimination of the national state as the only way out of its crisis and clearly set democracy up against the national

state, debasing to the utmost the role it had played in the democratization of European politics and society. "We believe that democracy is
condemned to remain a weak crisis formula in Europe unless it has the
courage to change the national state's historical scenario and then create a new political one in which democracy is not offered as a false formula but as a natural one." In other words, democracy was supposed to
carry out the function that the myth of the national power had performed in the building of the modern state. It was to become the institutional ideology of a federal European state. *Cronache sociali* granted
this future entity, the new myth of united Europe, quasi thaumaturgic
capacities in solving the fundamental problems that troubled European
society, ranging from the end of national rivalries to the stability of democracy, from the idealistic revival of public spirit to the merging of social groups and classes, to "overcoming the gap between middle and
working class," giving the middle class renewed faith in Christ and dis-
tracting the working masses away from being attracted to the Soviet
myth. "Wouldn't the myth of a strong Europe, united under the banner
of democracy, be able to shake off the myth of 'Holy Russia' or the
myth of the 'October Revolution' in the masses of workers?"

Eliminating the national state, abandoning the myth of the nation
and spreading the myth of a united Europe—this was the course of action needed to invigorate Europe, creating a unified political organization that ranged from the "Pyrenees to the Elbe and the Danube." Faith
in the feasibility of the unification plan came not only from certainty
that the national state's crisis was irreversible but also from the fact that
this crisis had weakened all the parties linked with the national state,
placing "political power in the hands of forces that had formed historically in opposition to the national state: the Christian Democrat Party
and Socialism." According to *Cronache sociali*, these were the only forces
that had "European open-mindedness, tradition and significance," because they had formed "outside the framework of the national state."
Taking for granted the vocation of these two forces to support Europeanism, *Cronache sociali* demoted the "various federalist movements" to the
by-now outdated role of forerunner: "These are no longer times for forerunners but builders, and the builders can only be parties, Socialist and
Christian Democrat." Obviously, of the two, the publication acknowledged the Christian Democrats as being "the only European People's
Party" because it had a long-standing tradition of idealistic and political
opposition to the myth and reality of the national state and the historical
function of carrying out the plan to unite Europe. Furthermore, unified

Europe could only rise out of the foundations of the ancient Christian civilization, with a return to Christianity.[12]

From National to Universal Country

The antinationalist dispute, waged under the banner of universalist ideals, also implicated patriotism, accusing it of being a potential generator of nationalism because it identified the country with the national state. For the more radical antinationalists, both lay and Catholic, the rejection of nationalism should, therefore, include any form of patriotic mythology that legitimized the division of peoples into national states.

The fear that patriotism might be the breeding ground of nationalism had already surfaced during the war of liberation, when there were some among the partisans who thought it raised suspicion to characterize the Resistance as being a patriotic war of liberation. We are referring above all to the partisans for whom the ultimate goal of the Resistance was not just the liberation of Italy from Nazi-Fascism but also the opportunity to carry out a political and social revolution. They had agreed to act under the banner of the national myth only as a tactical expedient, necessary to keep the heterogeneous anti-Fascist forces united. They considered acting in the name of the national myth a risk because it might have prevented the Resistance movement from becoming a revolutionary one that would have created a radically new Italian and European system with respect to the past. It would have been radically new especially because it would finally have ended the era of nationalism and the national states.

There were some partisans who had rejected the identification of "patriot" with "partisan," judging it ambiguous and equivocal. They had insisted, therefore, that a distinction be made, precisely because a "'partisan' is a patriot, but a 'patriot' is not necessarily a partisan," given the incompatibility between the "'nationalist' nature of the patriot" and the "'internationalist' nature of the partisan."[13] The need to make this distinction derived from the ambiguity of patriotism and its connections with nationalism: "The sentimental and rhetorical background of the ideal concept of country led to the degeneration and perversion of the bourgeois way of thinking, turning it into imperialist mysticism, fatal generator of the nation's destruction and spiritual decomposition." Therefore, partisans were to reject any form of nationalistic patriotism and accept only patriotism "dedicated, above all, to the destiny of the community of peoples" that fought for "a higher cause than miserable egoistical national interest" and which "subordinated a policy exclusively concerned with national interests to one—both national and international—concerned with world cooperation." A partisan was first of all a citizen of a "new universal fatherland" and did not acknowledge the "interests of his own country, its laws, institutions and war." He professed allegiance to "different laws, another war for another fatherland, common to all men, a fatherland without borders, common to all nations confronting each other in conflict, the fatherland of freedom. The partisan, or freedom fighter, fought for that universal fatherland and was one of its citizens."[14]

The distinction between "partisan patriotism" and "nationalistic patriotism" did not appear to other partisans to be sufficient to prevent the danger of a "national reaction" within the Resistance movement itself, brought about by the patriotic mythology of the nation's war of liberation. The partisans who professed European federalism, Action Party followers for example, were suspicious of the "national patriotism" professed by the other anti-Fascist parties. According to *Italia libera,* in 1944 the "greatest danger" for the anti-Fascist coalition government did not lie in the alliance between progressives and conservatives, but in the national orientation prevailing among the coalition parties. As a result, "the flow of the popular movement threatens to become fossilized once again in the traditional, national, patriotic platform, which, apart from the internal social system, basically reproduces the same world situation that led to the Fascist war, that is, a number of sovereign states that are mutually against each other." Giving the war against Nazism and Fascism a predominantly national imprint was, for the Action Party members, a risky expedient because, by doing so, the issue of "national egoisms" could receive new energy and legitimization and could become a fundamental condition for the reconstruction of Europe based on the division into national states, as in the past.

In other words, Action Party members feared that the war against Fascism, as a "reaction to Hitler's cosmopolitanism," might tend to consolidate into humanistic forms of national independence since "the very clear religious nature assumed by this war in the far-reaching strata of the underprivileged facilitates the reconstruction of myths, and the national myth, which is always there ready and waiting, is still the most convenient and best known." They denounced a certain "nationalistic reflux" in the principal Resistance movements in Europe, such as the French and the Yugoslav ones, which prevented the forming of effective internationalist support of the war against National Socialism and prevented vanquishing all forms of patriotic mythology in order to open the way to a new European order no longer founded on unlimited national state sovereignty. In Italy, according to the Action Party organ, the "nationalistic reflux" came from the "traditional patriotic military and conservative forces," whereas the Resistance movement "was far from being dominated by patriotic mythology, particularly where it was authentic, spontaneous and not adulterated by diplomatic and government worries." In fact, despite the "Communists' heated patriotic phraseology," the working class was animated by revolutionary ideologies that went "beyond even the shabbiest patriotism." As a result, the Action Party organ did not take any notice of the Communists' "patriotic phraseology," considering it only instrumental and "tactically advantageous," because "the link between the party and Russia and the party's acute sensitivity toward the international situation would be sufficient guarantees if there were to be a nationalistic shelving of the European federalist revolution."[15] Once liberated, not only from the German occupation, but also from the national myth, the new Italy could be the point of departure for such a European federalist revolution "against a return to an era of sovereign national states."[16]

Immediately following the war, the polemic against the nation was taken up again, mainly by the movement of *l'Uomo qualunque* (man-in-the-street), or *Qualunquismo*, headed by Guglielmo Giannini. Perhaps more than any other party *Qualunquismo* conducted a violent campaign using simple language, without complex arguments, to desecrate and demolish all forms of the idol of the national myth, including the most generic form of patriotism. According to *Qualunquismo*, with its focus on ethical authority, the myth of the nation and the national state bore nationalism written in their genetic codes. They believed in the servitude of citizens to the omnipotent state, the ambition to dominate other peoples and war as a means of satisfying that ambition. There was no other way to fight nationalism than to demolish the myth of the nation and the national state, aiming at the realization of a United States of Europe, in which the national states would disappear, thus annihilating the primary source of nationalism and war. Along with the myth of the nation and the national state, *Qualunquismo* also scrapped all idealistic tradition from the Risorgimento to Fascism. Nothing of the myth of Greater Italy survived *Qualunquismo*, not even a revised and corrected version. There was nothing to light the spark of national pride or revive even the tiniest bit of sentiment for the Italian national identity or a certain sense of state after the catastrophe of the war. In some ways,

Qualunquismo's antinationalism was the most coherent, albeit simplified, ideologization of the desire to "run from history" that had taken hold of the Italians after September 8, manifesting itself in that movement by condemning, without extenuating circumstances, the period in Italian history from 1914 on. It was during this period that a minority, obsessed with the desire to "attack history" with the myths of national patriotism, had "coerced and deceived the Italian people, sending them to die in two absurd and useless world wars, torturing them in two revolutions, the first of which lasted three years (1919–1922), the second, twenty-three (1922–1943)."[17]

The narrow world of civic values that the *Qualunquista* believed in did not harbor any sense of duty toward the state or devotion or allegiance to a fatherland that had the state and its national territory as its reference point. As far as the *Qualunquista* was concerned, we might say that his idea of fatherland coincided, in its resemblance to the maternal figure, with the horizon of personal feelings, closed within the boundaries of its existence, the object of filial affection only. *Qualunquismo* saw Italy as being completely devoid of the strong connotations that had been the nation's characteristics and given it the appearance of a supreme and eternal entity, just as it was depicted by the Risorgimento, the Liberals and the Fascists, surrounded by sacredness like a warrior divinity, descendant of noble Rome, glittering with ancient glory and grandeur, and destined by God to conquer new prestige and greatness. However, for *Qualunquismo*, the fatherland stripped of all rhetoric, was human and fragile: "If anything on earth is mortal, the idea of fatherland is the most mortal of all."[18]

Love Your Fatherland

As we have seen, the condemnation of nationalism also risked sweeping away the concept of fatherland, which had been subsumed by the idea of nation ever since the French Revolution and, at the same time, identified with the national state. The Fascists' use and abuse of the values of country and nation, the fear that showing patriotic feelings might arouse the suspicion of nostalgia for Fascism and the rebirth of neo-Fascist groups after 1945 under the banner of nationalism certainly contributed to discrediting the idea of fatherland.

Exponents of the lay culture who were linked to the Risorgimento tradition through ancient idealistic bonds made a desperate attempt to defend love for the fatherland against the tendency of the Italians to let it fall to pieces after the manipulation it had suffered under Fascism. According to the liberals it was a matter of "revising the concept of nation, denying certain groups the right to represent it and dictate their inexorable demands and honoring this concept as the greatest expression of solidarity that does not distinguish between elected and non-elected either at the national level or within a supra-European community to which our future is necessarily linked."[19] For this reason it was useful to suggest making a distinction between patriotism and nationalism, the latter to be seen as a form of total exaltation of the nation, of state authoritarianism, aggressive imperialism, and the claim to racial superiority. Patriotism, instead, should enhance devotion to one's own country as a sentiment that can coexist with recognition and respect for other countries, as Giorgio Fenoaltea wrote in 1944:

> For too long patriotism, nationalism and imperialism have been fused in a single hybrid concept: the idea of country has served to mask every kind of atrocity for too long. In the name of the country, liberty has been killed, citizens have been tortured, wars have been waged, so that what is called the land of our fathers, where our dead lie to rest, where our children were born, has lost its pristine sweetness by now calling up, instinctively, images of misfortune and destruction. It is time we separated the idea of country from the idea of war, which has been its inseparable companion for too long: it is time to eliminate nationalism from the meaning of patriotism, as if history had not recovered from the period of national unification, and from imperialism, as if it were not possible to love one's country without insulting, threatening and stealing from other people's countries. Last, it is time to substitute a world of countries at war with a world of countries in harmony.[20]

A month before the fall of Fascism, referring to what "our fathers taught us during the Risorgimento," Croce had made an appeal to bring back an "old-fashioned phrase," devotion to one's country, which "had not been corrupted, but rather substituted with the word nationalism." And resuming his criticism of nationalism, seen as perversion of the spirit, Croce affirmed that between patriotism and "cynical and stolid nationalism" there was "the same difference there is between the gentleness of human love for another human being and beastly lustfulness, or morbid lewdness or egoistic waywardness." In fact, while "the nationalist movements open their mouths to devour each other, countries cooperate with each other, and even the wars between them, when they cannot be avoided, are not aimed at reciprocal destruction but at mutual transformation and common elevation," because "the country is a moral idea," and it is in that, that "it has its intimate link with the idea of liberty." The philosopher entrusted the good fortune of the new Italy, with its parties that arose from the ruins of Fascism, to a return of devotion to the country.[21]

When in 1947, the philosopher began again to defend the sentimental, ethical and civilized values of love for one's country, he was not trying to avoid the moral and political problem of the relationship between love of fatherland and national state, particularly in the dramatic cases of schism between country and state, which he had experienced personally. According to Croce, the sense of duty toward the state arose from love for one's country, because "in fulfilling one's duty toward the state, what one really loves in all of this is not the state but the country." One loves "all of the moral values that the fatherland synthesizes and symbolizes, and its force and power only in relation to these values." Therefore, devotion to one's country cannot be identified with duty toward the state and does not subject itself to the state as if it were "an absolute duty," because this duty has a limit "in the idealistic principle that animates real love for one's country." According to Croce, the tragedy of the conflict between love of fatherland and duty toward the state, suffered by those who did not feel any moral obligation to the Fascist state arose precisely because individuals and people were bewildered by this distinction and "thought the commands of the state, whatever they were, were absolute." The result was that they accused those who did not bow down to these commands of deserting "the fatherland in a difficult period and during its most painful trials, while, actually, the deserters and traitors were on the other side, on the side of those who governed the country, abusing their power and its name."[22]

Influential voices also arose from the Catholic world in defense of devotion to the country, which, according to *La Civiltà Cattolica* in 1946, had been "the great inspirational element leading to so much sacrifice and which had obliged the best Italians to fight two wars at the same time, both little understood for different reasons, but in which it was obvious the only thing at stake was the country's greatness and its very existence, so they fought heroically."[23] The Church was not against devotion to one's country. On the contrary, it encouraged this sentiment: it only condemned its degeneration into exaggerated and exclusivist passion or worship of the nation, as had happened during Fascism.

Following the collapse of Fascism, there were some Catholics who felt the immediate need "to restore the defeated country," as Aldo Moro, a Christian Democrat, wrote in 1944, to give confidence and a sense of direction back to the Italian people who, having lost all feeling for the country, "are having difficulty in finding themselves," because "they have little faith in the value of our national life and its future."[24] Under Fascism "we were not modest or good enough because we imagined our fatherland and life as being heroic, and when we discovered it was noisy, pompous and without a bit of sentiment, we put out any flame of human passion that we had. Now we have a long and difficult road ahead; we must rebuild. We can begin here. Let us all go back to simply doing our duty, without losing sight of the values to be found in all jobs done by men for men. This is the way we can really serve our fatherland in distress." After the fall of Fascism it was necessary to reconstruct the fatherland in the consciences of the Italians, teaching them to understand it correctly as the symbol of "a series of human experiences like ours, a place to find ourselves in others, the self that belongs to us all the more, the more its touching human experience is repeated in other men as it was at the beginning."

In defending the reasons for patriotism, Moro used arguments and tones that recalled Gentile's conception of nation. More than on historic or cultural factors, Moro insisted on an essential human motive linking the idea of country to the real experiences of social life.[25] On the eve of the peace conference in London, Moro again brought up the matter of the fatherland, with ever greater passion because he had realized what punishment the allies would inflict on Italy and because he feared that the indifference with which the Italians awaited the decision of the winners would result in a definitive loss of their patriotism. "It is not the case to shrug our shoulders as if the matter did not regard us. It is not a matter of being cast out of the world. No, the country still exists, even if from now on its frontiers, which seemed too narrow, will be mutilated and a strong policy line will necessarily be reduced," because "the fatherland is a human reality, and it lives on in what is human and spiritual in us. Trampled, shamed and scorned by its own sons, divided internally, it has, however, a supreme resource in its mortification," which is "to develop fruitfully a profound spiritual life" that has reason to resurrect itself in the midst of such poverty and desperation. Moro ended his patriotic exhortation calling upon the Italians and, above all, the young to "be proud of their dignity as human beings and to look for the essential things at this crucial time: goodness, a pious life and consolation in beauty. That is the best way to face a peace agreement that is expected to have deficiencies and weaknesses, so that the country can continue its existence beyond, far beyond, the dangerous and inhuman game of power."[26]

The Communists were just as interested in advocating the cause of patriotism during the Resistance as the Liberals and Catholics. Having adhered to the national myth, which it had incorporated into the ideology of the self-styled *partito nuovo* (new party), to the extent that it was one of the fundamental propaganda motifs behind the Communist resistance, and the new strategy of *via italiana al socialismo* (Italian road to socialism)," the Communist Party declared itself defender of devotion to one's country, according to its leader. As a matter of fact, it claimed for the Communists and the working class the merit of having raised the nation's flag up out of the mud and of having given more substantial and authentic meaning to the sentiment of patriotic duty, as Palmiro Togliatti told young Communists on May 24, 1947:

> We have no intention of oppressing or obscuring the idea of fatherland and national sentiment in the consciences of the young. On the contrary, we have proved not only that we fuel this sentiment but also that we know how to bring it to the highest level ever. For example, up to now the country has been "served," according to the present expression, by the army and the other armed forces, and this indicates obligation. Together with the country's other democratic forces, we have been able to transform that obligation into an outburst of voluntary generosity on the part of tens of thousands of men. . . . We must teach our young people that not all of those who cry out "My fatherland, My fatherland!" are good patriots, but only those who do not separate but, rather, identify the national interest with the fight for the nation's social renewal.[27]

The Dilemma of "Two Fatherlands"

Actually, the petition in favor of devotion to one's fatherland could have been taken up by anyone opposed to the national state and who considered the idea of nation old-fashioned. In this case it was a matter of separating patriotism from nationalism, the idea of fatherland from the national state, and redefining the concept of fatherland in new, more modern terms in view of the new international scenario within which history after World War II was moving. The desire to raise national patriotism to a form of universal patriotism, clearly separating devotion to one's country from the idea of nation and national state, was generically present in all of the antinationalist opinions in Italy during the second postwar period and was also mixed with various ideologies. Even when this universal patriotism made reference to the Risorgimento's humanitarian patriotism, it had little in common with that tradition because it was sustained by other cultural motivations and moral values. The humanitarian patriotism of the Risorgimento placed the nation and the national state at the center, identifying them with the fatherland, as the primary values within the Italians' ethical and political universe. Conversely, republican Italy's universal patriotism had as its premise the dissociation of the fatherland from the state and removal of the nation from the apex of the citizens' civil and political values, replacing it with other entities identified with a universal country. Today, observed Arturo Carlo Jemolo in 1946, devotion to one's country is no longer unconditional, and above everything else: "One is devoted to one's own country, hoping to see the regime one thinks best come into power. In the eyes of some, this should have religious faith as the guiding principle; in the eyes of others, order and discipline; and others still, social justice and protection of the weakest." Ideological faith is the main factor of division or solidarity among citizens of the same state or the same nation, and "wherever you look, there is nobody anywhere any longer who feels closer to an internal political enemy than to a foreigner of the same political faith."[28]

This changed situation led inevitably to a new concept of the relationship between the individual and the nation, between the citizen and the state. It postulated the existence of "two fatherlands" that vied for supremacy and the citizens' whole-hearted allegiance: the "fatherland as state," represented by the national state to which loyalty was due as citizens, and the "ideal fatherland," that is, the constellation of principles and values (ideology, religion, philosophy, etc.) to which loyalty was due as human beings, and which, institutionally, could be identified with an entity other than the nation and state of which one was a citizen. In this sense, for example, an Italian Communist might see Soviet Russia as his "ideal fatherland." And in this sense we might also speak of party patriotism. In other words, a party member's loyalty to the party might prevail and predominate over his loyalty to the nation and the state. Supporters of a universal fatherland that stood above one's national state maintained that the "two fatherlands" could cohabit in the citizen's heart and soul as long as he recognized in the national state—in its regime, its government, its internal and foreign policy choices—his own ideals. But when the national state contrasts with the citizen's principles and values, then loyalty to the "ideal fatherland" must prevail over the citizen's loyalty to the nation state, as happened with many anti-Fascist Italians, even if that meant desiring, in the case of war, one's country's defeat. As we have seen, this was the troubling ordeal Italians experienced during World War II when men, brought up with the cult of country and devotion to the national state, found themselves torn by the conflict between "ideal fatherland" and the national state that was triggered by the Fascist war.

The consequences that influenced the real relationship between citizens and state or between individuals and the nation arose from the acknowledgment that the "two fatherlands" did exist and raised once again the question of the principles and values of national ethics on which the civic conscience of the Italian state had been based up to World War II. It also involved the national identity. Affirming the existence of "two fatherlands" meant undermining the basic pillars of the national myth as it had been conceived and experienced since the French Revolution, when the nation was first considered as having sacred characteristics, identifying the fatherland with the national state, which summarized the highest ethical and political values of men and citizens. In the name of this idea of nation, which was both fatherland and state, there had been an appeal for the "sacred union" of citizens in support of the country, above and beyond political divisions, as had happened in most of the belligerent countries during World War I. But by World War II the situation had changed. While during the 1914–18 war the national principle had prevailed over party ideologies, the Second World War had brought "the conflict between loyalty to the nation—in that it was represented by established powers—and loyalty to the universal sociopolitical idea, to an extreme," as the Catholic writer Fausto Montanari observed in 1950. Montanari rightly noted that in Italy this had already happened with Fascism, which, "while it exalted everything about Italy, in actual fact it placed itself above the country, because it acknowledged the right to full Italian identity only to those who were Fascist. It was actually Fascism that developed the practice of ideological universalism: the Fascist felt closer to and more friendly with the German Nazi than the Italian Democrat." Because of its nature, Fascism's totalitarian nationalism "projected itself onto a universal plane" as it tended to "create a super-country where the party was seen as the universal concept of life." In the world that emerged from World War II, ideological universalism appeared to predominate with respect to the national country: "The ancient concept of territorial country and loyalty to the sovereign was in fact subordinated to a more universal concept," a "new awareness of the world as universal fatherland" that represented "the beginning of more humane conditions the world over," because it tended to "cancel the nationalistic idol in favor of world unification, albeit, in a distant future." Therefore, it seemed legitimate for the author to query, in this situation, "what the effective role of the country is today, being that the citizens of the various countries often feel they are, first and foremost, believers in a universal creed rather than citizens of their country."[29]

This question brings us to a crucial period in the history of the Italian national myth, which appeared to be on the decline. The antinationalist debate, the radical criticism of the myth of the nation and the indictment of the national state, even if voiced in cultural and political circles, revealed an underlying general tendency, an educated and knowledgeable expression of the sentiments and state of mind of the population regarding the "nation" and the "national state," although some people were still able to nurture patriotic feelings, either because of lingering emotions or ideological choice. These attitudes revealed, from the early years of the Italian Republic, a progressive withdrawal of the Italians from the national myth, while their patriotic allegiance was projected toward other ideal, historic and political entities — from religion to ideology, from humanity to the party — considered ethically superior to the nation and the national state. Actually, while the desire for a universal country remained a vague and rather evanescent aspect of the idealistic unification of humanity worldwide that lacked practical effects for life in the new Italy, the supremacy of loyalty to the "ideal fatherland" with respect to the nation state favored dissociating the idea of fatherland from the reality of the national state, and, above all, encouraged, at the same time, a stronger ideologization of the national myth that began with the Fascists and continued in an entirely different context thanks to the political parties of the Italian Republic.

Although in the early postwar years there was still favorable talk of the fatherland, the nation and even the greatness of Italy, by the fifties the national myth gradually began to decline, taking devotion to the country and the "sense of state" with it.

Benito Mussolini. From *Vizione di Roma Imperiale—Ente Nazionale Industrie Turistiche* (Rome, 1934).

Mussolini speaks outside La Scala, Milan. From *Temoignages de Notre Temps: Dictatures et Dictateurs*, Paris, June 1934.

Benito Mussolini, accompanied by Adolf Hitler, inspects the Companions of Honor.

Young boys imitating Mussolini, Rome, 1940.

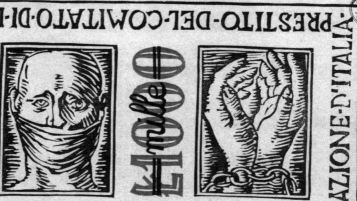

Partisan brigade on patrol. From *La neve cade sui monti—Memoire di un partigiano*, 1945.

Top left: Partisans parade in Montero. From *La neve cade sui monti—Memoire di un partigiano*, 1945.

Bottom left: Currency issued by Italian partisans.

ITALIA : RISORGI!

Italy Resurgent! May 1955. Supplement to *Il Secolo D'Italia*.

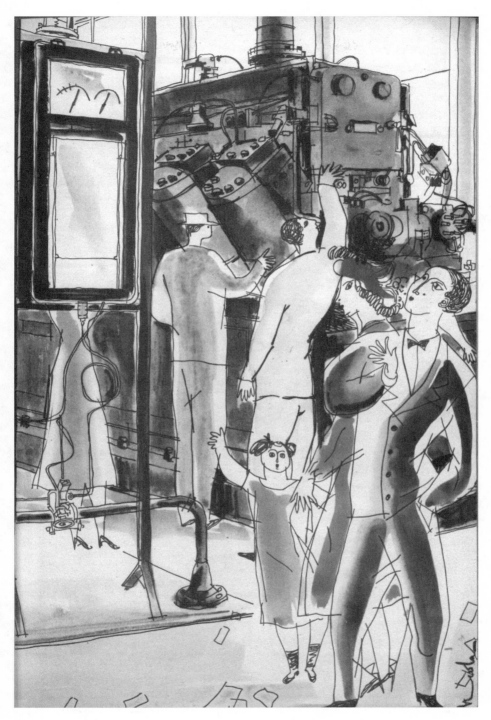

The Italian economic miracle. Exhibition catalog, *30th Fiera di Padova Internationale, June 1952.*

PART 5

THE COUNTRY OF
POLITICAL PARTIES

16

A Great but Small Nation

The Unity of the Nation Is Intangible

Defending devotion to the fatherland, meaning the national one, necessarily involved the political entity of the state. The dispute with the national state actually concerned only a minority of anti-Fascists while the majority of anti-Fascist parties, after the liberation, found themselves facing the urgent problem of safeguarding the territorial and political unity of the Italian state. At that time it was endangered by the moral collapse of the nation, by the expansionist desires of the French and Yugoslavs, and by separatist tendencies within the country. Defense of the national unity caused a common front of Christian Democrats, Liberals, Socialists, Communists, Republicans and also Action Party members to coalesce, alarmed that the Italian state was falling apart, which could have led to a distorted application of federalism. Augusto Monti warned against the type of federalism wanted by "the prosperous regions," in other words, Northern Italy: "We want the other regions, those of a poorer Italy—poverty is nothing to be ashamed of—the Southern regions, to say what they think."[1] We should not forget, observed the jurist Francesco Calasso, that centralization, "against which there is such a reaction, and there are good reasons for the reaction, was the administrative system that enabled a country like Italy, lacking a tradition of unification, to create one. Or better, to start creating one because, in these difficult times, our unification has shown that it has some weak spots." In saying this, Calasso was not referring to the separatist movements like the Sicilian one but, "rather, to national solidarity among the regions that, at a time of disaster, should have triumphed above everything else, and that evidently did not."[2]

The Liberals were the most decided in opposing any attack on the national unity. In 1944 *Risorgimento liberale* announced: "It is the duty of

279

the Italian state not to be indulgent with those who try to break up the unity after so much blood has been shed to achieve it. All kinds of liberties can be allowed, but not treason."[3] And despite Luigi Einaudi's regionalist orientation against institutional statism, some of the Liberal Party's most important exponents, like Benedetto Croce, were the proud adversaries of federalism, seeing it as an attack on the national unity. In 1947 Croce warned:

> After centuries of difficulties and great effort, our fathers left us an inestimable heritage that the foolish, disastrous war, which destroyed much of what they had created, did not take away and that not only allows us to resume an effective role in international politics in the future, but also allows us the widespread spiritual, intellectual and political freedom that we have enjoyed and fortunately continue to enjoy from the Alps to that beautiful island where Italian poetry originated. . . . How miserable are these ideas of separation, even if mitigated by self-government! How painful it is just to hear talk of such things at a time when saving the unified country is at stake![4]

Speaking to the Constituent Assembly on March 11 of that same year, Croce recalled that federalist conceptions "had never had much of a vigorous following in Italy where they were dreamt up by single individuals or small groups, only to be chased away by the gleam of unity. The philosopher launched a cry of alarm against the reawakening of antagonism between north and south and against "the claims and regional jealousies and demands for independence." Croce was firmly convinced that "the only thing still in one piece of what the Risorgimento achieved is state unity, which we must keep intact and strong even if, at the present time, the only comfort it gives us is to suffer together (and that is a kind of comfort) our common misfortunes."[5]

The arguments in favor of national unity put forth by Palmiro Togliatti were no different. He claimed that the work of the Risorgimento leaders and the construction of the unified state were something that rightly belonged to the working class. "Nobody can say today whether it was right to organize Italy as it was organized after 1860," said Togliatti in 1947:

> Could there have been another way? I don't know. That was the way history went, that's all. However, the fact is that by taking that course we made progress, we attained a certain position and basically we must say that, in any event, national unity has been maintained, thanks to a system that, doubtlessly, had serious, and even

very serious, defects. Therefore, national unity is a very valuable thing, above all for a country that has not had it for very long. How many years have we been a united country? Not more than seventy or eighty, and we fought, suffered, were defeated and humiliated for centuries in order to achieve that. Almost all the neighboring peoples defeated and humiliated us because we were not united, we did not have an army nor were we a single state, while they had had these things for centuries. We must be careful not to lose this unity now.[6]

Togliatti called upon the working class to defend the unified state at a time when national unity "had deteriorated and was greatly endangered," not only because of the reorganization of "our frontiers, . . . which were legitimately conquered, the result of the aspirations and work of generations of Italians,"[7] but because there are equally serious signs of "divisions and internal separations within the country that tend to jeopardize our national unity":

> Political and moral unity of the nation is a legacy that must not be lost. Therefore, when we hear people speak so lightheartedly about the North and South being opposing entities, or ones that should contradict each other, or hear people say that the regions would like to separate from the mother country, which would place the very existence of the nation and the Italian state in question, we become alarmed . . . we feel that a great national party like ours should take up the task not only of working to prevent the unity from being destroyed or seriously compromised but also of regaining and strengthening all of its aspects throughout the country as soon as possible.[8]

Thus the Communist Party became one of the most intransigent supporters of the national unity. In his opening speech at the Fifth Communist Party Congress on December 29, 1945, Togliatti said, "A federalist Italy would be a country where all the egoisms and local peculiarities would emerge and triumph, and this would hinder solutions to the nation's problems that pertain to the collectivity. A federalist Italy would be a country where the regions' economic and political systems would be outdated, governed by old reactionary groups or a bunch of old egotists, the same ones that have always been the ruin of Italy." Therefore, the Communists were ready to defend the national unity "against anyone who endangered it, whether due to doctrinal misinterpretation or for the sake of being a reactionary. The country's political and economic unity was hard won by generations of Italians. That unity belongs to all the citizens, and we deny anybody the right to jeopardize what is in the interest of everybody." For this reason, Togliatti declared, "We are convinced antifederalists and, as such, continue the great tradition of the Italian Socialist movement, which has always been a unified one, thus contributing to the creation of a new Italy, where the old regional rivalries no longer exist and the standard of living is higher."[9]

When the plans for regional decentralization were put before the Constituent Assembly, the Communist deputy from the south, Fausto Gullo, recalled the danger of dividing the country.

> Where is it going to end up? . . . It is audacious to think that the result will only be the creation of different regional laws, all effective within the same national territory and alongside which there will be the state legislation that will try in vain to coordinate so many different systems. Does anyone really believe that that would not jeopardize the country's unity, unless unity of the country only means having territory in common instead of the spontaneous and harmonious efforts to achieve the same goals for all the Italian people of any region, taking the same route in fraternal agreement to fulfill the same aims?[10]

The Socialist Party also espoused the antifederalist front in the name of the "great desire for unity" that had "animated all those fighting for liberty," because, as Pietro Nenni said before the Constituent Assembly on March 10, 1947, "The real significance of this battle has been the desire and will to safeguard the country's unity and independence with respect to foreign entities as well as internal movements, which include the separatist movements approved by Val d'Aosta and Sicily. The unity and independence of the country was the first and, to a certain extent, the main objective of the whole liberation movement."[11] The Socialist Party also saw federalism as a threat to the nation's unity, and Nenni praised the creation of the unified state, acknowledging the difficult task that its architects had undertaken and the problems that they had had to face. One might admit that the federalism proposed by Carlo Cattaneo and Giuseppe Ferrari was "progressive" compared to Mazzini's unitarianism, but as Nenni commented, "historically Mazzini was right, and Italy could never have been anything but a unified state. This is proved by the enormous difficulties Italy encountered after 1860 and again after 1870 in implementing the unified state, which reached full-fledged status only after the serious trials and tribulations our generation lived through from 1915 to 1918." Therefore, according to Nenni, since Italy could not have been created "taking any other form but a single, indivisible state, so today it would be a political and economic error to implement local administrative independence in the form of regional federalism."[12]

Rehabilitating the Nation

The national unity was a valuable asset that should be defended and preserved. It was not only a political and territorial reality like a piece of property that should not be broken up and sold off but an ideal and moral reality as well. From the early years of the Republic, defending the political unity of the state was combined with holding the nation up as an important example of collective solidarity and idealistic union, fortified by a common cultural and historic tradition. In this, laymen and Catholics, Christian Democrats and Communists shared in efforts to redeem and regenerate the idea of nation that had been contaminated by Fascism and nationalism. They could then repropose it to Italians as a value that was still valid and current and that they could not get rid of without losing their identity and individual characteristics. At a time when the population had lost its self-confidence, dispersed in its own isolated existence, the idea of nation could function as a merging factor, as a collective ideal, and could generate renewed energy in everyone to reconstruct Italy and put it back on the road to modern civilization. On July 18, 1950, the national secretary of the Christian Democratic Party, Alcide De Gasperi, said, "Italy, the cradle of civilization, must also be defended as the center from which national sentiment emanates, so as to fuel the cult of our history and traditions more and more, particularly among the young."[13] And a few months later he reiterated, "There comes a time when it is a moral duty to defend the character of a nation and the dignity of a population," granting "the word patriotism and the word nation . . . a meaning that befits our historic values, and above all, let's apply that word to the people."[14]

However, the most convincing and logical defense of the idealistic value of the nation, strongly contesting its summary elimination or wishes that it would die out, came from the secular, liberal and democratic cultural circles, heirs to the national tradition of the Risorgimento and liberal Italy. As Carlo Sforza stated in 1945:

> The idea of nation will be one of history's most vital forces for a long time to come, and it will not be by fighting or scorning what is noble, healthy and fruitful in the idea of country that the advent of an international spirit, capable of creating the foundation of a more fraternally Christian world, will be facilitated. Nations are

not only a reality; they are a valuable heritage and reflection—the bright reflection of what, today, is still the most splendid sentimental and spiritual ornament of Europe.[15]

From an historical and idealistic point of view, the nation's rehabilitation was motivated, on the one hand, by recalling the existing vitality of the Risorgimento's national myth, and on the other, by the conviction that the nation, according to the principle of nationality, represented a historic, idealistic and human value that could not be cancelled even by the prospect of European unification, because it was an essential asset of the modern conscience. It was a necessary step along the path to human emancipation that could not be eliminated. In the historicist vision of modernity, secular culture, as the progress of freedom, claimed that the preeminent characteristic in the development of freedom and human dignity was the principle of nationality, dissociating it from responsibilities of nationalism, considered a separate phenomenon not necessarily derived from the idea of nation as the more radical federalists sustained. In fact, even *La Nuova Europa* involved in fighting the idol of the nation, published a strong appeal made by the historian Eugenio Di Carlo in favor of the idea of nationality, "which responds to the true need for the legal regulation of relations between peoples and explains much of the history of the last century and of the present." The principle of nationality "that should not be confused with nationalism, is still a legitimate political and ethical exigence, a justified claim that must certainly be acknowledged proportionate to other rights and necessities," given that it is not an idea that is being forced on "historic reality but an idea and a sentiment that is founded on humanity's historic process. It is in the very conscience of peoples, who do not want to be subjected to foreign rule but aspire to the independence of their national entity, to preserve it wholly and purely from any foreign political subjugation and to be able to support it without impediments, much less constraints." The national conscience, concluded Di Carlo, as the "creator and transformer of states, is still an active force and still has a function to discharge in modern history."[16]

In order to support this concept, liberal intellectuals made a very clear distinction between the principle of nationality and nationalism, upholding the defense of the nation as a value because it had had a positive function in the progress made by mankind after the French Revolution. Theirs was also an attempt to demonstrate that the ideas of nation and nationalism were not related and did not even have a common genesis. Nationalism was a phenomenon with its own roots. It originated from a particular conception of the nation, typical of a given culture or historic political period, for instance, the imperialist era, and had little or nothing to do with the concept of nation that had given rise to the Italian Risorgimento. In a speech delivered on September 21, 1944, Croce attempted to absolve Italy from any responsibility linked to totalitarian nationalism by declaring as "historically false the affirmation that Italian history reveals evidence of nationalistic or imperialist tendencies during its course or during the Risorgimento" and as false the attempt to maintain, to the detriment of historic reality, that the Risorgimento "dissipated the cult, albeit rhetorical and not political, of Rome, and the Italians as Rome's sons and heirs." Nationalism and imperialism came to Italy through "foreign infiltration and were embraced by a few simple-minded people who lacked willpower and by many social climbers, until Fascism, which came into power without having an idea of its own, made them its *raison d'être*, welcoming the nationalists into the gang, where they did as much harm as the others."[17] The advent of Fascism, which Croce compared to the invasion of the Hyksos, shattered the "hopes of a freer and livelier life in Italy," but did not manage to distort the sincere Italian tradition of liberty: because it had suffered the nationalist disease, Italy returned to freedom after the Fascist experience, "definitely vaccinated against a new infection." Responsibility for Fascism's disastrous undertakings was not to be attributed to Italy's genuine tradition, which from the period of the Communes had been based on liberty, but only to the gang of dangerous individuals who had taken over authority, forcing the Italians into slavery. As Croce explained to Einstein on July 28, 1944, Italy

> has suffered a sad and painful vicissitude due to its collapse caused, as in other countries, by the previous war, . . . which made it possible for crazy, violent people to take over the state authority, to the great satisfaction and approval of the whole world, and to force Italy to take a course that was not congenial to it and was in contradiction with its centuries of history. Italy had never dreamt of having dominions in the world since the fall of the Roman Empire, and it had put into effect, and searched for, liberty and became a unified country of its own free will; its nationalism and Fascism came from foreign concepts that only those crazy, violent people could have adopted as a pretext for their misdemeanors.[18]

This was an attempt to rehabilitate the myth of the nation by rediscovering that originally it was associated with liberty and humanistic values. Proceeding along these lines, the theory of a genetic difference was restated between "voluntary nationalism," which foresees that its sustainers adhere freely and consciously, and "naturalistic nationalism," which does not consider freedom of choice because it postulates the existence of the nation as a given fact, circumscribed and enclosed within boundaries, determined by ethnic and geographical factors independent of its members' will. The matrix of brutal, authoritarian, imperialist, racist nationalism was identified within this second type of nationalism.

It was based on this distinction that the historian Federico Chabod developed his considerations on the idea of nation during the postwar period, starting with a university course held in 1943–44 at the University of Milan.[19] Keeping to strict historical fact in spite of his passionate attitude at the time, Chabod wanted to vindicate the humanistic and universalist value of the voluntary concept of nation, typical of the Italian way of thinking, by comparing it to the naturalistic concept, typical of the German school of thought that was the matrix of imperialist and racist nationalism.[20] The historian pointed out that the Italian culture of Mazzini and Mancini had contributed specifically to the original and fundamental development of the idea of nation combined with the idea of liberty and humanistic values, in an amalgamation of individualism and universalism that translated politically into conceiving the Italian nation as an integral part of European civilization. "Consequently, the distinction between nation and liberty made during the Risorgimento and the extremely spiritual idea of nation were such that the Italians considered the principle of nationality a universal value, not limited to their own land, but embracing all areas where there were oppressed peoples."[21] The Italian culture did not consider the nation as an "exclusive value to the detriment of others, rather as a means conducive to harmony and a way to move forward with others." And it was from this "widespread European humanitarian zephyr" that the phenomenon of Italian voluntary patriotism originated in favor of other oppressed nations.[22] The fulcrum of the Italian idea of nation was the "trinomial of values, liberty-nationality-Europe,"[23] from which only Francesco Crispi distanced himself when he embraced a naturalistic and imperialist concept of nation, conceived as "*a priori*, independent of the will of men, preconceived, unchangeable in time, eternal and indestructible."[24] According to Chabod, the "tragedy of the modern world" had been caused by breaking the trinomial liberty-nationality-Europe.[25]

By backtracking to the historic origins of the idea of nation, according to Chabod, one can find the "good" nation in pure Italian tradition, which the Italians could relate to in order to rebuild their identity, reviving their national conscience after the nationalist inebriation of Fascism and the bewilderment of wartime experience. It was necessary to go back to the healthy principle of nationality that had nothing to do with perverse nationalism, being "radically opposite" principles, as Fernando Vegas maintained in 1946. He used arguments that were almost identical to Chabod's to affirm that the idea of nation was not dead and not incompatible with a plan to unify Europe. Building a "European nation" on the principle of nationality and proceeding, at the same time, to "eliminate the national states" was not a contradictory formula, because "Europe, as we conceive it, will be based on the principle of nationality; the national states, instead, are based on nationalism." Nationalism had "degraded the principle of nationality, turning it into something beastly and uncontrollable, renouncing what had been its animating principle, that is liberty," in turn degraded "from being the conclusion and animating essence of a process to being a mere mechanical means to reach a particular end, that is not liberty itself but the nation, considered the supreme value." As for the sovereign national state, generator of nationalism, Vegas no longer considered it befitting "human dignity." Therefore, he quickly dismissed it as "a past stage overcome and behind us," meanwhile confirming the vitality of the national idea in its original essence, which had represented "a point in time during the progressive liberation of the human spirit, as a means whereby mankind could achieve ever greater freedom." The principles of nationality and liberty were, therefore, closely related originally; the former as the means subordinate to the latter, which was the end, the only end possible in the history of mankind." In this sense, the principle of nationality was not at all obsolete or dangerous. As a matter of fact, "Europe should be rebuilt taking into careful consideration what was fruitful and positive in the principle of nationality, given that this is a period of overall development of the spirit and not at all outdated."[26]

The "Good" Nation

During this same period, a convincing and passionate defense of the nation was made by the Church as well as the Catholics who followed the direction it was taking closely. In the first ten years after the war, the Catholic cultural community in particular concerned itself with the problem of the nation. On various occasions it treated the problem, expressing greater involvement than other cultural sectors did at that time, with the exception, perhaps, of the neo-Fascist right-wing group.

The two main reasons for such interest were closely intertwined and were the principal motivational factors that inspired the Catholic Church's activity throughout the world in the postwar period: the universal plan to Catholicize the modern world, and the national plan, connected with the former, to win back Italy to Catholicism. As we shall see later on, the Church wanted to take a primary role in the reconstruction of the national identity, basing it on the principles of Christian civilization and availing itself, in this undertaking, of all the new instruments that a society of the masses had to offer, as well as Fascism's experience in mobilizing the collectivity.[27] As regards the connection between the two plans, that is the aspects of a single plan to conquer modernity, it is significant to consider what Giovanni Battista Montini stated when he insisted on a "Catholic modernity" just at the end of a Catholic Jurists' meeting in 1954 on "The Nation and the International Community": "The legacy of the word 'Catholic' would appear to exclude us from this new, dynamic modernity, so plentiful with new creations. We are survivors of the Middle Ages who carry the heavy weight of a fine and glorious tradition that excludes us from taking part as an active force in the modern world's genetic thoughts." Montini did not accept such an exclusion, particularly at a time when the hopes of a unified world organization, based on the principle of collaboration among peoples, opened up new prospects for the worldwide activities of the Church, always universally oriented. With this prospect in mind, Montini proudly claimed modernity for the Catholics: "If the world aspires to becoming unified and if I am a Catholic, not only am I modern, but I am in the vanguard of the modern world. I precede the others; I can enlighten the others; I have the genius of the modern world's progress in my Catholicism; I can be proud and content; and I can thank God for having given me this, not only to experience and carry forward, but to enjoy, magnify and spread around me," because the very fact of being Catholic "is conducive to the probability of coinciding with the most significant and lively trajectories of the modern world." And most certainly the creation of the national states was among the trajectories of modernity. Their existence appeared to be in conflict with the desire to create a new international order, but Montini insisted that the "conflict did not exist, because it was not so much a question of changing the existing order as overcoming it, preserving the good things obtained through experience, especially of the nineteenth century when nationalities were determined, nationalities that would then establish the states," almost completing "this great, this huge, task" before the outbreak of World War II. "Everything achieved by this great task and carried out in the nineteenth and early twentieth centuries can remain; nobody should undo it," because the formula of a new universal peace is not "*la debella-tio . . .* but *fraternitas* and *societas* and the concerted effort of the various international entities that have come into being as a result of this laborious experience and that should create a super *civitas*, which would bring these units together. Sovereignty is still in force for everything that comes under its authority; sovereignty no longer prevails when there is something extra that unites it with other sovereignties as one."[28]

We do not think we are overstressing the significance of these statements when we take them as being the clearest evidence of the plan to promote a "Catholic modernity" by acknowledging the nation, and within certain limits the national state as well, even with its limited sovereignty, as the irreplaceable foundation upon which to build the future international, European or universal order. On the other hand, this attitude was consistent with what the Church had asserted regarding the problem of the nation, at least from World War I on. During Fascism, the Church had reiterated its condemnation of "false nationalism" or "exaggerated nationalism" that led to worshipping the nation and ideologizing the national state. However, the Church had always avoided condemning the idea of nation and devotion to one's country that constituted the main sentimental factor, supported and defended by the Church as long as it was compatible with Christian morality. After the war, the Church reconfirmed that it was a mistake to confuse "national life in its proper sense with nationalist policy," explaining that, whereas the former, being "a people's right and merit can and should be furthered," the latter was "the germ of infinite disaster [and] will never be rejected enough." In his 1954 Christmas message Pius XII said: "National life is all of the civilized values working together because they are particular to and typical of a given group, and they bind the group together as a spiritual unit. At the same time, national life makes its own contribution, enriching mankind culturally. Therefore, national life is not something political in its essence," but when "it began to be exploited as a means to a political end, it became one of the principles causing the decay of the human community; that is, when the dominating, centralized state made nationality the basis of its power to expand. The result was a nationalistic state, the germ of rivalry and source of discord." The only way to prevent a return of nationalistic activity is to look for "a common bond that should unite the single states," continued the pope, which for the European nations could only be the rediscovery of their unity through Europe's Christian tradition.[29]

The condemnation of "exaggerated" nationalism, that is, "a theoretical concept and practical activity that tend to overvalue the nation, making it a predominant and even absolute ethical-political principle,"[30] according to Luigi Sturzo, should not necessarily have involved the nation. Sturzo wrote that the nation was "a people's particular identity" that "cannot form without stable adjacent geographical surroundings, without a historical and cultural tradition or an economic interest." These are the initial conditions required so that the "collective personality that we call nation can develop when the people's awareness is added, to create one of those sociological combinations that only the great ideas such as religion, liberty and independence can arouse. . . . We believe a people's identity indicates only the difference of one ethnic group from another, while the personality indicates the active conscience that develops from the differentiated group, determining its own cultural and political imprint."[31] With this understanding, the nation "will not die" but can take part in the realization of "a kind of internationalism based on a moral code, and which respects and supplements the historical and cultural tradition of the single nations, enabling them to live side by side in peace and prosperity."[32]

The Catholic culture was naturally oriented toward a future world of peaceful cohabitation among peoples, but not all Catholics agreed on the role the nation should play in the future scenario. The confrontation between the different positions was very lively, a sign of the special interest in the nation and its future shown by the Church and the Catholics, but not without some apprehension regarding the decline of patriotic values that was starting to become noticeable at the beginning of the fifties. During the Catholic Jurists' meeting mentioned earlier, there were those, like Francesco Carnelutti, who asserted imperiously that the "national period of the community has been surpassed" by the existence of the supranational states and by the "desire of the movement for international unity to overcome the rights of the nation." "We created the nation and now we are surpassing the nation."[33] The attitude of Francesco Santoro-Passarelli was more moderate. He spoke of the "deep Christian significance of the march toward the nation and from the nation toward the international community," maintaining, first of all, that the nation was "a reaffirmation of the liberty and Christian dignity of all the partners with respect to the sovereign's power, even before it meant political independence for the national community."[34]

Actually, in order to highlight the nation's Christian origin, the Catholics proposed a revaluation of the "good" nation concept, to be realized at the society rather than the state level. By so doing, the nation and the national state would be separated, thus enhancing the truly Christian component within the national society as opposed to the national state's lay component. In the end, the nation could be defined as a natural, cultural and historical entity that could not be suppressed.

This was the predominant line of thought taken by the Catholics as regards the nation. At a meeting of the Italian Catholic University Federation in 1951 on *Nazione e prospettive sopranazionali* (The Nation and Supranational Prospects),[35] it became evident, as Franco Costa pointed out, that it was necessary to "react to an identification that plunges us back into a static vision of the nation that becomes inflexible within the state or vice-versa opposes it and undertakes an all-out struggle against it." However, Costa also recalled that from the time of the French Revolution, the coexistence of state and nation had been a "legitimate" aspiration of peoples. But he believed it was possible to overcome this problem of coexistence by moving "toward a supranational rather than a national unity" through a more dynamic vision of the nation. Of course, this process was not yet clearly defined, and therefore, Costa admitted, "I am not sure that history will evolve toward a legitimately unified Europe."[36]

Along with a stern condemnation of nationalism, the outcome of the federation's meeting was an overall favorable attitude toward the nation, highlighting the natural and historical characteristics that formed the fundamental grounds of solidarity: "The nation is not my God, nor my master, but my neighbor, my fellow human being, organized within a history, a culture and a complex of institutions. . . . Seen in this light, the nation is truly the total social expansiveness of all the capabilities of the individual himself,"[37] affirmed Fausto Montanari. The nation is a "reality," "a historical organism toward which I have concrete duties of justice and charity," which individuals cannot shirk, because one of "the most serious sins is to evade history."[38] The nation is the "healthy example of how the limits of a small community can be overcome" within a historical and ideal scenario that enhances the individuals but battles egoism: in this sense the nation should be defended and strengthened against the "dangers of individualism on the one hand and cosmopolitical universalism on the other."[39]

The Regeneration of a Great Nation

During the early years of republican Italy, in the midst of the new defense of the nation and the rebirth of devotion to the fatherland, the
myth of Greater Italy also reappeared in a moderate, revised and corrected version as did some of the other myths that had surrounded it,
such as the myth of primacy, the universal mission or the evocation of
past greatness as a good omen for future greatness. Rising up from the
catastrophe of the war, Italy could return to the forefront, maintained
the supporters of the new myth of the great nation. It could become the
leader of a new civilization for the progress of mankind because it had
a new universal formula for resolving modern conflicts. And right after
the war, the myth of regenerating the Italians also reappeared, this time
without any traces of racism or warlike models, but newly inspired by
the archetype of a free, responsible, civically virtuous citizen.

For many anti-Fascists, and above all, those who had experienced
and taken part in the Resistance movement, dissociating the Italians
from Fascism and describing the Fascists as a gang of indigenous invaders and enemies of Italy, did not at all reprieve the Italians from the
judgment passed by the early anti-Fascist Piero Gobetti, who in 1925
had defined Fascism as the "autobiography of the nation," born of the
womb of the Italian nation itself.[40] Therefore, after having "remade
Italy," what was left to do was to "remake the Italians once again," according to a Liberal brochure that appeared in 1943. "The subjects must
be transformed into citizens. . . . We must start with the primer on civilized living."[41] Consequently, a profound moral regeneration was necessary to recover from the state of corruption into which the nation had
sunk during the dictatorship and military occupation. More than a material disaster, what weighed heavily against the new Italy was a serious
"moral disaster," said Francesco Fancello, illustrating the Action Party's
platform, because there was not a "single institution that had escaped
the grip of misgovernment, nor was there a single aspect of life in Italy
that had not been polluted by corruption."[42] The Italians needed to be
regenerated, first of all, from the legacy of the Fascist experience and
influence of the nationalist mythology. By accepting the punitive conditions of the peace treaty with dignified humility, as proof of their expiation, the way would be opened for Italy to resume its place among the
democratic nations. As Adolfo Omodeo stated in 1944, "To save the
country we must eliminate the disgraceful actions that survived twenty
years of tyranny."[43]

The Christian Democrats were also convinced, as Alcide De Gasperi declared, that "the problem of reconstruction was mainly a moral one. Without a revival of the moral conscience of all classes making up the Italian people, a material and civilized reconstruction would be impossible, and even if it were realizable, it would be a short-lived job due to the internal corruption that would continue to gnaw away at and destroy the social fabric of the new state."[44] At the end of 1944 in the first issue of *Il Commento*, a Christian Democrat publication, Giuseppe Castelli Avolio wrote that it was the main duty of the parties that were getting ready to reconstruct the country, as well as restore freedom to the institutions and provide solutions to the most pressing economic problems, "to get busy renewing morality and creating a sound and healthy political conscience in the Italians so as to provide a solid foundation for the free institutions."[45] According to *La Civiltà Cattolica*, the moral regeneration of the Italians could only come about through "a sincere and lasting return to the faith that had always made the country glorious" and "not by giving in to the influence of exotic ideologies or systems alien to its nature" but by reviving the institutions "according to the needs of its native genius."[46]

However, with such peremptory requests for regeneration there was the risk that, by insisting too much on the decadence and corruption of the Italians, they might lose all confidence in their capability of rebirth. Monsignor Pietro Barbieri observed that many Italians "felt inferior and therefore denied their past for fear of being accused of imperialism and Fascism."[47] And in turn, Corrado Alvaro wrote that resignation to the condition of defeated nation, accepted as the punishment for a crime to be expiated, risked being transformed into a permanent state of passiveness; that withdrawing from history might make Italy renounce being part of a historical reality forever; that Italy's "rhetoric of greatness regarding the national conscience" might be substituted with the "rhetoric of impotence"[48] and "resignation to the catastrophe."[49] This might lead the Italians to accept degradation, humiliation and corruption as their irrevocable condemnation to a position of inferiority, which the nation could never rise above because it would be constitutionally incapable of recovering a place among civilized nations.

When a united Italy began life again as a national state, despite everything, the need to pull itself out of the abyss into which it had fallen became evident. We must "create new reasons to exist and find them in ourselves and in our national reality," warned Alvaro.[50] If the aim was to spark the glimmer of a national conscience in the Italians, humiliated by the defeat and the shattered national state, it was necessary now to bolster national pride.

That is what the anti-Fascist parties did. Starting from the experience of defeat, from the collapse of the nationalist ambitions, from the suffering, sacrifices and humiliations, they erected the pedestal on which to place the myth of a new Greater Italy, no longer a great power but a great nation because, more than any other, Italy had experienced the inebriation of power. It had paid to the very end for its crimes, making amends for and redeeming itself with pain and sacrifice, until it had gained freedom. The new Italian nation, symbolically represented by the successful self-image of the neorealist cinema, showed its sores, its miseries, its population in rags astonished among the ruins, but already hard at work to reconstruct, as an example of a population regenerated from pain and shame. The Italian nation revealed itself as being human and discovered, in this new humanness devoid of ambition, a new greatness.

All of the anti-Fascist, Catholic and secular movements encouraged Italy, in its resurrection, to hold its head high as it moved forward toward a future of renewed and more genuine greatness, not based on material power, armies and conquered territory but on moral power, ideas and the peaceful spread of civilization by means of example. *Il Commento* stated that no people were subject to irremediable decline, and even less so the Italian people, because the possibility of their rebirth "was innate in their native land, its history, in the great traditions, in the indelible memories and the tombs of its famous dead. . . . The whole secret of rebirth lies in putting the people back on the trajectories along which their history has developed. History rises out of the past and continues in the present and the two together, past and present, form the future."[51]

Italy could rise again and give the world the new modern formula for resolving the problems that have troubled humanity, creating "the harmonious collaboration of peoples," as Action Party leader Riccardo Bauer wrote. The formula developed out of the "very mortification caused by a trial that had lacerated and oppressed the country, almost disintegrating it, but had also rigorously selected its politicians, preparing them for modernist viewpoints," showing Italy the way to a new, more dignified and truer greatness than in the past, "when it wanted to play at being a great power." Because it was strengthened by a "shameful experience of pain and death, but also because it had shown that it was capable of recovery," Italy could once again aspire to having a role in the postwar world, wrote Bauer.[52]

Once the myth of the great power had collapsed, the new Italy was christened by its founders under the good omen of a great nation reborn, purified by suffering, redeemed by the blood shed during the war of liberation, ready to resume its own role in the international community and to carry out a mission for the progress of modern civilization, as was the tradition of its centuries-old civilization and in keeping with the ideals of peace, work and justice. The anti-Fascist parties agreed in acknowledging that the primary condition for Italy to achieve a new greatness was to reestablish a unified conscience among the Italians, creating a renewed national identity based on the values of a republican democracy in order to found the new state's political unity on a wider and more solid basis of spiritual and moral unity. Upon the birth of the Republic, Giuseppe Dossetti proclaimed, "We must build a new Italian unity."[53] In 1947 Togliatti told the Constituent Assembly that, after freedom, the supporting pillar of the new state was "the political and moral unity of the nation, in part to be saved, but largely to be consolidated."[54]

The anti-Fascist parties set right to work at this task, rivaling each other. However, the general agreement regarding this proposal developed into a radical conflict between opposite models of the national identity: in just a few months after liberation, the unified patriotism of the Resistance was shattered, sparking a new conflict over the differences among the national myths of the different Italies, embodied in the various parties, each claiming to be representative of the "true Italy" and implicating the others as the nation's enemies, who were trying to hinder its rebirth and return to greatness.

17

A Myth for the Republic

A Humble Birth

"The birth of the Italian Republic was unpretentious," wrote Corrado Alvaro the day after it occurred on June 2, 1946. "This is probably the first time an Italian regime has come into being without a heroic fanfare or delirious manifestations of greatness; the Italian Republic was born a poor creature, and like its poor country, is assisted by its poor relatives." However, even if the Republic's birth had none of the characteristics of a great event that, like all great events, are usually transfigured into the founding myth of new states, it was an event in that it marked a change in the history of the Italians. In fact, for the first time

> Italy is allowing itself a people's regime, letting the people partici-
> pate in the government. This revolution, seemingly brought about
> by the ballot, was actually prepared by the civil wars of 1943 and
> 1944. Today the problem is to give this newly emerged force some
> substance, ideals and tasks. This mass of people is so complex in
> its makeup that, for the most part, it eludes all parties. It is the
> foundation of a modern Italian state and cannot be the monopoly
> of anyone.[1]

In order to provide this mass of people with substance, ideals and functions, the newborn Italian Republic, like any new state, needed a founding myth for itself so that it could bestow upon its birth—in spite of the fact that it was "quiet and subdued"[2]—the characteristics befitting an event, charged with historic and symbolic importance for the future, that marked the beginning of a new era for the Italians. Symbols and myths in the condensed form of images and words were equally necessary to communicate to the masses their values, which were the idealistic principles legitimizing the new state.

Because of the unavoidable needs of mass politics, the founding parties of republican Italy found themselves faced with the task of giving the reborn Italian state a political myth. Naturally, they turned first to the common experience of the war of liberation. The myth of the Resistance was the only myth the Republic's founding parties had in common. From the moment of liberation, in the overall enthusiasm for the end of the war and the unity regained, attempts had been made to create a national mythology based on the Resistance and anti-Fascism. Everything utilizable of the previous national mythologies was adopted, starting with the description of the Resistance as a "second Risorgimento." Apart from being an idealistic reminder, this definition was historically unfounded,[3] but by recalling the Risorgimento idealistically, it was nevertheless an effective image that exalted the new movement for the liberation and independence of the Italian people. This movement had by itself secured the nation's political and idealistic unity once again. Actually, the "second Risorgimento" was depicted as truer than the "first" because it was a popular undertaking and not brought about by a minority group. The "second Risorgimento" gave birth to a national state in which the masses, excluded from the "first" Risorgimento and from the state that had ensued, were fully integrated, and they acknowledged it as their country. Another aspect of the myth of the Resistance was the victory of the "real Italy" over Fascism, which had taken on all of the ills and wrongdoings of the Italians' history and character, incarnating everything that represented the "false Italy." The deep-rooted antagonism between the "two Italies" that had made the existence of the state so precarious during the "first Risorgimento" had by now been overcome, because, finally, an "animate, true, eternal Italy" had triumphed, stated *La Nuova Europa* on April 29, 1945.

With the exaggeration typical of every mythical transfiguration of real events—no matter how great and significant they themselves might be—in the creation of the myth of the Resistance as a "second Risorgimento" there was soon a tendency to worship the Resistance as supreme, thus playing down or even concealing the decisive role of the Allies in defeating the Germans and republican Fascism. Although this was the trend, some realistic souls recalled that the liberation "was carried out by the Allied Forces and was not, unfortunately, carried out by us," wrote Francesco Calasso on May 6, 1945.[4] In the same way, what prevailed in the epic version of the war of liberation as the war for the regeneration of the Italians was the tendency to forget the moral proportions of the nation's collapse and the deep wounds that the destruction of the country and the shattering of the national identity had left in the souls of the Italians. Thus a mythical image was created of the Italian people, who, after being the recalcitrant victims of the Fascist dictatorship, had finally risen against the tyrant, demolishing the Fascist regime with all their strength, fighting and beating the German invader, rising again to freedom, morally regenerated and united, and ready to take up their place in the world again. The Resistance—wrote the historian Luigi Salvatorelli soon after the liberation—was "much more than a purely military feat, more than just complementary guerrilla warfare": "It was the affirmation of a population that knows it has a function in Europe and the world, the political affirmation of a nation that intends to take its destiny into its own hands."[5] Thus depicted, the Resistance became the new myth on which to found the national state, in the symbolic rhetoric of republican Italy. It was the beginning of a new era for the Italians.

"Patriotism based on the Resistance" seemed to provide a valid basis on which to create the Republic's national myth, one that represented all Italians, over and above ideologies and religious beliefs, symbol of the nation and the inspiring principle of a common, civilized, ethical code. There were those who imagined or hoped to create Italy's national myth by incorporating the ideological traditions of all the movements that had participated in the "second Risorgimento," thus combining it idealistically with the first. In light of this, on June 25, 1946, Alcide De Gasperi, speaking before the Constituent Assembly that was about to draft the fundamental Table of Laws of the Italian Republic said, "The forces at work within the Republic are the universalist tendencies of Christianity, Giuseppe Mazzini's humanitarian tendencies and solidarity among workers championed by the workers' organizations."[6] Such a combination of universalist and humanitarian ideals could not, however, elude the attraction of the myth of the nation as the source legitimizing the new state.

This was evident both to those drafting the new Constitution and to the parties taking a leading political role, even if the founding fathers did not place the myth of the nation at the top of the scale of values and principles that were supposed to inspire a new, more civilized ethical code, as did liberal and Fascist Italy, albeit with the differences we have seen. The Constitution reserved an eminent position for the national myth, where the existence of an Italian nation was evoked as the presupposition for the existence of the Italian state, although not explicitly. It is interesting to note that the Constitution makes no mention of the

Resistance and only marginally mentions anti-Fascism in the transitory and final provisions forbidding the reorganization of the Fascist Party.

The first reference to the nation is in Article 9, where it states that the Republic protects "the landscape and historic and artistic assets of the nation"; then it is mentioned again in Article 67, which reads, "all members of parliament represent the nation," and in Article 98, "all public officials are at the service of the nation only." More frequent in the Constitution is the adjective "national" ("national territory," "national policy," "national interest," "national security," "national unity"), whereas the word "fatherland" appears only once, in Article 52, where it affirms that "defending the fatherland is the sacred duty of the citizens": this is the only trace left in the culture of the Italian Republic of a "religion of fatherland."

The national myth was less evident in the symbols of the new Italy. In the public competition to establish the state's emblem, which was supposed to describe graphically "the idea of our Republic," as one of the members on the special committee in charge of examining the designs said, the idea that predominated was "labor—so as to establish the concept that our Republic is a Republic founded on work."[7] Most of the symbols proposed focused on the myths of peace, labor, and civilization, and there were references to Rome and the Italian civilization as well. The emblem chosen did not include symbols of the nation, for example, an "Italian Marianna" on the French model, as some suggested. The myth of the nation was evoked very discretely by the narrow band of three colors. On the whole, the new emblem looked like an "indisputable astronomic-industrial-botanic mixture" and that is how it was defined by *Risorgimento Liberale* on February 8, 1948.

The Indian Summer

Apart from the references to the nation made in the Republic's Constitution, where the national myth was concerned, the dawning of republican Italy was like the myth's Indian summer, marking its rebirth during a fertile season. The main architects of this rebirth were, as we have seen, the political parties that generated the Italian Republic. While it was true that the Italians had lost their sense of belonging to a common country due to the disaster of defeat, the hatred that had developed during the civil wars and the humiliation of foreign occupation, it is also true that the anti-Fascist parties did their utmost to restore prestige and dignity to the myth of the nation. They were determined to redefine the

characteristics of a new national identity in keeping with the principles
and values of the new Italian Republic. Except for the *Qualunquisti* and
the "universalists," all the Italian political parties spoke in favor of the
nation; they all declared they were the heirs to the genuine Risorgimento
tradition, epitomized in the binomial "unity and liberty"; all promised to
put Italy back on the road to modernity, now conceived according to
ideals of peace and justice and no longer power and conquest; everybody paid homage to the reborn nation, freed of the black shirts, once
again to be honored by all Italians as their common country. As Umberto Merlin said before the Constituent Assembly, "Our country is no
longer our stepmother but our generous mother, who accepts and wel-
comes all her children with the same heartfelt tenderness."[8]

It is certainly not easy to distinguish how much of the national
myth's rebirth was sincere and how much was insincere. There was definitely a great deal of propaganda; certainly it was used, particularly by
those who, like the Communists, Socialists and Christian Democrats,
were linked idealistically to universalist values that gravitated around an
"ideal fatherland" to which supreme allegiance was paid. On the other
hand, it is always difficult when analyzing any mythical representation,
to know where to draw the line between spontaneous conviction and the
artifice of invention. Almost always the two elements are mixed. Sometimes it is useful to make a distinction between old and new believers in
the myth of the nation. On one side we can place the parties that proposed the national myth again, following logically in the tracks of Risorgimento tradition and remaining faithful to political cultures such as
those of the Liberals and Republicans, which had always attributed to
the nation a primary value. On the other side we can place the Socialist
and Communist Parties that had "discovered" the national myth and
the Risorgimento only at a certain point in their history, because they
did not belong to their original cultural heritage. As a result of this, both
the national myth and the Risorgimento had remained foreign to their
world of values or had often been the target of violent attacks and now,
instead, were being incorporated into their ideological universe,
flaunted and defended with the fervor typical of a novice. However,
besides this distinction, each party, including the Movimento sociale
italiano (Italian Social Movement, the neo-Fascist party formed at the
end of 1946), claimed the privilege of representing the Italians as the
most authentic and faithful interpreter of the nation. Thus, right from
the beginning of the Republic, the Italians were once again both actors
and spectators of the deeply rooted antagonism between the parties,

each proclaiming, against the other, that it was the "nation's chosen son," as the *Corriere della Sera* described them ironically in 1947. The newspaper also admonished that "the desire to be given recognition as a people or elected party had never brought anyone good luck."[9]

The Liberal, Republican and Monarchic parties, the latter formed after the monarchy fell, could consider themselves genuine inheritors of the Risorgimento tradition. Each had its own legitimate reasons, although their concepts of the nation were extremely different, as were the models of the new Italy they proposed. The Republicans considered themselves the interpreters of the Risorgimento's "real Italy," the democratic Italy that had been taken over by the monarchy and Fascism. Therefore, they described themselves as the most legitimate representatives of the link between the "first" and "second" Risorgimentos. The link consisted in their intransigent opposition to the monarchy after the unification, in democratic interventionism and anti-Fascism. Founding the Republic was the final victory of the "real Italy," because the country, belonging to all Italians, could only have been a republican state.[10] Obviously the Monarchists were of the opposite view. They claimed that the dynasty of the House of Savoy had had a leading role in the Risorgimento as well as being the creators of the unified state. They considered the monarchy the best guarantee of national unity, over and above the parties. While they hoped for an improbable return of the monarchy, their attitude toward republican Italy was like that of a disinterested custodian of a form of patriotism without party ideology.[11] As for the Liberals, although divided when facing the institutional problem, they were united when defending their Risorgimento legacy, which they claimed included the fifty years of unification up to the advent of Fascism. They also defended the role of the ruling class that had built and governed the national state, laying the foundation of a free country for the Italians and bringing Italy closer to the level of modern European nations. All this had come about under the banner of a modern, secular idea of nation that the Liberals felt was still valid as an idealistic principle for republican Italy, against the dangers of clericalist influence over the state or the threat of Communist totalitarianism.

As the inheritors of the Risorgimento, the Liberals, Republicans and Monarchists expressed patriotic ideals dating from the past, but by now they were a minority compared to the new forces dominating the Italian political scene. These forces were boldly remaking the traditions of the Risorgimento and the history of united Italy according to their ideological needs. Even parties that had nothing to do with the Risorgimento and its traditions—the Socialist, Communist and Christian Democrat Parties, for example—competed for the role of authentic heirs to the Risorgimento. The discovery of the nation by the parties that had an internationalist ideology was, without any doubt, the newest and, to a certain extent, most important fact in the history of the myth of the nation after World War II. It was important, first of all, because it showed that the national myth did not have an obsolete meaning or function for the anti-Fascist parties, after World War II. It was also important because such a frequent and even widely publicized propaganda use of the national myth during the early years of the Republic, particularly by the major parties, meant that these parties thought the Italians were still responsive to the ideals of country and nation. They were so convinced of this that they ostentatiously included the national myth in their ideology, although it was carefully revised and adapted for this purpose. Besides the problem of sincerity, it was significant that the major parties of the Italian Republic turned to the previous national mythology, including, as we have seen, the myth of a Greater Italy presented under a new guise, and even went so far as to copy some of the tunes and rhythms of the Fascist rhetoric. Even if these parties did not admit it explicitly, they recognized that eighty years of unification in a single national state, where the nation was exalted as the supreme value of civilized ethics (albeit through different and contrasting means, first during the liberal regime and then during Fascism), had left in the people of the peninsula a kind of national conscience and patriotism that not even the trauma of defeat, the hatred of the civil war or the humiliation of the peace treaty had wiped out.

The Republic's political parties wanted to take advantage of this residual national sentiment, which still inflamed patriotic passion in discussions over the peace treaty or the matter of Trieste, to mobilize the Italians' energy and direct it toward the work of rebuilding the national state. Use of the national myth by the anti-Fascist parties was deemed necessary to prevent the neo-Fascists from taking it for their own use. The latter, in fact, tried to foment a rebirth of nationalism, not so much as part of their ideology but as a reaction to the defeat, humiliation and poverty that ensued. As Mario Ferrara observed in August 1945, they tried to exploit the "moral uprising" of the "lower and middle classes, who have given a lot and suffered a lot, who have nothing more to give but know they will have to suffer a great deal more, and who knows for how long, against the new snobbery that turns the nation's difficulties into an international social gathering." This uprising could have been "turned into a wily subterfuge aimed at renewing illusions of sacred egoism and absurdly abstract political realism in order to glorify a new dictatorship." Now, warned Ferrara, to defend ourselves from the risk of "nationalist poisoning" as a result of the country's frustration at being defeated and humiliated, it was necessary to "nourish in our minds the supreme importance of a national sentiment" as a sentiment of human dignity, which has reacted to the humiliation and defeat by showing the strength of collective solidarity and the will to redeem the country by working hard to reconstruct it. We must exalt the national sentiment "in the moral and material reconstruction process, transferring it to nation-wide social solidarity. We must be Italians united in the sorrow of Italy; we must change that sorrow into the joy of labor, which redeems and re-generates"; by so doing "we can prove we are capable of being a nation, that we have the structure and moral strength that allow us to be called a people and to claim our destiny for ourselves."[12]

This encouragement led to the revaluation of the national myth as a common collective myth and as the principle legitimizing the republi-can state. Undoubtedly, the competition raging among the parties that aspired to taking over command of the new Italy implied adopting a national policy in which the term "national" could not have had only an institutional and territorial meaning but idealistic value as well. This im-plied interpreting the history of Italy as a national one, seeing a national identity in its past, present and future, in other words, basically assum-ing the development of a national myth. However, in order to proceed in this direction, it was necessary to take into account what this myth had represented in the lives of the Italians, particularly during the total-itarian regime, when a modern national policy strategy was first imple-mented systematically in Italy, through the autocratic organization of a single party and through widespread ideological indoctrination aimed at all the social classes.

The Legacy of a Myth

As early as March 1945, the young Catholic intellectual Mario Nigro observed that it was definitely impossible for the major anti-Fascist par-ties to ignore the influence that the "atmosphere created by the totalitar-ian regime" had had on the Italians and particularly on the young, who had been educated exclusively by Fascism. This was especially impor-tant, since even the elderly, educated in different political beliefs, includ-ing anti-Fascist ones, "ended by letting themselves be swept up in the

mechanism, swearing faithfulness and devotion to the Fascist creed."
Considering the nature of totalitarian regimes, which "are not satisfied
just to take your body" but "tie up your soul in their totalitarian propaganda," Nigro warned that the new state should not underestimate the
mark left on the Italians by a regime that "had so completely permeated
the state, that had so profoundly wedged itself into the nation's life, cov-
ering it with a tightly woven network of interventions and controls, that
only a proud, solitary hermit could have escaped." In a particularly
shrewd way he made acute considerations about what might be termed
the "appeal of Fascism," exercised through nationalism, colonialism, the
myth of the totalitarian community and the ambition to see "Italy rise
proudly on the international scene." Last, Nigro recalled that for the
young, "Fascism was also a huge effort to propel the nation into a superpower configuration." For this reason, "living life fully and dangerously
meant establishing a relationship of solidarity, not with Fascism but with
the essential needs developing within the nation."[13]

The person who was particularly aware of the legacy left by Fascist
education in the minds of the generations that grew up under the regime was Palmiro Togliatti. "It would be rather surprising if eighteen
years of Fascist government and fourteen of totalitarian regime had not
left their mark," especially on the younger generations who did not have
any other political experience, observed Togliatti in 1941. Being convinced Fascists, the younger generations had followed Mussolini because they wanted "Italy to be great, strong and respected," and they had
accepted the dictatorship, considering it a necessary means to "achieve
the unity of the whole nation."[14] "The fall of Fascism," Togliatti remarked in 1944, "has left a void, yet to be filled, in many young people,
because they do not understand how their aspirations for regeneration
of the country and social justice can now be implemented. It is up to us
to show them that their ideals are the same as ours."[15] The Communist
Party's strategy aimed at filling the void left in these young people, who
had lost faith in the Fascist myths, by offering them a national myth and
a model of national greatness, repackaged in a Communist version. According to Togliatti it was necessary to explain to these young people
that their hopes for social justice and national greatness were not false;
that the Communists wanted the "well-being of the people and greatness for the nation"; that Fascism's imperialist ambitions had been false,
deceptive and illusory when they identified greatness with waging war to
plunder and conquer; that the choices, means and objectives of a vague
policy of power had been wrong and disastrous, subjecting Italy to

Germany and leading the nation not to greatness but catastrophe. Speaking to the young Communists in 1947, Togliatti repeated that the battle against the inheritance of Fascism should not be fought at the political level only but should also involve "ideology, the moral code, customs and everyday life," and he recalled that Fascism had risen to power by promoting "the most noble sentiments and highest ideals," such as the country's greatness and social justice.[16]

By operating throughout the nation in a systematic, widespread and uniform manner, Fascism had actually contributed to making the national myth popular among the Italians, more so than had liberal Italy up to World War I. Apart from its specific objectives, the totalitarian experiment had implemented a socialization process of policies for the masses that, despite their counterproductive outcome, had occurred under the banner of the national myth. Fascism's main problem had been "how to carry forward the national integration process of our people, at least at a fast pace," noted Camillo Pellizzi[17] in 1953, speaking more as a sociologist than former Fascist. Two decades of Fascism had left "behind very deep tracks," above all because it had "brought a certain type of crowd within the sphere of a national sentiment that was lively and genuine." Pellizzi acknowledged, however, that this "popular national sentiment, which Fascism had somehow helped to spread and take root, was not accompanied by any similar tradition or by any sure and unambiguous directive, no matter how elementary." It had not left "behind a 'well-constructed mythology' linked with that sentiment," because it had created a "single pedestal based on emotions and the support of the masses, which had been lacking in Italy for centuries and millennia," and it was upon "this pedestal that Fascism built a series of 'meanings' that were inconsistent or even contradictory in every way and in every field."

During the years leading up to World War I, the parties opposing the liberal state had not been able to ignore the nationwide importance given to the unified state but had had to accept it and even tried to take it and use it for their own ends. In the same way, after World War II the anti-Fascist parties as well as the two major parties could not ignore what Fascism's national policy had represented for the Italians: the disastrous outcome had not cancelled the mark of twenty years of totalitarian domination. For a major party that hoped to lead the state and acquire authority in the nation's society, the Fascist experience was a model to follow. And it was by taking that experience as their model that the Christian Democrats and the Communists both learned, not only how to organize and mobilize the masses through the party, which proposed itself for the leadership of the nation, but also how to develop a national ideology. Like Fascism, they needed a national ideology to create (within a certain framework and depending on the categories of their own ideology) their own national myth that would be an interpretation of Italian history, identify the characteristics making up a national identity, and determine the nature and purposes of the state, so as to relate them to the Italian nation, its role and its destiny in the world.

The need on the part of the Christian Democrats and the Communists to develop a national policy and ideology coincided with a growing prominence given to the role and function of the political parties, deemed the most genuine and authentic expression of the nation. This prominence was further fueled by the fact that each party claimed it was the most legitimate candidate to lead the state, being the only party capable of forming policies that were above party interests, of mending the wounds caused by the civil war, of completing the moral and spiritual unification of the Italians, and of putting Italy back on the road to modernity and greatness. Consequently, although they acted according to the procedures of a parliamentary democracy, both the Communists and the Christian Democrats retraced the steps toward the ideologization of the nation already taken by Fascism, each trying to claim for itself, to the detriment of the other, the monopoly of the national myth, claiming that the adversary did not have any lawful authority because it was antinational and subservient to a foreign entity.

Therefore, both the Christian Democrats and the Communists established themselves as republican Italy's predominant parties by popular consent and thanks to their mass organization, and each claimed the prerogative of being the leader of the new state. At the same time, both wanted to create a new national identity, shaping it according to the principles and values of their own ideology. In the midst of this contest, which all Italian political parties participated in, the national myth seemed to rise up out of the ruins of the war to take its place again at the center of Italian political culture, but only for a brief period.

18

The Italies of Republican Italy

The Orphans of Fascism

One of the reasons why the parties founding the Republic wanted to reevaluate the myth of nation was to prevent the Italians' lingering patriotic feeling, still present despite everything, from being exploited by the neo-Fascist movements to delegitimate the new state.

Fears that a Fascist-inspired nationalism might rise again were not unfounded. In fact, those who had been active in the Social Republic and those who had remained faithful to the myths of Fascism were in the forefront of the apologists of the nation in republican Italy, even if they were an isolated case. The attitude of those who took up the political struggle again was, in some ways, similar to that of the Mazzinians after unification: the neo-Fascists felt they were foreigners in a state that, to their eyes, embodied the betrayal of the nation with which they identified themselves.

The neo-Fascist movements that sprang up immediately after the Republic was founded aimed at exploiting resentment for the defeat, the humiliations of the peace treaty and the Trieste issue, the difficulties encountered by the new regime, the party clashes and the threat of communism. They also nostalgically evoked the memory of the Fascist regime's triumphs in order to foster new nationalism against the anti-Fascist republic. Most of the former Fascists had gotten themselves organized again into a party—the Movimento sociale italiano (MSI, Italian Social Movement)—claiming to be the only interpreters and authentic representatives of the "real Italy," against the anti-Fascist "false Italy." MSI was "the party of the country,"[1] "the only political party that guarded the idea of the unitary and independent national state."[2] The neo-Fascists believed that the republican state was completely illegitimate: it was a political regime born of the betrayal committed against the nation on September 8 and set up by antinational parties that had worked against the country, collaborated with the enemy to defeat the nation at war and demolished the national state in order to rebuild a state without a nation on its ruins, with the help of foreigners, subject to the United States or the Soviet Union.

The former Fascists carried the torch for the myth of nation as they had felt and understood it in the past, even though their nationalism was no longer fostered by enthusiasm for modernity and perhaps not even by faith in Italy's future as a great power. Dissociating the myth of nation from that of modernist nationalism may be the most important element in neo-Fascist ideology, which was strongly imbued with nostalgia for lost greatness. In many former Fascists, the myth of nation was tinged with regret for the ideal of a Greater Italy, something they had longed for in their youthful dreams of power, at that time supported by the vision of a nation walking proudly and boldly side by side with the great powers, ambitious to compete and surpass them. Their nostalgia for the past was mixed with contempt for the present and defeated Italy, which was no longer respected and whose territory had been broken up. Italy was now governed by parties that had ensconced themselves in power, ignoring the country's lacerations and the fact that it no longer counted in international politics.

It was mainly the MSI that took in the neo-Fascists, working out its ideology by mixing the various factions that had made up the regime's Fascism with that of the Salò Republic, all of which clashed violently, even bitterly, within the movement. However, the ideological cornerstone for all neo-Fascists was still the supremacy of the myth of nation or, as Carlo Costamagna called it, the dogma of nation, explaining that "it is only treating it as the dogma of nation that we can differentiate ourselves from all the parties of the democratic lineup, each of which denies the principle of nation for its own reasons, whether supranational or antinational."[3] Flaunting their loyalty to Fascism and its ideological legacy, the MSI's activists did not hesitate to call themselves "nationalists," repeating word for word the Fascist concept of nation as "moral, political and economic unity that is fully realized in the state, a political and ethical body par excellence."[4] Consequently, the neo-Fascists were against any plan to decentralize the country into regions, seeing it as an attack on national unity, just as they supported the necessary supremacy of state authority, which "transcends individuals and is the repository of the nation's permanent interests and will to exist."[5]

The neo-Fascists believed that the nation and nationalism were still the driving force of history, even when nationalism took on the ideological guise of internationalism, as in the case of Communist Russia. In 1949 Augusto De Marsanich maintained that it was always "the nation that absorbs and overcomes communism" when the two were face to face. However, when defining its nationalism, the neo-Fascist party wanted to distinguish it from generic patriotism, which was also the banner of the nostalgic Monarchists, in order to highlight the social element of its concept of nation to the extent of speaking of National Socialism once again as "a new intuition and meaning of the concept of nation." De Marsanich declared that "in Italy, it is always difficult to distinguish between country and nation, between feeling and reality," and for a long time "patriotic feeling has covered up social injustice, class domination and the supremacy of money with rhetoric." Different from country, the nation is not a feeling but "a moral and political idea, a historical fact and an economic system, which must be considered as independent of the natural love for one's birthplace." These make it possible "to fill in social distances" in the formula proposed by national socialism and "to go beyond class conflict, to finally give a historical and vital solution, not an ideological one that is easy and inconclusive, to the age-old issue of the economic relations between individuals and classes."[6] The MSI clearly evinced a return to the tradition of national trade unionism and the socializing Fascism of the Republic of Salò, proposing a populist version of the myth of nation, taking as its "guiding principle" a nation "that sums up the distress, suffering, work and the ideas of a whole people," not a nation "of fanfares and plumes on review days."[7]

Once again proposing the myths of anti-individualist and corporatist Fascism, the neo-Fascist Party also renewed the myth of Italian supremacy in creating a New Civilization, an "original concept of the world and life, a spiritual civilization and a new universal, Italian humanism," as an alternative to the materialistic civilization of Americanism and communism, as *La Lotta Politica* declared at the end of 1953. The neo-Fascists firmly believed "that there is a kind of natural cause-and-effect relationship between Italy and the idea of civilization, an eternal bond that makes Italy the guiding compass of all human history." However, this did not mean that they were inclined to prefigure going beyond the national state in the future, as totalitarian Fascism in the triumphant years had imagined. It is true that some neo-Fascist groups, closer to neo-Nazism than to neo-Fascism, dreamt of an Aryan

Europe, and that others debated the ideal of a Europe-nation, mixing nostalgia for the Middle Ages with romantic spiritualism and inciting Europeans to undertake a crusade against American and Russian materialism. However, most neo-Fascists remained strongly attached to the national state as an irrepressible spiritual and political reality and derided the "deceptive abbreviated abstractions," that is, the various international organizations from the UN to NATO and the European Community, which claimed to go beyond "national reality." "For the idea of Europe, the idea of European unity, not to be an abbreviated abstraction but a living reality, first of all the idea of nation must not be abstract either, but also a living reality. Denying the nation and judging nationalism from degenerate imitations of it, trying to go beyond this first fact to reach broader formations, means building on sand."[8]

Also those who, although belonging to the ranks of former Fascists, considered the Fascist experience over continued to believe that the nation and nationalism were eternal. However, they did not think it was dignified to deny how important, according to them, an ambitious and generous attempt to make Italy greater had been, even though this effort had ended in the most ruinous defeat in national history. The historian Gioacchino Volpe was an example of this, declaring he was proud of not having belonged "to the honored society of those who hope and work for the defeat of their own country at war, whatever the country may be." He confirmed his faith in Italy and its future, "the faith that has rarely died in the Italians' hearts since Roman times," even if he saw the Greater Italy reduced to "a heap of rubble" around him:[9]

> How momentously the war and the ruinous defeat have changed the face of present-day Italy, dashing so many hopes or prospects for the future. We shall build our houses, roads and bridges again and maybe our factories and the already promising farming industry, but what about our standing among nations? And our self-confidence? And our civilizing works begun in Africa? And our independence? These disasters have made us see yesterday's Italy with different eyes. I saw it moving forward, now I see it brought to a halt and pushed back, obliged to begin again from the main walls. Let us hope it will be on more solid foundations.[10]

The Italian Flag Below the Red Flag

It is likely that many of the doubts that gnawed at the nationalist historian also tormented the anti-Fascist politicians, who were committed to rebuilding the Italian state while at the same time trying to find workable formulas to rebuild the national identity on more solid foundations.

The socialist and communist left wing believed that there was only one solution to the problem of building the nation's political and moral unity, and that was social revolution, which had to destroy the roots of Fascism (that is, the capitalist economic structure) and lead to the real unification of the Italians, something that the liberal and Fascist regimes, as instruments of bourgeois domination, had prevented. Having fought in the front line in the war of liberation, the working-class parties thought they had originated the "second Risorgimento" more than any other. Furthermore, they believed they had won the title as the heirs of the "first Risorgimento" patriots, claiming their role as "the nation's favorite children," and that only socialism would realize a country for all the Italians in Italy and lead it back to the main road to modernity, that is, the way opened by the October Revolution and triumphantly carried on by Lenin's and Stalin's Russia.

In the new mythology of nation of the socialist and communist left, the coming of socialism, by then considered inevitable because of the irresistible crisis of Western capitalism, was described as the last stage of the national revolution that began with the Risorgimento. Thus, the myth of nation merged with the myth of socialism, and the hegemony of the working class became the essential and necessary means to achieve the Italians' political and moral unity. The myth of the Italians' rebirth also came up again within this process. The socialist revolution would be intellectual and moral, because bringing down and destroying the reactionary bourgeoisie that had dominated the country since its unification would destroy the economic and social conditions that had corrupted the Italians' character. Consequently, the social revolution would finally achieve the revival of the nation, giving birth to a "new Italian," similar to the Soviet "new man."

These were the dominant ideas of leftist national mythology, both socialist and communist. Actually the Socialist Party persisted in being largely indifferent to the myth of nation, something typical of its tradition and which completely ignored Carlo Rosselli's lesson. This was despite the patriotic appeals during the war of liberation and Pietro Nenni's defense of national independence, with his opposition to Italy's becoming a NATO member as an expression of anti-Americanism. However, traces of the lesson of liberal socialism can be found in the Social Democratic Party, which was born in 1947 of the Palazzo Barberini Party split. Here the myth of nation appeared as democratic patriotism

deriving from the Risorgimento, integrated with the myth of the Resistance as a "second Risorgimento."[11]

However, the Communists were much more loquacious and determined as supporters of the myth of nation. Not only did they want to
give proof of their complete conversion to the myth of nation by including the Italian flag in their symbol, though it was placed behind the red
flag with hammer and sickle, but they also did everything to appear as
the champions of the most genuine and authentic Italian nation, those
who had inherited the democratic values of the Risorgimento revolution that had been left unfinished owing to the reactionary bourgeoisie,
the monarchy and Fascism. The working class was the only really national class capable of creating "a national and people's Italy, great and
respected in the world,"[12] and of completing the Italians' political and
moral unity. In 1946 *Rinascita* explained that this was why it was up to
the party, which was the vanguard of the working class, to head the
country's government. "By proposing an immediate government program, the Communist Party, of all the Italian parties, has confirmed it is
the one with a broader and more precise vision of the nation's interests,
the most genuine expression of the working masses who, through their
nature and will, are decisive for the salvation and rebirth of Italy."[13]

Since his return to Italy in 1944, and in full agreement with the Soviet Union's policies, Togliatti had aimed at consolidating the "nationalization" of the Communist Party, begun with fits and starts during the
war of Ethiopia and intensified during the Second World War. "The
new party that we have in mind," he said in September 1944, "must be a
national Italian party, a party that brings up and resolves the problem of
emancipating work in the framework of our lives and national freedom,
making all the nation's progressive traditions our own."[14] After taking
part in the patriotic war of liberation and in founding republican Italy,
nobody could have doubted the Communist Party's Italianness, because,
said Togliatti in 1945, through it "the working class has now become established as a national class, as a class that can aspire to being the center
around which all the democratic forces are organized, all the sincerely
national forces, all the forces that want to take part in building a new
Italy."[15]

Italianness played the most important part in building a national
communist mythology, whose mainstays were, first, nationalizing the
Communist Party as the main heir of the Risorgimento revolution, of
the democratic tradition of united Italy, and of secular and humanist
culture that went from Francesco De Sanctis to Antonio Gramsci;

second, the mythical transfiguration of Gramsci, sanctified above all as a "great Italian"; and, last, the cult of personality bestowed on Togliatti, then leader of the Italian Communist Party and Gramsci's "best collaborator, who directly carries on his work." In 1947 the party's organ explained that "the most typical feature of Palmiro Togliatti's personality, together with his exceptional intelligence and culture, is his 'Italianness,' that is, his generous and profound feeling for the nation that enlivens his every speech, writing, and political and cultural activity, raising them to a higher level."[16]

Indeed, there was enough material to create a national communist myth in Gramsci's reflections on the history of Italy, reconciling it with internationalism, or rather, making the myth of nation part of the Communist Party's new internationalist strategy summarized in the formula "the Italian way to socialism." Gramsci had maintained that the Risorgimento movement was not at all destined to lead to nationalism and imperialism, because these were both contrary to "all Italian traditions, first Roman, then Catholic ones":

> Traditions are cosmopolitan. Besides, during the Risorgimento Mazzini and Gioberti also tried to graft the surging national feeling onto the cosmopolitan tradition, to create the myth of Italy's mission reborn in a new world and European cosmopolis. However, it is only a verbal and rhetorical myth, based on the past and not on the present situation, which is already established or developing (such myths have always been a stimulus for Italian history, even the most recent, from Q. Sella to Enrico Corradini to D'Annunzio).

Gramsci had come to assume that the Italians' mission could begin again as the mission of a new civilization, identifying communism as the cosmopolitan means of this vocation:

> The traditional Italian cosmopolitanism should become modern, so to ensure the best developmental conditions for the Italian worker, wherever he finds himself in this world. He should not be a citizen of the world as *civis romanus* or as Catholic but as one who produces civilization. . . . The Italians are a people "nationally" more interested in a modern form of cosmopolitanism. Not only workers but countrymen, and especially Southern ones, working together to rebuild the world's economy is a tradition of the Italians and their history, not to dominate the world hegemonically and appropriate the fruit of others' work, but to exist and develop as an Italian people. . . . The Italians' mission is to regain Roman

and medieval cosmopolitanism, but in its more modern and advanced form, even if this means a proletarian nation, as Pascoli
wanted—proletarian because the Italians have been the reserve
army of foreign capitalism, because together with the Slavs, they
have given workers to the whole world. Consequently, that is precisely why the Italian people must become part of the modern
struggle to reorganize the rest of the world, which it has contributed to creating with its work, etc.[17]

Making use of Gramsci's ideas according to the needs of national politics, the Communists worked out a new kind of Italianism in an "Italo-
Marxist" version.[18]

As the vanguard of the working class, the Communist Party was the
national party, which could interpret the destiny of the "country of the
Gracchi and Julius Caesar, of Dante and Machiavelli, Giordano Bruno
and Galileo Galilei, Mazzini and Garibaldi better than anyone else, the
cradle of Roman civilization and the Renaissance,"[19] and bring it back
to the forefront of modern civilization. "Precisely because we are a
Marxist party and therefore with the most advanced ideology and culture for interpreting history," said Togliatti in 1944, "we are able to
understand the greatness and true importance of all the facts of our history, woven on Italy's soil by the peoples that have inhabited our peninsula."[20] As Fascism had dragged the nation to ruin, and its myths of
greatness had failed miserably, reborn Italy could aspire to real greatness once again, entrusting its leadership to the "most advanced national forces, which are the working class and its vanguard in the present
period of history." Thus Italy could be reborn spiritually and prepare itself to be in the forefront in creating the new modern civilization begun
by the Soviet Union:

> A nation does not become great through speeches and not even
> through conquests when its progressive forces are humiliated and
> oppressed. England was great when it carried out its liberal revolu-
> tion, and the Russia of Lenin and Stalin is great, because the inter-
> nal renewal achieved in these countries through revolution by pro-
> gressive social and political forces had or has placed them in the
> vanguard of the whole civilized world. How could the Italian na-
> tion become great with a regime like the Fascist one, which kept
> the most backward reactionary social and political groups, those
> incapable of moral inspiration and social progress, in control of
> Italy's whole existence? Once again Italy can return to the fore-
> front and, despite today's disasters, be great, only if it is capable of

radically renewing itself spiritually. However, all those who bring
new principles of political and social progress, those who fight for
social justice and the emancipation of work, and all those who do
not just pretend to but really care about the future and greatness of
the nation must fight together for this renewal.[21]

Only by entrusting their destiny to the working class's party would
the Italians be able to complete the national revolution begun by the Risorgimento patriots, regaining their own modern identity and their national and cosmopolitan propensity. They would thus have a place in
the capitalist world, which is condemned to collapse, as the vanguard of
socialist modernity, in the same way they started off the modern age.

In some ways, communist national mythology could be considered
the latest lay metamorphosis of the myth of a Greater Italy and also the
latest version of modernist nationalism. Furthermore, it echoes quite a
few dominant ideas of national radicalism, from the interpretation of
the Risorgimento as an unfinished revolution to the radical hostility between the "two Italies," from the need of intellectual and moral reform
to the myth of a new state, from the universalistic leaning of the Italian
nation to the myth of supremacy and mission. The myth of a Greater
Italy, including reference to the Roman spirit in a national communist
version, was also one of the themes of Togliatti's rhetoric in liberated
Italy. "In the past we were a great people," Togliatti said at the Fifth
Congress of the Partito Comunista Italiano (Italian Communist Party)
in December 1945, "and we were so at the beginning of modern European and world civilization. At that time, in the Renaissance period, we
were in the forefront in all fields of peace-loving human activity, in artistic and scientific creation and in the field of work," because "the progressive forces that were then the first urban bourgeois groups had developed and established themselves in our society before anywhere else.
They were the first ever to give battle and begin eliminating the backward feudal regime, achieving remarkable results in all the fields of their
activities."[22] Communist Italianism even called up Romanness to work
out a national people's version of a myth of Rome. Speaking to the Romans in 1944, Togliatti explained:

> We reject Fascism's "Roman" rhetoric, but we cannot forget that
> Rome was twice the center of a world civilization, the city that the
> most advanced and progressive intellects of our nation turned to
> during our Risorgimento's struggle, seeing it as the destined capital
> of the Italian national state. However, Rome today is not only this
> for us: it is the city that resisted, which was not subdued, which

fought, which gave Italy hundreds of thousands of heroes and martyrs. Rome showed the whole of Italy the way that must be taken if we really want our country to rise again and our people to regain the place due to it among the free and equal peoples of the whole world.[23]

In 1947, when speaking to young Communists, Togliatti repeated that Fascism had used Roman rhetoric to hide "the main problem of our age" from young people, that is "creating and establishing new social forms and structures that foster the development of forces and the aspirations to freedom and justice of millions and millions of people." Therefore, the "greatness of our country depends today on our future capacity to advance in this direction, as the great Russian people did after the October Revolution."[24] The Communist Party proposed the myth of renewed greatness to the new Italy born of the Resistance, and this was to be achieved under the banner of communism:

> I do not know if or when we shall once again be considered a great power; however, I am convinced that we can return rapidly to being a great nation, a great people, thanks to our capacity to work and produce, both materially and intellectually. Only if the forces of labor triumph will Italy be given back a place worthy of the one it had in past centuries. We call on all good Italians to cooperate in this task. To reach this aim we want to restore unity to the Italian nation around the forces of labor.[25]

With the "Italian way to socialism," the Communists were offering the Italians a new formula to achieve modernity, indicating the Soviet Union and people's democracies as real models of the most advanced political, economic, social and cultural modernity. The Soviet Union was the vanguard of a new civilization, which should inspire the new Italy "if we do not want to go on being a backward province of Europe and if we aspire to reaching the forefront of economic and civil progress and of progressive social ideas. . . . We want Italy as well, like all civilized countries today, to march toward socialism."[26] This march would not come about by following the example of the October Revolution but by following the way of "progressive democracy," which, for example, could be the "Czechoslovakian model," carried out in Prague by the Communists with the February 1948 coup d'état. Ten years later, it is still celebrated by the Italian Communist Party's publication, as a particularly "eloquent example of how a country can reach socialism without a civil war, and how socialism can affirm its own superiority over capital, even where capitalism has reached very high levels."[27] According to the Communists, not all Italians were fully aware of the nation yet, due to the reactionary bourgeoisie's hostility. After causing the failure of the Risorgimento's revolution to create a nation, the reactionary bourgeoisie organized an oligarchic state. It then gave rise to Fascism and now, after preventing the anti-Fascist parties from uniting, it was trying to change the anti-Fascist republic into a new "clerico-Fascist" regime with the Christian Democrat election victory on April 18, 1948, thus placing Italy at the service of American imperialism and the Vatican. Building up national communist mythology reached its apex with a definition of the essential components of the new national identity.

The Communist Party declared it was the guardian and interpreter of the most coherent and rigorous anti-Fascism and postulated the principle of identifying the national conscience with anti-Fascism. "In Italy today, being national means being anti-Fascist," Togliatti declared in 1943.[28] This identification became the cornerstone on which the Communist Party developed its plan to gain the monopoly of the myth of nation and of anti-Fascism, presenting itself simultaneously as the most genuine interpreter of the nation, of anti-Fascism and democracy. Naturally, the Communist Party kept for itself the privilege of indicating, from time to time and according to the situation, those who were "real" anti-Fascists and those who were, or behaved like, Fascists, even if they had been or said they were anti-Fascists. Anti-Fascism thus became the nexus indissolubly binding the destinies of the nation and the Communist Party. In turn, the monopoly of anti-Fascism and the "spirit of the Resistance" was a prerequisite for claiming the monopoly of the myth of nation and democracy. Anticommunism "is a danger for democracy and the nation," Togliatti warned in 1945.[29] Being anticommunist meant betraying or insulting the "spirit of the Resistance," it meant being enemies of anti-Fascism and, consequently, enemies of the nation. Those who were against the Communist Party were against democracy, the Republic and Italy.

Under the Sign of the Cross

The Communist plan to monopolize the myth of nation, anti-Fascism and democracy was counterposed by a similar one of the Christian Democrats. In fact, if the Communists presented themselves as the vanguard of a nation that was still to be completed through the working-class party's rise to power, the Christian Democrats aimed at presenting themselves as the true expression and interpreter of an already completed nation, formed over many centuries, which had lost its way during liberalism and Fascism but which had now regained the most solid foundations of its identity in religion and Christian civilization. A motion of the Christian Democrat National Council in March 1945 stated: "As the Italians have eliminated every dark dream of imperialist nationalism, harbored only by their dominating tyrants, not by them, they are now straining toward a just peace, founded on the independence and fraternal cooperation of nations. . . . We believe that this universalist policy derives also from the deep and innermost springs of Christian Democracy. Our action must be Christian civilization in progress." Therefore the Christian Democrats had to work as "faithful and conscious interpreters of this great and outstanding tradition, with which our history is imbued and which makes this Italy of ours sacred and venerable, even in the midst of the outrages and bloody wounds of this tragic period"[30] in both internal and international politics. And the Italians, through the Christian Democrat Party, had to draw the ideal resources for rebuilding the national state from the wellspring of Christian doctrine. The program for a new constitution presented at the First National Congress of the Christian Democrats in April 1946 declared:

> (1) Constitutional liberties will be efficient if they have Christian inspiration, because Christianity is the leavening of all liberties, the promise and guarantee of a new and constructive experience after the failure of other systems that lay claim to freedom. (2) The Constitution must not be inspired either by a political party or by a religion but must be of the Italian people, which is Christian and therefore cannot want a lay or agnostic state. Besides, a state in conformity with Christian ethics is not a confessional state.[31]

Using the myth of nation not only for anticommunism but also in controversy with generic kinds of universalism and internationalism, which seemed too close to the Social Communist left, became one of the central ideas of Christian Democrat ideology, in tune with the Catholic doctrine of nation and love of country. Aldo Moro, in particular, disagreed with the "universalists," who insisted that the nation be abandoned to then enter a supranational dimension, where, with the end of national states, the kingdom of universal justice would be achieved. In 1945 he wrote: "Nationalist ideology is being substituted by an internationalist one. The outcome of the desire for renewal that has swept through the world is that the ungenerous exclusivism of the nation is condemned in the name of a farther-reaching human solidarity." Yet, Moro warned, when such tendencies appear, "there is the risk of being too abstract," and the only thing achieved is that one deceptive and dangerous mythology is substituted by another, just as deceptive and dangerous:

> We would not like the mythology of nationalism (let us speak of nationalism not of nation, which is not a myth but very human re-ality) to be substituted by another myth, with the dangerous illu-sion of having resolved the serious problem of peoples living in harmony. This other myth would be no better than the first one as regards suppressing freedom and life, even though disguised as at-tractive, even though it has the advantage of corresponding to the ideal, alive in all of us, of an all-embracing communion among people.

According to Moro, to prevent nationalism, there was no sense in contemplating "destroying the nation, or regions, or municipalities, or families, or the thousand other societies that free people create, follow-ing an innate impulse," since all "these experiences may be selfish and exclusive, as they may all be open and generous, and that is, instead of being an obstacle, an efficacious means to reach broader and broader associative forms. It is not by going beyond these experiences that uni-versal community living is achieved but by using them, making them personal and humane, in conformity with their reality." Consequently, he observed that "universal community living," carried out to the detri-ment of the nation, could be "dangerously overwhelming, a tyranny like all the others, disuniting people in their inalienable freedom. With the il-lusion of everlasting peace, it would bring us new wars in the form of minor and major revolutions."[32] Therefore, it was only right to try and end "nationalistic excesses, which have caused so much human suffer-ing;" nevertheless, it was necessary to conserve the nation for its human value as a shared life and as the historical unity of traditions, just as it was necessary to keep nationality as a still-valid principle to regulate so-cial relations among peoples:

> Although nowadays the word has become almost obsolete and is not at all popular in our times, the nation is still a guiding principle for setting out new laws for social relations. It should be reduced to terms of humanity, out of the love of simple and real things. In

short, the rightful claims to nation are only claims to people's insuppressible rights, and these rights are established by a particular
social means.[33]

On a more directly ideological level, it was mainly De Gasperi who
worked out the Christian Democrat myth of nation. De Gasperi, who
was a convinced antinationalist and supporter of European unity, both
as party leader and as prime minister, seemed to be likewise convinced
when defending Italy's historical, cultural and religious individuality,
which had to be protected also in view of future European unity. When
"we say we are not nationalists," he explained in 1950 as prime minister,
"we mean that we do not want all problems to be solved through the
strength of the nation, through national initiative, and we are not speaking of something that limits our real strength, which reduces, suppresses
and disheartens our feelings for the nation as Italians: the basis of all
kinds of cooperation is the nation, in an association of free nations."[34]
Fully aware of the myth's political function, as determined by Georges
Sorel, De Gasperi thought it was indispensable for a democratic state to
foster national feeling and love of country, as an ideal and moral myth
of collective unity, above the level of parties.[35]

De Gasperi considered the myth of nation indispensable to defend
freedom, seeing that, as he stated to the Senate on July 11, 1950, "country
and freedom are lost if they are not invigorated and defended by the unitary sense of national discipline and a profound feeling for our civilization, which over the centuries has created Italy and molded the Italians.
Consequently, for us, descendents of a glorious history and heirs to a
great mission, operating as Italians is an honor, and not doing so a defec-
tion."[36] A resolute supporter of the value of fatherland as the ideal foundation of the new republican state, which called for the allegiance and
loyalty of all the parties, De Gasperi taught the young Christian Democrats that the "fatherland belongs to all Italians, and young people, above
all, feel it must be given greater importance than petty considerations of
one-sided interests."[37] He reminded party leaders and activists that the
fatherland "and national pride should never be despised nor should
others be allowed to despise them, as they contribute to restoring our
moral unity,"[38] because the nation "is also history, tradition, a mass of
feelings and ideas that continually flow from generation to generation,
but the living country where we must work and that we must defend, is
the Italian people."[39] When building up the Christian Democrat myth
of nation, De Gasperi tried to make use of materials taken from various

national mythologies, selecting carefully, following closely (however consciously or unconsciously, as, after all, Togliatti also did) the Fascist method of assimilating the traditions and myths that seemed most suitable and efficacious to legitimate his own party as the most genuine heir of the national tradition and the interpreter of republican Italy's destiny, "a worthy heir to carry on its centuries-old and universal civilization."[40]

Once again the myths of mission and supremacy arose in a different ideological context, closely linked to the myth of ancient Rome. Both Roman and Christian civilization were the cornerstones on which, De Gasperi believed, the original features of the "Italic civilization," the essential factors of the Italian nation, were founded, giving rise to its special, unending mission in the world, the "centuries-old civilizing function" of the "Christian Italic civilization." "We serve and defend the Italic civilization where Christ is Roman; we defend the Italian people: workers, seafarers, discoverers, colonizers and the light of the Universe," declared De Gasperi in Rome in February 1948,[41] with rhetoric that echoed Mussolini's clichés. In 1947 De Gasperi urged the inhabitants of Trento to feel "they were part of the greatest civilization in the world, an Italian, Christian civilization."[42] De Gasperi's view of the myth of nation is summarized in a speech he gave in Trento in 1951, where he referred to the monument to Dante, the city tower and the cathedral as symbols "of our tradition, history and civilized life." These symbols of universal, Italian culture, of freedom and religion, showed that "our sense of nation, of the fatherland's unity and soundness is at the same time a sense of international justice and Christian universality."[43] The intermingling of the myth of nation and Christian universality with political unity made up the solid structure of the Italian nation, with its dynamic transformation based on tradition and modernity, where different and contrasting forces contributed to its formation, and De Gasperi acknowledged the merits of each force as an act of reconciliation. Although he firmly condemned Fascist totalitarianism, he was also understanding toward those who had been militants in the Social Republic in the name of honor and discipline, thus expressing his "intention to reconcile all the factions and rebuild the moral unity of the nation torn apart by the civil war by putting the past behind us," as he said in Parliament in 1951.[44]

The subject of political and moral unity was the predominant idea of the Christian Democrat mythology of nation. De Gasperi thought that the Italians' religious unity responded already to this idea. The Roman Catholic religion was the foundation of an identity that had been forming over the centuries through the symbiosis between Christian and Italic civilizations. Achieving political unity and building the national state, which De Gasperi acknowledged was the well-deserving work of the Risorgimento and the monarchy, had, in the end, strengthened the historical individuality of the Italian nation:

> Awareness of nation requires unity, above all. This awareness is nourished by traditions and continually draws on its cultural and civil wealth. This legacy is the fruit of the intelligence of our great intellects, of our inventors' experience, the labor of our workers and managers, our servicemen's sacrifice and our statesmen's ability. However, Italian civilization and its people's consciousness transcend the passing historical phases and continue to progress despite the different kinds of regime. For a century the monarchy had a great unifying influence: it helped open the way to universal suffrage, it held high the banner of legitimate continuity in the terrible crisis of defeat and, with a new constitutional agreement, ensured the end of a regime without fighting, without conflicts or bloodshed.[45]

This is how De Gasperi summed up his concept of the myth of nation in one of his last speeches at the Fifth Christian Democrat Congress in 1954. With moderate syncretism and excluding any kind of exclusivism or universalism, this concept tried to bring together the legacies of various myths of nation, to then blend them in a vision of the nation that De Gasperi proposed as a myth to found and legitimate the new state, brought back to the fold of Christian civilization.

In the early postwar years, the Christian Democrat ideology joined forces with the Roman Catholic doctrine of nation and once again paid great attention to the problem of determining the national identity, keeping in mind also, in our opinion, the complex mythology of Fascist nationalism. We refer particularly to the use of the myth of Italian civilization, a fusion of Roman, Catholic and Italian characteristics, to propose the myth of a Greater Italy again, in a Christian version, outlining the features of Italianism in the shadow of the cross. The Christian Democrat myth of nation imagined a reborn "democratic and peaceful" Italy with a leading role on the world stage—which was part of the Christian Democrat program worked out at the beginning of 1944—and saw Italy as

> a bridge between central Europe and the Mediterranean, and with its national independence and integrity restored, will find its

greatness again by keeping a balance and mediating between three important human factors: labor, through Italy's irrepressible emigration, which has already made the fields and factories of America fruitful; culture, through its civilization dating back three thousand years, the reason why Italy has gone down in history as mankind's most fertile land; religion, because three hundred million Catholics look to Rome from all the countries of the world, as Rome is a sacred city and the seat of the supreme papacy.[46]

Christian Democrat Italianism was established, above all, as anticommunist, while Roman Catholic doctrine laid down that absorbing the myth of nation was useful for justifying the Christian Democrats' hegemonic ambitions as republican Italy's leading party. Cradle and seat of Catholicism, Italy now had a new mission—to be the outpost of Western Christian civilization against the Communist empire and, at the same time, the vanguard bearing the key to reconciling national feeling with a universal ideal. This key had been confirmed by the people's vote on April 18, which had consecrated "the revival of the Italians' civic Christian conscience."[47]

Reconciled with its intrinsic religious nature, the Italian nation could once again achieve supremacy in the modern world by accomplishing "national democracy"[48] founded on Christian civilization, while Christian Democratic Italy could become a model for the whole of Europe, a "third force" alternative both to totalitarianism—right and left—and liberalism. On April 25, 1948, *Il Popolo,* the official periodical of the Christian Democrat Party, maintained that by entrusting its leadership to a party that worked under the sign of the cross, Italy had already taken the lead of the "flags marked with a cross" all over Europe, becoming the vanguard of Christian modernity. "A task and an enormous responsibility await us": "to consolidate peace, make Europe a modern 'Christendom' again and finally give meaning to freedom, and the strength to implement social justice."[49] It may seem that the Christian Democrat Party saw the April 18 victory as symbolically becoming the founding event of the new state of the Italian nation, reunited with Christian civilization after the liberal and totalitarian interludes, rather than April 25, the date of liberation, an event quickly and noisily monopolized by the Communist Party. Immediately after April 18, Mario Scelba proudly announced that the nation should be "eternally grateful to a party that had defended the freedom and independence of the country seriously threatened by Communist activities." Consequently, nobody should be surprised if, after its election victory, the Christian

Democrat Party also took on "managing the economic, industrial and financial activities of the country" as well as its political leadership, in order to continue working in the service of the nation. In short, the Italians had to get used to "also seeing Christian Democrats at the head of the great financial and industrial companies."[50] Therefore, identifying the Italian nation with Christian civilization fell from the ideal sphere of values and principles uniting Italy to God's will to the more earthly sphere of politics, state administration and the economy. And the Christian Democrat Party intended to make its hegemonic function felt in this sphere. In 1952 at the Fourth Christian Democrat Congress, De Gasperi stated, "Our party is the party of the nation and that is why we must have an all-embracing view of the interests involved and try to subordinate all of them to the interests of the community, directing them to the task of social justice. This means we support interclass collaboration."[51]

So also the Christian Democrat Party reached the point of identifying the nation's destiny with its own, like the Communist Party but by other ways. It attributed to itself the missionary function of "the nation's party," whose duty it was to safeguard the Italians' traditions, civilization and identity as well as the freedom and independence of the nation against a totalitarian antinational party that supported an ideology alien and hostile to the Christian nature of Italy, an enemy of the country because it was in the service of a foreign power, standard bearer of an atheistic, anti-Christian and anti-Western civilization. De Gasperi declared that the Communist Party could not in any way claim "to directly represent the ideas and interests of the Italians, because it was a party "that, thanks to its doctrine, has cut the umbilical bond uniting us, our generation of 1945–46, with other generations of the Italic and Christian civilization."[52] Only the Christian Democrats, the political expression of the Christian, Italian civilization could represent the Italians and guarantee the welfare and freedom of the nation. "We are the largest, most responsible party that the Italian nation has at present, and if the Christian Democrat Party's organizational, internal strength collapsed, democracy would be lost in Italy," De Gasperi declared in 1953.[53]

The Christian Democrat viewpoint was that turning the nation to account meant exalting the Catholic tradition as the essence of the Italian identity, and, therefore, this was the way to establish the hegemonic role of the Christian Democrat Party as the leading party of the new Italy.

"The Virgin Mary's Fief"

In support of the Christian Democrats' myth of nation, the Church of Pius XII resolutely entered the field, invoking the mystical union between Italianness and Roman Catholicism.

The myth of a new, Greater Italy—great because of its humble pride in the suffering endured and the spiritual strength of the Catholic faith, and not pride in might and material strength, as well as being the forerunner of a new civilization of cooperation and progress for all peoples—found a particularly fertile breeding ground in the Church. After all, exalting greatness as the sublimation of suffering, humiliation and cathartic expiation that purifies and ennobles was congenial to Catholic culture.

The Church was up front when competing to revive the Italians' national identity, which was part of its plan to recapture Italianness from the secular part of Italy. This also reflected the close ties between religion and politics, between the Church and the Christian Democrats, especially in their crusade against communism. When carrying out this plan, the Church worked by retrieving its own idea of the myth of nation and developing it, completely setting aside the controversy against the national state—but not its condemnation of liberalism—and exploiting fully the neo-Guelphic element of the Risorgimento. The political unification of Italy itself was now interpreted as a plan carried out by Divine Providence, one of whose instruments was assigning a special mission to Italy, and which fostered Italy's aspiration to renewed greatness, pursued with humility and piety. The Catholic Church, traditionally in conflict first with the liberal and then with the Fascist state, was not new to a neo-Giobertian defense of Italy's specific Christian characteristics. This gave Italy spiritual supremacy over other nations, "a spiritual mission in the world that tends to be a spiritual model for a country's people," as Giovanni Battista Montini described it in 1923.[54]

The Catholic church's plan to regain Italianness was resumed in republican Italy, picking up from the myth of mission. The Italian nation, *La Civiltà Cattolica* declared in 1947, had to become worthy of the gift that God had given to Italy, "entrusting it with the spiritual center of humanity, the true capital of the world!" Echoing Gioberti, the Jesuit publication revived the myth of supremacy, explaining that Italy's special missionary bent bestowed eternal greatness on the Italians, because it was even part of "the aim of the creative plan," which had prepared the choice of Italy as the seat of Christ's religion from the peninsula's beginning, a sacred place where God and man were reunited. "The cable that descends from God and that must connect the sensible world to God again, was planted by God in the earth of the city of Rome; and Christ became Roman." The "Christian mission" of the Italian nation, its incomparable greatness, derives from this: "no people on earth has its destiny so united with the work of Christ as ours: no people has its greatness bound so tightly to that greatness. We believe that there is only an alternative: either we rise high in faith to the mission that God entrusted to us when he gave us the center of the Church or be its traitors and, therefore, 'misfits.' And every misfit is a wretch." Regaining "our true nature as a Roman Catholic nation par excellence before the peoples that are watching us" was the only way to have a "renewed nationalism," "if our country wants to accept the glory of once again giving an example to the world by saying the new word; it has pronounced the word so many times over the centuries and has now been made wiser by suffering a deeper and more universal experience."[55] The indissoluble nexus between Church and the Italian nation was not only the fruit of an act of God, who had chosen the peninsula as the spiritual center of humanity, but has unfolded throughout the Italians' whole history, from the end of the Roman Age up to the present. From the first barbarian invasions up to the tragic period of the Second World War, there was not a period in Italian history when the Church did not intervene for the good of Italy, "in favor of its independence and freedom, to the benefit of its real progress and greatness." Therefore, "in order to be strong, glorious, free and independent, Italy must always be united and in agreement with the pope," because the "papacy, which has saved Italy from the uncivilized state and tyranny of its enemies so often over the centuries, will certainly save it again in the future from any kind of modern barbarians and tyrants, who attack its independence and freedom in any way they can." Identifying Italianness with Roman Catholicism reached its height in the charismatic union of the Italian nation with the pope, "the supreme apex of our country, the personification of Italian glory" and "the greatest defender of its independence and freedom, the heedful protector and tireless supporter of its prosperity," to which, "Italy owes its independence, freedom, glory, life, doctrine and beauty, that is, everything!"[56]

The renewed charismatic union between Italianness and Catholicism was the necessary bulwark against the advance of communism and took on a universal meaning for the Church in an apocalyptic vision of mortal challenge between the kingdom of God and the kingdom of

Satan: "The expression 'either Rome or Moscow,' which we understand here as antagonism between Church and anti-Church, is, unfortunately, a reality. On one hand there is Rome, which rises to defend the kingdom of God and Christian civilization; on the other, there is the capital of open and active atheism, which has rallied its forces to sustain and expand the kingdom of Satan." Therefore, Italy's new universal mission, which would give it back its faith in the future, thus beginning the age of a new Italian revival, was to lead the anticommunist crusade. "Italy's spiritual rebirth" would be "the work of the Virgin Mary." For Italy to rise strong and great in its Christianity before the world," the Jesuits' publication explained, "all the best Italians should fall humbly and opportunely to their knees before the Mother of God."[57] Through the mystical union with the Church, the dedication of Italy to the "immaculate heart of Mary" which took place in 1959, carrying out Pius XII's wishes, acquired the symbolic meaning of yielding the nation's sovereignty to the Mother of God. It was "a nationally significant gesture, with which [the Italians] officially recognize the Virgin Mary's sovereign dominion over them, as the Mother of God and Queen of the whole world." Consequently, "they voluntarily submit themselves to her as devoted and faithful subjects," entreating her "to be gracious and watch over and protect Italy as her eternal domain, to defend it from every national calamity and particularly from the danger of falling under the dominion of atheist communism."[58] And "the Virgin Mary's fief" could escape this danger only by entrusting itself to the political force that derived its inspiration from the Church, following the plan of Providence that had already revealed itself after the elections on June 2, 1946. The Jesuits' publication, the banner of a renewed "national-Catholic" unity, was triumphantly satisfied and celebrated the Christian Democrat election victory as definitively ousting liberalism from the Italian state, applauding, just over thirty years after the liberals celebrated the country's jubilee, the "rapid decline of an ideology that molded last century and particularly, we think, the Risorgimento." The liberal concept "is outdated and cannot spiritually and permanently regain what it has lost—because history does not turn back, whatever temporary variations, caused by contingent facts, there may be."[59] By voting for the Christian Democrat Party, the majority of Italians understood that "they could only be saved by the wellspring indicated by the centuries-old Christian tradition that has inspired so many generations." The Jesuits' publication wanted to confirm "the high and noble mission that Providence has assigned to Italy," approved by the people's expressed will, and once again acknowledged its "historical propensity" as "mother and mistress of civilization," which could only be fulfilled by following Christian inspiration.[60]

A War of Myths in a Mythless Republic

During Pius XII's papacy, a fervent attempt was made to make the myth of nation Catholic, which was very important historically in the final phase of the myth's decline. A singular feature of this attempt was the united action of the Church and the Christian Democrat Party that had taken on the responsibility of governing the Italian state. This combined effort considerably influenced the attitude of many Italians toward the national state during the half century that the undisputed Christian Democrats were in power. Indeed, if we consider the Christian Democrats' long hegemony in republican Italy in the nineteen hundreds, it is clear that a great number of Italians who were self-declared Catholics and who voted for the Christian Democrats identified Italianness with Roman Catholicism. This identification worked as a meeting-point between the "national fatherland" and the "ideal fatherland," and was based on the Church's open claim to the Catholic monopoly of Italianness. "Being a good Italian also includes being Catholic. We believe that being anti-Catholic includes being a traitor to the country."[61] This slogan, when expressed less bluntly, meant that, politically, Christian Democracy was necessarily central as the nation's leading party.

However, this was a meeting point that came about in both a party and a "universalistic" dimension, and, therefore, outside the national state. The Italian Communists ideologized the myth of nation within a "party" and "universalistic" dimension in the same way, by monopolizing anti-Fascism and the "Resistance spirit." The Communists glorified the Resistance with repeated, ritual appeals for anti-Fascist rallies and by more frequently using street politics, considered the expression of the people's real will against the revival of Fascism, which always lay in wait. These were the Communists' main weapons, used for decades to undermine the Christian Democratic governments and their allies, even though they were governments supported by a majority of voters, consensus that, in truth, was the only legitimate expression of the people's will in a parliamentary democracy. If Catholic Italians believed that the "two fatherlands" converged in the ideal supremacy of the Church, Communist Italians believed that the political and ideological entity that substantially represented their "ideal country" was the Soviet Union.

However, this led the Communists to see the split between the "national fatherland," which was the Italian state governed by the anti-Communists, and the "ideal fatherland" not only widen but actually become, so to speak, institutional, turning into a permanent attempt to undermine the authority of the state in real politics. Although the state declared it was anti-Fascist, it was governed by anticommunist parties, accused by the Italian Communist Party of being traitors to the Resistance, the Republic and the country, as they either restored a clerico-Fascist regime in the service of American imperialism or were its accomplices. The Communists reacted with hostility to the government's choices in foreign policy, from Italy becoming a member of NATO to its role in building a European union and the Trieste issue. Always lined up and permanently mobilized beside the Soviet Union, the Communists did not hesitate to threaten revolt and civil war if there were a conflict, and the Italian state entered the field against the Soviet Union. If "our country were really dragged into a war, we know what our duty would be. Nowadays the answer to an imperialist war is revolt, an uprising to defend the peace, independence and future of our own country," Togliatti warned in 1948.[62] The Communist leader was convinced that a threat of war could only come from American imperialism, a capitalist remake of Hitler's ambitions to dominate the world, because the threat of war was "immanent in capitalist society."[63]

On the opposite side, De Gasperi, as prime minister, denounced a "systematic and organized" "fifth column" in Italy, "which, during emergencies, tends to aggravate the internal situation by introducing disruptive factors," as he said in 1950. It has an "insidious, psychological preparation" aimed at "forming a collective will outside the state, which, if a conflict occurs, denies the democratic state's right and duty to demand that citizens carry out civil and military duties, protesting that the state does not satisfy the rightful social needs of the workers." "Furthermore, it would be a disaster for Italy if we were allowed to wait for the country to become politically red, white or green before obeying its laws. The Italian flag holds good for everyone."[64]

The Cold War contributed to the rapid decline of the myth of nation's Indian summer. The center of a universal religion actively supporting the Western bloc, which included the Italian state, but also the center of the strongest European Communist Party, which actively supported the Eastern bloc, republican Italy was born and lived in a permanent state of "ideological war," as the Socialist leader Rodolfo Morandi called it. It was both a national and international war, whose main protagonists in Italy were the Christian Democrat Party and the Communist Party but that involved all republican Italy's parties.

The ideological war between communism and anticommunism was, in fact, an expression of new kinds of "religious war," fought between opposing political myths and caused by ideologizing politics, which had already been typical of the struggle between Fascism and anti-Fascism. Like wars of religion, the ideological war crossed the borders of national states and divided citizens within them, making them take opposite sides in the name of opposite ideals of country, nation and state. Once again ideology prevailed over nation, in the sense that the essence of the nation coincided with an ideology, at the same time weakening the sense of allegiance and loyalty to the national state as a political and ideal entity above governments and parties. Arturo Carlo Jemolo, one of the most acute observers of the national state's crisis in republican Italy, realized what was happening early on and in 1954 noted:

> History reminds us that in times of conflict the group in power is always tempted to proclaim that the state can be fully identified with the majority's ideology and [can] resort to outlawing, expelling or suppressing dissidents, according to the times and customs.[65]

The Party as Fatherland

The ideological and political clash among the anti-Fascist parties became radicalized and rapidly destroyed the patriotic unity of the Resistance, while it made the two major parties each claim, ever more aggressively, to identify the myth of nation with its own ideology. Faced with this antagonism, Resistance patriotism turned out to be completely ineffectual as the basis of a myth of nation for the citizens of republican Italy.[66]

Resistance patriotism was intrinsically fragile, considering how profoundly different the anti-Fascist parties were ideologically, beginning with how they conceived the idea of nation, as we have seen. It was, so to speak, a trucelike patriotism, a truce among parties with contrasting principles, ideals and values that had become allies in the name of their country to face a common enemy together. Once the latter was defeated, the truce was no longer necessary, and the profound ideological differences came to the surface. Resistance patriotism broke up with the end of the anti-Fascist parties' unity, each of which claimed to embody the "real Italy," and this contributed to making the divisions among the Italians wider, breaking up every remaining national bond in common.

After all, because it was an ideal contingent movement, Resistance patriotism could not survive in a democracy so soon torn by radical hostility among the parties, which hurled at each other the infamous accusations of having betrayed the "spirit of the Resistance," of reincarnating Fascism or totalitarianism, of being in the service of foreign powers, in short, of betraying the nation. If Resistance patriotism did not succeed in becoming the ideal foundation of national patriotism for the Italians of the Republic, those above all responsible were the anti-Fascist parties themselves, which competed to monopolize the legacy of the Resistance. Although the major parties defended and even glorified the nation, the myth of nation ended up by being confused, belittled and overcome by an increasingly imperious and arrogant party patriotism, which substituted national patriotism in the minds, behavior and aims of political militants. In fact, the two major parties closely followed the Fascist Party, both in claiming the monopoly of the myth of nation and in the militants' tendency to consider the party itself "the ideal fatherland," ethically and politically superior to the fatherland identified with the state.

The major parties' tendency to absorb the myth of nation, to the point of making it little more than a rhetorical ornament of their own ideological identity and transforming themselves into the country's party, was clear right from the early years of republican Italy. In 1949 Mario Ferrara spoke of "party patriotism," highlighting the negative consequences it would have on the democratic state:

> The mysticism of party has substituted the mysticism of the ethical state, of the chosen people and the ruling race. From this point of view we must recognize that the democratic forces have fallen completely into Fascist and Communist ideology, and when they appeal to "party patriotism," to the "active party members," to enchanting and disenchanting the masses, they speak the language of Communism, Fascism and National Socialism. . . . The party has also become a closed and tyrannical world for those who call themselves democratic and liberal, and they cannot do without it, giving up all moral dignity and sometimes pure and simple human dignity in its name. Parties that were once understood and accepted as associations of citizens looking for something in common to resolve some of the state's problems and defend some of its features, or to change them and give the state specific tasks, today are nothing more than small chapels where mysterious rites are practiced in homage to a rhetorical faith that disguises and protects very obvious interests, even if they are not always permissible. When these

parties are at the height of their popularity, they refer to apocalyptic expectations and prescribe Messianic aims for themselves. . . .
And indeed all the parties are demagogically capable of making
promises and fostering hopes, but they carefully avoid proposing
solutions. On the contrary, the real function of the parties should
not be appealing to the great laws of humanity but offering people
various possibilities of resolving every kind of difficulty in which
they constantly get entangled, so they can help themselves to find
their way in this world: because everyone looks for and finds the
way to Paradise by himself.[67]

Subordinating the myth of nation to party ideology was certainly
one of the main factors that prevented republican Italy from having its
own myth of nation, in which anyone, regardless of political party affili-
ation, could recognize in it those values and principles common to all
citizens, worthy of protecting and handing down to future generations.
A few years later Jemolo observed that the parties were certainly free
to "strengthen the ideological ties with the ones that come from 'community living,'" and each of us was free "to isolate himself and not keep
company with those who do not have the same ideas, and say, 'how nice it
is to be together, without the others.' However, this weakens a nation."[68]
    The extraordinary result of materially rebuilding the country, car-
ried out with admirable tenacity and energy by the Italians in the space
of ten years, was not successful in recreating the shared feeling of a collective, national identity based on the new values and ideals of republican Italy. From 1949 Primo Mazzolari, an anti-Fascist priest, was dis-
tressed to note that a shared feeling of fatherland had not been revived
in the Italians' hearts:

> Everything is being rebuilt: roads, bridges and factories. We are
> not. Even if our numbers are increasing, even if we speak the same
> language as the men of our revival, we cannot really say that we
> are Italians again. . . . If Italy moves, it means that it still exists. It
> changed from a monarchy to a republic, from dictatorial to demo-
> cratic and from imperialist to remissive. Each of us forces himself
> to dress Italy the way he likes so he can love it, almost as if they
> were the clothes that bind us to our mothers, while today there are
> few who dare to love Italy for itself, and also those few often lack
> the courage to admit it, almost as if this humble love were shame-
> ful. . . . Many are afraid of being bypassed by history if they profess
> their love for their own country, if they speak respectfully of it, if
> they reverently and approvingly think of its dead and its glories,

and if they do not get lost in a universalism that is still not clearly defined and that, coming from certain people, has an ambiguous and false meaning. The Communist proletarians call Russia their country, while the others look to America: Slav or Eastern universalism, Anglo-Saxon or Western universalism. The Italians are still on a September 8 level, when some became rebels for love of freedom. The Resistance continues but in the name of those who are against the fatherland, carrying on and widening the split. . . . How can tension be eased when we lack a shared political conscience, a shared affection and altar where we can lay down our fratricidal arms. I can see that nobody feels at ease, that there is widespread poverty that could soon become ruin, but I cannot see a shared fatherland: I see Fascists and partisans, not brothers and Italians. . . . If the Resistance had not lost its initial nobility thanks to the parties, if it had kept the spiritual wealth of its dead intact, if it had built a bridge instead of digging a trench, it would have saved Italy. . . . Fascism wore the Italians out, anti-Fascism threatens to wipe them out. In an Italy that is no longer a home, it is easier to be a Fascist or a partisan than Italian. Russia and America, the East and West are talked about, not Italy. Yet our dead died for Italy.[69]

The revival of the myth of nation at the dawn of republican Italy did not at all mean that a common national identity had been born for the Italians on a new ideal basis, or that it was above the differences in ideology, religion and social class. Ideologizing the nation, carried out above all by the two major parties, made it increasingly difficult to rebuild a common fatherland based on democracy and freedom for the Italians, made the Italians' national identity even weaker and more precarious and made the myth of nation slip even more quickly into oblivion. "We no longer have a people, a fatherland, a common good or ideal. The memory of the Resistance is not only distant but is used as a rhetorical pretext by both sides," Mazzolari repeated in 1950.[70]

The ideological war, conditioned and aggravated by the Cold War, created or deepened the rifts that divided Italians and was certainly one of the main reasons why a myth of nation was not created for republican Italy. The ideological war prevented the collective sense of a national state from being created, as it was inseparable from the myth of the nation in its modern sense, and also universalistic ideologies, party patriotism and the ideals of federalism and Europeanism hindered the rebirth of the myth of nation.

However, the fact that a myth of nation common to all the citizens was not revived was also largely due to a fundamental weakness, a

pretense, as Altiero Spinelli wrote in 1959, that was inherent in republican Italy's conception and in the very consciousness of its creators,
making the ideal foundations and legitimacy of the new Italian state intrinsically fragile and precarious. This weakness was a consequence of
the "depressing way the new regime was born." Spinelli observed that,
"while the liberals were strongly aware of their having been the founders of the Italian state," and Mussolini and his followers as well "felt
they themselves had created the Fascist regime with their armed squads
and their 'revolution,'" the "men of the Republic" lacked any awareness
of being the real founders of the state, because they knew "very well that
it was false," even if they proclaimed that "the new state was founded by
the men of anti-Fascism, of the Resistance and of the war of national
liberation." "It was the Americans and the British who broke up the
Fascist regime and brought back democratic freedom to Italy."

> Democracy was not regained by the Italians nor by any other Eu-
> ropean nation freed from Nazi-Fascist domination. It was given
> to them by the Anglo-American conquerors. The Italians limited
> themselves to deciding whether to have a king or a president of a
> republic, a centralized or decentralized state. The American and
> British troops went away, but when the young democracy was
> threatened by the wave of communism, once again it was America
> that held it back, and the democratic Italian forces were left with
> carrying out the national details of policies that were actually su-
> pranational. These events reflected the new world reality, but also
> partly explained why the Italian politicians did not feel that they
> themselves had created their own state, but felt they were simply
> the modest administrators of a nation that had been conceived and
> supported by foreigners.[71]

The Catholics lacked this awareness of being the real "builders of
the state," in its strict meaning, differently from the Liberals and Fascists. However, it was the Catholics who now had the responsibility of
recreating "the old national state": which they did, according to Spinelli, "not because they believed in its value, but because it had been
given to them to govern." Thus structured, the Italian state seemed "economically strengthened" after fifteen years, but was a state

> without a soul because it does not know its purpose, and in fact its
> purpose is little more than waiting for something new to be born in
> the world. It is up to them, the governors, to kindle a new political
> spirit in the Italians. But they do not know what to say. Not even the
> Socialists or the parties for renewal, and every day that passes not

even the Communists know any longer, but none of these has the responsibility of governing a people, and they will not have it for quite a while.[72]

The parties of republican Italy did not know how to foster and transmit to the Italians an awareness of their nationality, a national consciousness, love of fatherland and a sense of state, uniting these with the principles and values of social democracy, which was the foundation of republican Italy. During the fifties the ideas of fatherland and nation as the "soul" of the state, as ideals and values of the Italians' common identity and civic conscience, and as higher principles to inspire the government's and the parties' policies, were inadvertently put aside. Nevertheless, appeals to the fatherland, the nation and the state were still heard for some time in the government's official public speeches and in the parties' rhetoric, though less and less frequently. With time, the outcome was that the Italians' collective conscience was without ideals, a void that was not filled by any other moral factor of unity and national identity. When commenting on the centennial of Italian unity in 1961, Ugo D'Andrea wrote: "it is a void, although there are all the objective conditions for the progress and development of the people. Celebrating the Risorgimento centennial cannot fill this void."[73]

Conclusion

The Jubilee of the Simulacrum

"Italy '61": The Last Performance

In 1961 Italy celebrated the centennial of its unification. There were ceremonies, messages, speeches, public events, conferences, television shows, the unveiling of plaques and busts and the inauguration of monuments. Booklets recalling the ideals and events of the Risorgimento were distributed in schools, while a film about the Expedition of the Thousand, *Viva l'Italia,* was shown in all the movie theaters. The centennial ceremonies officially began on March 25 with a message from the president of the Republic, the Christian Democrat Giovanni Gronchi, read at Montecitorio before the joint Chambers. On March 27 the president paid homage to the Unknown Soldier. That same day, the prime minister, Amintore Fanfani, a Christian Democrat, placed a laurel wreath on the tomb of Victor Emanuel II at the Pantheon. The wreath bore the inscription "The Italian Republic to Victor Emanuel II, Father of the Fatherland." Meanwhile other Christian Democrat ministers paid homage to Cavour, Garibaldi and Mazzini at their tombs. A second visit by the president to pay his respects to the Unknown Soldier and a television appearance of the prime minister delivering a speech to the Italians closed the centennial's official ceremonies.

Turin was granted the honor of organizing the centennial exhibitions, not only because it had been Italy's first capital but because it was the symbol of new Italy's "economic miracle." The exhibitions included a history of Italy's unification, which recalled aspects and stages of the process "that had led to the triumph of free institutions and the proclamation of a unified Italian State"; an exhibition by the regions showing

337

how they had developed in a century and "the different historic voca-
tions of each region"; and an international exhibition dedicated to
labor "illustrating at the world level the most important feature of this
era—the rapid technological and social progress being made."

The purpose of the exhibitions was mainly to demonstrate and
highlight the economic and social progress made by republican Italy.
Just fifteen years after the end of the disastrous war, united Italy had
risen from destruction and poverty and climbed back to the top with
extraordinary vitality and the desire to reconstruct the country. "Italy is
alive and on its feet; it is more prosperous or, better, not so poor as we
were; the population has increased and it is more often in lively ferment.
The years 1959 and 1960 were the best for our industrial development
and economic expansion; they marked the highest indices in our currency's value, in the volume of transport and trade and in the size of our
reserves,"[1] wrote the conservative *Il Borghese* in 1961. The right-wing conservative magazine was not at all indulgent toward the republican regime and the predominant party. On the opposite side, the democratic
La Stampa said the same thing: the Italians were experiencing "a period
of profound and rapid transformation. We are becoming a great industrial country." And even if the State still had to deal with the imbalance
between North and South, the inequality of wealth between the classes
and regions, the agricultural crisis, unemployment, education and the
public administration, the Italians in 1961 could look toward their future
"reasonably optimistically."[2]

The source of inspiration for these celebrations was the reference
made to the national values. Giuseppe Pella, the Christian Democrat
chairman of the national committee for the celebrations, said, "Once
again the value of the Fatherland is considered of primary importance,
not at the level of nationalistic political doctrine but, rather, in understanding that unless national values are duly praised we shall have little
to pass on to those who will be leading our fatherland in the future."
Praising the patriotic values in a free and democratic context did not
"conflict with the wider-ranging objectives of European and international solidarity" nor did it affect the differences between the regions because, "while we are so proud of the unity that has withstood many difficulties, at the same time we feel that devotion to the different regions
does not clash with allegiance to the nation but is a kind of contest to see
which one, within the framework of regions, knows how to serve our
mother country best."[3] It was necessary to renew and intensify praise of
the country, added the chairman of the organizing committee for the

celebrations in Turin, to "confirm its significance and importance in a historical period when class rights tend to prevail over those of the nation and family."[4]

The most solemn moment of the celebrations came when the Republic's president read his message, which was moderately patriotic for the occasion. Gronchi briefly recalled the events of the Risorgimento, again depicting a "harmonious plan" carried out by forces that, although diverse and contrasting, had fought for a "common cause"—the nation's independence and unity—realized thanks to the discordant but functional cooperation agreement among the creators of the Risorgimento. Equally general were the president's remarks regarding the century of unification. Without making any specific reference to Fascism or the Resistance, the president briefly mentioned the country's progress, recalling that "despite the drama of two world wars, the range of Italy's human capabilities had almost doubled in a hundred years, and its inherited productive capacity had increased almost fivefold, and was now large enough to grow independently in order to become competitive at the world level." Gronchi wanted to devote more space to the list of open problems the state had to face. First among these was the social problem "that, strictly speaking, limits the effective completion of political unification." He listed suggestions for solving these problems and the time needed. This speech regarding the program that Gronchi himself acknowledged might seem to be "enlarging the constitutional functions of the president" was interpreted by many observers as an inappropriate electoral speech by the president, who, having reached the end of his mandate, made no mystery of the fact that he hoped to be reelected. He let his presidential aspirations show when he exalted the president's role as the supreme interpreter of the nation, whose task it was "to set the direction when he thought it necessary in the interests of the nation, doing so more as a duty than as a right."[5]

On the whole, the celebrations of the national state's second Jubilee, bureaucratically called "Italy '61," were less numerous, less sumptuous and not so clamorous as the fifty-year celebrations had been. They also appeared to be less pervaded by patriotic enthusiasm and national pride. Looking back, the centennial Jubilee was actually the last time the national myth appeared as the most important protagonist of the Italian political scene, in an event that symbolically was more a self-glorification of the predominant Christian Democratic Party as the enlightened leader of "the Virgin Mary's fief" than a celebration of the country's unification into a national State.

The Jubilee of Divine Providence

Besides the official rhetoric praising personalities and events relative to Italy's unification, the real protagonists of the Christian Democrat Jubilee were not the fatherland, the nation and the national state, as they had been in 1911, but Divine Providence, which the Christian Democrat government leaders, supported by the pope, indicated as the true inspiration and creator of Italy's unification process. Through celebrations for "Italy '61" the Christian Democrat ruling class tried to carry out their national political plan, offering the Italians a completely new version of unification, presented as the accomplishment of a Divine plan achieved by reconciling the national State with the Church.

This interpretation of the history of Italy's unification was illustrated by Pope John XXIII during the prime minister's visit to the Vatican as part of the centennial celebrations. The pope said:

> The celebrations held these past few months to commemorate one hundred years of unification, which have given Italy reason to be joyful, find us on both sides of the Tiber feeling the same gratitude to Divine Providence, which, while there were times when it seemed to vacillate, as has always happened throughout the ages, has guided this chosen part of Europe toward a respected and honorable arrangement, in agreement with the nations where, thank God, there is still a civilized society that takes its name and lifestyle from Christ.

The intransigent Catholic opposition to the unified State and the long conflict between the State and the Church in liberal Italy were forgotten in the pope's commemoration. In spite of some "reasons for turmoil," the movement to unify the nation had been successful mainly thanks to the intervention of the Church and Pope Pius IX. Pope Pius IX had been able to interpret the "most noble significance" of the plan devised by Divine Providence. And the Lateran Pacts, signed by the Church under Pius XI with the Fascist government, marked another "victorious page of history," prelude to the "final celebration" for having achieved a "truly perfect unity of race, language and religion."[6] The pope's speech did not say so expressly, but the reference to the achievement of a "truly perfect unity" of the Italian nation made it clear that the pope included in Providence's plan entrusting the State's leadership to a party that saw its "ideal fatherland" in the Church.

Confirmation of this indirect consecration of the predominant party's charismatic role came also from the Italian prime minister, who not only shared the interpretation regarding Divine Providence's part in the unification, as suggested by the pope, but also cooperated, on more than one occasion, in his position as a statesman in celebrating this symbolic act of devotion to Divine Providence by the national state. When he opened the exhibitions in Turin, the prime minister wanted to associate the ceremonies celebrating the unification and its architects with a "celebration of April 11, when we gathered wild flowers on the Vatican hill, at the beginning of spring, also clearly a sign consolidating our national unity from a point of view that in the past had known troubled periods and conflict."[7] On the other hand, the prime minister's devotion to Divine Providence had already manifested itself in the good wishes sent on March 27 to the president of Italy in which he expressed his gratitude "to God for the help given to the Italian people."[8] And again in his speech to the Italians on November 4, after recalling "the number of heroic sacrifices made by our big family for more than a century to unite all the Italians around a single hearth," the prime minister felt it was his duty to remind everybody that, while the secular ceremony was taking place to honor the Unknown Soldier during the celebrations closing Italy's Jubilee, almost at the same time

> the representatives of populations all over the world were gathered on another hill in Rome to pay their respects to an eighty-year-old Italian, today head of the Roman Catholic Church but from 1914 to 1918 one of the chaplains who comforted our soldiers and consecrated their sacrifices to God, elevating first the passion to fight and then the joy of victory through prayer. Two different celebrations this morning, both demonstrating the serious work done by our forefathers to give Italy lifelong unity supported by democratic liberty with the continuity of the Christian tradition.[9]

By viewing Italy's unification as providential, it was possible to finally achieve the reconciliation of the Church and the state, drained and purified of any ideological slant and secular influence, backtracking to the moment it was conceived in the womb of the Roman Catholic religion.

Both the Catholic and the Christian Democrat press undertook to spread the new interpretation of the national movement that had led to the birth of the Italian state. Great emphasis was given to the pope's speech during the prime minister's visit, in which he referred to "the Risorgimento, the most spontaneous, popular and creatively fertile and harmonious movement, and although various subsequent events have been able to cover that fact, they cannot, however, cancel it or make people forget, and that shows us that the Church and the Roman

Catholics not only are not hostile or estranged but also participate enthusiastically and are almost the precursors of the great movement."[10] In the undertaking to retrospectively Catholicize the Risorgimento, the roles of unification's real architects and the unified state's effective builders were drastically belittled. As *Studium*, the Catholic university review, explained, "although some wanted the contrary, none of the protagonists of the secular event saw their own plan fully implemented," while "unintentionally and unknowingly everybody served only Divine Providence," since even "the events that seem, at this time, the most distressing and unacceptable can become an element of progress in the game played by Divine Providence." According to this concept, the main protagonists of Italy's unification had not been the lay, liberal and democratic patriots, but the Church and the Catholics.

In addition to the new legitimizing of the national state as the work of Divine Providence, a considerably negative description of Italian history after the unification up to the time when the Christian Democrats came into power was promulgated. The Catholic press depicted the events that occurred in Italy during the liberal regime as a continuous series of "difficulties and inefficiencies" caused by the "Gordian knots that the rapid and sudden diplomatic and military solution to the Italian question" had not been able to untie, knots that made "new types of traps and intricacies possible" and, above all, made "confusion and a blood-stained experience such as Fascism possible."[11] In the same tone *Il Popolo* commemorated one hundred years of unification speaking only about disasters. "From Novara to Caporetto to the Resistance, the Italians have grown to realize what fraternity is through a series of tragic events." The main cause of all the ills was to be found in the very origin of the Italian state. The way in which it was created had triggered "all the ills of our country and, first of all, the abyss dug out between the central power, the groups of political leaders and the citizens, the fact that the lower classes were alien to political events that should have interested them, the widespread parliamentary practice of shifting party allegiance, and the widening of the gap between North and South." There was no acknowledgment made at all to the builders and liberal governors of the unified state, and nothing was said about the social and cultural progress made by the Italians during the liberal regime. Of course, the Christian Democrat paper mentioned only the worst aspects, for example, the repression of the popular uprising in 1898, which became symbolic of the liberal governors' policies. The leaders, it was said, had betrayed the ideals of the Risorgimento. *Il Popolo* wrote, "Just a few decades after the unification, cannon were shooting at the hungry population"; it seemed that "the dream of the Risorgimento's patriots, poets, enlightened politicians and historians was to be dissolved in an atrocious hoax, owing to the foolishness of an incapable, corrupt ruling class, and the population was to pay the penalty." The paper ended the commemoration of the centennial singing the praises of the Christian Democrat Party, the real architect, thanks to God's will, that achieved the Risorgimento's ideals:

> Having mended the conflict between state and Church, it was up to the "outcast Catholics to seriously unify Italy by introducing far-reaching solutions to the imbalance between North and South, bringing the institutions closer to citizens, making every institution a reflection of the citizens' ideals and needs, guaranteeing everybody a good job and the national community a peaceful existence among free nations. . . . This Italy was born a hundred years ago. . . . It was there in God's mind. . . . He wanted our history to be full of great sorrows perhaps because then our people, who had learned the lesson the hard way, would always remember and remind all other peoples that Man's destiny is to be free.[12]

However, now that they had crowned themselves the principle standard-bearers of Italy's unification, the Catholics could joyfully declare that "for decades the peninsula's political unity has been accepted by everybody as a final and irreversible fact, and what is more important, it is acknowledged without any doubt as positive." They even went so far as to admit "it was undeniable that it had also been possible for the movements that had, at first, remained on the sidelines, to grow and fortify themselves so that they could achieve their current full participation in the life of the state, specifically in the unified state, in the lawfulness that it had guaranteed and in the liberty it had brought, although sometimes frail."[13] Thus, fifty years after the blasphemous celebration of the "Fatherland's Holy Year," all traces of the Catholics' longtime hostility toward the national state, which was so bitter at the time of the first Jubilee, had disappeared from view in the nation that, under Christian Democrat guidance, had returned to its original spiritual matrix and found its spiritual unity. According to *La Civiltà Cattolica*, it was the Italians' duty to celebrate unanimously "those events from which, depending on the point of view, the unity of the country that now belongs to all of us was derived."[14]

The New Lie about the Nation

The way the Christian Democrats officiated at the "Italy '61" celebrations seemed to consecrate, with the pope's blessing, both the Catholic leadership of the national state and the reappropriation of the nation by the Catholics, who returned it to the Church's folds. The governing party was leading the country toward modernity under the emblem of Christ, moderating conservatism and progress, conciliating modernization and Christian tradition. At the same time, the Jubilee celebrations allowed the Christian Democrats to claim they were the legitimate winners of the competition with the Communist Party for the monopoly of the national myth.

Obviously the Communist Party's reaction was to denounce the mystification of Italian history, perpetrated by the Christian Democrats as they celebrated their self-glorification in the centennial ceremonies. *Rinascita* commented ironically on Amintore Fanfani's visit to the Vatican, saying that "the delightful wildflowers the prime minister went to gather in the Vatican gardens appeared as a sign of homage by the Italian leadership to the authority that inspired it: from 'monarchy conquest' to 'papal conquest,'" when actually the prime minister's gesture was part of a "process to mystify and disguise," so as to conceal the "struggle for democracy carried out in Italy by the working class, the Socialist- and Communist-organized workers' movement."[15] According to the Communists, the centennial celebrations and the exhibitions in Turin were a costly pretence to enhance the party in power and the capitalist potentates who supported it. "The dominating Christian Democrat and employer groups and their spokesmen let themselves go in an orgy of rhetoric and self-exaltation," wrote *L'Unità*. Even before becoming "imbued with clericalism, the 'Italy '61' celebrations were and are imbued with the most shameless exaltation of monopolistic capitalism."[16]

Togliatti himself denounced the "by now clear tendency to depict the unification process and the past century of our history very differently from the real situation, both as regards the superficial optimism that aims to hide grave facts and problems and the dominant party's attempts to shift the focus so as to always be the protagonist no matter the cost, even when it should only play the part of exploiter." As the Communist leader recalled, "the ecclesiastical executive hierarchies were against our Risorgimento, and while they were able, they tried to prevent the creation of the unified state." "The Catholic political movement was against this state for almost half a century as the opposition," and after having been chosen to govern, the Catholic Party used any means "to prevent the masses of blue-collar and female Socialist and Communist workers from having access to state leadership." And he further accused the Christian Democratic Party of being at the service of the privileged classes that "effectively hindered the historical and political processes that began with the Risorgimento from reaching their legitimate goals." Togliatti countered the Catholic–Christian Democrat interpretation of Italy's unification with the Communist interpretation, which pointed to the avant-garde working-class party as the legitimate heir to the democratic aspirations of the Risorgimento patriots and as the national party that could really achieve the moral and political unity of the Italians. Therefore, unlike the Socialists in 1911, the Communists participated in and "acknowledged" the centennial celebrations because they considered the unification of Italy a "great revolutionary event," since "Italy's most politically advanced although less fortunate groups entered the battlefield and fought for several decades with a different program to make all of Italy an independent, unified state."[17]

However, despite acknowledging positively some of the progress made during the century within the unified state, the Communists basically ended by siding with the Catholics in describing the postunification history of Italy as dominated only by the struggle between the reactionary middle class and the proletariat. They saw only the working class and the party, considered avant-garde, as the real protagonists of an authentic national revolution, yet to be accomplished.

Intellectuals who considered themselves the most faithful heirs to the lay and liberal matrix took the floor against such criticism of the unification process and the liberal state, which came from opposite fronts but converged on the same target, that is, "to put the Risorgimento on trial" (*il processo al Risorgimento*) so as to uproot the Italian state from any connection with that matrix. While in 1911 the intransigent Catholics had bitterly contested the Jubilee celebrations, rising up against the "lie about the unification" perpetrated by the liberal rulers, in 1961 it was secular intellectuals, who felt it their task to defend the Risorgimento's lay and liberal tradition, who rose up against the new "lie about the unification" perpetrated by the Catholics and the Christian Democrat leadership. The Liberals and Democrats contested both the historical truth and the values and ideals used by the Catholics and Communists to depict the Italian unification. The historian Rosario Romeo deplored a somewhat ambiguous atmosphere that surrounds this centennial, in which widespread propaganda, endowed with extensive means ranging from the control of large publishing houses to weeklies, dailies and the movies, is anxious to remind the Italians of Cavour and the Risorgimento's liberal state with approximately the same distortion as that with which Radetzky and the Hapsburg Empire were presented to our fathers, . . . in other words, maximum obstacles on the way to magnificent destinies and developments that without them would have come the way of the Italian people.[18]

The main target of their protest was obviously the Catholic–Christian Democrat description of the national revolution as a Providence-inspired revolution spiritually led by the papacy. The publication *Nord e Sud* commented ironically: "The most recent discoveries in history have informed us that Italy was created through an agreement with Pope Pius IX and that the disagreements that took place with imprisonments, firing squads and hangings, etc., 'as has always happened,' were only slight misunderstandings, and in fact, everything was settled with the sublime Italian Concordat between the pope and the Fascist Duce. Today, all of Italy is happy, with permission from the Vatican."[19]

Particularly hostile toward the "ecclesiastical version of the history of the Risogimento" was *Il mondo*, a radical magazine published by Mario Pannunzio. It ridiculed the inauguration of the exhibitions in Turin, comparing them to a "nice company party at which children in school smocks wave flags, stars are distributed to the most deserving workers, where neocapitalism is extolled and those ruling the country are thanked for their devotion." The publication questioned the "monopoly of the evocations," which had condemned the celebrations to failure: the tone was "falsely and nauseatingly rhetorical, artificial and not convincing"; "the attempt to overturn positions was frankly intolerable"; the effort "to disguise the truth and turn the meaning around was too shameless"; the mystification of historical fact was "disgusting" because "the whole sense of the Risorgimento is falsified when you try to make people believe that the Catholics were precursors of the Risorgimento, a movement that was—like it or not—anticlerical in its most profound essence and anticlerical in what it actually carried out."[20] The publication denounced the "historical falsification served with a disgusting rhetorical sauce,"[21] noting that if the Risorgimento could appear in the end as the result of a "providential" plan, it was also true "that the interpreters authorized by Divine Providence desperately opposed that plan to the very end."[22]

One of the most vigorous protesters against the "pseudo-interpretation of the Risorgimento's Catholicization" was Vittorio De Caprariis. The liberal historian recalled that the state whose "birth was being celebrated or should be celebrated" was "the liberal, lay state that brought our country up to the level of contemporary European civilization," struggling against "Roman Catholic theocratic absolutism." And the Christian Democrats' rhetorical praise of the Risorgimento and the birth of the Italian state were not sufficient to hide the fact that they had no connection with the principles and values at the origin of the national state. According to De Caprariis, this transpired from the "unusual coolness and remoteness" of the celebrations, conducted with the stiffness "of a bureaucratic duty being performed instead of the deeply felt, joyful participation in celebrating the past." Pointing his finger at the Communists, the historian wondered "where the logic was in mixing their ovation with that of the others" or even claiming "to be the authentic heirs to or the only party continuing the Risorgimento," after they had declared that "a long red line" traversed, uninterrupted, "the history of Italy from the Risorgimento to Fascism." However, not even the "sound of their acclaim" could make people forget "the lengthy obsessive polemics conducted by the Communists against the Risorgimento," said to be "a failed revolution, a revolution that stopped halfway" because it had not achieved "that unification of the people necessary to make the new state a real nation" but had given birth to a unified state that "was a bourgeois state par excellence, ruled by a small conservative oligarchy that responded only to its own class interests."[23]

Behind the Facade

By countering the manipulation of history carried out by the Christian Democrats and Communists, De Caprariis did not intend only to safeguard what he considered the historic truth about the Risorgimento—a liberal, secular movement—and about the unified state that originated the national state, created by a ruling class that aimed to place Italy among the modern European civilizations. He also intended to highlight a more serious problem that was revealed in the way Italians participated in the centennial events. Celebrating the birth of a national state, he noted, was worthwhile if the celebrations "serve to remind ordinary individuals, concerned with problems of the present day, that they are the offspring of the past, a past that belonged to their fathers and fathers' fathers and that belongs to them as well," therefore inducing them to search their souls about their existence as a national collectivity. This did not occur with the centennial celebrations, characterized by "unusual disinterest and remoteness, which leads one to think that the protagonists felt it was their bureaucratic duty instead of feeling profound joy in commemorating the past. And, frankly speaking, there is something hypocritical about the unanimous rhetoric that has been created around these celebrations."[24]

Above all the rhetoric about the unity of the Italians and the vitality of their national sentiment rang a hypocritical note. The Christian Democrats officiating at the Jubilee ceremonies had exalted the country's political and moral unity, claiming the merit for having completed the creation of a national conscience among the Italians after a century of misfortunes, failures and divisions brought on by the previous ruling class. "Today the political and moral unity of our country is sound; however, to make it unassailable by decay we must now complete social and economic unity," said the prime minister in Turin.[25] Actually, *Il Mondo* commented, "the disinterest shown by the Italians in the centennial celebrations and the gap between public opinion and the opinion of official circles" belied such affirmations, because it was obvious that "the 'political and moral' unity of the country is only a facade for outside appearances, raised just to prevent that soul-searching that the Risorgimento's centennial calls for."[26]

That the Italians were basically disinterested in the centennial celebrations was the only point on which the most realistic observers agreed, whether Catholic or lay, conservative or liberal. The indifference, noted *Studium*, was prevalent particularly among the younger generations, who seemed totally detached from the values and ideals evoked by the commemoration of the Risorgimento. Their elders looked on

> sadly, surprised by the cool and embarrassed reception given by the middle-aged generation that, completely recovered from any leftover nationalist spirit after the disastrous experiences of the last decades, does not know how to find even a historical and cultural interest in the national Risorgimento, let alone a sentimental one. And yet that era was the incarnation of a noble and lengthy passion, as if fraught with the desire for religious and moral redemption. . . . Today, all of that is gone, and there is no possibility of recovering it.[27]

On the conservative front, *Il Borghese* commented that as regards the celebrations, all is well formally, but the crowds are not feeling their heartbeats quicken and people are distracted and remote. Why? There is no feeling for the tradition of the recent past, which seems to be dead; there is no longer the monarchy around which the great reality of Italy's unification revolved; yes, Rome is the capital of the state, but confusion and agitation by the parties reign supreme there. Something has happened these past fifteen years to make us consider this the end not the rebirth of the Risorgimento.[28]

From this point of view, the spontaneous reaction was to make a comparison with the ideal atmosphere of the first Jubilee. Rosario Romeo pointed out that in 1911 there had been a "widespread participation acknowledging the national sentiment because it was expressed by the ruling classes. Moreover, there was a close correspondence, visible in the symbols, institutions and ideals, between the Italy that was confident in recalling and celebrating the achievements made in fifty years of unification and the historic tradition it related to, still functioning as an idealistic and moral reality closely linked to the country's ethical-political conscience." In 1961 "within the grandiose framework of official events" there was a certain feeling of detachment, not only among the masses but also among the educated and ruling classes, and the sensation was that, when confirming some traditional values, the Italians found it difficult to link the present with the past, which, however, is still the only central theme that the whole country can relate to as a sign of its unity."[29]

The journalist Domenico Bartoli, writing for the *Corriere della Sera,* also recalled the "greater enthusiasm, the spontaneous and joyful participation in the fifty-year celebrations," despite the divisions that still existed among the Resistance veterans. "The fifty-year celebrations mirrored the feelings and enthusiasm of many people and, above all, the principles that sustained the state and were to be found within the constitutional monarchy, the parliament and among the majority of the politicians brought up to cherish those memories and who were profoundly convinced they would continue the work of the Risorgimento, even if in a mediocre way."[30]

Actually, the Italians of "Italy '61" had almost nothing in common with those who had celebrated the "country's Holy Year" in 1911. The way the Italians saw themselves, their past and their future had changed radically and so had the attitude of Italy's rulers and subjects in regard to the nation and the national state, seen as institutions and idealistic values. Italy in 1961 was a totally different country from Italy in 1911, from every point of view. The tumultuous economic development of the fifties accompanied by widespread internal migration from the South to the cities driving the "economic miracle" in the North had triggered an unprecedented social and cultural upheaval that was to decidedly influence the future of society and the national state, considerably modifying not only the economic system in an increasingly industrialized country but also the social structures, traditions, customs, mentality and Italians' basic values. In 1961 the Italians were experiencing a mass anthropological revolution in their attitudes and behavior— this time effective and not ideological. The result was an Italian who belonged to a new civilization based on welfare and consumerism. This Italian was completely different from the "virtuous citizen" of liberal Italy or the "soldier citizen" of Fascist Italy. He was also very different from the model of the Italian regenerated by liberty, or the "democratic citizen" dreamt of by the anti-Fascist parties during the Republic's early years, whether in the guise of actively devout Christian believer or Socialist revolutionary activist or emancipated and free lay-democracy supporter.

The Nation's Oblivion

Looking at the nation from this point of view, it did not seem to be in such good health, despite the excellent results of its productive capacity on view at the Turin exhibitions, posited as tangible evidence of Italy's progress:

> Material progress, increasing welfare and economic growth are all important developments and must be welcomed by all. But it is necessary to have a common basis, a unified foundation, most of all a state that is the moral center, one that arouses loyalty and spontaneous obedience. These are things that, once destroyed, are difficult to improvise no matter the regime. However, an attempt should at least be made to reconstruct them little by little, patiently and willingly, making sacrifices and abiding by the principles that sustain public life, that is, those of liberty and a parliamentary system. We did not do this during the fifteen years that followed the war and the Resistance. Will this centennial be the beginning of a new era?[31]

The answers to this question, given by those who thought about the moral consistency of the national state during the centennial period, were anything but positive. *La Stampa* warned against excessive optimism, recalling that nothing "will be possible unless there is a breath of new idealism, an idealistic passion for some very important steps that will inspire our political scenario as during the Risorgimento."[32] According to *Studium* "the Italians' somewhat slow, if not indolent, reaction to such an exceptional event as the centennial of the country's unification" could "be taken as a lack of ethical vigor."[33] Romeo spoke more harshly of an "ambiguous atmosphere surrounding this centennial," the symptom of "how serious the present crisis in our country's political and cultural conscience is."[34] *Il Borghese* exacerbated the pessimism by maintaining that "never as in this dangerous year 1961 had the dissolution of Italy's unity been more evident; never had it developed with such disruptive fatalism right under our noses."[35] These pessimistic considerations were confirmed by Mario Scelba, then Minister of the Interior and one of the most important exponents of the Christian Democrat Party. Speaking in Milan on March 27, 1961, during a centennial ceremony, he said, "The country is still too deeply divided on moral issues and we lack political traditions; it is necessary to anchor life in the country to sound traditions and thus reinforce the connective tissue. Today, the political divisions are so strong that they could affect Italy's influence in the world."[36]

Actually, the centennial celebrations themselves revealed that Italians were totally detached from the world of values and myths that had originated their national unification, which caused them to lose a common ideal image of reference as citizens of the national state. Domenico Bartoli noted that:

> For many years now the continuity of our history has been interrupted and the breach has not been mended. Fascism, the war, the catastrophe of the monarchy and then a state that does not have the moral and political strength to fully assert itself, its independence and prestige. These are the events we are all familiar with because we experienced them and suffered through them. If we consider these situations, it is easy to understand that the people's lack of fervor, of spontaneous enthusiasm for the centennial celebrations, is the result of recent historical occurrences, some of which are still in progress and stand between us and the great events of a century ago.[37]

The polemics regarding the Risorgimento and the unification of Italy highlighted "the lack of a common foundation or a national tradition accepted and interpreted by everybody in the same way, as is the case in the United States with the American Revolution led by

Washington and in Great Britain regarding a hundred other events."[38]
The detachment of the Italians from the Risorgimento tradition also
severed the last bonds with the myth of the nation and the set of ideas,
values, beliefs and ideals that it stood for.

The most evident sign of this detachment from the Risorgimento
was the decline in patriotism among the Italians. Many had "the impression that in Italy, today, devotion to the fatherland is not given due
importance,"[39] as *Studium* noted in 1957. In 1960 in the same publication, Giancarlo Zizola analyzed "the current lack of patriotism, intended as the sentiment of allegiance to a community made up of memories, cultural inheritance, a permanent territory, customs and usages
that create a kind of familiarity, which makes us feel we are foreigners
outside our country": "The obligation to love one's country 'above all
else' is breaking down in consciences. Patriotism is considered an obstacle to creating more extensive communities capable of offering groups
the guarantees that the state is not able to provide. The confusion between state and fatherland, the original sin of the liberal era, leads to
the devaluation of the community that is the backbone of a free society."[40] Believers in the European myth or in universalistic myths thought
that by separating patriotism from the national state the result would be
a form of democratic patriotism purified of any residual nationalistic or
state-controlled tendencies, placing the fatherland in a "universalistic
perspective, enlightened by Christian principles" according to which
"the fatherland is neither depreciated nor deified."[41] This was Zizola's
suggestion. However, the hope of creating a supranational form of patriotism as a new perception of a collective identity for the Italians, dissociating devotion to fatherland from the national state so as to project it
toward a supranational entity such as a hypothetical united Europe, appeared to the most realistic observers a benevolent illusion that could
actually lead to destroying the sense of country as well as the national
state associated with it since the Risorgimento. In 1957 Arturo Jemolo
had voiced his skepticism regarding the possibility of overcoming the
national state:

> There are those who hope that the national state will be like an old
> shoe that you don't like any more and Europe the new shoe that
> will get all your attention. I am not confident that this will ever hap-
> pen. I am still skeptical, despite the many agreements and real fac-
> tors that have given populations an ever-increasing number of
> interests in common, about the creation of a new union; without a
> common language, or commonly shared political and religious

ideals like those that cemented the national unities established in
the nineteenth century, there is no place where the rich want to
share their money with the poor and workers are willing to accept
any kind of reduction so that their peers in the poorer countries
can find work: even the single governments are not strong enough
to impose sacrifices or the measures needed to implement the
changeover. I cannot see the creation of a Europe that will take the
place of the national states.[42]

On the eve of the centennial it was evident that the myth of the
nation, devotion to the country and sense of the national state were disappearing from republican Italy's civil conscience and not being substituted by new values and new common ideals, nor by a sense of collective identity. "The decline of patriotism is so obvious that almost nobody
talks about it," wrote Bartoli in 1959, describing the Italians' lack of
interest in the commemoration of the 1859 centennial, proof that the
Risorgimento "no longer has anything practical to teach us in a changed
world. In our tradition there is a breach that we cannot seem to mend."[43]
In this sense, the decline of patriotism could be linked to the effects of
the "economic miracle" and the forming of a consumerist mentality
typical of an affluent society, which made the world of civil values iden-
tifiable with patriotism appear obsolete. Bartoli rightly observed that the
causes of the decline should be looked for elsewhere and not just in the
egoism of the recently achieved welfare. They could be traced back to
the frustration and delusion inherited by the Italians after the country's
defeat in World War II. "Our patriotism stayed buried under the ruins
of Fascism and the war as the victim of nationalistic exasperation. . . .
The Resistance was not able to revive it despite the sacrifices of some
and illusions of many. It would be too long and painful to explain why.
The Republic, born frail and unsteady, was not able to restore vitality to
the patriotic sentiment, due to the extremely weak monarchy, more than
its own weakness." If national devotion was based on pride in the
country's history, then it was not surprising that patriotism declined in
Italy. As Bartoli noted, among Italians inhabiting the Republic there
was a consolidated vision of the nation's history as being a series of failures and disastrous aspirations, populated by the ghosts of ambitions
that never became realities. "Italy did not know how to be a liberal country, progressing toward more equal and more open forms of political organization, nor a militarily powerful nation on equal standing with its
Western neighbors." The liberal ghost "is the companion, the enemy
brother of another ghost—the myth of a great power, a nationalistic

illusion. And the fact that our literature, art and culture are still given some importance, makes it all the more difficult and bitter to accept our political inferiority, which for the last century has been confirmed decade after decade." Bartoli's was a sharp, clear-cut prophetic analysis of the profound crisis republican Italy was slipping into: "We are not capable of being the kind of state or nation that we are, or were, as a civilization or culture. This incapacity exasperates particularly the intellectuals, active minorities and those who should be the ruling class, and turns everybody toward extreme pessimism or evasion, which almost always ends up in cynical indifference as soon as the first moments of fury have passed." And Bartoli perceived a threat to democracy with the decline in the sense of nation and state:

> A democracy without patriotism has a hard life. It is easier for a society governed according to authoritarian methods to survive under these conditions, because the wounds and cracks can be covered up and kept under control. But patriotism cannot be imposed, it cannot be taught mechanically, even to children. One has to find it in oneself. And to find it one has to reduce egoism, have a sense of duty as a citizen and be ready to make some sacrifices in the name of solidarity. Once the dangerous nationalistic illusions have disappeared forever, the only kind of patriotism that is good for us, furthermore the most genuine, is similar to the envied national sentiment of the Scandinavians, Swiss and even the English nowadays. Pride in the reforms carried out or to be carried out, in the orderly lifestyle and progress made. There is no patriotism without good policies. But there can be no good policies without patriotism.

The warnings of those who considered the decline of patriotism, the sense of state and myth of the nation a risk for the future of the democratic state went unheeded. The question of the nation, which had tormented the consciences of the Italians for more than a century, at least while they had dreamt of a new, great, united Italy on equal standing with, or even in the forefront of, the most modern nations, was now crossed off the agenda by the ruling class and lost importance, even from a cultural point of view. The national myth was pushed more and more onto the sidelines of the new constellation of values considered important among the Italians, as was evident during the centennial celebrations. It was obvious then that the myth of the nation was disappearing from the Italians' civil conscience, taking devotion to the country and sense of state with it. From this point of view, the history of the myth of the nation in Italy in the twentieth century actually ends with its last appearance on the scene during the centennial celebrations. During the decades that followed, the nation—in the modern definition as an idealistic entity that is actualized in the national state, identifying itself with the fatherland—became a simulacrum that was exhibited when necessary for the established celebrations but was incapable of arousing ideals, sentiments or collectively shared emotions in the Italians, nor was it able to evoke memories or commonly shared pain and hope.

NOTES

Prologue: The Fatherland's Jubilee

1. Camera dei Deputati, *Raccolta degli atti stampati. Legislatura VIII, Sessione 1861–1863*, stampato n. 2.

2. Giustino Fortunato, *Il Mezzogiorno e lo Stato italiano* (Florence, 1974), vol. 2, 144.

3. Id., *Carteggio 1865–1911*, ed. Emilio Gentile (Rome-Bari, 1978), 68.

4. Quoted in *Corriere della Sera*, 28 March 1911.

5. "1° Maggio 1911," *Critica sociale*, 16 April 1911, 113.

6. Alfredo Oriani, *La rivolta ideale* (Bologna, 1912), 71–72.

7. "L'Esposizione di Torino inaugurata dai sovrani," *Corriere della Sera*, 30 April 1911.

8. Various authors, *La Patria risorta. Cinquant'anni dopo (1861–1911)* (Milan, 1911), v.

9. Luigi Einaudi, "Cinquant'anni di vita dello Stato italiano," *Corriere della Sera*, 2 April 1911.

10. Napoleone Colajanni, *Il progresso economico* (Rome, 1913), 8.

11. Richard Bagot, *Gli italiani d'oggi* (Bari, 1912), 30–31.

12. Quoted in *Corriere della Sera*, 26 March 1911.

13. Ernest Lémonon, *L'Italie économique et sociale 1861–1912* (Paris, 1913), quoted in Ernesto Ragionieri, *Italia giudicata, 1861–1945*, vol. 2 (Turin, 1976), 261–71.

14. Giuseppe Sergi, "Dopo altri cinquant'anni," *La Vita Internazionale*, 20 June 1911.

15. Arturo Carlo Jemolo, *Italia tormentata* (Bari, 1951), 10.

16. Angelo De Gubernatis, "Il cinquantenario del Regno d'Italia," *La Vita Internazionale*, 5 April 1911.

17. Nino Berrini, "L'esposizione di Torino," *Nuova Antologia*, 1 May 1911.

18. "L'Esposizione di Belle Arti inaugurata alla presenza dei Sovrani," *Corriere della Sera*, 28 March 1911.

19. Paolo Picca, "L'esposizione di Roma," *Nuova Antologia*, 16 March 1911.

20. Quoted in Enzo Forcella, "Roma 1911. Quadri di una esposizione," *Roma 1911* (Rome, 1980), 28.

21. Guglielmo Casetti and L. Cavallari, *Il giubileo della Patria* (Milan-Rome-Naples, 1911), 5.

22. *Atti Parlamentari, Senato del Regno, Legislatura XXIII, 1ª Sessione 1909–1910, Documenti, Disegni di legge e relazioni,* tornata del 4 July 1910, n.339-A, p. 2.

23. Alexander Robertson, *Victor Emmanuel III, King of Italy* (London, 1925), 104.

24. Giovanni Pascoli, *Patria e umanità* (Bologna, 1914). Quotations taken from 1–15.

25. *Atti Parlamentari, Senato del Regno, Legislatura XXIII, 1ª Sessione 1909–1910, Discussioni,* tornata del 12 March 1910, p. 1988.

26. Ernesto Nathan, "Nell'anniversario della morte di Mazzini," *La Ragione,* March 1911.

27. "The Commemoration in Milan. Speech by the Hon. Vecchini at the Scala," *Corriere della sera,* 18 March 1911.

28. *Atti Parlamentari, Camera dei Deputati, Legislatura XXIII, 1ª Sessione, Discussioni,* tornata del 5 May 1910, pp. 6630–31.

29. "La spedizione dei Mille commemorata solennemente alla Camera," *La Stampa,* 6 May 1910.

30. "Vibrazioni patriottiche," *Corriere della Sera,* 6 May 1910.

31. *Atti Parlamentari, Camera dei Deputati, Legislatura XXIII, 1ª Sessione, Discussioni,* tornata del 5 May 1910, pp. 6627–28.

32. *Atti Parlamentari, Camera dei Deputati, Legislatura XXIII, 2ª Sessione, Discussioni,* tornata del 27 March 1909, pp. 17–18.

33. See Niccolò Zapponi, "I miti e le ideologie. Storia della cultura italiana, 1870–1960," *Storia dell'Italia contemporanea,* ed. Renzo De Felice, vol. 7 (Naples, 1983), 38 ff.

34. See Bruno Tobia, *Una patria per gli italiani: spazi, itinerari, monumenti nell'Italia unita (1870–1900)* (Rome-Bari, 1991); Umberto Levra, *Fare gli italiani. Memoria e celebrazione del Risorgimento* (Turin, 1992); Emilio Gentile, *Il culto del littorio* (Rome-Bari, 1993), 5–38.

Chapter 1. Modernity, Freedom, *Italianità*

1. Camillo Benso di Cavour, *Discorsi parlamentari,* vol. 15, ed. Armando Saitta (Florence, 1973), 412.

2. Giuseppe Mazzini, *Scritti politici,* ed. Terenzio Grandi and Augusto Comba (Turin, 1972), 884.

3. Bertrando Spaventa, *Unificazione nazionale ed egemonia culturale,* ed. Giuseppe Vacca (Bari, 1969), 203.

4. Emilio Gentile, "The Conquest of Modernity: From Modernist Nationalism to Fascism," *Modernism/modernity* (September 1994), 55 ff.

5. Camillo Benso di Cavour, *Le strade ferrate in Italia*, ed. Arnaldo Salvestrini (Florence, 1976), 69.

6. Giuseppe Mazzini, *Scritti politici*, 881.

7. Ibid., 253.

8. Gian Domenico Romagnosi, *Vedute fondamentali sull'arte logica* (1832), ed. Lorenzo Caboara (Rome, 1936), 446.

9. Id., *La scienza delle costituzioni* (Florence, 1850), 227.

10. Giuseppe Mazzini, *Scritti politici*, 882–83.

11. Ibid., 677.

12. Pasquale Stanislao Mancini, *Saggi sulla nazionalità*, ed. F. Lopez de Onate (Rome, 1944), 7.

13. Ibid., 61.

14. Ibid., 44.

15. Ibid., 62. The italics are in the original.

16. Ibid., 84.

17. Giuseppe Mazzini, *Scritti politici editi ed inediti*, vol. 30 (Imola, 1941), 92–93.

18. Pasquale Stanislao Mancini, *Saggi sulla nazionalità*, 36–37.

19. Niccolò Tommaseo, *Dizionario dei sinonimi della lingua italiana*, ed. Paolo Chiglieri, 4 vols. (Florence, 1973), 1381–83.

20. *Nuova enciclopedia popolare ovvero dizionario generale di scienze, lettere, arti, storia, geografia, ecc. opera compilata sulle migliori di tal genere, inglesi, tedesche e francesi coll'assistenza e col consiglio di scienziati e letterati italiani*, vols. 9–10 (Turin, 1847–48).

21. Professor Gerolamo Boccardo, *Nuova enciclopedia italiana ovvero dizionario generale delle scienze, lettere, industrie, ecc.* (Turin, 1883).

22. *Dizionario di cognizioni utili. Enciclopedia elementare di scienze, lettere, arti, agricoltura, diritto, medicina, geografia ecc. fondata sui programmi delle scuole secondarie e ad uso delle famiglie colte*, ed. Dr. Mario Lessona, vol. 4 (Turin, 1914).

23. "Pasquale Stanislao Mancini e la teoria psicologica del sentimento nazionale. Discorso commemorativo del Socio Giuseppe Carle letto nella seduta del 78 maggio 1890," *Atti della R. Accademia dei Lincei*, 1889, fourth series (Rome, 1889), 559.

24. Ibid., 566.

25. Francesco Crispi, *Ultimi scritti e discorsi extraparlamentari (1891–1901)*, ed. Tommaso Palamenghi-Crispi (Rome, n.d.), 371.

26. Celso Ferrari, *La nazionalità e la vita sociale* (Palermo, 1896), 262.

27. Ibid., vi.

28. Napoleone Colajanni, *Latini e Anglo-Sassoni* (Rome-Napoli, 1906[2]), 25.

29. Ibid., 25–26.

30. Alfredo Niceforo, *Italiani del Nord e Italiani del Sud* (Turin, 1901), 8, 11.

31. See Giulio Bollati, *L'Italiano. Il carattere nazionale come storia e come invenzione* (Turin, 1983).

32. Giacomo Leopardi, "Discorso sopra lo stato presente dei costumi degl'italiani," *Tutte le opere*, ed. Walter Binni (Florence, 1969), vol. 1, 975.

33. Ibid., 979–80.

34. Ibid., 977–78.

35. Ibid., 981.

36. Francesco Lomonaco, *Opere*, vol. 6 (Lugano, 1835), 141.

37. Quoted in Carlo Curcio, *Nazione Europa Umanità* (Milan, 1950), 58–59.

38. Ibid., 66.

39. Vincenzo Gioberti, *Del primato morale e civile degli italiani* (Brussels, 1843), vol. 1, 80.

40. Massimo d'Azeglio, *I miei ricordi* (Rome, 1959), 5–6.

41. Silvio Spaventa, *La politica della Destra* (Bari, 1910), 302.

42. Augusto Alfani, *Il carattere degli italiani* (Florence, 1878).

43. Ibid., 245.

44. Ibid., 244–45.

45. Francesco De Sanctis, *I partiti e l'educazione della nuova Italia*, ed. Nino Cortese (Turin, 1970), 515.

46. Id., *Saggi critici*, ed. Luigi Russo, vol. 3 (Bari, 1957), 10.

47. Ibid., 7.

48. Ibid., 21.

49. Ibid., 23.

50. Id., *Storia della letteratura italiana*, ed. Luigi Russo, vol. 2 (Milan, 1960), 463–64.

51. Id., *La scuola liberale e la scuola democratica*, ed. F. Catalano (Bari, 1953), 449.

Chapter 2. Complex of Greatness

1. "Excelsior," *La Stampa*, 20 April 1911.

2. Vincenzo Gioberti, *Del primato*, vol. 1, 19. The italics are in the original.

3. Ibid., 43.

4. Ibid., 44.

5. Ibid., 46.

6. Ibid., 44.

7. Ibid., 76.

8. Giuseppe Mazzini, *Scritti politici*, 964.

9. Ibid., 554.

10. Ibid., 885.

11. Vincenzo Gioberti, *Del primato*, vol. 1, 4–8.

12. Quoted in Federico Chabod, *Storia della politica estera italiana dal 1870 al 1896. Le Premesse*, vol. 1 (Bari, 1951), 286.

13. Vincenzo Gioberti, *Del primato*, vol. 1, 1.

14. Giuseppe Mazzini, *Scritti politici*, 1012.

15. Ibid., 885.

16. Quoted in Luigi Salvatorelli, *Il pensiero politico italiano dal 1700 al 1870* (Turin, 1935), 244.

17. Camillo Benso di Cavour, *Discorsi parlamentari*, ed. Delio Cantimori (Turin, 1942), 240.

18. Ibid., 250.

19. *Atti Parlamentari, Camera dei Deputati, Legislatura XV, 1ª Sessione, Discussioni*, tornata del 10 March 1883, p. 2998.

20. Ibid., 4363.

21. Ibid., 14 March 1881 session, 4354.

22. Ibid., 4353–54.

23. Ibid., 4249.

24. Ibid., 4293.

25. Ibid., 4245–46.

26. Ibid., 4269.

27. Ibid., 4371.

28. Ibid., 4295.

29. Mario Morasso, *Uomini e idee del domani. L'egoarchia* (Milan, 1898), 127.

30. Ibid., 131.

31. Ibid., 158.

32. Ibid., 160–61.

33. "La commemorazione del cinquantenario dello Statuto," *Corriere della Sera*, 5–6 March 1898.

34. "Il discorso di Vittorio Emanuele III," *Corriere della Sera*, 28 March 1911.

35. See Gioacchino Volpe, *Italia moderna*, vol. 1 (Florence, 1973), 70.

36. See Federico Chabod, *Storia della politica estera*, 206–89.

37. Francesco Crispi, *Ultimi scritti e discorsi extra-parlamentari*, 64.

38. Ibid., 309.

39. Ibid., 163.

40. Ibid., 239–40.

41. Ibid., 17.

42. Ibid., 308–9.

43. Giovanni Rapisardi, *La libertà la patria e la scuola* (Florence, 1868), 273.

44. *I discorsi della Corona*, ed. Antonio Monti (Milan, 1938), 101–2.

45. Ibid., 190.

46. Ibid., 212.

47. Ibid., 223–24.

48. *Atti Parlamentari, Senato del Regono, Legislatura XXIII, 1ª Sessione, 1909–1911, Discussioni*, tornata del 26 March 1911, p. 4849.

Chapter 3. The Italies of Monarchic Italy

1. Giovanni Ansaldo, *Diario di prigionia*, ed. Renzo De Felice (Bologna, 1993), 226.

2. Giovanni Giolitti, *Discorsi extraparlamentari,* ed. Nino Valeri (Turin, 1952), 254–56.

3. Ugo Ojetti, "Roma e l'Italia," *Corriere della Sera,* 5 June 1911.

4. "Caratteri e significato di una giornata storica," *La Stampa,* 5 June 1911.

5. Diego Angeli, "La giornata dell'inaugurazione," *L'Illustrazione Italiana,* 11 June 1911.

6. "Significati," *Corriere della Sera,* 5 June 1911.

7. "La buona giornata," *Corriere della Sera,* 6 May 1910.

8. "Caratteri e significato," *La Stampa,* 5 June 1911.

9. Giovanni Rabizzani, "Cinquant'anni di vita italiana in una recente pubblicazione," *Il Marzocco,* 18 June 1911.

10. Annibale Gabrielli, "L'inaugurazione del Monumento a Vittorio Emanuele II," *Rivista di Roma* (June 1911).

11. Benedetto Croce, *Cultura e vita morale* (Bari, 1955³), 163.

12. Annibale Gabrielli, "L'inaugurazione del Monumento a Vittorio Emanuele II," *Rivista di Roma* (June 1911).

13. "Le commemorazioni patriottiche del 1911," *La Civiltà Cattolica,* vol. 2 (1911).

14. "Un anno di lutto," *La Civiltà Cattolica,* vol. 1 (1911).

15. "27 marzo 1862–27 marzo 1911," *L'Osservatore Romano,* 28 March 1911.

16. "Sciopero e patriottismo," *L'Osservatore Romano,* 27 March 1911.

17. "I due cinquantenari," *Avanti!* 27 March 1911.

18. "1° maggio 1911," *Critica Sociale,* 16 April 1911, 113.

19. Giuseppe Mazzini, *Scritti politici editi ed inediti,* vol. 91, 162.

20. *La Ragione,* 11 March 1911.

21. "Il cinquantenario e il caro viveri," *La Ragione,* 14 March 1911.

22. *La Ragione,* 12 March 1911.

23. "Le feste giubilari," *La Ragione,* 19 March 1911.

24. *La Ragione,* 5 June 1911.

25. "L'usurpazione monarchica delle feste della Patria," *La Ragione,* 18 March 1911.

26. "Il cinquantenario e il caro viveri," *La Ragione,* 14 March 1911.

27. "Il partito Mazziniano e il Cinquantennio," *La Ragione,* 5 June 1911.

28. Giuseppe Prezzolini, "Italia mia," *La Voce,* 9 March 1911.

29. "L'annata triste," *La Voce,* 24 August 1911.

30. Antonio Anzilotti, "Per il programma della «voce»," *La Voce,* 14 September 1911.

31. *La Voce,* 9 March 1911.

32. Giustino Fortunato, "Le due Italie," *La Voce,* 16 March 1911.

33. See Alberto Asor Rosa, "La cultura," *Storia d'Italia dall'Unità ad oggi,* vol. 4, book 2 (Turin, 1975), 1234 ff.

34. Eduardo Cimbali, *Esiste l'idea di patria e di patriottismo?* (Rome, 1912), 21–22.

35. Scipio Sighele, *Ultime pagine nazionaliste* (Milan, 1912), 29.

36. Bernardino Varisco, *La patria* (Rome, 1913), 9–29.

37. Enrico Corradini, "Dal Campidoglio a Montecitorio," *Il Marzocco*, 2 April 1911.

38. "Le elezioni," *Il Regno*, 22 May 1904.

39. Giuseppe Prezzolini, "Le due Italie," *Il Regno*, 22 May 1904.

40. See Emilio Gentile, *Il mito dello Stato nuovo dall'antigiolittismo al fascismo* (Rome-Bari, 1982), 54–60.

41. "Cinquantenario," *Corriere della Sera*, 27 March 1911.

42. Alfredo Oriani, *La rivolta ideale*, 256.

Chapter 4. The Metamorphosis of a Myth

1. Adolfo Omodeo, *Momenti della vita di guerra* (Bari, 1934), 24.

2. Scipio Sighele, *Ultime pagine nazionaliste*, viii–ix.

3. Dante Diotallevi, "Italia nova," *La Vita Internazionale*, 20 December 1911.

4. Giustino Fortunato, *Carteggio 1912–1922*, ed. Emilio Gentile (Rome-Bari, 1979), 25.

5. Ibid., 89.

6. See Giulio Cianferotti, *Giuristi e mondo accademico di fronte all'impresa di Tripoli* (Milan, 1984).

7. Dante Diotallevi, "Italia nova," *La Vita Internazionale*, 20 December 1911.

8. Giuseppe Prezzolini, "Italia 1912," *La Fiera Letteraria*, 26 November 1961.

9. Roberto Michels, *L'imperialismo italiano* (Milan, 1914), 4.

10. Ibid., 107.

11. Ibid., 178.

12. See Rosario Romeo, *L'Italia liberale: sviluppo e contraddizioni* (Milan, 1987), 22 ff.; Giuseppe Galasso, *Italia nazione difficile* (Florence, 1994), 48 ff.

13. Guido De Ruggiero, *Scritti politici 1912–1926*, ed. Renzo De Felice (Bologna, 1963), 487–91.

14. For a list of the varieties of nationalism, see Paolo Arcari, *La coscienza nazionale in Italia* (Milan, 1911), *Il nazionalismo giudicato da Letterati, Artisti, Scienziati, Uomini politici e giornalisti italiani*, ed. Arturo Salucci (Genoa, 1913).

15. Paolo Arcari, *Il nazionalismo giudicato*, 106.

16. Gioacchino Volpe, *Italia moderna*, vol. 3 (Florence, 1973), 274 ff.

17. Edoardo Giretti, "Nazionalismo?" *Critica e Azione* (October 1909).

18. Giovanni Vidari, "Nazionalismo e . . . nazionalismo," *La Vita Internazionale*, 20 October 1910.

19. Pantaleo Carabellese, "È necessaria una democrazia?" *L'Unità*, 2 March 1912.

20. Rodolfo Savelli, "Ripresa," *L'Unità*, 14 April 1913.

21. Gaetano Salvemini, "Alla ricerca di una formula," *L'Unità*, 14 March 1913.

22. Giuseppe Donati, "Gioberti e i nazionalisti," *L'Azione*, 25 May 1913, now in id., *Scritti politici*, ed. Giuseppe Rossini (Rome, 1956), 157.

23. See *Pro e contro la guerra di Tripoli. Discussioni nel campo rivoluzionario* (Naples, 1912).

24. Paolo Arcari, *Il nazionalismo giudicato,* 175.

25. Arturo Labriola, *Il sostanziale e l'accidentale nel socialismo* (Naples, 1914), 63–64.

26. See Karl Dietrich Bracher, *The Age of Ideologies,* trans. Ewald Osers (New York, 1984).

27. Guido De Ruggiero, *Scritti politici 1912–1926,* 549–50.

28. Emilio Gentile, *Il mito dello Stato nuovo,* 3–28.

29. *Parliamentary Acts, Chamber of Deputies, 24th Legislature, 1st Sitting, Debates,* 9 December session, 1913.

30. Adolfo Omodeo, *Lettere 1910–1946* (Turin, 1963), 14.

Chapter 5. Italianism and Modernity

1. See Stelio Zeppi, *Il pensiero politico dell'idealismo italiano e il nazionalfascismo* (Florence, 1973).

2. See Emilio Gentile, "Breve storia delle storie d'Italia," *Storia d'Italia,* ed. Renzo De Felice, vol. 7 (Naples, 1983), 253 ff.

3. See Giorgio Chiosso, *L'educazione nazionale da Giolitti al primo dopoguerra* (Brescia, 1983).

4. See Emilio Gentile, *"La Voce" e l'età giolittiana* (Milan, 1972), *Futurismo e politica,* ed. Renzo De Felice (Turin, 1983); Walter L. Adamson, *Avant-Garde Florence: From Modernism to Fascism* (Cambridge, Mass., 1993).

5. *I discorsi della Corona,* ed. Antonio Monti (Milan, 1938), 230.

6. Alfredo Oriani, *La rivolta ideale,* 78.

7. Francesco Saverio Nitti, *L'Italia all'alba del secolo XX* (Turin-Rome, 1901).

8. Ibid., 184–85.

9. Mario Morasso, *L'imperialismo nel secolo XX* (Milan, 1905), 327.

10. Ibid., 330.

11. Ibid., 325–26.

12. The expression is Angelo Oliviero Olivetti's, "Sindacalismo e nazionalismo," *Pagine libere,* 15 February 1911.

13. Giovanni Amendola, "Il convegno nazionalista," *La Voce,* 1 December 1910.

14. Id., "La guerra," *La Voce,* 28 December 1911.

15. Alfredo Oriani, *La rivolta ideale,* 157.

16. Ibid., 102–3.

17. Giovanni Amendola, "La vague allemande," *Il Regno,* 25 July 1905.

18. Giuseppe Prezzolini, "Il risveglio italiano," *La Voce,* 30 November 1911.

19. Giovanni Amendola, "Il Mezzogiorno e la coltura italiana," *La Voce,* 7 January 1909.

20. Giuseppe Prezzolini, *Amendola e «La Voce»* (Florence, 1973), 138.

21. Ibid., 59.

22. Umberto Boccioni, "Contro la vigliaccheria artistica italiana," *Lacerba*, 1 September 1913.

23. Id., *Opere complete* (Foligno, 1927), 39.

24. *Archivi del futurismo*, ed. Maria Drudi Gambillo and Teresa Fiori, vol. 1 (Rome, 1959), 271.

25. See Emilio Gentile, *Il futurismo e la politica. Dal nazionalismo modernista al fascismo (1909–1920), Futurismo, cultura e politica*, ed. Renzo De Felice (Turin, 1988), 107 ff.

26. Giovanni Papini and Giuseppe Prezzolini, *La coltura italiana* (Florence, 1906), 84.

27. Giovanni Amendola, "Il Mezzogiorno e la coltura italiana," *La Voce*, 7 January 1909.

28. Benedetto Croce, *Cultura e vita morale* (Bari, 1955), 166.

29. "Verso la più forte Italia," *Corriere della Sera*, 28 November 1908.

30. Bernardino Varisco, *La patria*, 66–67.

31. Gabriele D'Annunzio, *Tutte le opere*, ed. Enrica Bianchetti, vol. 3 (Milan, 1961), 400 ff.

32. "Presentazione," *Pagine Libere*, 15 December 1907.

33. Benito Mussolini, "Un grande amico dell'Italia: Augusto von Platen," *Il Popolo*, 3 July 1909.

Chapter 6. Italian Imperialists

1. Giuseppe Are, *La scoperta dell'imperialismo* (Rome, 1985).

2. Olindo Malagodi, *Imperialismo. La civiltà industriale e le sue conquiste* (Milan, 1901), 25.

3. Ibid., 31.

4. Ibid., 32–33.

5. Roberto Michels, *L'imperialismo italiano*, 105.

6. See Giovanni Sabbatucci, "Il problema dell'irredentismo e le origini del movimento nazionalista in Italia," *Storia contemporanea*, no. 4 (1970), 467 ff.; no. 1 (1971), 53 ff.

7. See Carlo Curcio, *Nazione Europa Umanità*, 163 ff.

8. Scipio Slataper, *Scritti politici*, ed. Giani Stuparich (Milan, 1954), 290–94.

9. Arturo Carlo Jemolo, *Crispi* (Florence, 1922), 122–23.

10. Mario Morasso, *L'imperialismo artistico* (Turin, 1903), 26.

11. Giovanni Amadori Virgilj, *Il sentimento imperialista. Studio psicosociologico* (Milan, 1906), 94–95.

12. Ibid., 121.

13. Enrico Corradini, *Scritti e discorsi 1901–1914*, ed. Lucia Strappini (Turin, 1980), 64–65.

14. See Franco Gaeta, *Il nazionalismo italiano* (Rome-Bari, 1981), particularly 239–50.

15. Enrico Corradini, *Nazionalismo italiano* (Milan, 1914), 230.

16. Id., *Discorsi politici (1902–1923)* (Florence, 1923), 87.

17. Ibid., 101.

18. Id., *Nazionalismo italiano*, 156.

19. Luigi Valli, "Che cosa è e che cosa vuole il nazionalismo" (Florence, 1911), in Francesco Perfetti, *Il movimento nazionalista in Italia (1903–1914)* (Rome, 1984), 190.

20. See Emilio Gentile, *Il mito dello Stato nuovo*, 167 ff.

21. Alfredo Rocco, *Scritti e discorsi politici*, vol. 1 (Milan, 1928), 35.

22. Ibid., 238.

23. Ibid., 51.

24. Bernardino Varisco, *Discorsi politici* (Rome, 1926), 128–29.

25. "La necessità del Nazionalismo per il progresso dell'Italia," *La Grande Italia*, 2 October 1910.

26. Mario Viana, *Sciopero generale e guerra vittoriosa* (Turin, 1910), 57.

27. Ibid., 53.

28. Scipio Sighele, *Il nazionalismo e i partiti politici* (Milan, 1911), 23–24.

29. Enrico Corradini, *Discorsi politici*, 47.

30. Mario Morasso, *L'imperialismo artistico*, 121.

31. Michele Pericle Negrotto, "Principi e direttive del nazionalismo," *La Grande Italia*, 12 May 1912.

32. Enrico Corradini, *Discorsi politici*, 261.

33. Alfredo Rocco, *Scritti e discorsi*, vol. 2, 489.

34. Enrico Corradini, *Discorsi politici*, 7.

Chapter 7. The Man and the Patriot

1. Benedetto Croce, *Memorie della mia vita* (Naples, 1966), 39.

2. Id., "Un vocabolario della lingua filosofica italiana," *La Voce*, 25 February 1909.

3. Giovanni Amendola, "Il convegno nazionalista," *La Voce*, 1 December 1910.

4. Emilio Gentile, "Italianismo e umanismo. Le ambivalenze de «La Voce»," *«La Voce» e l'Europa*, ed. Diana Ruesch and Bruno Somalvico (Rome, 1994), 21–38.

5. Giovanni Amendola, "Il libro non letto," *La Voce*, 9 May 1912.

6. Giuseppe Prezzolini, "Risposta ai nazionalisti," *La Voce*, 13 April 1911.

7. Id., "Il liberismo come azione morale," *La Voce*, 3 July 1913.

8. Antonio Anzilotti, *La crisi spirituale della democrazia. Per una democrazia nazionalista* (Faenza, 1912), 85.

9. Giuseppe Prezzolini, "Come faremo «La Voce»," *La Voce*, 7 November 1912.

10. Id., "Relazione del Consiglio," *La Voce*, 6 March 1913.

11. Antonio Anzilotti, "Dalla classe alla nazione," *La Voce*, 6 June 1912.

12. Giuseppe Prezzolini, "Perché siamo anticlericali," *La Voce*, 21 January 1909.

13. Id., "Il risveglio italiano," *La Voce*, 30 March 1911.

14. Id., "I fatti di Romagna," *La Voce*, 11 August 1910.

15. Id., "Contro Roma," *La Voce*, 25 August 1910.

16. Giovanni Boine, *Carteggio*, vol. 3, book 1, ed. Margherita Marchione and S. Eugene Scalia (Rome, 1977), 462.

17. Scipio Slataper, "Gli Slavi meridionali d'oggi," *La Voce*, 13 April 1911.

18. Id., "Oggi," *La Voce*, 15 December 1910.

19. Ibid.

20. George G. Herron, "Roosevelt," *La Voce*, 28 April 1910.

21. "Le «atrocità» italiane," *La Voce*, 16 November 1911.

22. Fausto Torrefranca, "In Germania. Civiltà di seconda mano," *La Voce*, 18 January 1912.

23. Giuseppe Prezzolini, "Tripoli," *La Voce*, 6 March 1913.

24. See Giovanni Belardelli, "«L'Azione» e il movimento nazionale liberale," *Il partito politico nella Belle Époque. Il dibattito sulla forma-partito in Italia tra '800 e '900*, ed. Gaetano Quagliariello (Milan, 1990), 293–327.

25. "La propaganda nazionale liberale. A Milano. Il discorso di Gioacchino Volpe," *L'Azione*, 20 December 1914.

26. Giovanni Vidari, *Nazionalismo e . . . nazionalismo*.

27. Angelo Crespi, "Patriottismo ed industrialismo," *La Vita Internazionale*, 5 April 1908.

28. "Patria ed Umanità," *La Vita Internazionale*, 5 February 1904.

29. Ernesto Teodoro Moneta, "Patriottismo più alto, più vero e più fecondo," *La Vita Internazionale*, 20 October 1910.

30. Id., "Due patriottismi," *La Vita Internazionale*, 20 June 1910.

31. Arcangelo Ghisleri, *Che cosa è una nazione* (Florence, 1919), 12.

32. Pietro Bonfante, "Stati-città e Stati-nazioni," *L'Unità*, 16 February 1917.

33. Giuseppe Prezzolini, *Vittorio Veneto* (Rome, 1920), viii–ix, xi.

34. Giovanni Amendola, *La nuova democrazia* (Naples, 1951), 92.

35. Ibid., xxv.

36. See Francesco Traniello, "Religione, nazione e sovranità nel Risorgimento italiano," *Rivista di Storia e Letteratura religiosa*, no. 2 (1992), 319 ff.; Giovanni Aliberti, "Nazione e Stato nei federalisti cattolici del Risorgimento, Balbo, Taparelli, D'Ondes Reggio," *Ricerche di Storia sociale e religiosa* 45 (1994), 127 ff.

37. "Equivoci di nazionalismo: «Martiri» in guerra e «preti in zaino»," *La Civiltà Cattolica*, vol. 2 (1915), 423 ff.

38. Agostino Gemelli, *Principio di Nazionalità e amor di Patria nella dottrina cattolica* (Turin, 1918), 60–61.

39. Ibid., 57–58.

40. Ibid., 44.

41. Ibid., 67.

42. Ibid., 52.

43. "Nazionalismo e amor di patria secondo la dottrina cattolica," *La Civiltà Cattolica*, vol. 1 (1915), 129 ff.

44. "Patria e patriottismo," *La Civiltà Cattolica*, vol. 4 (1923), 486 ff.

45. "Patria e patriottismo," *La Civiltà Cattolica*, vol. 1 (1924), 10 ff.

46. "Il nazionalismo e le presenti lotte politiche," *La Civiltà Cattolica*, vol. 3 (1924), 97 ff.

47. Gabriele De Rosa, *L'Azione Cattolica. Storia politica dal 1905 al 1919*, vol. 2 (Bari, 1954), 305 ff.; Luigi Ganapini, *Il nazionalismo cattolico. I cattolici e la politica estera in Italia dal 1871 al 1914* (Bari, 1970).

48. Luigi Sturzo, *I discorsi politici* (Rome, 1951), 357.

49. Ibid., 359–60.

50. Ibid., 368.

51. Quoted in Gabriele De Rosa, *Utopia politica di L. Sturzo* (Brescia, 1972), 33.

52. Luigi Sturzo, *Riforma statale e indirizzi politici* (Florence, 1923), 79.

53. Ibid., 170.

54. Ibid., 31–32.

55. Agostino Gemelli, *Principio di Nazionalità e amor di Patria*, 65–66 for all the quotations.

56. See Tullio Rossi Doria, *Socialismo e patriottismo* (Milan, 1912).

57. Cesare Battisti, *Scritti politici e sociali*, ed. Renato Monteleone (Florence, 1966), 18.

58. Ibid., 19.

59. Ibid., 244.

60. Ibid., 281.

61. Ibid., 507.

62. Tullio Rossi Doria, *Socialismo e patriottismo*, xi.

63. Ibid., 149.

64. Ibid., 10.

65. Ibid.

66. Ibid., 47.

67. Benito Mussolini, *Opera omnia*, ed. Edoardo and Duilio Susmel, 35 vols. (Florence, 1951–63), vol. 2, 169–70.

68. See *La politica estera italiana dal 1897 al 1920* (Milan, 1923).

69. Enrico Leone, "L'idea di nazionalità e l'avvenire delle guerre," *Critica sociale*, 1–15 January 1915.

70. Giovanni Zibordi, "Per la personalità della nazione italiana," *Critica sociale*, 1–15 December 1916.

71. Carlo Treves and Filippo Turati, "Proletariato e resistenza," *Critica sociale*, 1–15 November 1917.

72. Benito Mussolini, *Opera omnia*, vol. 6, 428–29.

73. Id., *Opera omnia*, vol. 7, 147.
74. Ibid., 237.
75. Giuseppe Prezzolini, "Facciamo la guerra," *La Voce*, 28 August 1914.
76. Benito Mussolini, *Opera omnia*, vol. 7, 196–97.
77. Giovanni Gentile, *Guerra e fede* (Naples, 1919), 119.
78. "I nuovi orizzonti della vita operaia italiana," *Il Rinnovamento*, 6 June 1918.
79. Giovanni Gentile, *Dopo la vittoria* (Florence, 1920), 71.
80. Ibid., 61–62.

Chapter 8. Italy in Black Shirts

1. Benito Mussolini, "Italia e Francia," *Il Popolo d'Italia*, 3 December 1918.
2. See Emilio Gentile, "Un'apocalisse nella modernità. La Grande Guerra e il Mito della Rigenerazione della politica," *Storia contemporanea* (October 1995), 733 ff.
3. Benito Mussolini, *Opera omnia*, vol. 15, 214.
4. Id., *Opera omnia*, vol. 18, 457.
5. Ibid., 314.
6. See Emilio Gentile, *Le origini dell'ideologia fascista* (Bologna, 1996), 25 ff.
7. Benito Mussolini, "Breve preludio," *Gerarchia* (January 1922).
8. Id., *Opera omnia*, vol. 18, 160.
9. See Emilio Gentile, *Storia del partito fascista. 1919–1922. Movimento e milizia* (Rome-Bari, 1989), 36–37, 387 ff.
10. Benito Mussolini, *Opera omnia*, vol. 18, 434.
11. See Pier Giorgio Zunino, *L'ideologia fascista* (Bologna, 1985), 107 ff.
12. Benito Mussolini, *Opera omnia*, vol. 19, 94.
13. Carmelo Licitra, "Proemio," *La Nuova Politica Liberale* (January 1923).
14. Massimo Rocca, "Il fascismo e l'Italia," *Critica Fascista*, 15 September 1923.
15. Roberto Cantalupo, "Società nazionale e Stato nazionale," *Gerarchia* (November 1925).
16. Gioacchino Volpe, *Italia che fu* (Milan, 1961), 183 for all the quotations.
17. Id., *Scritti sul fascismo*, vol. 1 (Rome, 1976), 142.
18. Id., *Nel regno di Clio* (Rome, 1977), 289.
19. See Emilio Gentile, *Le origini dell'ideologia fascista*, 207–12, 283–94.
20. Camillo Pellizzi, *Problemi e realtà del fascismo* (Florence, 1924), 73.
21. In Luigi Federzoni, *L'Italia di ieri per la storia di domani* (Milan, 1967), 17–18.

Chapter 9. Remaking the Italians

1. Maurizio Maraviglia, *Alle basi del regime* (Rome, 1929), 14–15 for all the quotations.

2. See Renzo De Felice, *Mussolini il fascista*, vol. 2 (Turin, 1968), 293 ff.

3. Benito Mussolini, *Opera omnia*, vol. 21, 45.

4. Id., *Opera omnia*, vol. 25, 15–16.

5. Augusto Turati, *La dottrina fascista* (Rome, 1929), 18.

6. Giuseppe Maggiore, "Nazione e popolo: mito e realtà," *Atti della Reale Accademia di Scienze Lettere e Arti di Palermo*, series 4, 3, part 2, file 1, 1942, xxvii–xxix.

7. Proof given to the author.

8. Texts republished in *Credere Obbedire Combattere*, ed. Carlo Galeotti (Rome, 1996).

9. Giovanni Gentile, *La riforma dell'educazione* (Florence, 1955), 9–10.

10. Ibid., 12–13.

11. Giovanni Gentile, *Dopo la vittoria*.

12. Id., *Guerra e fede*, 48–59. ·

13. Id., *Origini e dottrina del fascismo* (Rome, 1929), 44 ff.

14. "Fascismo," *Enciclopedia italiana di scienze, lettere ed arti*, vol. 14, 847–48.

15. To give an example, see what one of the harshest anti-Gentile critics, Giuseppe Attilio Fanelli, wrote: "The nation as conceived by the Fascists therefore transcends the individual and as such is an objective reality, objectively perceived by the individual. Therefore it is not in Gentile's immanent nation that the subject discovers awareness of self and nothing else by himself. It is not a result but a principle." "L'equivoco attualista," *Roma fascista*, 4 October 1931. Doubts about Gentile's concept were also expressed by Sergio Panunzio, *Popolo Nazione Stato* (Florence, 1933), 36.

16. Julius Evola, "Elementi dell'idea europea," *Lo Stato* (November 1940). For a summary of Evola's criticisms of the idealistic concept of nation, see id., "In alto mare," *Vita Italiana* (November 1942).

17. Carlo Costamagna, "Stato," *Dizionario di politica*, vol. 4 (Rome, 1940), 393.

18. Id., "Nazione," *Dizionario di politica*, vol. 3, 263.

19. Antonino Pagliaro, "Politica," *Dizionario di politica*, vol. 3, 451.

20. Giovanni Gentile, *La riforma dell'educazione*, 12.

21. "Il divenire del Regime," *Il Legionario*, 10 September 1927.

22. See Renzo De Felice, *Storia degli ebrei italiani sotto il fascismo* (Turin, 1988⁴).

23. Ottavio Dinale, *Quarant'anni di colloqui con lui* (Milan, 1953), 100.

24. Benito Mussolini, *Opera omnia*, vol. 22, 100.

25. Id., *Opera omnia*, vol. 19, 266.

26. Id., *Opera omnia*, vol. 22, 145.

27. Id., *Opera omnia*, vol. 24, 283.

28. Giuseppe Bottai, *Diario 1935–1944*, ed. Giordano Bruno Guerri (Milan, 1982), 187.

29. Ibid., 111.

30. Ottavio Dinale, *Quarant'anni di colloqui con lui*, 181.

31. Galeazzo Ciano, *Diario 1937–1943*, ed. Renzo De Felice (Milan, 1980), 394.

32. Giuseppe Bottai, *Diario*, 210.
33. Ibid., 242.
34. Galeazzo Ciano, *Diario*, 444–45.
35. Ibid.
36. Giuseppe Bottai, *Diario*, 356–57.
37. Galeazzo Ciano, *Diario*, 458.
38. Antonino Pagliaro, *Politica*, 452.
39. Carlo Costamagna, *Nazione*, 264.
40. Balbino Giuliano, *L'esperienza politica dell'Italia* (Florence, 1924), 200.
41. Benito Mussolini, *Opera omnia*, vol. 17, 161.
42. Giovanni Gentile, "Il Giappone guerriero," *Civiltà*, 21 January 1942.
43. Antonio Messineo, "Il culto della nazione e la fede mitica," *La Civiltà Cattolica*, vol. 3 (1940), 212 *ff*; Id., *La nazione* (Rome, 1942), 189.
44. See Emilio Gentile, *Il culto del littorio*.
45. Carlo Costamagna, *Nazione*, 265.
46. Paolo Orano, *Il fascismo*, vol. 2 (Rome, 1939), 143.

Chapter 10. A New Imperial Civilization

1. "Verso l'Europa," *Critica fascista*, 15 August 1930.
2. Delio Cantimori, "Fascismo, rivoluzione e non reazione europea," *Vita Nova* (September 1931).
3. Quoted in Delio Cantimori, "Fascismo, nazionalismi e reazioni," *Vita Nova* (January 1931).
4. Berto Ricci, "L'universale," *L'Universale* (January 1931).
5. "I nuovi doveri," *Il Legionario*, 19 May 1934.
6. U. I., "Verso una gerarchia delle nazioni," *Roma Fascista*, 15 May 1941.
7. Giovanni Gentile, *Opere*, 46: *Politica e cultura* (2), ed. Hervé A. Cavallera (Florence, 1991), 116.
8. Ibid., 316–37.
9. Ibid., 343–44 (speech at the Istituto nazionale di cultura fascista, 19 December 1936).
10. Delio Cantimori, "Fascismo, rivoluzione e non reazione europea," *Vita Nova* (September 1931).
11. Mirko Ardemagni, "Critica dei nazionalismi. Il nazionalismo francese," *Gerarchia* (March 1934).
12. Id., "Critica dei nazionalismi. II. Il nazionalismo germanico," *Gerarchia* (May 1934).
13. Carlo Curcio, "Nazionalismo," *Dizionario di politica*, vol. 3, 241–42.
14. Mario Rivoire, "Il fascismo non è nazionalismo esagerato," *Dottrina fascista* (May 1939).
15. Carlo Costamagna, "Nazione," 265.
16. Id., "Nazionalità," *Dizionario di politica*, vol. 3, 249.

17. See Dino Cofrancesco, "Il mito europeo nel fascismo," *Storia contemporanea* (February 1983), 5 ff.

18. Walter Maturi, "Nazione, Storia del principio di nazionalità," *Enciclopedia italiana*, vol. 15 (Rome, 1934).

19. Ernesto Sestan, "Europa," *Dizionario di politica*, vol. 2, 119.

20. Augusto De Marsanich, *Civiltà di masse* (Rome, 1940), 333.

21. Istituto nazionale di cultura fascista. Primo convegno nazionale dei gruppi scientifici. Roma 23–26 November 1942. *I Tema. "Idea dell'Europa"* (Resoconto stenografico), bozze di stampa riservate per i collaboratori dell'INCF, 11.

22. Ibid., 48.

23. Ibid., 79–81.

24. Giuseppe Bottai, "Il problema della ricostruzione," quoted in Renzo De Felice, *Autobiografia del fascismo* (Rome, 1978), 553–66.

25. Fantasio Piccoli, "La Nazione e l'ordine nuovo," *Gerarchia* (July 1942).

26. Carlo Costamagna, "Nazionalità," *Dizionario di politica*, vol. 3, 249.

27. Carlo Morandi, "Equilibrio," *Dizionario di politica*, vol. 3, 57.

28. Giuseppe De Matteis, *Verso l'equilibrio della nuova Europa* (Florence, 1941), 160–61.

29. Carlo Curcio, "Di questa guerra," *Lo Stato* (August–September 1940).

30. Julius Evola, "Elementi dell'idea europea."

31. *Spunti (o motivi) della lezione inaugurale che il prof. Camillo Pellizzi si propone di tenere all'istituto italiano di cultura in Vienna il 7 novembre 1941, XIX su* "Tradizione e rivoluzipone nella cultura italiana contemporanea," in Archivio Pellizzi.

Chapter 11. The Fascist War

1. "La guerra mondiale per l'ordine nuovo," in *Due anni di guerra*, suppl. to "PNF Press Office Weekly Bulletin," year 2, 17.

2. Carlo Morandi, "Questa guerra e il Risorgimento," *Primato*, 1 April 1941.

3. Dino Pasini, "Parallelo fra la guerra del 1914 e quella odierna," *Gerarchia* (July 1940).

4. Giovanni Gentile, "Il Giappone guerriero."

5. "La guerra nella rivoluzione," *Civiltà fascista* (May 1941).

6. Sirus (pseud.), "Funzione imperiale delle ideologie," *Civiltà fascista* (January–February 1937).

7. Renato Famea, "Dalla «questione sociale» alla guerra-rivoluzione fascista," *Gerarchia* (September 1940).

8. *Nuova civiltà per la Nuova Europa* (Rome, 1942), xiv.

9. Quoted in "Punti di incontro," *Roma Fascista*, 24 July 1941.

10. Luigi Fontanelli, *Sentimento della rivoluzione* (Rome, 1941), 247. See Giuseppe Parlato, *Il sindacalismo fascista. II. Dalla «grande crisi» alla caduta del regime (1930–1943)* (Rome, 1989), 134 ff.

11. Emilio Dusi, "Le basi politiche del nuovo ordine europeo," *Il Campano* (March–April 1941), now in *Il Campano*, ed. Paolo Nello (Pisa, 1983), 289–91.

12. Vittorio Frosini, "I convegni di Catania e di Pescara. Evoluzione della coscienza politica europea," *Il Campano* (August 1941), now in *Il Campano*, ed. Paolo Nello, 302–6.

13. Mariano Pintus, "I giovani all'opposizione," *Roma Fascista*, 10 July 1941.

14. Pellizzi Archives.

15. Giuseppe Bottai, "Latinità e germanesimo," *Primato*, 1 January 1941.

16. Giovanni Selvi, "Il mito della razza," *Gerarchia* (October 1934).

17. Giuseppe Bianchini, "Mistica della razza ossia la religione come materia umana," *Il Campano* (May 1934), now in *Il Campano*, ed. Paolo Nello.

18. Carlo Costamagna, "Nazionalità," 249.

19. Ugoberto Alfassio Grimaldi, "Razza e nazione," *Civiltà fascista* (February 1943).

20. Delio Cantimori, "Nazionalsocialismo," *Dizionario di politica*, vol. 3, 250.

21. Carlo Costamagna, "Nazione," 263.

22. Carlo Costamagna, "Razza," *Dizionario di politica*, vol. 4, 26.

23. Ibid., 24.

24. Lorenzo La Via, *Popolo, nazione, nazionalità, razza, civiltà* (Rome, 1942), 80.

25. Ibid., 81 ff.

26. See Vincenzo Mazzei, *Razza e nazione* (Rome, 1942). On this book and the controversy that it caused in comparing different interpretations of Fascist racism, see Renzo De Felice, *Storia degli ebrei italiani sotto il fascismo*, 393 ff.

27. Aldo Capasso, "Corpo e spirito nel razzismo italiano," *Augustea*, 1–15 April 1942.

28. Camillo Pellizzi, "Italia e Germania. Problemi del nuovo ordine," *Civiltà fascista* (November–December 1941).

29. Antonino Pagliaro, "Politica," 449.

30. Aldo Capasso, "Corpo e spirito nel razzismo."

31. Camillo Pellizzi, *Principi e orientamenti della politica fascista. Schizzo di conferenza,* in Pellizzi Archives.

32. In 1941 Hitler forbade mention of the "German race," because that would have led to sacrificing the racial idea "in favor of the mere principle of nationality." Meanwhile, Himmler was setting up the "German SS" in various countries, asking its members to subordinate "your national ideal to the higher racial and historic ideal, the German Reich." See Hannah Arendt, *Le origini del totalitarismo*, Italian trans. (Milan, 1978), 565 note.

33. In April 1943, Giuseppe Bastianini put forward to Mussolini, who approved it, the text of an Italian-German statement in which the two countries affirmed that the future order of Europe would be enacted in respect of the principle of "national individuality" and state sovereignty. See Renzo De Felice, *Mussolini l'alleato 1940–1943*, vol. 1, book 1 (Turin, 1990), 458 ff.

34. Renzo Bertoli Salis, "Nazionalità e razza nell'ordine nuovo," *Dottrina fascista* (February–March 1942).

35. Francesco Orestano, "Del nuovo ordine europeo," *Gerarchia* (May 1943).

36. Giovanni Gentile, "Il Giappone guerriero." The italics are the author's.

37. Vincenzo Buonassisi, "La rivoluzione sul piano sociale," *Dottrina fascista* (October 1940–January 1941).

Chapter 12. The Failed Identity

1. For the observations of Renzo De Felice, see *Mussolini l'alleato 1940–1945,* vol. 1, book 2, 677–79.

2. Ugo Spirito, "La guerra rivoluzionaria," *Annali della Fondazione Ugo Spirito* (1989), 137–38.

3. See Emilio Gentile, *Il culto del littorio,* vi.

4. Renzo Bertoli Salis, *Nazionalità e razza nell'ordine nuovo.*

5. Ardengo Soffici-Giuseppe Prezzolini, *Diari 1939–1945* (Milan, 1962), 170.

6. Archivio Centrale dello Stato, Ministero della Cultura popolare, folder 32, file "Giuseppe Mastromattei," notes for the minister, 10 December 1942.

7. Yvon De Begnac, *Taccuini mussoliniani,* ed. Francesco Perfetti (Bologna, 1990), 39–40.

8. Galeazzo Ciano, *Diario,* 598.

9. It is interesting to note that the words "patria" and "patriottismo" were not included in the *Enciclopedia italiana* or in the *Dizionario di politica.* In the latter, the word *patria* referred the reader to the word *terra.*

10. Giovanni Gentile, "Discorso agli italiani," 24 June 1943, in Benedetto Gentile, *Giovanni Gentile* (Florence, 1954), 67.

11. Ibid., 72.

12. Ardengo Soffici-Giuseppe Prezzolini, *Diari 1939–1945,* 66.

13. Dino Grandi, *25 luglio. Quarant'anni dopo,* ed. Renzo De Felice (Bologna, 1983), 287.

14. Luigi Federzoni, *L'Italia di ieri per la storia di domani,* 300.

15. Piero Calamadrei, *Diario 1939–1945,* ed. Giorgio Agosti, vol. 2 (Florence, 1982), 145–46.

16. Pietro Nenni, *Vento del nord,* ed. Domenico Zucaro (Turin, 1978), 18.

17. Carlo Rosselli, *Scritti dell'esilio,* vol. 2, ed. Costanzo Casucci (Turin, 1992), 101.

18. Ibid., 354.

19. Id., *Scritti dell'esilio,* vol. 1, ed. Costanzo Casucci (Turin, 1988), 210.

20. Id., *Socialismo liberale,* ed. J. Rosselli (Turin, 1979), 134–35.

21. See Salvatore Sechi, "Togliatti e la questione nazionale: un pretesto per la legittimazione," *Storia contemporanea* (December, 1994), 983 ff.

22. Palmiro Togliatti, *Opere,* ed. Luciano Gruppi, vol. 5 (Rome, 1984), 205.

23. Carlo Bozzi, *La tragedia degli italiani* (Rome, 1947), 29.

24. Adolfo Omodeo, *Libertà e storia. Scritti e discorsi politici* (Turin, 1960), 62.

25. Benedetto Croce, *Scritti e discorsi politici (1943–1947),* vol. 1 (Bari, 1973), 51.

26. Mario Albertini, *Lo stato nazionale* (Naples, 1980), 10.
27. Giovanni Gentile, "Ripresa," *Nuova Antologia*, 1 January 1944.

Chapter 13. Where Is Italy?

1. See Domenico Bartoli, *8 settembre 1943. l'Italia si arrende* (Milan, 1983); Elena Aga Rossi, *Una nazione allo sbando* (Bologna, 1993).
2. Pietro Nenni, *Diari 1943–1956,* ed. Giuliana Nenni e Domenico Zucaro (Milan, 1981), 38.
3. Leo Longanesi, *In piedi e seduti* (Milano, 1948), 216.
4. Vittorio Bachelet, "I maestri, i giovani e la storia," *Studium* (March 1952).
5. Corrado Alvaro, *L'Italia rinunzia* (Palermo, 1986), 41.
6. Benedetto Croce, *Scritti e discorsi politici (1943–1947),* vol. 1 (Bari, 1973), 223–24.
7. Ugo La Malfa, "Per la rinascita dell'Italia," *Quaderni del partito d'azione* (n.p., n.d.), 4.
8. Salvatore Satta, *De profundis* (Milan, 1980), 182. The idea of the "death of the country" after September 8 was taken up again from a historical point of view by Renzo De Felice, *Rosso e nero,* ed. Pasquale Chessa (Milan, 1995), and by Ernesto Galli Della Loggia, *La morte della patria* (Rome-Bari, 1996).
9. Salvatore Satta, *De profundis,* 16–17.
10. Piero Calamandrei, *Diario 1939–1945,* vol. 2, 284.
11. Ibid., 154–55.
12. See Claudio Pavone, *Una guerra civile* (Turin, 1991), 169–220.
13. Giovanni Gentile, "Ricostruire," *Corriere della Sera,* 28 December 1943.
14. Dante Livio Bianco, *Guerra partigiana* (Turin, 1954), 7–10.
15. Tullio Giannetti, "È necessario parlare chiaro," *La Stampa,* 4 February 1944.
16. Giovanni Gentile, "Ricostruire."
17. "Vita nuova," *Il Campano,* 10 November 1943.
18. See Maria Fraddosio, "Per l'onore della Patria. Le origini ideologiche della militanza femminile nella RSI," *Storia contemporanea* (December 1993), 1155 ff.
19. *Lettere di caduti della Repubblica sociale* (Milan, 1960), 193.
20. Ibid., 76.
21. Tullio Giannetti, "Guerra di popolo e non lotta di partito," *La Stampa,* 16 February 1944.
22. See Sergio Cotta, *La Resistenza come e perché* (Rome, 1994), 99 ff.; Angelo Ventura, "La Resistenza nella storia d'Italia," in *Mezzo secolo fa. Guerra e resistenza in provincia di Varese* (Milan, 1995), 17 ff.
23. Palmiro Togliatti, *Opere,* vol. 4., ed. Franco Andreucci and Paolo Spriano (Rome, 1979), book 2, 485.
24. Piero Calamandrei, *Diario,* 154–55.

25. Sergio Cotta, *La Resistenza,* 101.

26. See Claudio Pavone, *La guerra civile,* 179–80.

27. *Lettere di condannati a morte della Resistenza italiana,* ed. Piero Malvezzi and Giovanni Pirelli (Milan, 1965).

28. Ibid., 27.

29. Ibid., 31.

30. Ibid., 65.

31. Ibid., 83.

32. Ibid., 160.

33. Leo Valiani, *Tutte le strade conducono a Roma* (Florence, 1947), 357.

34. Pietro Nenni, *Vento del Nord,* 38–39.

35. Franco Calamandrei, *La vita indivisibile. Diario 1941–1947* (Rome, 1984), 131.

36. Alfredo Pizzoni, *Alla guida del CLNAI* (Turin, 1986), 16.

37. Ibid., 278–79.

38. Corrado Alvaro, *Quasi una vita* (Milan, 1986), 327–28.

39. Alba De Cespedes, "Pagine di diario," *Mercurio* (December 1944).

40. Piero Calamandrei, *Diario,* 259–60.

41. Ibid., 270.

42. Pietro Nenni, *Vento del nord.*

43. Piero Calamandrei, *Diario,* 220.

44. Corrado Alvaro, *Quasi una vita,* 296.

45. Ibid., 345.

46. Curzio Malaparte, *La pelle* (Florence, 1969), 10.

47. Pietro Nenni, *Vento del nord,* 141.

48. Lorenzo Barbaro, "L'Italia perduta," *Il Risorgimento liberale,* 31 October 1944.

49. Corrado Alvaro, *Quasi una vita,* 393.

50. Curzio Malaparte, *La pelle,* 28.

51. Corrado Alvaro, *Quasi una vita,* 341–42.

52. Ibid., 341–43, 354.

53. Guido De Ruggiero, "Questo popolo. La crisi morale," *La Nuova Europa,* 8 April 1945.

54. Ignazio Silone, "Come ricostruire? (appunti per un dialogo tra socialisti e cattolici)," *Mercurio* (May 1945).

55. Pietro Barbieri, *Il travaglio della democrazia italiana 1943–1947* (Rome, 1948), 69–72.

56. Ranuccio Bianchi Bandinelli, *Dal diario di un borghese* (Milan, 1962), 114.

57. Piero Calamandrei, *Diario,* vol. 1, 223.

58. Corrado Alvaro, *Ultimo diario (1948–1956)* (Milan, 1959), 161.

59. Ibid., 28.

60. *Diario 1945 di Nicolò Carandini,* ed. di G. Filippone-Thaulero, in *Nuova Antologia,* January–March 1983, 217–18.

61.   Fabio Cusin, *L'Italiano. Realtà e illusioni* (Rome, 1945); Giorgio Fenoaltea, *Storia degli italieschi dalle origini ai giorni nostri* (Florence, 1945); Ranuccio Bianchi Bandinelli, *Tre (tentativi di) diagnosi,* in id., *Dal diario di un borghese;* Silvio Guarnieri, *Il carattere degli italiani* (Turin, 1948); Giuseppe Prezzolini, *The Legacy of Italy* (New York, 1948) (Italian trans. *L'Italia finisce,* Milan, 1981).

62.   Fabio Cusin, *L'Italiano,* 36.

63.   Giuseppe Prezzolini, *L'Italia finisce,* 24.

64.   Giorgio Fenoaltea, *Storia degli italieschi,* 20.

65.   Ibid., 52.

66.   Ibid., 24–25.

67.   Ibid., 185.

68.   Fabio Cusin, *L'Italiano,* 110.

69.   Ranuccio Bianchi Bandinelli, *Dal diario,* 114.

70.   Francesco Flora, "Quel che ha rovinato l'Italia," *Mercurio* (January 1946).

71.   Giovanni Ansaldo, *Diario di prigionia,* ed. Renzo De Felice (Bologna, 1993), 32.

72.   Ibid., 81.

73.   Quoted in Pietro Scoppola, *La repubblica dei partiti* (Bologna, 1991), 90.

74.   Giacomo Perticone, *La democrazia in Italia* (Rome, 1946), 96.

75.   Mario Albertini, *L'amore dell'Italia e l'Europa,* in *Lo Stato Moderno,* nn.18–19, 1947.

Chapter 14. Pull the Idol Down

1.   Paolo Santarcangeli, "Decadenza del nazionalismo," *Mercurio* (July 1949).

2.   Ibid.

3.   Corrado Alvaro, "Dopoguerra," *Mercurio* (November–December 1946).

4.   Edward H. Carr, *Nationalism and After* (New York, 1946).

5.   *Nazionalismo e oltre* (Milan, 1947), 51.

6.   Ibid., 75.

7.   *Nations ou Fédéralisme* (Paris, 1946), i.

8.   Alberto Moravia, "La Borghesia," in *Dopo il diluvio. Sommario dell'Italia contemporanea,* ed. Dino Terra (Cernusco sul Naviglio, 1947), 214.

9.   Alberto Savinio, *Sorte dell'Europa* (Milano, 1977), 55.

10.   Giovanni Ansaldo, *Diario di prigionia,* 36.

11.   Roberto Ducci, *Questa Italia* (Milan, 1948), 193–94.

12.   Augusto Monti, *Realtà del partito d'azione* (Turin, 1945), 24.

13.   Paolo Santarcangeli, "Decadenza del nazionalismo," *Mercurio* (July 1949).

14.   Guido De Ruggiero, *Il ritorno alla ragione* (Bari, 1946), 202.

15.   Ibid., 69–70.

16. Ibid., 135–36.

17. Ibid., 70.

18. Ibid., 203.

19. Arturo Carlo Jemolo, "Fine del nazionalismo," *Comunità*, 29 November 1947.

20. Antonio Messineo, "La coesistenza nell'errore. l'errore nazionalista," *La Civiltà Cattolica*, 26 November 1955.

21. *Mercurio* (November–December 1946).

22. Silvio Trentin, *Stato nazionale federalismo* (Milan, 1945 [illegal edition]), 10.

23. Ibid., 16.

24. Ibid., 40–41.

25. Ibid., 23.

26. Ibid., 71–72.

27. Ibid., 107–8.

28. Ibid., 204.

29. Ibid., 110–11.

30. Paolo Santarcangeli, "Decadenza del nazionalismo," *Mercurio* (July 1949), 243.

31. Alberto Savinio, *Sorte dell'Europa*, 21–22.

32. "Federarsi o perire," *L'Italia libera* (Lombard edition), 20 October 1944.

33. Giampiero Carocci, "Superamento della nazione," *La Nuova Europa*, 14 October 1945.

34. Altiero Spinelli, *La crisi degli Stati nazionali. Germania, Italia, Francia*, ed. Lucio Levi (Bologna, 1991), 47.

35. Ibid., 74.

36. Guido De Ruggiero, *Il ritorno alla ragione*, 191–92.

37. Mariano Maresca, "Stato democratico e stato nazionale," *La Nuova Europa*, 23 September 1945, all of the citations.

38. Agostino Trabalza, "Nazionalità e nazionalismo," *La nuova Europa*, 19 March 1946.

Chapter 15. In Search of a Fatherland

1. Benedetto Croce, *Storia d'Europa nel secolo decimonono* (Bari, 1964[11]), 370.

2. Movimento Liberale Italiano, *Per una federazione economica europea* (n.p., 1943), 7–8.

3. Luigi Einaudi, "La sovranità è indivisibile?" *Risorgimento liberale*, 22 June 1945.

4. Vincenzo Mazzei, *La repubblica dei repubblicani* (Rome, 1947), 23–25.

5. Adolfo Omodeo, *Libertà e storia*, 61.

6. Manlio Rossi Doria, *Il problema politico italiano e il Partito d'Azione* (Rome, n.d.), 30.

7. "Federarsi o perire," *L'Italia libera*, 20 October 1944.

8. Giuseppe Dossetti, *Scritti politici* (Genoa, 1995), 314–15.

9. Ibid., 359.

10. Ibid., 273–74.

11. "Per una democrazia cristiana europea" (2), *Cronache sociali*, n.21 (1949).

12. "La democrazia cristiana e l'unità europea" (1), *Cronache sociali*, n.20 (1949).

13. Valentino Marafini, "Una distinzione necessaria. «Partigiani» e «Patrioti»," *il partigiano*, 4 September 1944.

14. Bruno Valerj, "Il partigiano della libertà e la patria," *il partigiano*, 18 December 1944.

15. "Unione nazionale e federalismo europeo," *L'Italia libera* (Lombard edition), 10 August 1944.

16. "I movimenti di resistenza e l'unità europea," *L'Italia libera* (Lombard edition), 10 August 1944.

17. "Non solamente anticomunisti," *L'Uomo qualunque*, 18 July 1945, quoted in Giuseppe Parlato, "La nazione qualunque. Riformismo amministrativo ed europeismo in Guglielmo Giannini," *Storia contemporanea* (December 1994), 1144.

18. Guglielmo Giannini, *La Folla* (Rome, 1945), 119.

19. Movimento Liberale Italiano, *Primi chiarimenti* (n.p., 1943), 15.

20. Giorgio Fenoaltea, *Sei tesi sulla guerra con note per i fascisti onesti* (Florence, 1944), 215–16.

21. Benedetto Croce, *Scritti e discorsi politici*, vol. 1, 95–97.

22. Benedetto Croce, "L'amore verso la patria e i doveri verso lo Stato" (1947) in id., *Filosofia e storiografia* (Bari, 1949), 241–45.

23. V. Migliorati, "A servizio della patria," *La Civiltà Cattolica*, vol. 2 (1946).

24. Aldo Moro, *Scritti e discorsi*, ed. Giuseppe Rossini, vol. 1 (Rome, 1982), 26.

25. Ibid., 55–57.

26. Ibid., 193–96.

27. Palmiro Togliatti, *Opere*, vol. 5, 304–5.

28. Arturo Carlo Jemolo, *Fine del nazionalismo*.

29. Fausto Montanari, "Patria e concezione politica universale," *Civitas*, n.5 (1950).

Chapter 16. A Great but Small Nation

1. Augusto Monti, *Realtà del partito d'azione*, 51.

2. Francesco Calasso, *Cronache politiche di uno storico (1944–1948)* (Florence, 1975), 186–87.

3. "Separatismo siciliano," *Risorgimento liberale*, 23 September 1944.

4. Benedetto Croce, *Scritti e discorsi politici*, vol. 2, 324.

5. Ibid., 370.

6. Palmiro Togliatti, *Opere*, vol. 5, 257–58.

7. Ibid., 180–82.

8. Ibid., 181.

9. Ibid., 206–7.

10. *La Costituzione della Repubblica nei lavori della Assemblea Costituente*, vol. 3 (Rome, 1970), 2011.

11. Pietro Nenni, *Discorsi parlamentari (1946–1979)* (Rome, 1983), 27.

12. Ibid., 29.

13. *Atti e documenti della Democrazia cristiana (1943–1967)*, ed. Andrea Damilano, vol. 1 (Rome, 1968), 134.

14. Alcide De Gasperi, *Discorsi politici*, ed. Tommaso Bozza (Rome, 1969), 297.

15. Carlo Sforza, *Panorama europeo. Apparenze politiche e realtà psicologiche* (Rome, 1945), 93.

16. Eugenio Di Carlo, "Un avversario del principio di nazionalità," *La Nuova Europa*, 8 July 1945.

17. Benedetto Croce, *Scritti e discorsi*, vol. 2, 101–2.

18. Ibid., 83.

19. Federico Chabod, *L'idea di nazione* (Bari, 1967), and id., *Storia dell'idea di Europa* (Bari, 1967). The subject was taken up again and widely developed by Chabod in *Storia della politica estera italiana*.

20. Id., *L'idea di nazione*, 66–68.

21. Id., *Storia della politica estera italiana*, 136–37.

22. Id., *L'idea di nazione*, 81.

23. Ibid., 135.

24. Ibid., 75–76.

25. Ibid., 135.

26. Ferdinando Vegas, "Principio di nazionalità e nazionalismo," *Stato moderno*, nn.16 and 17 (1946), all citations.

27. See Renato Moro, "Il «modernismo buono». La «modernizzazione cattolica» tra fascismo e postfascismo come problema storiografico," *Storia contemporanea* (August 1988), 625 ff.

28. *Nazione e comunità internazionale* (Rome, 1954), 156–58.

29. "Messaggio natalizio di S. S. Pio XII sulla pacifica coesistenza dei popoli del mondo" (24 December 1954), *La Civiltà Cattolica*, vol. 1 (1955).

30. Luigi Sturzo, *Nazionalismo e internazionalismo (1946)* (Bologna, 1971), 21.

31. Ibid., 10–11.

32. Ibid., xvi.

33. *Nazione e comunità internazionale*, 22.

34. Ibid., 18.

35. Federazione Universitaria Cattolica Italiana, *Nazione e prospettive sopranazionali* (Rome, 1954).

36. Ibid., 123.

37. Ibid., 89.

38. Ibid., 94–95.

39. Ibid., 99.

40. Adolfo Omodeo, *Libertà e storia*, 61.

41. Movimento Liberale Italiano, *Primi chiarimenti* (n.p., 1943), 11.

42. Ibid., 13–15.

43. Francesco Fancello, *Il Partito d'Azione nei suoi metodi e nei suoi fini* (Rome, 1944), 33.

44. Alcide De Gasperi, *La democrazia cristiana e il momento politico* (n.p., n.d.), 33.

45. Giuseppe Castelli Avolio, "Lotta di partiti e rinnovamento morale," *Il Commento*, 1 December 1944.

46. La Direzione, "Per un'Italia migliore," *La Civiltà Cattolica*, vol. 2 (1946).

47. Pietro Barbieri, *Il travaglio della democrazia italiana*, 231.

48. Corrado Alvaro, *L'Italia rinunzia*, 93.

49. Ibid., 73.

50. Corrado Alvaro, *L'Italia rinunzia*, 92.

51. Giovanni Taranto, "L'ora presente e il dovere dei giovani," *Il Commento*, 1 January 1946.

52. Riccardo Bauer, "La posizione e la funzione internazionale dell'Italia," *Mercurio* (January 1946).

53. Giuseppe Dossetti, *Costituzione e Resistenza* (Rome, 1995), 79.

54. Palmiro Togliatti, *Opere*, vol. 5, 254.

Chapter 17. A Myth for the Republic

1. Corrado Alvaro, "Repubblica Italiana," *Mercurio* (March–April 1946).

2. Alba De Cespedes, "In casa e fuori," *Mercurio* (March–April 1946).

3. Vittorio De Caprariis, "Scritti," 3, *Momenti di storia italiana nel '900*, ed. Tarcisio Amato and Maurizio Griffo (Messina, 1986), 99–107.

4. Francesco Calasso, *Cronache politiche*, 48.

5. Luigi Salvatorelli, "Italia libera e una," *La Nuova Europa*, 6 May 1945.

6. Alcide De Gasperi, *Discorsi parlamentar*, vol. 1 (Rome, 1985), 87.

7. Archivio Camera dei Deputati, Assemblea Costituente, Incarto di Segreteria, busta 136.

8. *La costituzione della repubblica nei lavori preparatori della Assemblea Costituente*, vol. 3 (Rome, 1970), 1849.

9. "Due giugno," *Corriere della Sera*, 1 June 1947.

10. See Mario Toscano, "Dalla democrazia risorgimentale all'Italia nuova: il Partito Repubblicano Italiano e il problema della nazione (1943–1946)," *Storia contemporanea* (December 1994), 1059 ff.

11. See Cesare Degli Occhi, Piero Operti, *Il partito nazionale monarchico* (Milan, 1958).

12. Mario Ferrara, "Sentimento nazionale," *Risorgimento Liberale*, 19 August 1945.

13. Mario Nigro, "I giovani e il fascismo," *Il Commento*, 16 March 1945.

14. Palmiro Togliatti, *Opere*, vol. 4, book 2, 145–46.
15. Id., *Opere*, vol. 5, 35.
16. Ibid., 298.
17. Camillo Pellizzi, "Elementi per un riepilogo," *ABC*, 16 June 1953.

Chapter 18. The Italies of Republican Italy

1. Carlo Costamagna, "Il partito della patria," *La Rivolta Ideale*, 14 September 1950.
2. Movimento Sociale Italiano, "Programma elettorale," *La Lotta Politica*, 11 April 1953.
3. Carlo Costamagna, "Il partito della patria," *La Rivolta Ideale*, 14 September 1950.
4. Giorgio Almirante, Francesco Palamenghi-Crispi, *Il Movimento Sociale italiano* (Milan, n.d.), 122.
5. Movimento Sociale Italiano, "Programma elettorale," 4.
6. Augusto De Marsanich, "Il nostro nazionalismo," *La Lotta politica*, 3 December 1949.
7. Giorgio Almirante, Francesco Palamenghi-Crispi, *Il Movimento Sociale Italiano*, 119.
8. Anacleto Del Massa, "Nazionalismo perenne," *La Lotta Politica*, 5 December 1953.
9. Gioacchino Volpe, *L'Italia che fu come un italiano la vide, sentì, amò* (Rome, 1960), 361.
10. Gioacchino Volpe, *Italia moderna 1815–1898* (Florence, 1973), x–xi.
11. Mario Buonajuto, "Socialismo e nazione," *Mondo Operaio* (June 1986).
12. Palmiro Togliatti, *Opere*, vol. 4, book 2, 405.
13. Mario Montagnana, "Nell'interesse della Nazione," *Rinascita*, n.7 (1946).
14. Palmiro Togliatti, *Opere*, vol. 5, 79.
15. Ibid., 118.
16. Mario Montagnana, "L'eredità di Antonio Gramsci," *L'Unità*, 27 April 1947.
17. Antonio Gramsci, *Quaderni del carcere*, vol. 3, ed. Valentino Gerratana (Turin, 1975), 1988–89.
18. Giulio Bollati, *L'Italiano*, 196–97.
19. Palmiro Togliatti, *Opere*, vol. 4, 395.
20. Id., *Opere*, vol. 5, 56.
21. Ibid., 301.
22. Ibid., 184.
23. Ibid., 56.
24. Ibid., 299.
25. Ibid., 216–17.
26. Ibid., 212–13.

27. "Il 25 febbraio del '48," *L'Unità,* 25 February 1958.

28. Palmiro Togliatti, *Opere,* vol. 4, 320.

29. Id., *Opere,* vol. 5, 131–32.

30. *Atti e documenti,* 134.

31. Ibid., 233.

32. Aldo Moro, *Scritti e discorsi 1940–1947,* 215–17.

33. Ibid., 109–11.

34. Alcide De Gasperi, *Discorsi parlamentari,* vol. 2, 793.

35. Ibid., 1154.

36. Ibid., 784.

37. *Atti e documenti,* 491.

38. Alcide De Gasperi, *Discorsi politici,* 281.

39. Ibid., 299.

40. Id., *Discorsi parlamentari,* vol. 1, 356.

41. Id., *Discorsi politici,* 202.

42. Ibid., 142–43.

43. Ibid., 334.

44. Alcide De Gasperi, *Discorsi parlamentari,* vol. 2, 893.

45. Id., *Discorsi politici,* 621–22.

46. *Atti e documenti,* 33.

47. *Il Popolo,* 24 April 1945.

48. Francesco Maria Dominedò, "Democrazia nazionale," *Il Popolo,* 27 April 1948.

49. Piero Malvestiti, "La ragione della libertà," *Il Popolo,* 25 April 1948.

50. "La libertà è la premessa della giustizia sociale," *Il Popolo,* 27 April 1948.

51. Alcide De Gasperi, *Discorsi politici,* 436.

52. Ibid., 118.

53. Ibid., 454.

54. Quoted in Ennio Di Nolfo, *Le paure e le speranze degli italiani (1943–1953)* (Milan, 1986), 199.

55. Riccardo Lombardi, "L'ora presente e l'Italia," *La Civiltà Cattolica,* vol. 1 (1947).

56. A. Oddone, "Il Papato e l'indipendenza e libertà d'Italia," *La Civiltà Cattolica,* vol. 4 (1949).

57. D. Mondrone, "Colei che salverà l'Italia," *La Civiltà Cattolica,* vol. 1 (1948).

58. Id., "La consacrazione dell'Italia al cuore immacolato di Maria," *La Civiltà Cattolica,* vol. 3 (1959).

59. Riccardo Lombardi, "L'ora presente e l'Italia," *La Civiltà Cattolica,* vol. 1 (1947).

60. La Direzione, "Per un'Italia migliore," *La Civiltà Cattolica,* vol. 2 (1946).

61. Riccardo Lombardi, "L'ora presente e l'Italia," *La Civiltà Cattolica,* vol. 1 (1947).

62. Palmiro Togliatti, *Opere*, vol. 5, 488.
63. Ibid., 381.
64. Alcide De Gasperi, *Discorsi parlamentari*, vol. 2, 780–81.
65. Arturo Carlo Jemolo, *La crisi dello Stato moderno* (Bari, 1954), 160–61.
66. See Gian Enrico Rusconi, *Se cessiamo di essere una nazione* (Bologna, 1993); id., *Resistenza e postfascismo* (Bologna, 1995).
67. Mario Ferrara, "Nuovi orientamenti," *Nuova Antologia*. August 1949.
68. Arturo Carlo Jemolo, *Società civile*, 511.
69. Primo Mazzolari, "Ritorniamo italiani," *Adesso*, 15 March 1949.
70. Primo Mazzolari, "Patria terra di nessuno," *Adesso*, 15 July 1950.
71. Altiero Spinelli, *La crisi degli stati nazionali*, 239.
72. Ibid., 260.
73. Ugo D'Andrea, "Il vuoto del «Centenario»," *Il Borghese*, 16 March 1961.

Conclusion: The Jubilee of the Simulacrum

1. Ugo D'Andrea, "Il vuoto del «Centenario»."
2. "1911–1961," *La Stampa*, 7 May 1961.
3. *La celebrazione del primo centenario dell'Unità d'Italia* (Turin, 1961), xxxii.
4. Ibid., ix.
5. Ibid., 43–51.
6. Ibid., 81–82 for all of the quotations.
7. Ibid., 75.
8. Ibid., 51.
9. Ibid., 95.
10. Sigma, "Lezione di umiltà e di fiducia," *Studium*, April 1961.
11. Ibid.
12. Angelo Narducci, "Uniti attraverso le sventure," *Il Popolo*, 27 March 1961.
13. Sigma, "Cento anni di esperienza unitaria," *Studium* (March 1961).
14. Salvatore Lener, "Nell'anno secolare dell'unità d'Italia," *La Civiltà Cattolica*, vol. 1 (1961).
15. p.s., "Italia '61," *Rinascita* (June 1961).
16. "Siamo tutti italiani?" *L'Unità*, 9 May 1961.
17. Palmiro Togliatti, "Il centenario dell'unità," *L'Unità*, 26 March 1961, all of the citations.
18. Rosario Romeo, "Gli abusi feudali," *Il Mondo*, 25 July 1961.
19. Eva Omodeo Zona, "Il Risorgimento sotto processo," *Nord e Sud* (June 1961).
20. "Il risorgimento fu un'altra cosa," *Il Mondo*, 28 March 1961.
21. "Un sindaco impudente," *Il Mondo*, 4 April 1961.
22. "Il Papa, Fanfani e l'unità," *Il Mondo*, 25 April 1961.
23. Vittorio De Caprariis, "Senza eredi," *Il Mondo*, 11 April 1961.
24. Ibid.

25. *La celebrazione del primo centenario,* 75.

26. "Italia '61," *Il Mondo,* 16 May 1961.

27. Gina Borghese Provasi, "Alla ricerca di una tradizione," *Studium* (September 1961).

28. Ug o D'Andrea, "Il vuoto del «Centenario»."

29. *La celebrazione del primo centenario,* 191.

30. Domenico Bartoli, "Italia centenaria," *Corriere della Sera,* 18 April 1961.

31. Ibid.

32. "1911–1961," *La Stampa,* 7 May 1961.

33. "Centenario dell'unità," *Studium* (June 1961).

34. Rosario Romeo, "Gli abusi feudali."

35. Corrado Pecci, "Roma dei Mille e l'Italia '61," *Il Borghese,* 27 April 1961.

36. *Corriere della Sera,* 28 March 1961.

37. Domenico Bartoli, *Italia centenaria.*

38. Ibid.

39. f.m., "Patria e Pace," *Studium* (May 1957).

40. Giancarlo Zizola, "Patria e patrie," *Studium* (October 1960).

41. Ibid.

42. Arturo Carlo Jemolo, *Società civile,* 111.

43. Domenico Bartoli, "Patriottismo," *Corriere della Sera,* 20 April 1959.

ILLUSTRATIONS CREDITS

The Fry Collection of Italian History and Culture, courtesy of the
    Department of Special Collections, Memorial Library, University
    of Wisconsin–Madison: pages 131, 140, 269, 271 (top), 272 (top and
    bottom), 273, 274, 275.
*The Exhibition of 1911 Torino, Florence, Rome: Illustrated Periodical of the
    Temporary Exhibit in the Three Capitals for the Solemn Jubilee of the "Regno
    d'Italia"* compiled by Guido Treves (Milan: Fratelli Treves Editore, 1911):
    pages 132, 133, 134 (top and bottom).
The collection of John Tortorice: pages 135, 136, 137, 138, 139, 270.
The Richard Vowles Collection, courtesy of the Department of Special
    Collections, Memorial Library, University of Wisconsin–Madison:
    page 271 (bottom).

INDEX

Action Party, *xiii*, 219, 237, 244–45, 252, 258–59, 279, 292, 294

Alatri, Paolo, 241

Albertini, Mario, 208

Alberto, Carlo, 10–11

Alfani, Augusto, 37

Alfieri, Vittorio, 35

Alvaro, Carrado, 212, 221, 222, 223, 225, 232, 293–94, 296

Amendola, Giovanni, 87, 89, 90, 97, 107, 115

anarchism, 47, 90

Ansaldo, Giovanni, 51, 229, 236

anthem, national, *vii, viii, xi–xii*

anti-Fascism: antinationalism linked to, 237; Catholics and, 120, 162, 262–63, 289; civil war and, 80, 215–19, 221; communism and, 218, 317, 328–29; cult of fatherland and, 206, 217, 237; "denationalization" of anti-Fascists under Fascism, 165, 207; factionalism and disintegration of, 330–31; freedom and, 221–22; as heterogeneous coalition of parties, 219, 250, 257–58, 279, 301–2, 305, 317, 328–31; humanist nationalism and, 115; imperialism rejected by, 205; myth of nation and, 205–6, 214–21, 237, 297, 299–303; patriotism and, 214–21, 330–31; and perceived weakness of Italian character,

223–25, 228; rebuilding of national state and, 225, 310–11, 334; regeneration project of, 292–95; rejection of responsibility for war by, 204–7, 222, 266; the Resistance and, 206, 219, 292, 297, 299, 330–31, 332–33, 334

"anti-Italian" moralists, 227–28

antinationalism: anti-Fascism linked to, 237; of Catholics or the Church, 119, 240–41, 319; Croce and, 90; decentralization and, 242–43, 250; defeat during WW II and, 208–9, 222, 236–37; fatherland concept and, 260–67; federalism and, 241–44; myth of nation and, 74–75, 233–35, 237–40, 244–49; national pride and, 237, 239, 259–60; patriotism rejected by, 257–60; *Qualunquismo* and, 259–60, 300; universalism and, 255, 257–58, 264–67, 300, 318, 352

anti-Semitism, 166, 190–91

Anzilotti, Antonio, 107, 108

authoritarianism, 108; authoritarian nationalism, 242–43, 286; imperialism and, 94, 99, 105, 155; monarchy and, 5, 14, 49; nationalism and, 242. *See also* Fascism; National Socialism

the avant garde, 58, 82–84, 89–90

Avolio, Giuseppe Castelli, 293

Axis powers, 233

Jesuits, 55, 117–18, 241, 327

John XXIII, 340

Jubilee celebrations of the nation (1911), x, 3, 10–13, 46; dedication of monument to "founding fathers" during, 10, 51–55, 57, 59, *134;* exhibition pictured, *134;* as patriotic ceremony, 52–53; protests and demonstrations during, 56, 345; resistance to monarchic state and objection to, 55–58; universal value of Italian revolution as theme of, 40–41

justice: coexistence of free nations as formula for, 24

Labor Charter (*Carta del Lavoro* of Fascism), 157, 159

labor unions, 76

Labriola, Arturo, 76, 80

La Malfa, Ugo, 213

land (*paese*): conflated with nation and fatherland, 25; fatherland (*patria*) as distinct from, 26

language: national identity and, 28–29, 122

La Nuova Europa (periodical), 246, 247–48, 253, 284, 297

La Via, Lorenzo, 193

"La Voce" group, 83, 107–12, 127

La Voce (newspaper), 58, 89, 107

League of Nations, 176–77, 232

Leone, Enrico, 124–25

Leopardi, Giacomo, 33–34

liberalism or Liberal Party, 111, 152, 260, 334, 345, 353–54; Catholic opposition to the liberal state, 53, 55–56, 71, 116, 117–18, 325, 327; civic and economic progress linked to liberal state, 72–73, 83–84; democratization and, 72; establishment of liberal political regime, 4–5; federalism and, 252; freedom and nation linked in, 48–50; liberal socialism, 206;

Libyan war and crisis of the liberal state, 66–68; modernity and progress linked to liberal state, 72–73, 83–84; monarchy and support of, 6, 8; nation perceived as distinct from nationalism, 284–85; national myth and, 70–74, 78–81, 219; patriotism and, 55–56; principle of nationality and, 96; regeneration project of, 292; as relative success compared to Fascism, 201; Risorgimento traditions and, 300–302; statism and, 252, 255, 280; unitary nation and, 279–81

libertarianism, 90, 149–50

Libya, 6, 8, 62, 65–68, 76, 104, 110–11, 119–20

Lomonaco, Francesco, 35

Longanesi, Leo, 211

l'Uomo qualunque (man-in-the-street movement), *xiii,* 259–60, 300

Luzzatti, Luigi, 13

Machiavellianism, 199, 225–26, 227–28

Maggiore, Giuseppe, 158–59

Malagodi, Olindo, 94–95

Malaparte, Curzio, 223

Mancini, Pasquale Stanislao, 23, 25, 286

man-in-the-street movement (*Qualunquismo*), *xiii,* 259–60, 300

Maraviglia, Maurizio, 156–57

Maresca, Mariano, 246–47

Marinetti, Filippo Tommaso, 90

Mastromattei, Giuseppe, 200–201

Maturi, Walter, 176

Mazzini, Giuseppe, 313; concept of nation of, 19–25, 128; and faith in Italian supremacy or universality, 41–42; as founder of Risorgimento and national hero, 10–14, 40–42, 47–48; Giovanni Gentile and, 159, 161, 165, 173; humanitarian nationalism linked to, 76; monarchy opposed by,

during WW II as destructive of, 230; as political rather than cultural, 19; pride and, 43; provincial or regional identity and, 109–10; as racial, 77–78

National Institute of Fascist Culture, 178, 185

nationalism: as assertion of supremacy, *xiv;* and civil war, 78–81; as compatible with left-wing values, 112–13; competing ideologies and formulations of, 75, 78–81, 83; as distinct from nationality, 284; Fascism and, 285; "good" *vs.* "bad" nationalisms, *xiv,* 248; imperialism and, 241; intolerance of minorities linked to, 240; modernity and unified national identity, 21–22; myth of nation and, 239–40, 248; patriotism compared and contrasted with, *xiv,* 239, 261; *Qualunquismo* and rejection of, 259–60, 300; rhetoric of, *ix, xi;* rise of Fascism linked to climate of, 235–36; as rudimentary stage of political development, 247; sacralization of ("religion of the fatherland"), 10–11, 14, 22, 52–53; Socialism as compatible with, 121–26; use of term, *xiii–xiv,* 75; war and cultivation of, 238, 241; WW II and decline of European, 231–35, 237–38

nationality: Catholic critiques of, 240–41; conflated with nation and fatherland, 25, 248, 249; as distinct from nationalism, 284; evolving meaning of, 27–29, 69; freedom linked to, 287; imperialism and, 97, 120, 176–77; industrial civilization and rejection of, 95; Mazzini's concept of, 23, 24–25; racial constructions of, 69, 240; as rational basis for the rights of peoples, 23; supranational aspirations and rejection of, 178, 187,

233–34, 290–91, 308; value of principle of, 284; WW I linked to concept of, 68

National Liberal group, 111

National Socialism (Nazism): Fascism's ideological differences with, 163, 181–82, 188–89, 190, 192, 195–96; Fascism's similarity to, 143, 217–18, 266, 309–10; nationalism as barrier to Resistance movements, 258–59; as political ally of Fascist Italy, 182, 188–89, 217–18; racism and, 166, 189–90

national state: antinationalism and rejection of, 239–44

nationhood: competing views of, 55–56; human dignity and, 21–22

naturalism: Fascism and rejection of, 157, 159–62, 192, 194; nation and nationalism as naturalistic, 31, 98, 100, 102, 155, 157, 159–62, 192, 242, 286; racism and, 191, 194

nazione (nation), *ix, x,* 25–26; use of term, 28

Nenni, Pietro, 204–5, 211, 220–21, 222, 223, 282–83, 311

neo-Fascism, *ix,* 226, 236, 260, 288, 300–303, 307–10, 317

neo-Guelph movement, 19, 325

Niceforo, Alfredo, 33

Nigro, Mario, 303–4

Nitti, Francesco, 6, 84

North Atlantic Treaty Organization (NATO), 310, 311, 329

North/South geographic regions, 56, 279, 281

Olivetti, Angelo Oliviero, 76

Omodeo, Adolfo, 65, 80–81, 207, 252, 292

Orano, Paolo, 170

Orestano, Francesco, 196

Oriani, Alfredo, 5–6, 62, 84, 88

GEORGE L. MOSSE SERIES
IN MODERN EUROPEAN CULTURAL AND
INTELLECTUAL HISTORY

Series Editors

Stanley G. Payne, David J. Sorkin, and John S. Tortorice

Of God and Gods: Egypt, Israel, and the Rise of Monotheism
Jan Assmann

Collected Memories: Holocaust History and Postwar Testimony
Christopher Browning

Cataclysms: A History of the Twentieth Century from Europe's Edge
Dan Diner; translated by William Templer with Joel Golb

La Grande Italia: The Myth of the Nation in the Twentieth Century
Emilio Gentile; translated by Suzanne Dingee and Jennifer Pudney

*Carl Schmitt and the Jews: The "Jewish Question," the Holocaust, and
    German Legal Theory*
Raphael Gross; translated by Joel Golb

Confronting History: A Memoir
George L. Mosse

Nazi Culture: Intellectual, Cultural, and Social Life in the Third Reich
George L. Mosse

What History Tells: George L. Mosse and the Culture of Modern Europe
Stanley G. Payne, David J. Sorkin, and John S. Tortorice

The Jews in Mussolini's Italy: From Equality to Persecution
Michele Sarfatti; translated by John and Anne C. Tedeschi

*Jews and Other Germans: Civil Society, Religious Diversity, and Urban Politics
    in Breslau, 1860–1925*
Till van Rahden; translated by Marcus Brainard